Politics in Hungary

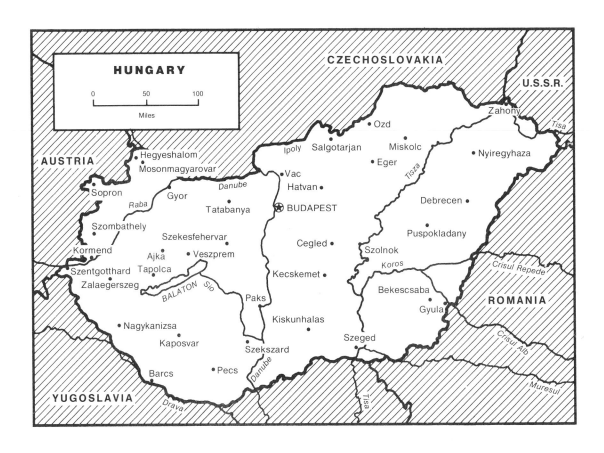

HUNGARY

0   50   100
Miles

CZECHOSLOVAKIA

U.S.S.R.

AUSTRIA

Zahony

• Ozd

Ipoly   Salgotarjan   Miskolc   • Nyiregyhaza

Hegyeshalom   • Eger

Mosonmagyarovar   • Vac

Sopron   Hatvan •   Tisza

Danube   Debrecen •

Gyor   ⊛ BUDAPEST

Raba   Tatabanya   Puspokladany •

Szombathely   Szekesfehervar   Cegled   •

Kormend   Szolnok

Ajka •   • Veszprem   Koros   Crisul Repede

Szentgotthard   Tapolca   Kecskemet •

Zalaegerszeg   BALATON   Sio   Bekescsaba   ROMANIA

• Nagykanizsa   Paks   Kiskunhalas •   Gyula •

Kaposvar   Crisul Alb

Szekszard   Szeged •

Barcs   • Pecs   Danube   Muresul

YUGOSLAVIA   Drava   Tisa

Toma, Peter A.
Politics in Hungary / Peter A. Toma and Ivan Volgyes. San Francisco : W. H. Freeman, c1977.
x, 188 p. ; 24 cm.

Politics in Hungary

Peter A. Toma
University of Arizona

and

Ivan Volgyes
University of Nebraska

W. H. Freeman and Company
San Francisco

Library of Congress Cataloging in Publication Data

Toma, Peter A
   Politics in Hungary.

   Bibliography: p.
   Includes index.
   1.   Hungary—Politics and government—1945-
I. Völgyes, Iván, 1936-   joint author.   II.   Title.
DB956.T63   320.9′439′05   76-29613
ISBN 0-7167-0557-5

Printed in the United States of America

9 8 7 6 5 4 3 2 1

Contents

Preface

This study is neither a miniature nor an enlargement of the Almond and Powell model of structure-function analysis; because of its "genetic characteristics," it is an approximation of the Almond-Powell comparative politics model presented to us by Eastern European scholar Jan F. Triska of Stanford University.

As explained by participants in a panel on "comparing East European Political Systems" at the 1970 American Political Science Association meeting in Los Angeles,[1] there are at least three methodological problems with the Triska version of the Almond-Powell approach.[2] First, the comparative politics model assumes that each political system develops within specific environmental restrictions. However, we demonstrate in the chapters that follow that the Hungarian political system is not independent of other political systems—especially the USSR and other Warsaw Pact countries. Therefore, it is both difficult and unscientific to clearly differentiate (as the Almond-Powell model would call for) between the Hungarian political culture and that of the other Eastern European socialist cultures in the Soviet bloc. For example, it is inaccurate to equate the Soviet oppression of Hungarian revolutionaries in 1956 with the rule application of the system existing at that time; evidence indicates that the Nagy regime in power in Hungary during the revolution was vehemently opposed to Soviet intervention in November 1956. Similarly, we cannot argue that the 1956 revolution (or counterrevolution) was a manifestation of a conversion function aimed at improving the policy-making process; in our opinion, the revolution represented the breakdown of a system that was alien to the overwhelming majority of the Hungarian people. Because the revolution failed, the Soviet leadership has continued to influence Hungarian policy making. Hence, although the Hungarian political system is perhaps less dependent than the other socialist systems under Soviet hegemony, it must, in the final analysis, be viewed as a subsystem within the international socialist system developed by the USSR, because the Hungarian regime is manipulated, if not controlled, by the Kremlin.

The second methodological difficulty arises from Almond and Powell's assumption that the developmental process in a Communist state automatically leads to an increase in "capabilities" and greater independence in state and nation building. If we measure Hungary's capabilities in terms of "opportunities or limitations," as we do in Chapter 2 of this volume, then we must conclude that Hungary has developed considerably in the last 25 years, but the country is not necessarily more independent. Furthermore, the economic reforms instituted in Hungary since 1968 have liberalized some of the economic and political processes, but the reform movement has not resulted in a pluralization of political control similar to that found in the West. As we explain in Chapters 4, 5, and 10, Hungary is pursuing genuine, extensive economic and political reform. It is the first country in the Soviet bloc to attempt to implement such far-reaching basic changes. However, it would be wrong to assume that these changes are weakening or challenging Party control. Quite the contrary. The Hungarian Socialist Workers' Party (HSWP) initiated and supported the New Economic Mechanism (NEM) because the Party expected that the NEM would bring about greater social mobility, economic opportunity, and Party legitimacy.

A problem related to the second methodological difficulty generated by the Almond-Powell model is the equation of political culture with integration. Since integration is dependent on purposeful and active citizen political initiative, it is problematic whether Hungary, which (as pointed out in Chapter 5) is still operating by political command, will ever achieve political integration. Because of this uncertainty, the ruling elite lacks complete self-confidence and the Hungarian citizenry lacks the institutional guarantees that its socialist democracy is legitimate.

The third methodological problem stems from Almond and Powell's supposition that all functions in the model of structure-function analysis affect the operation of the system equally. Some functions of the Hungarian political system are more important to the operation of the system than others. For example, Chapters 3 and 4 on the Communist Party and the problems of legitimacy describe additions to the model that provide a key to understanding both the conversion and the system-maintenance functions of the Hungarian system.

As far as the periodization in Part I of this study is concerned, we have adhered to an artificial and somewhat arbitrary delineation between a mobilization period (1949 to 1962)—subdivided into an early totalitarian phase (1949–1953) and a late national mobilization phase (1957–1961)—and a postmobilization period (1962 to the present). The shift from one period to the other occurred at the time of the Eighth Party Congress in November 1962, when the Party officially endorsed a new policy that left the machinery of mobilization intact but replaced the goal of using it to produce revolutions from above with that of encouraging voluntarism for the achievement of greater economic output. In its effort to mobilize citizen support and unite the political and social forces of the system, the Hungarian regime began to search for legitimacy by guaranteeing greater material rewards and greater political freedom. The turning point in Hungary's socialist development came in 1968 with the introduction of the New Economic Mechanism. Since that time, the regime has sought to modernize Hungary's economy by gradually dismantling the mobilization system, even at the risk of giving rise to new institutions (enterprises) with interests, loyalties, and dynamics of their own. At present, Hungary finds itself halfway between a society that is value-oriented and one that is goal-oriented. Despite various setbacks suffered since 1972, the regime is committed to reform. The road ahead, however, will be rough. Whether or not the Kadar leadership will make it to the finish remains to be seen.

We would also like to draw the reader's attention to the conceptual difficulties that relate to our chapters on the conversion functions of the Hungarian political system. In Hungary, as in most other Communist political systems, the leadership has attempted to abolish genuine citizen participation in "politics," by placing controls on the "feedback loop" of the political process as well as on governmental outputs. In short, in such societies the Party elite has tried generate those demands it is interested in satisfying and to stifle those demands it cannot meet. Yet, in the post-Stalinist era of rule application, the Party has not accomplished these tasks by the use of terror. Rather, it has relied on the distribution of welfare and the process of political socialization to create a willing and rewarded citizenry whose values and activities lie within the perimeters tolerated by the rule-making elite.

Consequently, functions such as rule adjudication, which are independent of partisan politics in the democratic societies of the West, contribute to the regulation of political behavior in Communist societies. These functions in fact serve the purpose of creating the "Communist man of the future," the perfectly socialized Hungarian Communist citizen, who will live in the ideal Communist political culture of Hungary. Such a culture does not yet exist in Hungary. Indeed, our examination of the prevailing political culture discloses that what exists in Hungary today can scarcely be considered a Communist political culture. It is, of course, easy to classify Hungary as a Communist state on strictly ideological grounds, but that description is inadequate for analytical purposes. The Party has a monopoly of political power, but Hungarian society is not yet politically homogeneous. One of the main reasons for this is that socialist morality is by no means universally accepted. Consequently, the ruling elite claims only "hegemony" over socialist morals. In the absence of a Communist political culture, the polity continues its pragmatic existence and its positive goal orientation toward making a better life for all Hungarians. The motto of the present political culture of Hungary is *"Navigare necessere est"* and not "Workers of the world unite!"

When in the fall of 1970 we began work on this study of the Hungarian political system, our approaches and points of view were slightly at variance with one another. However, our fieldwork, carried out between 1970 and

1975, enabled us to test certain propositions and to compile material that presents a blend of cognitive, evaluative, and affective orientations.

The work for this volume was divided equally between us. Peter A. Toma wrote Chapters 1–5; Ivan Volgyes wrote Chapters 6–12, with the exception of the evaluation of the NEM in Chapter 10, which was written by Professor Toma. (An earlier and incomplete version of Chapters 8 and 9 appear in Ivan Volgyes, *Political Socialization in Eastern Europe*, New York: Praeger, 1974.) Professor Toma prepared the conceptual framework and wrote the preface; Professor Volgyes wrote the conclusions and prepared the selected bibliography. Whereas the notes to each chapter cite the primary sources on which we based our conclusions, the selected bibliography lists readings that will enable English-speaking readers to pursue their interest in the Hungarian political system.

There are a number of individuals and institutions that deserve a credit line. Peter A. Toma wishes to acknowledge the support he received from the Inter-University Committee on Travel Grants (now IREX), which enabled him to do research in Hungary in the summer of 1967; part of that research is included in this study. He would also like to express his gratitude to the Committee on the International Exchange of Persons for permitting him to take time out from other scholarly duties to complete this study while in Belgrade, Yugoslavia during the 1972–1973 academic year as a Fulbright Senior Research Fellow.

Ivan Volgyes would like to express his appreciation to Professors Barbara Smith of the University of Nebraska and Peter Shockett of the University of Cincinnati for their helpful criticism, and to the International Research and Exchange Board for support during the 1974–1975 academic year to complete the study of Hungarian political socialization processes. He would also like to thank the Research Council of the University of Nebraska for the research leave it extended to him during the 1970–1971 academic year.

Finally, we would like to express our deepest gratitude to Professor Jan F. Triska of Stanford University for his early encouragement and guidance; to Professor Andrew C. Janos of the University of California, Berkeley, and William F. Robinson, senior analyst of RFE, for their helpful comments; and to Ruth Veres, manuscript editor, for her valuable assistance.

June 1976

Peter A. Toma and Ivan Volgyes

Politics in Hungary

PART I

The Development of the Hungarian People's Political System

1

The International and Domestic Environment Before 1949

Before invading the Danubian basin in the ninth century A.D., the ancestors of the Hungarian people were nomadic herdsmen and warriors who roamed the territory of the Khazar empire between the Don and Volga rivers near the Black Sea. They were organized in a loose confederation of archer tribes known collectively as the Turanian peoples of Asia, who mingled with a variety of cultures, plundering towns and villages in search of booty and territory to colonize. In the 870s, according to the legend, the chiefs of seven tribes chose the strongest tribe, the *Megyer* (later known as the *Magyar*), and its chief, Almos, to lead them to a new home. Hungarian historians have designated 896 A.D. as the year the Magyars, under the leadership of Arpad (son of Almos), conquered the territory roughly equivalent to the present area of Hungary. Under the rule of the Magyars, the seven tribes evolved from a pagan society of wandering raiders, mercenaries, and cattle breeders to a Christianized, feudal, agrarian society.

The princedom of Hungary became an apostolic kingdom in 1001 A.D. when (Saint) Stephen I, who had previously converted the "nation" to Christianity, received the royal crown from Pope Sylvester II. Subsequently, the kings of the House of Arpad consolidated the feudal order in Hungary. In 1241, the Mongol hordes of Batu Kahn devastated the country, which was later rebuilt under the leadership of the great King Bela IV. During the reign of King Matthias (Corvinus) of Hunyad (1458–1490), Hungary became one of the leading cultural centers in Europe.

Other highlights of Hungarian history include the year 1526 when invading Turkish armies from the Balkans won the battle at Mohacs. This defeat caused the disintegration of medieval Hungary. The country was thereafter divided in three: the largest subdivision fell under Turkish rule; the northern and western regions yielded to the German emperors from the Austrian House of Hapsburg, who became the recognized kings of Hungary; and Transylvania became an "independent princedom" under the Turkish Protectorate. Between 1683 and 1699 imperial and Hungarian troops drove the Turks out of the country.

The Turkish domination was followed by that of the Hapsburgs whose yoke the nation was unable to throw off, despite several uprisings. The national freedom war of 1703–1711, led by Ferenc Rakoczi II, ended in defeat, as did the 1848 war for independence, led by Lajos Kossuth. In 1867 the Hungarians concluded a compromise agreement with the House of Hapsburg that marked the beginning of the Austro-Hungarian Monarchy.

During the half century of the Austro-Hungarian Empire, Hungary remained a feudal aristocracy ruled by magnates and the gentry. Industry was weak, commercial policy protected the interests of the landlords, the administration was corrupt, and the countryside was economically underdeveloped. More than half the population of the country was illiterate. The national minorities, who constituted a majority of the population, were deprived of all their rights, which in the final analysis proved to be the principal cause of the disintegration of the empire.

With the collapse of the Hapsburg monarchy in October 1918, the national minorities were emancipated and Hungary became a republic encompassing 38 percent of the territory and 46 percent of the population of the former kingdom. The coalition government headed by Count Michael Karolyi, which followed the reign of the last Hapsburg king (Karl), tried desperately to turn doomsday into kingdom come. However, the Karolyi government was unable to resolve any of the major problems facing the new republic (e.g., establishing peace, carrying out agrarian reform), and there was general unrest and deprivation throughout the country. Under such conditions, Bolshevism, which had been brought to Hungary by prisoners of war returning from Russia, gained a substantial following in industrial areas. Against this background, one sudden blow brought down the whole, precarious structure of Hungarian democracy. On March 20, 1919, the armistice commission in Budapest informed the government that it must relinquish still more territory to newly created neighboring states. Karolyi could not and would not accept these terms. Negotiations between the Social Democrats and the Communists were initiated to deal with the problem. The following day, March 21, 1919, the Karolyi government was forced to resign

and the Hungarian Soviet Republic was formed. Under its commissar of foreign affairs, Bela Kun, the socialist-Communist coalition government allied itself with Lenin and opted to support world revolution. In so doing, the regime hoped to salvage "Saint Stephen's kingdom" from complete destruction by the Entente forces who were backing Czechoslovakian and Rumanian claims to Hungarian territory. Although Kun's army successfully withstood initial attacks by the Czechs, on August 6, 1919, the Rumanian army marched into Budapest and the 133-day Hungarian Soviet Republic came to an end. The cruelty and number of victims of the Red Terror of Bela Kun were surpassed only by those of the White Terror of Rear Admiral Miklos Horthy von Nagybanya (supreme commander of the Hungarian National Army, which had fought alongside foreign forces to defeat the Kun regime.)[1] By 1920 Hungary had lost not only the war and the greater part of her territory, but also all aspirations for democracy. After the demise of the Kun regime, Hungary became a kingdom without a king: the Hapsburgs were prohibited by law from assuming the throne. On March 1, 1920 the Hungarian National Assembly made Horthy regent of the Hungarian kingdom and thus began a period of authoritarianism that lasted for a quarter of a century.

The Horthy regime restored the traditional values, institutions, and authorities that had evolved under the feudal, monarchical system. Belief in God and country as well as in the sanctity of family ties and private property were placed above everything else; the rights of "gentlemen" over the common people were reaffirmed. The Hungarian upper (or ruling) class—comprising remnants of the old aristocracy, landowners, higher-level members of the clergy, military leaders, and industrialists—constituted about 6 percent of the post-1920 population. The middle class—consisting of bureaucrats, professionals, and business people—constituted about 8 percent of the population. About 37 percent were workers and artisans, and 49 percent belonged to the peasantry. Social stratification was based on such attributes as ancestry, race, wealth, type of residence, and national origin. The prevailing spiritual outlook or *Zeitgeist* of the country before World War II was chauvinistic, religious, introverted and traditionalistic.[2] The secret ballot was not reestablished until 1939, when Hungary was already moving into the Nazi camp. For her collaboration, Hungary received from Hitler approximately 80,000 square kilometers of "lost territory" with about six million inhabitants. "Great Hungary," as it was called during the war, reciprocated by rendering diplomatic as well as military support to the Axis Powers. (In 1945 Hungary again lost all of the territory she had regained during World War II.)

Following the Nazi attack on the Soviet Union in 1941, Hungary ordered a contingent of about 350,000 soldiers to fight against the Russians. However, the Soviet victory at the battle of Stalingrad in February 1943 demoralized the Hungarian army and forecast the ultimate defeat of Germany. In the autumn of 1944, when the Soviet army was pushing through the Carpathian Mountains, Admiral Horthy made an attempt to surrender to Moscow, but he was seized by the Gestapo and forced to abdicate. The Nazis installed a puppet regime of fascist fanatics under the direction of Ferenc Szalasi, leader of the Hungarian Arrow Cross Party. The Szalasi government committed the Hungarians to fight with the Nazis until the end of World War II.[3]

In December 1944 the Soviet army laid siege to Budapest. At the same time (and with encouragement from the Soviet army), the Hungarian Communists—most of whom had lived in exile in the USSR until 1944—met at Debrecen and established a Provisional National Assembly composed of a Communist-controlled coalition of four non-Fascist parties (Smallholder, Social Democratic, National Peasant, in addition to Communist). This Assembly formed a Provisional National Government with General Bela Dalnoki-Miklos as premier. (Dalnoki was the only general under Horthy who succeeded in surrendering to the Soviet army in October 1944.) It was with representatives of this government that the three Allied Powers signed an armistice in Moscow on January 21, 1945.[4]

The cost of the war in Hungarian lives (nearly one-half million military casualties) and material (40 percent of the national income) was staggering. Budapest was besieged for two months. Only Warsaw and the German cities suffered such horror and destruction. In April 1945, when the Russian army drove the German and Hungarian armies into Austria, the towns and villages as well as the people of Hungary had been totally devastated. Although Hungary was ostensibly governed by an Allied Control Commission composed of British, American, and Soviet representatives, in reality it was under the

control of the occupying Soviet army. By Article 22 of the Peace Treaty, the Russians were in full occupation until the treaty came into force in September 1947.

At the end of World War II, Hungary had a semi-feudal agrarian economy and a rigid class structure. There had been almost no industrial development since the disintegration of the Austro-Hungarian Empire. In 1945, more than three times as many people were employed in agriculture as in industry; industrial workers accounted for only 21 percent of the labor force. The main reason for this was that the country's interwar ruling elite had consisted of large landowners interested in the preservation of the status quo, rather than industrialization.

Under the Horthy regime, almost a quarter of Hungary's arable land belonged to a few estates of 500 hectares or more, which were owned by only 0.1 percent of the landholders, including the Catholic church. Because of these conditions, land reform and industrialization were the two main objectives pursued by the Hungarian Communists after the Soviet army began to drive out the Nazis in 1944.

The program advocated by the Provisional National Government had been prepared well in advance of the armistice by the Hungarian Communists in exile, under the auspices of the Soviet Party leaders, and propagated by the Hungarian Communist Party (HCP) ever since its reemergence in November 1944. The purpose of the program was to implement national-democratic revolution; the Stalinists applied similar strategies to other Eastern European countries. When the Soviet army took Debrecen in December 1944, there were less than 3,000 Hungarian Communists in liberated Hungary. (Some of them had been in exile in the Soviet Union during the Horthy regime.) By the end of World War II, Communist Party membership was 150,000; by March 1947 it had risen to 650,000; and by the time it merged with the Social Democratic Party in 1948, the HCP had an estimated 1,500,000 members.[5] "The Hungarian Communist Party was the first to start organizing life and popular power; it was the only party capable of mapping out a democratic revival. It invited the other parties, which were slowly organizing, to accept the program and to cooperate in its fulfillment."[6] The primary task of the Hungarian Communists after the war was to build Communist strength across the country. In practice this meant the organizing of a mass Communist party controlled by a Communist elite; the placing of administrative power in the hands of the Communist-controlled Committees of National Liberation; the formation of a new people's security system and army, built on the Soviet model; the prohibition of the revival of the political parties and organizations that had represented reactionary interests in prewar Hungary; a systematic purge of the political, economic and cultural life of the country; the expulsion of the German minority; and other measures enabling the Hungarian Communists to consolidate their control.

For example, after the Hungarian Communist Party machine had become well established (i.e., after December 1944), the Soviet Military Command allowed only the leaders of non-fascist parties to organize; the result was a progressive, democratic coalition (the National Independence Front) that included the Social Democratic Party (SDP), the National Peasant Party (NPP), and the Smallholder Party (SP), in addition to the HCP. Cooperation among the leaders of the three non-Communist parties dated back to May 1944, when Hungary was occupied by Nazi Germany. Furthermore, as early as October 10, 1944, the HCP and the SDP agreed to pursue a united front policy against reactionaries and to merge the two parties eventually. With regard to the systematic purge of undesirable political elements, in 1945 and 1946 approximately 25,000 Hungarian citizens were tried as war criminals by the people's courts; about 2 percent of them received the death penalty. Between January 1945 and March 1, 1948 a total of 39,514 Hungarians were brought to trial for political crimes, and 19,273 were convicted.[7]

In their well-organized bid for power, the Communists first created pressure from below through the agitation of "the masses" and then exerted pressure from above through the influence of Communist-dominated governmental units and the initiation of legislation. Both types of pressure kept the opposition constantly on the defensive. The aim of this "pincer tactic" was to force rivals to yield to pressure from both above (the National Independence Front, representing political unity) and below (the workers and peasants, representing national social and economic unity) so that adversaries could eventually be manipulated into a vulnerable position for the final assault. The Stalinists applied the pincer tactic throughout Eastern Europe. In Hungary the final seizure of power occurred on June 13, 1948, when the expurgated rump of the Social Democratic Party was absorbed by the Hungarian Communist Party. On that date, Hungary began a systematic transition from capitalism to socialism with no organized opposition in sight.[8] Between 1945 and 1948 the Hungarian Communists skillfully employed the pincer technique described above in a complex process of power struggle. Aided by Soviet authorities, they kept alive the struggle against the former fascists and collaborators, against black marketeers and opportunists, against those hostile to Hungarian friendship with the Soviet Union, and against the landed class of large-estate owners. As a matter of fact, while fighting was still going on in March 1945, one of the first acts of the Provisional National Government was the declaration and implementation of a land reform. Under the Communist Minster of Agriculture, Imre Nagy, the Chairman of the Land Reform Council, Peter Veres, more than a third of the agricultural land of Hungary was distributed among some 640,000 small or new farmers.[9] "The peasants who had thus been given land put their confidence in the working class and its revolutionary party."[10]

At the same time the Communists encouraged private enterprise within certain bounds, and through their auxiliary organizations and the cooperation of left-wing Social Democrats, they rallied support for greater civil, political, and economic rights for all strata of Hungarian society. The Communist Party did not promote "class struggle" on such issues as "reactionary forces," the slow pace of legislative work, sabotage, espionage for a "reactionary power," and the so-called conspiracy against people's democracy until several months after the first, national, postwar parliamentary elections which took place in November, 1945.

Because of their increasing efforts and hard work, the Communists were confident of victory at the polls. Nevertheless, to play it safe, they decided to hold municipal elections before November in Budapest, where they anticipated the support of the working class. (Two-thirds of Hungary's manufacturing industry and the majority of the country's working class were concentrated in and around Budapest at that time.)[11] The strategy backfired: in the October 7 municipal elections, the Smallholder Party, which represented small farmers, catholic clergy, and an assortment of political opportunists, received 51 percent of the vote, making the two workers' parties (the HCP and the SDP) and the National Peasant party members of the minority. After this defeat, Marshal Voroshilov, head of the Allied Control Commission, in an effort to exert some control over the November election, tried to coerce the leaders of the Smallholder Party into accepting a common list of the four coalition parties that specified a predetermined number of seats for each party. He offered the leaders of the Smallholder Party first 40 percent of the coalition's seats, then 45 percent, then 47.5 percent, but they refused to commit their party to anything beyond the promise that, whatever the results of the November election, the Smallholders would continue to work within the coalition of the National Independence Front.[12] Hungarian and foreign observers have agreed that the first parliamentary elections were freely conducted by secret ballot. The Smallholder Party won 57 percent of the seats in Parliament. For the next two years the aim of Smallholder leaders (such as Ferenc Nagy and Bela Kovacs), was to prevent further sovietization of Hungary. The aim of Communist and Soviet policy in Hungary, however, was to break the Smallholders' power and to speed up the development of a Hungarian People's Democracy. Communist pressure on the Ferenc Nagy government was well coordinated. What the Hungarian Communists could not achieve through the left-wing bloc of the National Front—a political alliance of the HCP, SDP, NPP and the National Council of Trade Unions, the Soviet occupation authorities accomplished for them.

The first significant attempt to weaken the Smallholder Party in Parliament came in January 1946, when the left-wing bloc sponsored a bill for the nationalization of mines.[13] Although the Smallholder Party had enough votes to block the passage of the bill, it failed to do so because its left-wing members had threatened to bolt the party (which they eventually did in July 1947). Two months later, the Smallholders' leaders again yielded to the demands of the left-wing bloc of the National Front and convinced the party to expel (on the basis of trumped-up charges) 21 of its members holding seats in Parliament. The left-wing bloc made more demands: support of land reform; state control over banks and heavy industry; nationalization of the flour mills; the Three-Year Plan; struggle against conspirators, exploiters, and speculators; and many others.[14] The climax of the Smallholders' crisis came late in February 1947 with the arrest of Bela Kovacs, general secretary of the Smallholder Party. Soviet security forces arrested Kovacs on February 26, 1947; they

charged that he had organized espionage on behalf of a foreign power, against the Soviet army. It was later revealed that this was a trumped-up charge, but at the time it was accepted at face value. After his arrest, Kovacs was held in captivity in the Soviet Union. (He did eventually return from his Soviet internment; in October 1956 he participated in Imre Nagy's government, and after the Soviet invasion he joined the Hungarian refugees in the West.) Before his deportation, however, he was reported to have incriminated his friend Ferenc Nagy.[15] In May 1947, while Nagy was is Switzerland, Soviet authorities produced "evidence" against him. The inevitable result was the expulsion of Nagy and most of his associates from the Smallholder Party. Ferenc Nagy was succeeded by a fellow traveler, Lajos Dinnyes.

In early June 1947, Hungary was invited to participate in the Marshall Plan. However, after Soviet authorities had exerted considerable pressure against participation, the Dinnyes government rejected the plan, and on August 1, the implementation of the Hungarian Three-Year Plan began. In December 1946, the Central Committee of the HCP had announced an overall plan for the development of the national economy and had put out the directives of the Three-Year Plan for national reconstruction. The plan was endorsed by the left-wing coalition of the National Front and a segment of the Smallholder Party, which made open agitation against the plan by Nagyists futile. Thus, the country embarked on a state-planned economy which, according to the former Director of the Agricultural Research Institute, the late Ferenc Erdei, "became a highly effective weapon of socialist transformation."[16] Thereafter, the National Planning Office had the right to demand the death sentence for proven sabotage of the plan, and the National Bank gradually assumed control of industry, foreign trade, and savings and loan institutions. By the end of March 1948, 73.8 percent of the industrial workers in Hungary had become state employees.

In the summer of 1947, Hungary made preparations for new parliamentary elections. The Communists were so confident of victory that they encouraged all parties to go to the polls on separate lists. They also initiated a new electoral law that disqualified voters who had been convicted of offenses against the republic or against democracy. As a result, six percent of the electorate, or 333,000 persons, lost their right to vote. In comparison to the first national elections, the August 31, 1947 elections were a fraud. The Hungarian Communist Party, which received almost 23 percent of the vote, became the largest party in Parliament. Its success was due largely to support received from the Soviet army and to such underhanded tactics as stuffing ballot boxes, voting more than one time, and other irregularities. The Smallholder Party received only 15.4 percent of the vote, primarily because after a July split, the party represented only one faction—the left wing—at the polls.

Two months before the August 31 election, Communist authorities had sanctioned the formation of six opposition parties to insure that the anti-Marxist vote would be divided among various factions; these parties were the Independence Party, the Democratic People's Party, the Hungarian Workers' Party (referred to by the Communists as the Radical Party), the Freedom Party, the Independent Hungarian Democratic Party, and of course, the Smallholder Party. However, before the election, the rump of the Smallholder Party joined the left-wing coalition. As a result, the opposition parties together received only 1,955,419 or 39 percent of the votes as against 3,042,919 or 61 percent cast for the government groups. The Social Democratic Party polled 14.9 percent and the National Peasant Party 8.3 percent of the electorate. Thus, in the new Parliament, the left-wing bloc held 271 seats whereas the opposition held only 140 seats. In contrast to the 2–1 split in the legislature, the new government itself was 100 percent left wing; the opposition had no representation in it whatsoever. The new regime of the National Independence Front therefore encountered no opposition when it adopted and proceeded to implement the Communist program for Hungary's socialist development. Although all major programs were based on parliamentary legislation, government continued to be largely by decree. For example, on March 26, 1948, all factories that had more than 100 employees as of August 1, 1947 were taken over by the state.[17]

In the fall of 1947, a campaign against "reactionary parties" resulted in the dismemberment of the Independence Party on charges of "illegal activities." One year later, the Democratic People's Party was dissolved "of its own accord"; at the same time, Catholic schools were nationalized and Cardinal Jozef Mindszenty was arrested. The Hungarian Worker's Party joined the government coalition in November 1947. The only non-Communist political party that still had any influence after the 1947

election (and therefore posed a potential threat to the Communists) was the Social Democratic Party. Hence the Communists moved to discredit right-wing members and to assimilate the left wing of the SDP. In November 1947, Karoly Peyer, a right-wing Social Democratic leader who had spent the last part of the war in the Nazi labor camp at Mauthausen, was accused along with thirteen others of espionage. Peyer fled Hungary in 1947; a score of other anti-Communist Social Democrats were purged.

By late 1947 Communist victory in Hungary was practically within reach; therefore in February 1948 the HCP decided not to admit any new members. The date of the fusion of the HCP and the SDP had already been secretly agreed upon and a further increase in Party ranks would have meant risking the creation of a mass party when the June 1948 merger occurred. Since the seizure of power was close at hand, the creation of a mass party (as opposed to the consolidation of a ruling elite) was no longer a goal of the Communists. In March 1948 a special Social Democratic Party congress decided on fusion with the HCP. As it happened, after the fusion, the new party—the Hungarian Working People's Party (HWPP)—had more than 2.5 million members. The ceremony giving birth to the HWPP was held June 12–14, 1948.[18] In fact, it was the culmination of policies carried out by left-wing members of the SDP under the direction of Arpad Szakasits. First as vice-premier and later as president of the republic, Szakasits was instrumental in converting the National Independence Front into a Communist-front organization. Since, in the bipolar system of the National-Front Government, Social Democrats were the pivotal factor, the anti-Communist Smallholders, eager to win Social Democratic support on specific issues (e.g., wage policy, land reform, educational policy, and religious tolerance), were willing to yield to certain Social Democratic demands, even though after November 1947 these demands represented Communist interests.

The postwar Social Democratic Party served both as a catalyst of the Communist consolidation of power and as a national unifier in the political arena of new Hungary. Considering the strength of the prewar SDP, especially in the labor movement, the reason for organizing two postwar workers' parties (HCP and SDP), instead of just one, becomes obvious. Because the HCP had been outlawed in August 1919, following the brutalities of the White Terror, the SDP became the only labor outlet for political socialization in Hungary between the two wars.[19] The pre-World War II (or old) SDP ceased to exist during the Nazi occupation of Hungary in 1944. To capture the support of the more than 100,000 union members who had belonged to Social Democratic unions before the war and to prevent right-wing leaders from usurping the potential power of the Social Democrats, left-wing leaders (supported by the Soviet army and the Communists) built a new SDP, which in reality became an indispensable tool of Communist strategy. Between 1945 and 1948 the voting strength of the SDP fluctuated between 112,-000 and 325,000. Without SDP support, Communist pressure from above would have been a fiasco and the "peaceful" seizure of power in June 1948, unattainable.[20]

The socialist transformation period between the June 1948 *Gleichschaltung* and August 20, 1949, when the Constitution of the Hungarian People's Republic was adopted, was effectively used by the Communists to win over to their side the "orphans" of capitalism and to consolidate the power of the dictatorship of the proletariat. To achieve these ends, the Communists employed the following means: they initiated a new agricultural program which led to collectivization and the organization of state farms; they expanded the network of state schools and welfare organizations; they converted the National Independence Front into the People's Front of National Independence (which meant replacing the alliance of political parties with mass organizations such as the National Council of Trade Unions, the Federation of Working Youth, and the Hungarian Federation of Democratic Women); they removed all "enemies of the people" from responsible positions in the state; and, on May 15, 1949, they held a new election. This time the single list of candidates of the People's Front received 95.6 percent of the total votes cast (the rest were either opposition votes—about 3 percent—or votes invalidated on technical grounds;[21] the election legitimized the power the Communists had acquired in May 1947. After May 1949 the road was open for the Communists to travel with full speed toward the complete establishment of a monopoly of power in Hungary.

Summary

Considering that in 1944, when the Provisional National Government came into being, the HCP had less than 3,000 members, Communist victory in 1948 must be viewed as a surprise. It is even more surprising if we bear in mind that non-Communist forces received an overwhelming majority in the first postwar parliamentary elections. The question therefore arises: what enabled the Communists to consolidate their power between 1944 and 1948?

The Hungarian Communists employed two main tactics in their postwar pursuit of power: first, they skillfully used the old political device of *divide et impera;* and second, they took advantage of possible intervention by Soviet occupation authorities. Most historians agree that Communist power in Hungary was acquired by peaceful means but under duress from Soviet occupation authorities. Until the autumn of 1947, when the bulk of the Soviet occupation forces was withdrawn in accordance with Article 22 of the Peace Treaty, the Russians in Hungary exerted direct political pressure favoring indigenous Communist interests. However, since the occupation forces were only in Hungary *ad interim*, the leaders of the HCP had to make certain that the Communists were securely in power by the time the major part of the Soviet occupation army withdrew. To this end, the HCP engaged in a power struggle that lasted from December 1944 to August 1949.

Hungarian historians delineate three tactical phases of this struggle: (1) the national democratic revolution (December 1944 to May 1947); (2) the socialist revolution (May 1947 to June 1948); and (3) the socialist transformation (June 1948 to August 1949).[22]

During the first phase, the Communists worked with members of the bourgeoisie to eradicate the remnants of fascism and semi-feudalism in the country. The organizational vehicle for this struggle was the National Front, composed of citizens from various classes and social strata: workers, peasants, petty bourgeois, and intellectuals. The workers, through their vanguard, the HCP, headed this left-wing bloc whose program included land distribution, nationalization of key industries and banking, expulsion of the German minority, friendship with the USSR, et cetera. The strategy was to build a strong base of support and then to accelerate the development of class struggle. The tactics were to demoralize the opposition and cause the disintegration of its political organizations through pressure from above and below. Matyas Rakosi, veteran Stalinist leader of the HCP, once referred to this scheme as the "salami tactics."

The second phase of the struggle was similar in content and approach to the first, except that during this period the left-wing bloc had a clear majority and the opposition (labeled the class enemy) only a small minority in the government of the National Front. During the period of socialist revolution, the thrust of Communist and Communist-supported pressure was applied against the right-wing Social Democrats and the rump of the "reaction parties." The program of the left-wing bloc included further nationalization of land, industry, and banks; socialist planning of the national economy; and struggle against the "millionaire enemies of the people."

During the third and final phase of the struggle, the unopposed People's Front, led by the HWPP, brought the socialist revolution to an end by imposing a dictatorship of the proletariat. After the parliamentary elections of 1949, the principal task of the new regime was to prepare the country for "socialist construction." Before this goal could be achieved, however, Hungarian society had to be reorganized.

The Communists achieved political hegemony in Hungary in 1949 through the skillful political maneuvers of trained leaders; their success was imposed from above and led to a domination (rather than an integration) of Hungarian society by the Stalinist faction of the indigenous Hungarian Working People's Party. The attainment of power was guaranteed by the Soviet occupation forces. As Rakosi once put it, "the Soviet army was both the originator and protector of the 1949 version of proletarian dictatorship."[23]

2

State and Nation Building

The Hungarian Communist Party came to power in 1949, not under the circumstances predicted by Karl Marx and Friedrich Engels in *The Communist Manifesto*, but under the singular conditions created by the postwar social, economic, and political disarray and the Soviet military occupation. There are, of course, different views and interpretations of when and how the Communist Party seized power; some writers claim it was in 1947, others maintain it was in 1948. Our claim of 1949 is based on the fact that not until the third postwar elections, held in May 1949, were all opposition parties eliminated from the contest, and not until after these elections were Hungarian Communist leaders able to establish the dictatorship of the Party.

The following factors contributed significantly to Communist political hegemony: first and foremost, the Soviet military command imposed severe limitations on the capabilities of the old ruling elite; secondly, non-Communist party leaders were unable to perceive and interpret correctly the environing conditions within which the rules of the game were constantly revised; thirdly, the atrophy of the role and structures of the old pseudodemocratic political culture induced many urban workers and landless peasants to seek economic security and social justice under a Communist-propagated people's democratic culture;[1] fourthly, Hungarians welcomed the opportunity to eradicate all vestiges of fascism; and lastly, Hungary yearned to participate in a credible international security system under the protection of an aggressive, neighboring power (the Soviet Union) instead of under the aegis of a distant and passive Western coalition. The protection secured by participation in the Soviet camp of the international power struggle was viewed by some Hungarians as a prerequisite for Hungary's continued existence and viability as a nation; this fact of political survival made the transition from one type of dictatorship to another more plausible for many Hungarians than a more complex and ambitious program of political development.

After the Communist victory in the 1949 parliamentary elections, the Hungarian Working People's

Party (HWPP), through its auxiliary the People's Front, promised to correct the wrongs perpetuated by previous political regimes and to establish a Communist utopia. To achieve this goal, the revolutionary directorate of the HWPP relied heavily on ideology's transfer culture, which also provided the norms for policy decisions.

Building the Foundations of Socialism

The formal process of social transformation in Hungary was accomplished chiefly by the People's Front Parliament which enacted a number of new laws to institute socialist norms. The old laws forbidding women and youth to do heavy labor were repealed and the new ones permitting the practice of forced labor were enacted. (The Government could both force people to work and specify the type of labor they must perform.) At the end of 1949, enterprises with more than ten workers were nationalized. (As a result, between 1948 and February 1953 the number of artisans dropped from 339,000 to 53,000.)[2] Tenement houses and other income property were also nationalized in late 1949. By 1950 all large-scale industry had been socialized and 81.8 percent of all employees were working for the state.[3] In the first year of the Rakosi regime, Parliament also passed laws imposing heavy penalties for negligence and damage to state property, forbidding workers to change jobs without written permission, and making absenteeism an anti-state act. The new legislation was designed to improve industrial and agricultural production; projects of social reform received secondary consideration. Yet there was no unemployment: women, children, senior citizens, and unskilled laborers from villages provided the raw muscle which in many instances served as a substitute for skill and machines.

In 1949, equipped with the new capabilities of a totally mobilized labor force and a reliance on the use of police terror and the promise of utopia, the Hungarian Communist regime launched its first Five-Year plan. This plan, unlike the three-year recovery plan which preceded it, emphasized the development of heavy industry and capital rather than the growth of agriculture or consumer goods industries. Its purpose was to build the foundations of socialism. It did not acknowledge the fact that Hungary was much better equipped to expand her diverse base of light industry than to support the development of heavy industry.

The initial implementation of the plan was very successful. However, as soon as the first goals were fulfilled, new and more ambitious ones were set.[4] Announcements of increased investments, stepped-up industrial production, and a growing labor force were followed by promises of a higher standard of living and improved labor productivity, but in 1951 and 1952 the standard of living fell below that of 1949. The exodus of manpower from rural into urban areas caused a severe housing shortage in the cities and at the same time slowed agricultural production. There were also inconsistencies in the industrial sector of the economy. Hungary had to import most of the fuel and iron ore required for the growth of heavy industry. While the manufacturing industry developed rapidly, the volume of industrial production and power generation fell far behind expectations. This, in turn, created a greater demand for imported goods. The result was an unfavorable balance of trade. By March 1953, when Stalin died, most leaders in the Party and the Government were convinced that the first Five-Year Plan was in serious trouble. "The mistakes," according to Ferenc Erdei, "resulted from inexperience, and were made still more serious by the dogmatic view that began to prevail in the leadership of the Hungarian Working People's Party."[5]

The mistakes in economics were, above all, mistakes in politics. Party politics dominated not only the economic scene but the social and cultural ones as well. The Party leaders' interpretation of Communist ideology, imposed in part through surveillance and political reprisals, affected every aspect of private and public life. The totalitarian style of politics did not change significantly until Kadar initiated the postmobilization period in 1962.

During the early mobilization phase (1949–1953), the new cultural goals—which were not at all popular—were imposed by a revolution from above. The results were domination of a displaced society by the state, censorship, suppression of initiative, transformation of the HWPP into a bureaucratic organization, and the emergence of a dictator, Matyas Rakosi, who held the top positions in both the Party and the Government. This pattern of political development was copied from the Soviet Union with a few modifications to permit Hungarian pecularities to play a role in the process. Because of the Rakosi personality cult and the widespread repression of dissenters, the early phase of mobilization has been described as the period of Sovietization or Stalinization.[6]

Rakosi and his followers believed that a sharpening of the class struggle would inevitably bring about war between the socialist and capitalist camps. In conformity with their Stalinist model, they determined to develop a heavy industrial base, build up a modern army, complete the socialist transformation of the economy, and eradicate all class enemies. Records from the Hungarian Party archives document, for example, the intent to more than double the production of heavy machinery to meet the demands of the army and the war industry, and the decision to scrap investment plans for housing in favor of an investment of 2 billion forints in a new subway system, which was meant to serve as an air raid shelter as well as an underground military warehouse.[7] What Rakosi's extreme dogmatism actually accomplished was a series of grave errors that, after Stalin's death, left the nation in a state of confusion and Party leaders quarreling among themselves.

The economic and social situation in Hungary the spring following Stalin's death was very serious; it had been a particularly hard winter. Government exactions, especially those levied on farmers in the great Hungarian plain—the country's granary, touched off peasant demonstrations, which made Russian leaders apprehensive. As a result, Rakosi, who was both general secretary of the Party and prime minister, was summoned to the Kremlin and urged to follow the Soviet lead in announcing a "new course" and effecting a division between Party and Government leadership. Instead of following the Kremlin's edict, Rakosi (in collaboration with his deputy, Erno Gero) embarked on a new Five-Year Plan that pursued the same ambitious goals as its predecessor, without making the slightest concession to consumer interests.

This leap in the dark by Rakosi and Gero elicited severe criticism of the Government's economic policy from the anti-Stalinist faction of both the Hungarian and the Soviet Communist parties. Anastas Mikoyan, for example, accused Rakosi of rashly developing iron smelting (and related industry) when Hungary had neither iron mines nor coke. This was precisely what Imre Nagy had been saying since 1948. After receiving a tongue-lashing from Mikoyan, Khrushchev, and others, Rakosi yielded to Soviet demands to initiate a new political and economic course by stepping down from the premiership of the Hungarian government.

Characteristics of the Hungarian People's Democratic Republic

When in late June 1953 Matyas Rakosi was replaced as premier by Imre Nagy, the foundations of the People's Democratic Republic had already been firmly established and the Communist system was fully operational. The transfer from the old to the new government (through the habit of obedience) had for all practical purposes been completed: the Rakosi regime had nationalized the main means of production and established basic socialist institutions to regulate every aspect of Hungarian political, social and cultural life.

The August 1949 Constitution of the Hungarian People's Republic legalized the building of socialism through administrative measures decreed by the dictatorship of the proletariat. It asserted that the "working class" comprised all individuals employed by state-owned economic units and declared that the working class, through its vanguard, the Party, was the sole authority invested with the power to lead the society toward the fulfillment of the socialist program. Anybody or anything that stood in its way was to be eliminated. The traditional separation between the activities of the state and those of the society, which existed in Hungary prior to the establishment of the dictatorship of the proletariat was replaced by an interlinked, homogeneous system of government dominated by the Party. The major guiding principle that determined the relation between the Party and all state and social organizations was democratic centralism, according to which the Party controlled the state organizations and the latter, in turn, dominated the social organizations. Although this centralized system permitted some local initiative in implementing top-level Party decisions, it was not possible to challenge these decisions. Other guiding principles of the people's democratic society were socialist equality and socialist legality. Both placed the value of the collective above that of the individual and gave precedence to the interests of the government in the enforcement of law and justice. Finally, it must be kept in mind that socialist justice was based on the Marxist principle, "from each according to his abilities, to each according to his needs." In Hungary, Party leaders used this maxim as a basis for granting state authorities the power to assign workers such employment as the state deemed appropriate. Since the Five Year Plan emphasized industrialization, most manual workers were assigned jobs in the industrial sector of the economy even if they were more qualified to perform other types of work.

Under the direction of the Party, all political authority in Hungary originated in the state executive and legislative organs, the state administration, the state judiciary, and the public prosecutor's office. These four sources of power mandated (either directly or indirectly) and controlled all other political authority and activities. Of the many institutions in the above four categories, the Presidential Council and the Council of Ministers carried the greatest influence. The Presidential Council acted as a collegial head of state; it also possessed *interim* legislative authority (the right to issue decrees), some judicial authority (the right to interpret laws), and the right to supervise local authorities. The Council of Ministers formed the cabinet, which was responsible to the Assembly. While the former took the place of the unicameral National Assembly when it was not in session, the latter had the power to quash or reverse decisions passed by any organ of the state administration, even if there had been no infringement of the law. Members of these two councils were nominally elected by the National Assembly. Both organs were fairly small and therefore viable decision makers. As might be expected, the top layer of the state organization was managed by Party leaders.

Just as the state political organs were coordinated under Party auspices into one socialist institution, so the various Hungarian social and cultural organizations were politicized and united into a conglomerate of socialist-type organizations, including the People's Front, the trade unions, the Young Communist League, women's organizations, the peace movement, sports organizations, national and local civic societies and associations, professional organizations, the Hungarian Academy of Science, the churches, and the schools. In 1953, there was not one institution in Hungary that had not evolved under the direct influence of the Hungarian Working People's Party. In the brief period of four years, the Party elite had created new structures and organizations designed to regulate all aspects of Hungarian society by orienting all the activities of the citizenry toward the achieve-ment of socialist goals. People's democracy in reality meant Party control.

The Impact of Sovietization

In June 1953 when the Hungarian delegation returned to Budapest from Moscow with a mandate to initiate a new political and economic course immediately, the leadership of the HWPP called a meeting of the Party's Central Committee (June 28, 1953). The two main issues confronting the Party were the dissatisfaction of workers and peasants, and a lopsided Hungarian economy that had resulted in an unfavorable balance of trade and a decline in both real wages and the standard of living. Rakosi's poor economic management and expedient inflationary measures were responsible for the failures that had created these issues, which reflected the real state of affairs in Hungary. Nonetheless, the new regime had achieved one of its major objectives: by using the totalitarian mobilization process, it had changed a principally agricultural society into a semi-industrial one. In spite of this accomplishment, the Soviet leadership sanctioned the appointment of Imre Nagy as premier effective July 1953. (Rakosi remained first secretary of the Party.) Under Nagy (1953–1955) forced collectivization of agricultural production ceased, projects representing Stalinist megalomania (such as the iron works at Dunaujvaros) were suspended, and the wages of the workers were increased. Nagy also criticized the police terror of the Rakosi regime and called for the consolidation of the rule of law and the rehabilitation of political prisoners. During Nagy's term, however, labor productivity decreased and the pace of industrialization slackened. Not until the end of 1955, nine months after Nagy had been replaced as premier (by Rakosi) and removed from both the Party and the Government leadership, did industrial production begin to pick up, increasing by eight percent in 1955 alone. Similar results were again achieved under Rakosi in the first half of 1956.

What we are suggesting is that while under Rakosi the primary Stalinist goal of industrialization was achieved at the expense of human rights and welfare, under Nagy, the welfare of the proletariat came first and the development of heavy industry second. This contrasting choice of values between the two Party leaders had a profound effect on the rank-and-file members of the HWPP: each version of socialist construction had its supporters within the Party, but

Rakosi's repressive totalitarian measures generated support for Nagy's "new course." In July 1956, five months after Nikita Khrushchev had exposed Stalin's crimes at a closed session of the Twentieth Congress of the CPSU, "anti-dogmatist," anti-Stalinist Hungarian Party members demanded and received the resignation of Rakosi as first secretary of the Party. However, Rakosi's replacement was Erno Gero—another staunch Stalinist—not Imre Nagy or some other liberal Communist leader. Consequently, from July to October 1956 Government policies were nothing but a continuation of the old Rakosi line. It is therefore not surprising that this stubborn and extremely rigid position of the Party and Government triggered a response from the rank and file which led to a spontaneous revolt and the establishment of a revolutionary government headed by Imre Nagy.

In the process of Stalinization, Rakosi had effectively disbanded all political and social opposition. Organizations critical of his totalitarian methods began to recoalesce after the liberalization of the first Nagy regime. In November 1956 divergent nationalist elements joined the revolutionary freedom fighters in calling for the withdrawal of Soviet troops, de-Stalinization, and the reinstitution of a pluralistic political system responsive to the needs of the workers. (Since it is not the objective of this book to examine historical events, the Revolution of 1956 receives only a cursory consideration. The theme has been examined in depth in several outstanding studies.[8])

The short period of the revolution revealed two unexpected facts about Hungarian society. First, it demonstrated that in spite of the regime's great efforts at political socialization only a small segment of the Party membership accepted the dogmatic values of the Stalinist prototype of Marxism-Leninism as taught during the Rakosi period. Secondly, it became evident that the workers' demands for material advancement were much more capable of unifying diverse social strata and interests than the totalitarian values implemented in Rakosi's version of the Hungarian People's Democratic Republic. The thrust of the revolutionary movement was to rid Hungary of Stalinism. At no time, however, did the revolutionary government or the numerous political groups that reemerged during the revolt contemplate the abolition of socialism. The two basic revolutionary demands were political freedom (meaning independence and nonalignment in foreign affairs) and the establishment of democratic rights (i.e., the abolition of police terror and the restoration of a rule of law).

It took Soviet tanks and Soviet soldiers to stop the revolutionary development of national democratic socialism in Hungary in November 1956. To Soviet leaders, the rapid disintegration of the Hungarian Working People's Party in October 1956 and the reestablishment of opposition parties in Hungary during Imre Nagy's second rule indicated that the Soviet-type political system, erected between 1948 and 1956, had collapsed. The declaration of Hungary's neutrality and withdrawal from the Warsaw Pact convinced the USSR that Hungary would no longer be a "buffer zone" against the West. However, Soviet leaders were divided on the issue of military intervention. The final Soviet decision to use Russian troops against the Hungarian insurgents and to install a pro-Kremlin government came after Khrushchev won his argument against the Soviet military elite who opposed the move.

Socialist Reconstruction and the Hungarian National Interest

Most writers who have carefully examined the 1956 Revolution are in agreement that the despotism of Rakosi caused the development of a negative loyalty and commitment to the Hungarian People's Democratic Republic among alienated citizens. Opposition to the political authority vested in the dictatorship of the proletariat had been suppressed by police terror, but it reappeared as soon as the terror (used by Rakosi and his clique to maintain power) subsided. Although Rakosi escaped to the Soviet Union during the 1956 revolt and was not allowed to return to Hungary until 1970, surveillance and selective brutalization by the security police as well as political trials continued long after the revolt. So did the spreading of a Communist utopia. However, the third ingredient that typified the Rakosi regime, namely despotism, ended with Rakosi's departure. Rakosi's postrevolutionary successor, Janos Kadar, who had suffered torture in jail from 1951 to 1954 under Rakosi, had neither charisma nor the pretension of practicing the cult of personality. Kadar has been a member of the interim revolutionary government headed by Imre Nagy, but in early November 1956 he left Budapest to join the revolutionary Workers' and Peasants' Government that had been established in the Soviet city of Uzhgorod. Although this government asked for Soviet intervention to quell the revolution, once in power Kadar was careful not to allow outside influences to undermine the authority of the revived Party, which had been renamed the Hungarian Socialist Workers' Party (HSWP). He sought to "humanize" the regime in a cautiously conceived manner that would assure both the confidence of Moscow and the loyalty of his peers. Kadar prudently listened to the counsel of his associates, many of whom were economic experts and intellectuals who fought both the Stalinist and "revisionist" factions within the Party.

In June 1957, at the first conference of the newly organized Hungarian Socialist Workers' Party (HSWP),[9] Kadar introduced his "alliance policy." According to this policy, any office—except for Party functions—could be held by a non-Party person provided that he or she had the necessary qualifications. The main purpose of the policy was to forge, in spirit if not in reality, an alliance of Party and non-Party people in which workers, peasants, the intelligentsia, and the *petite bourgeoisie* would work

cooperatively in the pursuit of common goals. All who were loyal to their homeland and who were interested in helping to achieve the goals established by the Party in conjunction with the Government were encouraged—without regard to family background, past activity, or personal philosophy—to participate in Hungary's socialist construction. Indeed, in terms of job prestige and remuneration, Party members were no longer to have an advantage over others. Even though prior to 1962 Kadar had little opportunity to implement this conciliatory policy, its proclamation nevertheless had a positive effect on the population at large by eliminating mistrust, suspicion, and indifference. To emphasize the new goal of alliance, the pre-1956 Party slogan representing the concept of class struggle—"Whoever is not with us is against us" (a paraphrase of *The Bible: Matthew XII, 30*)—was changed to: "Whoever is not against us is with us."

As in the prerevolutionary period, similarly after the revolution, the principal goal of the regime was industrialization. However, Kadar was perceptive enough to learn from past mistakes; he realized that economic planning initiated by Party leaders with

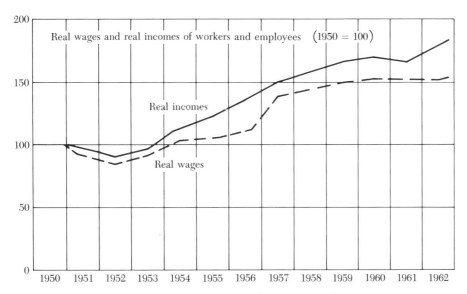

Figure 2.1. Real wages and real incomes of Hungarian workers and employees, 1950–1962.
Source: Central Statistical Office, *Statistical Pocket Book of Hungary* (Budapest: Statisztikai Kiado Vallalat, 1968), p. 153.

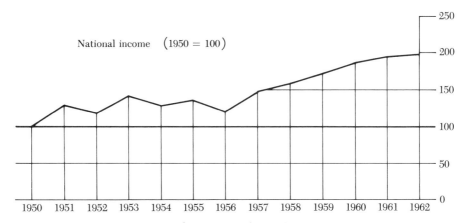

Figure 2.2. Hungarian national income, 1950–1962.
Source: Central Statistical Office, *Statistical Pocket Book of Hungary* (Budapest: Statisztikai Kiado Vallalat, 1968), p. 33.

the sole aim of implementing socialist construction through industrialization produced alienation rather than satisfaction on the part of the workers. Although still geared primarily to Soviet interest, industrialization under Kadar was managed on a more rational basis than before; it took into account national economic resources and capabilities and was closely

linked to a second major goal of the regime, namely, a steady rise in the standard of living. In 1957 the real wages of workers and employees rose by 18.6 percent over the 1956 level (which made them 32 percent higher than they had been in 1955). (See Figure 2.1.) Furthermore, in 1957 the net industrial output rose to its highest peak since 1949. (See Figure

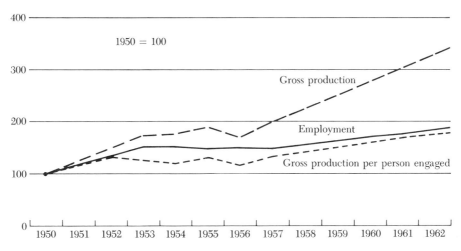

Figure 2.3. Gross production, individual productivity, and employment in the state industry in Hungary, 1950–1962.
Source: Central Statistical Office, *Statistical Pocket Book of Hungary* (Budapest: Statisztikai Kiado Vallalat, 1968), p. 58.

2.2.) By the mid-1960s the industrial sector provided 40–45 percent of the national income.[10]

During his last trip to Budapest in the spring of 1964, Khrushchev referred to a newly initiated economic policy of Kadar as "goulash politics," commenting to workers that it was wrong to believe revolution was the only important consideration; instead, he said "the important thing is that we should have more to eat—good goulash, schools, housing and ballet."[11] Kadar's "new course" reflected these goals. It must be added that the normalization of the Hungarian economy benefited from aid from other nations in the Council of Mutual Economic Assistance (Comecon or CEMA).[12] Yet the basis of Kadar's postrevolutionary success was his policy of moderation and unity. (See Figures 2.3 and 2.4)

Not everybody in Kadar's regime, however, approved of his "new course"; some Party leaders resisted liberalization of any kind. To enhance their influence within the Party, these "dogmatists" sought to scapegoat prosperous independent farmers for the retardation of the socialist transformation of the countryside. In December 1958, they convinced the Central Committee of the HSWP to lash out against the Hungarian kulaks in a campaign to reorganize

Hungarian agriculture to bring it more in line with socialist principles. (In 1957, 89 percent of arable land was in the private sector.) The recollectivization of the countryside had been decided in April 1958 at a top-level Party meeting held after the Khrushchev-Kozlov visit to Hungary. However, Party leaders disagreed as to the most effective method for achieving collectivization. The dogmatists supported the plan of Imre Dogei, then minister of agriculture, who proposed to force independent peasants into collectives by levying extremely heavy taxes on them. Lajos Feher, supported by Kadar and other moderates, proposed the use of propaganda, tax incentives, and government loans to encourage collectivization. Feher even suggested that reimbursement—or a small rent—be paid to collective farm members. While the moderates considered the "socialist transformation of the countryside" synonymous with the new economic policy aimed at strengthening the worker-peasant alliance, the dogmatists thought of collectivization as an attempt to reverse the hitherto liberal trend of the regime. For the next two years, the dogmatists prevailed and a large number of peasants were forced into agricultural producers' cooperatives, but in 1960 Kadar replaced Dogei with Pal Losonczi (a moderate) and by 1962, when 92.5

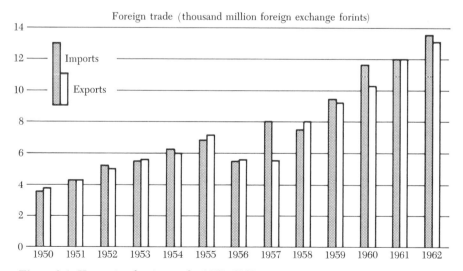

Figure 2.4. Hungarian foreign trade, 1950–1962.

Source: Central Statistical Office, *Statistical Pocket Book of Hungary* (Budapest: Statisztikai Kiado Vallalat, 1968), p. 91.

percent of Hungary's arable land was in the socialist sector,[13] Kadar was able to gain control over collectivization and thus alleviate unnecessary brutality. However, he was unable to assert his influence over district and local Party organs in rural areas until after the Eighth Party Congress convened in November 1962. By then, of course, Nikita Khrushchev's victory over the hardline dogmatists at the Twenty-second Congress of the CPSU in October 1961 had signaled the green light for an attack on dogmatism in the Eastern European countries under Soviet influence. The repercussions of Kadar's struggle with the dogmatists over the issues of leadership skills, expertise, the exploitation of talent, and reconciliation were impressive. His victory triggered a new movement of liberalization that brought about a reduction in the number of forced labor camps, the release of political prisoners, a change in the judicial process, a relaxation of travel restrictions, and an end to the jamming of Western radio stations. These were the key noneconomic elements of a reform instituted to gain the much-needed loyalty and support of "the masses."

Kadar sought to make modernization in Hungary work by persuasion rather than by coercion. The consolidation of his control at the Eighth Congress of the HSWP in 1962 signaled the beginning of a new period of Hungarian political development, identified as the postmobilization period; its main characteristics were the political participation of the citizenry and the regime's attainment of legitimacy.

Summary

The political system established by Matyas Rakosi in 1949 functioned under a trinity of despotism, police terror, and the promise of utopia. It contained all the elements of the Stalinist type of dictatorship. Despotism, based on the principle of one will, one leader, was the *modus vivendi* of the Hungarian Working People's Party. Doctrinal differences within the party were resolved by the terror of the secret police which was in the employ of the despot himself. Through terror, Rakosi was able to eliminate all of his rivals, and in a short time, to impose the "cult of his personality" on rank-and-file Party members. Through an appeal to utopianism, Rakosi's regime was also able to impose the values of a command economy as inspiration for "the masses." The elimination of surplus value, the establishment of

socialist equality and justice, and the total mobilization of the labor force gave many class-conscious proletarians a feeling of recognition and pride. However, these opinions were short lived because workers soon discovered that they were being denied the benefits of their hard work, which were derived instead by the despot and his bureaucracy. By 1956, the workers also discovered that Rakosi had fabricated a war hysteria through his mechanical application of Soviet economic practices and his oppressive implementation of the theory of the unconditional sharpening of the class struggle.

Overcentralization and the growth of an inefficient bureaucracy resulted from an imitation of the Soviet management system that led the Hungarian economy, under Rakosi, down the path to disaster. The emphasis on heavy industrial production and continually raised quantitative norms increased output, but quality suffered so badly that a large number of Hungarian state-owned enterprises were operating at a deficit. In addition, there was a great shortage of competent managers and skilled workers, caused partly by emigration and the precipitate rate of industrialization. To conceal the negative effects of rapid industrialization, the regime engaged in the methodical falsification of cost of living indexes, artificially inflating statistics relating to the growth of real wages. As Ivan T. Berend discovered in his research (see Note 7), Rakosi always subordinated economic factors to political considerations, making corruption, incompetence, suspicion, fear, and irresponsibility endemic to his regime. The demoralization resulting from the inhumanity of Rakosi's rule contributed to the economic stagnation and social apathy characteristic of the early fifties.

It is not too surprising, then, that in October 1956 betrayed workers, students, and the intelligentsia in Budapest revolted against the despotic practices of Rakosi and his clique. After the revolution (or "counterrevolution," according to Communist ideology), Rakosi's successor, Janos Kadar, searched for honest answers to the fundamental problems facing Hungarian society. Relying on collective leadership, Kadar developed his own "new course," which resembled that of the revolutionary leader Imre Nagy and consisted of policies aimed at achieving an improved standard of living to be shared by all in a new alliance between Communists and non-Communists. The immediate abolition of despotism and the gradual elimination of terror generated new patterns of socialization and Party behavior (de-Stalinization) that emphasized persuasion rather than coercion. After purging the reorganized small Party of "those directly responsible for past crimes," Kadar realized that it was not enough to get rid of the criminals; he also had to remove the cause of crime. Thus, his regime gradually introduced new incentives and practices that produced a mixture of nationalism and Communism peculiar to Hungarian conditions. As a result, the long-promised improvements in the standard of living began to materialize and Hungarians developed some control over their own fate.

In the early 1960s, however, the Kadar regime came to the conclusion that economic benefits alone could not generate enough popular support to sustain steady progress in modernization; it therefore sought to build a base of tangible reliable support by allowing increased citizen participation in the processes of government. Legitimacy thus became a primary goal.

3

The Communist Party

The key factor in the development of the post-World-War-II Hungarian political system was the Communist Party—first under Rakosi and then, after the abortive revolution of 1956, under Kadar. Since 1949, in addition to its mobilization function, the Party has directed, guided, and coordinated all activities of state and social organs. The 1972 Revised Constitution of the Hungarian People's Republic formally acknowledges both the existence and the leading role of the Party: "The Marxist-Leninist party of the working class is the leading force in society."[1] Although the Old (1949) Constitution did not mention the Party by name ("the leading force in political and social activities is the working class, led by its vanguard"[2]), in both theory and practice, the Communist Party has played a special and privileged role in the evolution of the Hungarian People's Republic. Its authority, according to Party historians, is not derived from legal measures, but from "revolutionary struggles [pursued] in the course of a century-old historical development.[3]

The Hungarian Communist Party (HCP) was formed on November 20, 1918 when a group of about 100,000 former Hungarian prisoners of war, who had been in Russia during WWI and who constituted the Hungarian division of the International Section of the Russian Communist Party (Bolshevik), joined forces with the left wing Social Democrats, anarcho-syndicalists, and intellectual revolutionaries of diverse philosophies. On March 21, 1919, after merging with the much larger Social Democratic Party (SDP), the HCP established without bloodshed the Hungarian Soviet Republic (headed by Bela Kun), which lasted 133 days.[4] Because of its dogmatic application of the Soviet prototype of "war Communism,"[5] the Bela Kun regime lost the support of the trade unions, and on August 1, 1919 the regime disintegrated as the Rumanian army closed in to occupy Budapest. The White Terror of Admiral Horthy, which followed the Red Terror of Tibor Szamuely (who had been People's Commissar for Internal Affairs under Kun), forced the HCP to go underground and drove several of its leaders into exile. During the interwar years only weak Communist cells existed in Hungary, while the leadership of the Party (including Bela Kun) was decimated by Stalin's purges.

Membership and Composition

The contingent of Hungarian Communists returning from the Soviet Union in 1944 was small and insignificant insofar as the international Communist movement was concerned. In 1945, for example, the Hungarian Communist Party had only 2,000 members. However, by May 1949, when the Communists achieved effective political control through the Parliamentary elections in which all parties participated in a coalition headed by the Communists, the newly formed Hungarian Working People's Party (HWPP) claimed a membership of 1,500,000. Because the bulk of this membership came from the "incorporated" SDP and therefore lacked the attributes of "good communists" the Rakosi leadership decided to reduce the membership systematically through a series of purges; by 1954 only 864,607 members remained in the Party. Just before the October 1956 Revolution, the membership rolls of the HWPP included 900,000 names. Yet in December 1956, the revived Party, called the Hungarian Socialist Workers' Party (HSWP), had only 108,000 members.[6] In postrevolutionary Budapest the Communists fared even worse; out of 330,000 members of the former HWPP, only 28,000 were recovered by the HSWP.

After 1956, the task of rebuilding the HSWP was monumental. Any success was due to duress imposed by the Soviet occupation forces and to Kadar's power of persuasion. In any case, Party membership grew slowly. The greatest increase occurred in April 1957 when, after an ultimatum to rejoin the HSWP was issued by the February plenary session of the Provisional Central Committee,[7] 118,313 members of the former HWPP enrolled in the HSWP. At its June 1957 National Conference, the HSWP claimed a total membership of 345,733 persons, 38.4 percent of the prerevolutionary HWPP. In 1960, as the Kadar regime began to stabilize, a new membership drive attracted more people, especially industrial workers. Then, as Kadar's regime moved cautiously toward reform, Party membership began to appeal to intellectuals and technocrats. By 1967,

the Party had 584,849 members and 37,900 candidate members. After the Ninth Party Congress (November 28–December 3, 1966) abolished candidate membership, 35,250 persons became full-fledged members; an additional 42,298 joined the HSWP between 1967 and 1971, at which time Party membership stood at 662,397: 6.6 percent of the entire population, 9.2 percent of the adult population, and 13.5 percent of all wage earners.[8] By 1974, another 91,956 members had been added to the Party rosters. Thus, according to the main report delivered at the Eleventh Party Congress (March 17–22, 1975) by Janos Kadar, the Party had 754,353 members as of December 31, 1974. (See Table 3.1.) Sixty-seven percent had joined the Party since 1956. However, between the November 1970 Tenth Party Congress and the March 1975 Eleventh Party Congress, 26,247 members died,

Table 3.1. Party Membership

Date	Numbers of Members
1. December 1919 (in exile)[1]	8,000
2. May 1945	2,000
3. May 1948	884,000
4. May 1949	1,500,000
5. February 1951	862,114
6. June 1954	864,607
7. October 1956	900,000
8. June 1957	345,733
9. June 1959	417,000
10. November 1962	512,000
11. December 1966	585,000
12. November 1970	662,000
13. December 1974	754,353

Sources: 1 and 2, Matyas Rakosi, *A bekeert es a szocialismus epiteseert* [For Peace and the Building of Socialism] (Budapest: Szikra, 1951); 3, 4, and 5, Ernst C. Helmreich, ed., *Hungary* (New York: Praeger, 1957), p. 126; 6, "Third Congress of the Hungarian Working People's Party," *New Hungary* (Budapest) 4, no. 6 (1954), 87; 7, *New Times* (Moscow), 50 (December 6, 1956), 11; 8 *Vsevengerskaia konferentsiia Veungerskoi Sotsialisticheskoi Rabochei Partii* [All-Hungarian Conference of the Hungarian Socialist Workers' Party] (Moscow: Gospolitizdat, 1958), p. 74; 9, *World Marxist Review* 11, no. 6 (1959), 72; 10 and 11; *A Magyar Szocialista Munkaspart IX kongresszusanak jegyzokonyve* [Minutes of the Ninth Congress of the Hungarian Socialist Workers' Party] (Budapest: Kossuth Konyvkiado, 1967), p. 480; 12, *A Magyar Szocialista Munkaspart X. Kongresszusanak jegyzokonyve* (Budapest: Kossuth Konyvkiado, 1971), p. 102; 13, *Nepszabadsag*, March 15, 1975.

7,478 left the Party of their own accord, and 15,474 had their membership revoked for not paying their dues; an additional 7,133 Party members were expelled for political reasons, bringing the total loss of membership in those five years to 56,332.[9] Kadar's figures do not take into account the losses sustained by the Party between the two congresses.

Anyone above 18 years of age may become a Party member, and even after retirement from work, members may continue to be active in the Party. (The age of compulsory retirement varies according to occupation: for miners and women it is 55, for other workers it is between 60 and 62.) The fact that in 1971 the average age of Party members was 44 implies that many of them were in their late fifties and early sixties. The social composition of the Party, detailed in Table 3.2, is informative. Although

Table 3.2. Social Composition of the Party in 1967 Compared to that of the Labor Force°

Social Stratum	Party	Labor Force
Industrial Workers	34.9%	39.5%
Peasants	7.8	30.8
Total: Workers and Peasants	42.7	80.3
Intellectuals	38.1	14.3
Retired	9.0	13.9
Armed Forces	7.9	2.8
Students and Others	2.3	0.8

°Adds up to more than 100 percent because some retired workers continue to work.

according to official statements issued in 1967, 70 percent of the membership was of working-class origin, only 34.9 percent of the membership actually held jobs requiring physical labor.[10] Between 1967 and 1971 the number of laborers in the Party decreased by 4.5 percent, even though overall membership increased by 20 percent in the same period. However, since the Party shifted from promanagement to proworker policies in 1971, the number of blue-collar Party members is likely to increase by 1980.

Another incongruity between the goals of the Party and the composition of the membership is the lack of adequate representation of the peasantry. In 1966 only 7.8 percent of the members were peasants; their number has not increased significantly since then. The disparity between peasant membership in the Party and peasant participation in the economy can be explained by three factors. First, the peasants have never engaged in politics to the extent that other social strata have. Although it is true that peasant movements and the Naional Peasant Party were important in the immediate postwar era, the agrarian segment of Hungarian society is isolated and generally apathetic toward politics; economic well-being has always been more important to the peasants than political participation. Secondly, a relatively low level of education combined with isolation from urban centers have not been conducive to the development of a political consciousness that would, in turn, result in a high propensity for political participation.[11] Thirdly, the disappearance of local, middle-level administrators at the end of World War II in conjunction with the coercive agrarian policies of the Rakosi regime (which imposed political direction from above) induced peasants to develop an anti-Government attitude and to place more emphasis on immediate, local political problems than on the national political scene.[12]

Although it is difficult to ascertain the extent of student participation in the Party, a recent survey revealed that at five leading Hungarian institutions of higher learning, HSWP membership was very low: only 1.1 percent of the students registered at these institutions were Party members in 1971. Although the number of student members remains low, perhaps one sign of change is an increase in the number of Party members among high school and college teachers. For example, a study of four towns selected by Hungarian sociologists as representative of the rural community revealed that in 1968 Party membership among high school teachers had reached influential proportions. In the high schools of Vasarosnameny 32.4 percent of the teachers were party members; in Nyiregyhaza it was 34.4 percent, and in Baktaloranthaza 35 percent. In the colleges of Budapest the percentage of faculty belonging to the Party grew from 26.4 percent in 1960 to 34 percent in 1968; the gains were registered largely on the associate and professorial levels.[13]

In 1971 only 22.9 percent of Party members were women, even though women constituted 51.64 percent of Hungary's population and 39 percent of all wage earners.[14] Since most Hungarian women bear the dual burden of jobs and household management, they have little time to spend in Party activity; nonetheless, the low level of participation, especially by younger women, creates a significant problem for the Party. It appears that the predominant "male-chauvinist" attitude of the general Party membership discourages women from becoming more of a force in Party affairs. As Julia Turgonyi stated in the official manual for students at the Party Higher School, "The political activity of women, in spite of the accomplished social changes, remains considerably less important than their role in the socioeconomic activities of the state." At the Szeged Attila Jozsef University of Sciences, where 75 percent of the students are women, women account for less than 10 percent of the total membership of the Party.[15]

The Party leadership has tried to rectify the shortage of female members by implementing policies aimed specifically at recruiting more women. In 1970, for example, the leadership assigned 32,000 specially designated functionaries the task of increasing female representation in the Party; and to accelerate the participation of women in political affairs, 160,000 volunteers of the People's Front sought political support from women in the community. In its drive to attract more women, the Party had to overcome three main obstacles: (1) the Hungarian woman's traditional opposition to participating in activities that reduce her already small amount of leisure time; (2) the negative image of Party membership among women who view political success as less desirable than other, more socially productive goals; and (3) the traditionally conservative attitudes of most male Party members.[16] Despite repeated encouragement from the Party leadership, however, the number of women in leading posts is still very low.

Organization

The organization of the Hungarian Socialist Workers' Party replicates that of the Communist Party of the Soviet Union. The Party operates on the principle of democratic centralism; indirect elections from lower to higher bodies, majority decisions, and the top-down enforcement of decisions from higher to lower bodies are operative tenets of decision making. At times, however, Party members in higher positions violate the principle of democratic centralism by their arbitrary and subjective interpretation of the resolutions passed by the Central Committee and the Party Congresses. Janos Kadar raised this criticism at the Eleventh Party Congress held in March, 1975. To cope with the problem, the Congress sanctioned an exchange of Party books (which is another term for "purifying" Party ranks). By March 1976, the attitude of every Party member regarding the policy and organization of the Party will have been examined.[17]

In reality the membership meetings, the conferences, and the Party Congresses, which are supposed to be the legislative arms of the Party, usually rubber-stamp decisions already made by the executive arms of the Party.

The Party has a hierarchical structure. At the base of the pyramid are the primary organizations, the local cells, which are formed in each production unit—factory, office, or collective farm—and in territorial subdistricts (for those who cannot belong to a production-unit cell). On December 31, 1974, there were 24,000 primary organizations at the base of the Party, and the average primary cell had approximately 32 members. Since the primary village organizations average around ten members, it is safe to say that most city cells have considerably more members. In fact, because of the high concentration of Communist leadership in the capital, it is estimated that close to 45 percent of all Party members work in Budapest. Just above the primary organizations in the pyramid are the local and district delegates conferences, which operate within the territorial subdivisions of the urban and rural districts and elect delegates to county conferences. These latter bodies send representatives to the national Party Congress which, in turn, elects delegates to the Central Committee. Table 3.3 outlines the territorial and functional organization of the Hungarian Socialist Workers' Party.

Theoretically, the highest organ of the HSWP is the Party Congress; however, it meets only about once every four years and its primary function is to elect the officials who rule the Party. At the Tenth Party Congress, in 1970, a total of 1065 delegates—685 voting and 380 nonvoting—participated in the deliberations. At the Eleventh Party Congress, in 1975, the total number of delegates was only 843. According to Party statutes, the members of the executive organs elected by the Congress are responsible for the actual operation of the Party while the Congress is not in session.

Table 3.3. Territorial and Functional Organizations of the HSWP

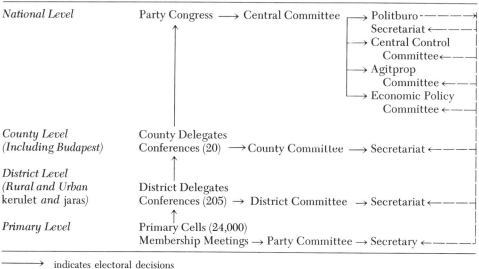

———→   indicates electoral decisions
-- ——→   indicates chain of command

The Central Committee (which was enlarged in 1975 from 105 to 125 members) meets approximately three to four times a year; its meetings usually last two days. Although little is known about the actual functioning of this body, its general purpose is elective and advisory. It elects its own secretaries and the members of its most important permanent subdivisions: the Politburo, the Economic Policy Committee, the Agitation and Propaganda (Agitprop) Committee, and the Central Control Committee. It also confirms the appointments of the various department heads of its permanent office (who together constitute the Secretariat of the Central Committee). These elections and confirmations, however, always take place on the basis of nominations submitted to the Central Committee by the Politburo, and there is no known contest of candidates for these nominations.

The advisory capacity of the Central Committee is clear from its rather passive behavior. It hears speeches, and its members participate in policy debates. Only when serious disagreements occur among the leadership (e.g., in the collectivization debates of 1959–1962) does the Central Committee play a key, decision-making role. In such instances, the full membership of the committee must decide the course of future policies.

Membership in the Central Committee carries a great deal of prestige, and to be in the inner core of decision-making one must be a member of this committee (although such membership does not assure this privilege); however, even those Central Committee members who are not at the top level of the decision-making elite can exert some influence on specific policies by virtue of their important posts in the administration. Furthermore, each member of this committee has relatively easy access to the leadership.

An analysis of the composition of the Central Committee reveals that in 1971, out of a total membership of 105, only 9 were women. Thus, the percentage of female representation on the Central Committee in 1971 was 8 percent—significantly below the percentage of women in the Party, which was approximately 23 percent. In 1975, however, when the membership of the Central Committee was increased to 125, 6 additional women were elected to that body, bringing the number of woman members to 15 and the percentage of female representation to 12 percent. The occupational breakdown of the Central Committee in 1972 is listed in Table 3.4.

The categories in this table are self-explanatory except perhaps for the category referred to as "mem-

Table 3.4. Composition of the Central Committee of the HSWP in 1972

Members of the Government	31
Parliamentary Representatives	31
Members of Regional Party Organizations	19
Members of Central Party Organizations	17
Managers, Directors of Cooperative or State Farms	7
Retired	7
Trade Unionists	6
Researchers at Academic or Technical Institutions	6
Active Worker	1
Total	125°

°The total number of representatives add up to more than 105 people because several members of the Party and Government fulfilled more than one function.

bers of the Government." This group included the holders of the following offices: the president and secretary of the Presidential Council, the president and three vice presidents of the Council of Ministers, nine ministers and five deputy ministers, the president of Parliament, the president and vice president of the People's Front, the president of the Planning Office, the commander of the Workers' Guard, the procurator general, the president of the Central Control Committee, the president of the Hungarian Radio and Television Service, and the Hungarian Ambassador to Moscow. It should be noted that the ministers of Construction, Heavy Industry, Light Industry, Transportation and Postal Services, and Finance were excluded from membership. At the same time, the armed services were represented by the minister and first deputy minister of the Department of Defense and the commander of the Worker's Guard. The organization of the Central Committee is shown in Table 3.5.

The Politburo of the Central Committee is the Party's highest rule-making body, which makes it the most important single Party organ. It's leaders are the actual decision makers who control the fate of the country and give a general direction to the policies of the state and government. The deliberations of the Politburo, usually held twice a month, are kept secret, but it is known that all major matters affecting

general policy are discussed here first; decisions emanating from this body carry the absolute authority of the Party.

The Politburo is composed of 15 members. In 1975, immediately after the Eleventh Party Congress, only one of its members (Valeria Benke, editor of the party's ideological journal) was a women. Four members were secretaries of the Central Committee (Janos Kadar, Bela Biszku, Karoly Nemeth, and Miklos Ovari). Although prior to the Eleventh Congress it had been rumored that Kadar would retire, he remains Party leader. In March 1975, the Council of Ministers had four representatives in the Politburo: the prime minister (Jeno Fock), two deputy prime ministers (Gyorgy Lazar and Gyorgy Aczel), and the president of the Parliament (Antal Apro). On May 15, 1975, however, Fock was released from his post at his own request. He was replaced by Lazar whose position as deputy premier was then assumed by Gyula Szeker and whose chairmanship of the National Planning Office was taken over by Istvan Huszar, another deputy premier. Then, on July 2, 1975, two new Politburo members were co-opted: Deputy Prime Minister Istvan Huszar and long-time Chairman of the Presidential Council Pal Losonczi. Although Huszar's unexpected election to the Politburo was intended to strengthen the economic team of that body at a time when Hungary's economic problems were growing in scope and magnitude, the inclusion of Losonczi, a peasant by origin, can be construed as a move to strengthen the position of the head of state and give the highly important agricultural sector of Hungarian society a voice in the Politburo.

The mass organizations were represented in the Politburo by the secretary-general of the Patriotic People's Front (Istvan Sarlos) and the general secretary of the National Trade Union Council (Sandor Gaspar). In the spring of 1975, the membership of the Politburo also included the dean of the Party Academy (Dezso Nemes), the first secretary of the Budapest Committee of the Party and Chairman of the Economic Working Collective (Karoly Nemeth) and the first secretary of the Communist Youth League (Laszlo Marothy).

The most surprising case of reelection to the Politburo at the Eleventh Party Congress was that of Aczel, who was dismissed from the Secretariat along with Nyers in March 1974. Since he had been

Table 3.5. Organization of the Central Committee

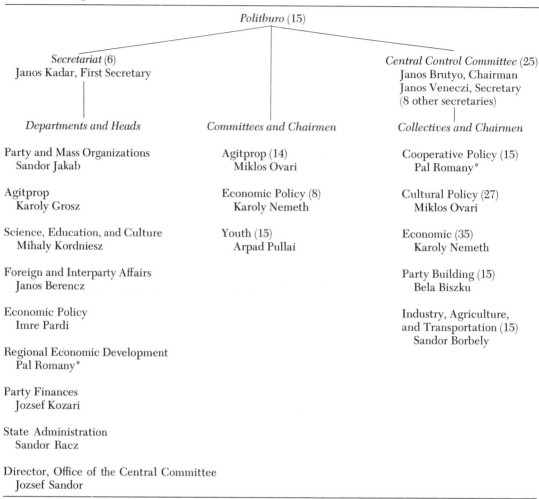

Politburo (15)

Secretariat (6)
Janos Kadar, First Secretary

Central Control Committee (25)
Janos Brutyo, Chairman
Janos Veneczi, Secretary
(8 other secretaries)

Departments and Heads	Committees and Chairmen	Collectives and Chairmen
Party and Mass Organizations Sandor Jakab	Agitprop (14) Miklos Ovari	Cooperative Policy (15) Pal Romany°
Agitprop Karoly Grosz	Economic Policy (8) Karoly Nemeth	Cultural Policy (27) Miklos Ovari
Science, Education, and Culture Mihaly Kordniesz	Youth (15) Arpad Pullai	Economic (35) Karoly Nemeth
Foreign and Interparty Affairs Janos Berencz		Party Building (15) Bela Biszku
Economic Policy Imre Pardi		Industry, Agriculture, and Transportation (15) Sandor Borbely
Regional Economic Development Pal Romany°		
Party Finances Jozsef Kozari		
State Administration Sandor Racz		
Director, Office of the Central Committee Jozsef Sandor		

Institutes	Publications
Party Academy Dezso Nemes, Director	*Nepszabadsag* Istvan Katona, Editor-in-Chief
Social Science Sandor Lakos, Director	*Tarsadalmi Szemle* Valeria Benke, Editor-in-Chief
Party History Henrik Vass, Director	*Partelet* Vera Lajtai, Editor-in-Chief

°Relieved of his post on July 2, 1975 to assume new duties as Minister of Agriculture and Food (replacing Imre Dimeny).
Source: *Nepszabadsag*, March 23, 1975.

the Party's chief spokesman on ideological and cultural affairs, it was rumored that because of his liberal policies he would be removed from the Politburo at the Congress. To date, Aczel has lost only his post in the Secretariat, the chairmanship of the Agitprop Committee, and the chairmanship of the Cultural Policy Working Collective. As deputy premier in charge of education and public culture, Aczel works under Valeria Benke and Miklos Ovari—two conservative hard-liners in the Politburo and the Secretariat.

Four new members were elected to the Politburo in March 1975 to replace the deceased Zoltan Komocsin as well as Rezso Nyers, Lajos Feher, and Gyula Kallai, who were removed for political reasons. The departure of Nyers and Feher from the Politburo had been expected after Nyers' dismissal from the Secretariat of the Central Committee in March 1974 and Feher's early retirement as deputy premier in 1974 at the age of 57. Nyers had been in charge of economic affairs, while Feher had supervised agricultural and cooperative matters, state administration, and the armed forces. Nyers' position on the Central Committee had been assumed in March 1974 by Politburo member Nemeth, who now serves as both a member of the Politburo and a secretary of the Central Committee. Lazar, a well-trained economist who is both premier and the Government's planning chief, joined Nemeth on the economic team of the Politburo in 1975. While the departure of Feher (who was relieved of all his duties) deprived the Politburo of the main architect of the Party's successful agrarian policy, the demotion of Kallai (who remains president of the Patriotic People's Front and a member of the Central Committee) had no significant effect on Party affairs. Kallai's political fortunes had been declining for several years (in part because of ill health): in 1967 Fock replaced him as premier, and in 1971 Apro replaced him as speaker of the Parliament. The four new members elected to the Politburo in 1975 are Gyorgy Lazar, Laszlo Marothy, Istvan Sarlos, and Miklos Ovari. They and Istvan Huszar are the youngest of the group and perhaps the most aggressive, but the Politburo can hardly be considered a young group; in 1971 the average age of its members was 57 (compared to the average age of all Party members, which was 44), and in 1975 the average age was 56. The functional composition of the Politburo in 1976 is shown in Table 3.6.

Table 3.6. Functional Composition of the Politburo in 1976

Four Party Secretaries (Kadar, Biszku, Nemeth, Ovari)
Chairman of Council of Ministers (Lazar)
Deputy Chairman of Council of Ministers (Huszar)
Deputy Chairman of Council of Ministers (Aczel)
Chairman of Presidential Council (Losonczi)
President of Parliament (Apro)
Secretary-General of Patriotic People's Front (Sarlos)
President of Trade Union Council (Gaspar)
Dean of Party Academy (Nemes)
First Secretary of the Communist Youth League (Marothy)
Editor of *Tarsadalmi Szemle* (Benke)
Chairman of Agitprop Committee (Ovari)
Chairman of State Planning Committee (Lazar)
Chairman of National Planning Office (Huszar)
Chairman of Economic Policy Committee (Nemeth)
Chairman of Cultural Policy Working Collective (Ovari)
Chairman of Economic Working Collective (Nemeth)
Chairman of Party Building Working Collective (Biszku)
Without Portfolio (Fock)

Although the Politburo is the highest organ of actual decision making, the permanent, full-time executive functions of the Party fall on the shoulders of the seven secretaries of the Central Committee. These men—Janos Kadar, Bela Biszku, Andras Gyenes, Imre Gyori, Karoly Nemeth, Miklos Ovari, and Arpad Pullai—are responsible for various, specific areas of activity, and are in constant control of Party and state affairs. The secretaries exercise their leadership functions through their direction of the permanent organization of the Secretariat of the Central Committee, which has a permanent staff with offices in a huge building called the "White House," located in the center of Budapest. The Secretariat is divided into nine departments whose permanent heads (nominally appointed by the Central Committee) report directly to one of the seven secretaries of the Central Committee (see Table 3.5).

The actual day-to-day operation of the Secretariat is accomplished through the nine department heads. These men have an immense amount of power. The Finance and the Mass Organizations Departments are in charge of the Party's finances and contact with mass organizations, and they are therefore in a position to handle personnel matters. The Agitation and Propaganda, and the Science, Education, and Cultural Departments are in charge of the propaganda activities of the Party; they also are responsible for transmitting Party messages through the media, setting guidelines for the development of the arts and the sciences, and imposing limits in each of these areas. The Foreign Affairs Department is in charge of foreign relations; a special section is responsible for liaison with the other Communist parties. A notable task of this section is to maintain continuous contact with a representative of the Soviet embassy in Budapest. Although it is unknown at what level contact is maintained, speculation persists that all people working in the department— from Central Committee Secretary Pullai down to the chauffeur on the one hand, and from the ambassador himself to the third secretary of the Soviet embassy on the other—are involved in this secretive process of communication. The Economic Policy and the Regional Economic Development Departments aid in the formulation and enforcement of economic policies, while the State Administration Department is in charge of the activities of the Ministry of the Interior and the armed forces. In May 1975, a Collective of Industry, Agriculture, and Transportation was created to ease the burden of the Economic Policy Department.

In addition to electing the members of the Politburo and supervising the activities of the Secretariat, the Central Committee elects the members of the Central Control Committee, the Economic Policy Committee, the Youth Committee, and the Agitation and Propaganda Committee. The Central Control Committee has 25 members and is charged with overseeing the credentials of delegates to the Central Committee, settling legal disputes within the Party, and generally insuring the legality of Party proceedings. This body, which usually meets just prior to the Central Committee, is not a part of the central decision-making apparatus of the Party.

The Economic Policy and the Agitprop Committees are by far the most important subdivisions of the Central Committee as far as the implementation of policy is concerned. (These are not to be confused with the Agitprop and Economic Policy Depart-

ments of the Secretariat of the Central Committee. See Table 3.5.) In contrast to the Politburo, which is in charge of planning the overall policy that affects all areas of public life, these committees have considerably narrower areas of responsibility, but they are empowered to implement policy as well as formulate it. The eight-member Economic Policy Committee (headed by Politburo member and Party secretary Nemeth) is composed almost entirely of economic specialists, all of whom occupy important positions in the Government. This committee is in charge of providing guidelines for the future development of the country's economy and for implementing all Party decisions related to economic policy.

The 14-member Agitprop Committee (headed by Politburo member and Party secretary, Ovari) is in charge of supervising the entire gamut of the country's intellectual, scientific, educational, and cultural life. Since its area of concern is so broad, this committee is less unified than the Economic Policy Committee and therefore less subject to control. It is instrumental in assigning the cultural and educational goals of the state and in placing limits on noneconomic contacts with the West.

The 15-member Youth Committee, headed by Arpad Pullai, is the least important of the committees elected by the Central Committee. Although Pullai is a Party secretary, his main activities (which are also the main charges of his committee) are the supervision of the political socialization of young people, the preparation of Hungary's youth for participation in public affairs, and the organization of the country's young people into meaningful "transmission belts" of socialist ideology.

There are several other organs under the supervision of the Central Committee, including the Political Academy, the Social Science Institute and the Institute of Party History. The Political Academy is in charge of the ideological education of the Party membership. The Social Science Institute is charged with research on the application of Marxist-Leninist theories; it is also the speechwriting arm of the Central Committee. The Institute of Party History conducts research into the past of the Hungarian labor movement and maintains the Party's archives.

Within the Party's Central Committee there are separate departments charged with the direction of the Party's three publications. *Nepszabadsag* is the Party's daily news organ. The monthly *Tarsadalmi*

Szemle deals with the idological questions of Party policy, while *Partelet*, which is a monthly aimed largely at the full-time functionaries of the Party, is concerned with the Party's internal development and the problems related to the implementation of various policies.

The tightly knit organization of the HSWP remains the basic instrument of Hungarian power. The country's ruling elite of perhaps as many as 1,000 people consists of those holding key Governmental and Party positions and includes most of the leaders of auxiliary organizations such as the National Women's Council as well as the leaders of the Academy of Science and the Writer's Union. The *nomenklatura* is a list of the approximately 1,000 most important Party offices that cannot be filled without the specific approval of the Party's personnel division. Persons holding these positions receive occasional special privileges and have access to privileged information, but their activities are closely scrutinized by the Party cadres' division. No position on the *nomenklatura* can be assigned to any person who has not obtained prior clearance by the apex of the Party leadership.[18] Even today, when economic expertise is highly prized by the regime and technical skills are at a premium, Party membership provides access to important decision-making functions. These all-important, decision-making functions remain the most zealously guarded and coveted prerogatives of the Party's ruling elite.

In addition to the high command of 1,000 or so people, the Hungarian power elite comprises several thousand "cadres" who exert an influence over the affairs of state far greater than that exerted by ordinary citizens. According to Sandor Jakab, head of the Department for Party and Mass Organizations, the cadres include 32,000 leaders who are at the disposal of the Party for both work in the Party and Government and after-hours activity.

A 1975 profile of this group indicates that 80 percent of them had completed political schooling of various levels, as had 42 percent of state leaders, 51 percent of economic leaders, and 42 percent of agricultural cooperative leaders. An analysis of the political education of Party and Government leaders reveals that only 14.5 percent of the leading officials in the ministries and central offices have a higher political education; among their economic counterparts, 9.7 percent of the directors and deputy directors possess a higher political education and 28

percent possess an intermediate political education. Among council leaders, the corresponding figures are 8 percent and 32 percent. More than 58 percent of agricultural cooperative leaders have no political schooling, and 24 percent have only an elementary political education. More than 62 percent of institutional leaders have no political education behind them. According to Jakab, these deficiencies are due to the fact that, in the past, the Party did not require a political education of anyone but Party officials and politicians in positions of power.[19]

The Cult of Matyas Rakosi

In 1949, as a result of the elimination of opposition parties from the political arena, the Hungarian Working People's Party (HWPP) became, in the Stalinist tradition, the unchallenged authority occupying the apex of the Hungarian polity. The task of the Party was to create conditions favorable for socialist construction. The chief architect and designer of post-World-War-II socialism in Hungary was Matyas Rakosi, first secretary of the HWPP. The Rakosi regime considered itself the legitimate heir to power by force of historical circumstances. It functioned as a classical example of autocracy—a self-ruling body with unlimited power; in this case, the decision makers accepted the ideological dictates of the Soviet example evolved through Stalin's interpretation of the writings of Marxism-Leninism. They ruled without consulting the ruled, ignored public opinion, and thwarted popular desire for a higher standard of living by Party decisions. Yet, they explained, rationalized, and justified the rule of the Party through constitutional and legal arguments and arrangements reflecting the prevailing ideology.

By assuring the leading role of the Party in all aspects of public life, the Hungarian Communist leaders hoped to insure strict Party control over all input to the decision-making process so that all issues could be resolved on strictly ideological grounds. Even decisions that were economic in nature were arrived at through predominately ideological considerations. For example, the 1950 decision to build a new steel plant at Sztalinvaros—later renamed Dunaujvaros—was justified by the Rakosi regime on purely ideological grounds. The fact that Hungary had neither iron nor coal to fuel such a plant was overlooked because the Stalinist road to socialism called for building heavy industry in the country. Thus, in this and similar cases, the Party controlled both the input and the output resulting in policy decisions and their implementation. The governmental structure erected by Rakosi was used merely as a rubber stamp to fulfill the Party's, not the public's desires.

Rakosi devised a policy based on the fanning of a war of hysteria, the unconditional sharpening of class struggle, and the mechanical application of Soviet economic practices. It was a policy of absolute subordination to Joseph Stalin and his policies. When Stalin unleashed his attack on Titoism in 1950, Rakosi indicted and tried scores of loyal Social Democrats and Communists (among them Laszlo Rajk and Janos Kadar) as Titoists, making them the scapegoats for the mistakes committed by Rakosi's regime in its effort to implement Stalinist dogma.

From 1949 to 1953, during the first period of socialist construction in Hungary, the Party's primary function was to mobilize society for industrialization. The blueprint for this plan was the Soviet economic model imposed by Stalin, not only on Hungary, but on all the other people's democracies under Soviet hegemony. To accomplish its Stalinist goals, the Rakosi regime forcedly collectivized the farms; nationalized all means of production; recruited women, youth, and senior citizens into the ranks of laborers; and imposed a crash program of heavy industrialization. Under the popular slogan of "building a material base for socialism," the Communist leadership moved quickly to wipe out all remnants of a market economy. The chief motivation for this revolutionary change was the Marxist teaching that public ownership eliminates exploitation of the many by the few. However, the leaders of the HWPP relied on the elimination of exploitation as a panacea for economic problems that could not be resolved through the Soviet economic model. Inefficiencies in the highly centralized industrial enterprises appeared as soon as the shifting of manpower from agriculture to industry and the mobilization of women for work was completed. The planners allocated their country's resources politically and set prices arbitrarily; the national goal was simply to produce goods regardless of their quality or marketability.[20] The development of production on a quota basis resulted in a tremendous waste of material and human resources. The industrial inefficiency was so overwhelming that the goods produced were of shoddy quality and were scorned by even the poorest consumers in the country. Much of the capital invested in an attempt to lay the material basis for socialism proved to be the wrong kind of investment, at the wrong place, and at the wrong time. The new Hungarian factories consumed a lot of resources for which they only produced statistics. By March 1953, when Stalin died, Hungary was using more and more capital to obtain the same increase in real output. Hungary's prewar standard of living (in terms of per capita consumption) was 87 percent of West Germany's 1955 living standard; Hungary's standard of living had dropped by 1955 to 52 percent of West Germany's 1955 standard.[21] Yet, the net industrial production of Hungary in 1955 reached 262 percent of the 1938 level.[22] Consequently, some Party leaders began to realize that the economic road upon which they had embarked was leading nowhere; that there was a limit to the positive returns from a command economy operated from one center; and that the revolution from above based on despotism; terror, and a promise of utopia had its limitations in terms of its capacity for achieving socialist goals. Therefore, after Stalin's death, and the introduction of the Kremlin's de-Stalinization and desatellitization policies, several Party leaders took a new look at the country's economic conditions and decided to make some drastic changes.

In June 1953, after the Central Committee of the HWPP disclosed the major economic and political errors made by the Rakosi regime, Imre Nagy replaced Matyas Rakosi as prime minister, and thus began the brief period of the "new course." During the subsequent months, several of the mistakes made in the immediate past were corrected: the forceful method of building agricultural cooperatives was abandoned; several Party leaders—including Janos Kadar—who had survived the 1951 anti-Titoist purges were released from prison and rehabilitated. However, economic conditions in Hungary failed to improve to any significant measure. When in February 1955, Khrushchev removed Georgi Malenkov from the premiership, he set a precedent for placing the Party above the Government and heavy industry above light industry. A month later, Rakosi accused Nagy of reversing these priorities and engineered his expulsion from the Party's Central Committee for "rightist deviation"; soon afterwards Nagy was also expelled from the office of the premiership. He was replaced by Rakosi whose return to the Government signaled a return to Stalinism in Hungary.

Rakosi's attempt to continue Stalinism in Hungary was partially successful in 1955, but it failed the following year. He not only purged Nagy's supporters from Party and Government positions, but in order to quiet the anti-Soviet outbursts in Budapest, he also placed pro-Communist police and troops on 24-hour duty. While Rakosi was reviving old Stalinist practices Khrushchev was systematically abolishing Stalinism in Soviet Russia. His speech exposing Stalinist crimes, given at the 20th Congress of the CPSU, encouraged and increased the determination of many loyal Hungarian Communists to reverse the trend toward Stalinization in Hungary and seek de-Stalinization. In March 1956, on instructions from Moscow, the national Communist leader, Laszlo Rajk, who had been executed by the Rakosi regime in 1949, was "rehabilitated" at a graveside ceremony, and in July, Rakosi was replaced as first secretary of the Party by his trusted deputy, Erno Gero. On October 23, after months of open criticism by writers, students, and other intellectuals, and under the stimulus provided by Poland's struggle for greater independence, Hungarian popular discontent erupted in student demonstrations. Street fighting broke out in Budapest between demonstrators and opposing Soviet-Hungarian forces. As soon as the Soviet troops withdrew from Budapest, Rakosi and Gero left for the Soviet Union where they were granted political asylum. Imre Nagy was returned to the premiership, and Gero was replaced as first secretary by Janos Kadar.

The coalition government, headed by Nagy, responded to the demands of the revolutionaries: on November 1, 1956, Nagy proclaimed Hungary's neutrality, the country's withdrawal from the Warsaw pact, and the Government's intention to hold free, multiparty elections. At about the same time, several members of the Nagy coalition, including Kadar, left Budapest for the Soviet city of Uzhgorod where, under Soviet tutelage, they formed the Revolutionary Worker-Peasant Government, which was responsible for requesting Soviet military intervention in Hungary. On November 3, 1956, Soviet armed forces invaded the country and crushed the rebellion. Nagy, who had been promised safe conduct from Hungary by the new Kadar government, was seized by Soviet military officers as he was leaving his sanctuary at the Yugoslav Embassy. He was executed several months later.

Kadar's Alliance Policy

According to the December 1956 resolution of the reorganized Hungarian Socialist Workers' Party (HSWP),[23] the October uprising was caused by: (1) the sectarian and dogmatic errors of Rakosi and his group; (2) the agitation of revisionists; (3) the activity of counterrevolutionary forces in Hungary; and (4) counterrevolutionary action abroad.[24] Workers' demands that Imre Nagy take over the leadership of the government, that there be a multiparty system allowing other parties based on socialism to function, that Hungary be a neutralist state, and that free elections by secret ballot be held after a specified lapse of time[25] were completely rejected by Kadar. Instead, on December 9, 1956, his regime abolished the workers' councils (above the factory level) that had been established during the revolution and jailed many of the workers who were passively resisting the new regime through strikes. Yet, although Kadar adhered to policies initiated by Khrushchev, he was bold enough to acknowledge the Hungarian populist movement for national identity and internal reform, and after a short period of severe reprisals, he introduced a systematic policy of conciliation aimed at restoring and reaping the benefits of national unity. At no time, however, did Kadar diminish the role of the Party in the affairs of state.

In an effort to gain the confidence of the population and at the same time maintain a pro-Soviet (anti-third-road) orientation, the Provisional Central Committee of the HSWP issued a compromise resolution excluding both active supporters of Rakosi and all supporters of Nagy from membership in the Party. As a result, only a small group of "neutrals" and civil servants registered as members of the HSWP during the first months following the revolution. By the end of 1956, the official party organ, *Nepszabadsag*, reported that 12 percent (108,000) of the former HWPP (900,000) had been recovered by the new Party and that Party organizations had been set up in 42 percent of the nation's villages.[26] This disclosure revealed that HSWP organizations still did not exist in a majority of villages and that most Hungarian workers did not support the new Party.[27] Therefore Kadar and his associates in the party hierarchy immediately launched a campaign to expand the base and strengthen the unity of the Party.

Whereas Rakosi's loyalty was to Stalin and his policies, Kadar's loyalty was to the Post-Stalinist Kremlin and its policies. However, unlike Rakosi, Kadar was more concerned about the welfare of his people than about proletarian internationalism. An apparatchik's apparatchik, Kadar always tried to persuade the Soviet elite that his party's decisions were the most palatable expressions of Marxism-Leninism and that they were in complete conformity with the interests of the international socialist community. Since Kadar was both anti-Stalinist and antirevisionist, he had the confidence not only of the Kremlin, but also of those in the Hungarian Party hierarchy whose past had been compromised by either Rakosi or Nagy. Thus, the basic political and cultural principles introduced in Hungary after 1956 mirrored those formulated in the Soviet Union; in both countries, a new regime aimed to de-Stalinize an oppressive and unpopular system that had been created by despots.

As in the Soviet Union under Khrushchev, so in Hungary under Kadar, the Party stood at the apex of all activities. However, after the Hungarian Revolution of 1956, the aim of the HSWP was to unify the various interests and organizations of Hungarian society. To assure a firm and responsive position for the Party, Kadar skillfully maneuvered between moderate purges in Party and Government ranks and a steady improvement in the Hungarian standard of living. "The first nine months," stated Kadar, "constituted a period of very intense class struggle. The Party-guided proletarian dictatorship was forced to take extremely severe measures." The fifteen months following this period of intense class struggle were devoted to internal struggle between factions within the Party, according to Kadar. The struggle waged against extremists on both the left and the right resulted in "enforcing the Marxist-Leninist ideals in their original purity, free of dogmatic, revisionist distortions."[28]

By the end of 1961, Kadar was confident of the strength of the Party and began to seek legitimacy for his socialist regime. Legitimacy, according to Kadar, depended upon the voluntary participation of a majority of citizens in the decision-making process in order to stimulate a positive response on the part of the citizenry toward the implementation

of decisions. After 1961, Kadar fought hard to keep this philosophy alive, placing constant emphasis on the needs of the masses, the development of national unity, and the alliance between Party and non-Party people. For example, in November 1962, at the Eighth Congress of the HSWP, Kadar reiterated the June 1957 Party principle that "people shall be judged by their competence" and announced a new application of the principle, namely that qualifications for admission to Hungarian universities would no longer be based on class origin. He also requested greater tolerance toward former "kulaks" and support for the "private plot." Between 1962 and 1975, the Kadar doctrine of legitimacy through participation produced several positive results, including a purge of Stalinists and all those involved in Rakosi's purge trials; amnesty for political prisoners; abolition of the system of internal exile and security internment without trial; reduction in the number of forced labor camps; elimination of the jamming of Western radio stations; greater freedom of criticism and inquiry; improved civil rights; more humane, more responsive, and more flexible Party leadership; and a socialist market economy. All of these reforms, including the economic one (discussed in the second half of Chapter 10), helped to consolidate the role of the Party in Hungarian society, and the increase in citizen participation and initiative resulting from the reform movement provided the Party elite with a gauge for measuring both the effectiveness of its policies and the cohesiveness of the new socialist society.

Economic Stagnation and the Challenge from the Dogmatists

However, before Janos Kadar and his acolytes could continue on the road to liberalization, which in 1968 led to the establishment of the New Economic Mechanism (NEM), they had to overcome several obstacles in the Party and the Government. Probably the most serious obstacle was the opposition of hard-line Party "dogmatists" to Kadar's pragmatic policies.

Throughout 1964 and the first half of 1965, Hungary experienced a temporary economic setback—the first interruption of its steady economic growth since the October 1956 revolt. A 1965 decrease in wages coupled with a rise in comsumer prices hit industrial workers very hard. Resentment spread when the salaries of Hungarian bureaucrats and officers of the armed forces were also cut. A few months earlier, in October 1964, Kadar's mentor in the USSR, Nikita S. Khrushchev, was forced to resign from both the Party and the Government. Several Hungarian dogmatists, especially those in smaller cities and villages who had been under criticism from Kadar ever since 1962, seized the opportunity to counterattack; they questioned the orthodoxy of Kadar's goals, arguing that his alliance policy had weakened the strength of the Party by permitting it to share its power with an "alien stratum." They also charged that the Party had lost its role as the vanguard of the working class, because workers engaged in physical labor constituted only 34.6 percent of the Party membership, whereas employees performing nonmanual labor and professionals made up 39 percent of the membership.[29]

Kadar defended his political line on two fronts. He attacked the Right (the "extreme reactionaries") for falsely applauding his reforms as a "restoration of capitalism" or a "bourgeois liberalization," and he condemned the Left (the "Rakosi-type dogmatists") for being blinded by the "petit bourgeois radicalism and a lot of mixed-up ideas."[30]

The first secretary warned his critics that in 1956, the counterrevolution had started with suspicion and innuendo, which gave rise to incitement. "But every rational person must understand," said Kadar, "that the entire nation cannot be suspect."[31] He praised the alliance between Party and non-Party people as the correct line. In the fall of 1964, when the dogmatists were hoping that the ouster of Kadar would follow that of Khrushchev, the Hungarian first secretary assured his followers that "the political attitude of the HSWP and the Government of the Hungarian People's Republic has not changed one iota, nor will it change."[32] It is true that the Soviet Union continued to seek detente with the West, while Kadar's regime pursued its former policies with undiminished energy, in the spirit of what Kadar called "the ideas of the 20th Congress of the CPSU and the 1957 and 1960 international Communist conferences."[33] By March 1966, Kadar had dispelled all of the dogmatists' hopes for political change in Hungary. At the 23rd Congress of the CPSU, the Hungarian first secretary was not only recognized as the Kremlin's man in Budapest, but for his statement that "there never has been, and there will never be, an anti-Soviet Communist," Kadar was also given a public bear hug by Brezhnev himself.[34] After that, Kadar felt secure enough to get rid of some of his leading opponents such as Gyorgy Marosan, Istvan Kossa, Imre Dogei, Ferenc Munich, and Istvan Dobi. There were many lesser-known workers, particularly in the provinces, along with many non-Party people, who were also either purged from the Party or arrested for "anti-state" activities, "incitement," "conspiracy," etc. It is difficult to say whether these "belt-tightening" measures by the Kadar regime were the direct or indirect consequence of pressures exerted by the Hungarian dogmatists. One thing is clear, however, the hard-liners continued to make every effort to undermine Kadar's liberalization policies. One such effort was apparently made at the May 1966 Central Committee meeting during a debate on the details of the New Economic Mechanism. According to Rezso Nyers, Kadar had laid his prestige on the line by supporting the NEM. The differences of opinion on several issues concerning the economic reforms ran deep. For example, there were members of the Committee who thought that Hungary had been economically stronger in the early 1950s than she was in 1966.[35] Kadar won approval of his reform by a very narrow margin, after which he carried out a campaign aimed at persuading rather than purging the opposition.

The Ninth and Tenth Party Congresses

To pacify the anti-alliance-policy dogmatists, the Ninth Congress of the HSWP decided not to publish the guidelines for discussion customarily included in the final report of each congress; this move precluded any participation by non-Party specialists in the pre-Tenth-Party-Congress discussions. In other actions, the Party amended its statutes to (1) permit Party organs to require performance reports from the heads of state, cooperative, and mass organizations within their territorial functions; and (2) require that Party organs be consulted on all important appointments to posts in their areas.[36] It seems logical to argue that in order to appease the dogmatists, Kadar chose a compromise solution: he strengthened the prerogatives of the local Party leaders in exchange for maintaining his alliance policy, which had already prompted many economic and political reforms. Moreover, between the Ninth and Tenth Party Congresses, the Kadar regime introduced many measures that gave the alliance policy renewed legitimacy. One of the most significant changes on this road to socialist democracy was the elimination of the legacy of dogmatism in the social sciences. In March 1967, for example, Ferenc Pataki argued in *Tarsadalmi Szemle* that ideology (meaning Marxism-Leninism) could not by itself explain human behavior: the expertise of social psychology and similar disciplines was considered a precondition for understanding human conduct.[37]

The tenets of Hungarian socialist realism, which attempted to de-ideologize several of the new spheres of endeavor that were developing in a liberalized Hungarian society, were challenged by Party conservatives (leftist dogmatists) during the preparatory discussions for the Tenth Party Congress held in November 1970. These critics of the Kadar regime raised a number of issues in debates that, according to *Nepszabadsag*, caused "impassioned arguments."[38] All of these issues centered on the welfare of the proletariat, namely, on whether the proletariat was sufficiently represented in Party, state, and mass organizations; whether it was favored over managers and peasants; and whether the proletariat was receiving the benefits of the scientific-technological revolution. The Kadar regime was subjected to renewed ideological criticism for the way it had exercised its leading role in Hungarian society. Most of this criticism had a familiar ring (dating back to the early 1960s). This time, however, the criticism was not so much directed against his program itself as against the impact of its implementation and emphasis. There was very little doubt that the standard of living of workers was improving at a much slower rate than that of bureaucrats, peasants, artisans, or members of the new managerial groups. According to official figures, during the Third Five-Year Plan (1966–1970) the real income of peasants increased by 42 percent, while that of workers rose by only 31 percent.[39] In addition, friction between workers and managers, which in 1969 had caused the abolition of the profit-sharing system, was still prevalent before the Tenth Party Congress convened in November 1970. Apparently, the new, "more equitable" system of management was equally unsatisfactory to the workers. Thus, price stabilization and income equalization remained major issues in 1970. Furthermore, two months before the Party Congress, the Central Statistical Office issued a study on income and consumption that confirmed the workers' suspicions: they were, after the

pensioners, the lowest-income group in the country.[40] Despite explanations that more time was needed and admissions of errors by the regime, worker dissatisfaction continued, and Kadar's critics skillfully exploited the situation at the Congress. It was probably for this reason that Kadar himself offered reassurances that more equitable state norms would be instituted to regulate the formulation of prices and profits.[41]

Another problem that angered Hungarian workers and thus became an issue at the Tenth Party Congress was corruption among the lower-level Party officials. Several charges were made that "money-grubbing and influence-peddling had been witnessed among those in positions of trust within the Party ranks."[42] In the opinion of some Party leaders these members were, in Communist jargon, "careerists" and "opportunists." The outcry for the expulsion of such culprits was understandable.

While some Party leaders charged that Party members and officials had been corrupted by the NEM, others criticized the very source of economic reform in Hungary, namely, the alliance policy. In September 1970, Janos Siklos, editor-in-chief of the trade union daily *Nepszava*, published an article in which he called for an intensification of the struggle against "bourgeois, lower-middle-class liberalism" in Hungary. Siklos claimed that this phenomenon was an outgrowth of the alliance policy, which minimized the "Marxist substance and class character" of socialist construction.[43] In October 1970, the National Trade Union Council (NTUC) submitted its report on the Party Guidelines, in which it questioned Kadar's policy of judging people and their loyalty to the socialist system by their competence and efficiency in their jobs. The document stressed that professional training or general culture are qualities that are "easily acquirable, while an alert worker's spirit is not."[44] No one took direct issue with the NTUC document at the Congress, but before the congress opened, Siklos' criticism of the alliance policy was condemned by his peer, Peter Renyi, deputy editor-in-chief of *Nepszabadsag*. Renyi accused Siklos of creating a "leftist intolerance" among the public and cautioned him about the repercussions that might follow from such irresponsible behavior.[45] At the Tenth Party Congress, Kadar himself addressed the question of the "leading role of the working class." He maintained that although "the workers' presence is indispensable in many places; nevertheless, numerical proportion is not the essence of the matter."[46] It is interesting to note that this explanation by the first secretary was more orthodox than the ones he had given on previous occasions when he had defended his alliance policy against the same charges. In his report, Kadar, of course, gave full support to the NEM and criticized those who blamed the system of economic management for "temporarily unsolved or unsatisfactorily solved problems."[47]

As it happened, however, these problems were persistent, not "temporary." In October 1971, after the economic reform had been in operation for nearly four years, Premier Jeno Fock had no choice but to reveal the existence of serious economic difficulties characterized by inefficiency and a critical lack of balance within vital sectors of the economy. Fock admitted that investment spending had gotten totally out of control and that state subsidies had increased at an unacceptable rate. He also complained that labor turnover was much too high and that Hungary had an excessive foreign trade deficit. The conference of economic activists, an *ad hoc* gathering, was convened to deal with this near crisis. Although it is customary for the Central Committee to deal with such a crisis in a plenary session, the Party elite apparently felt that an open discussion concerning the NEM at a time of economic disarray would be politically dangerous, and thus, they opted for tackling the problem in an ad hoc gathering. The conference recommended that investment expenditures be curbed, a credit ban on new investments in commercial enterprises be put into effect, limited restrictions on the free movement of labor be imposed and imports from the West be cut considerably. These recommendations resulted in the adoption of an effective stabilization program and by the middle of 1972, the economic difficulties had largely subsided, although they had not disappeared. In November 1972, the Central Committee of the HSWP met to tackle a large number of political, economic, social, and ideological problems that had accumulated in the course of putting the NEM into practice and that called for immediate action.[48]

The November 1972 and November 1973 Party Plenums

The changes endorsed by the November 1972 plenum of the Party's Central Committee took into account a number of lessons learned in the first five years of

the economic reform, and as such, they seemed to dovetail with the recommendations made by well-meaning critics of the NEM. By voting a one-time wage increase for some 1,300,000 workers in large industrial enterprises and construction firms, the plenum killed two birds with one stone: it raised the standard of living of an important segment of the labor force, thereby eliminating a crucial source of political tension that made itself felt nationwide; and it pulled the rug out from under the feet of conservative Party members who opposed the NEM.

The plenum also passed a resolution that singled out a section of the Party membership (the conservatives) and "certain Party organizations" for particularly severe censure. It charged that some Party organizations had failed to require their members to represent the Party's stand at all times and reprimanded Party members who went so far as to oppose the Party's position outside Party forums. The resolution warned such elements to uphold and respect the Party line, or else face expulsion. It also reminded Party members to cease debating issues that had been declared settled and to concentrate their energies on implementing the resolutions adopted "unanimously" by the plenum.[49] Although it is doubtful that a two-day session healed all wounds and reunited the dissidents of the Right and Left with the Center, a rundown of domestic developments in 1973 indicates that Party members worked together to implement the 1972 plenum resolution.

In January 1973, the Party convened a national conference on information and culture in Budapest, at which Central Committee Secretary Gyorgy Aczel discussed current ideological issues in terms of the November 1972 plenum resolution. He accused sociologists Andras Hegedus and Maria Markus and philosophers Agnes Heller and Mihaly Vajda of violating the fundamental tenets of Marxism-Leninism. Hegedus, Vajda, and philosopher Janos Kis were expelled from the Party in May 1973, and together with Markus, Heller, and the philosopher, Gyorgy Bencze (all non-Party persons), they were subjected to a scorching rebuke; the Party document on the subject referred explicitly to the section on ideology in the plenum resolution and quoted from it to justify the Party's action.[50]

With regard to the Party's economic policies, after the November 1972 plenum vigorous steps were taken to control and coordinate the planning process (particularly at the ministerial level). For example, the state acted directly to transform the production structure of six of the country's largest enterprises, which had previously been faced with bankruptcy.[51] Fifty economic units (responsible for 55 percent of the gross industrial production) employing one half of all of Hungary's industrial workers were affected by this transformation of production. One spillover of modernization has been the preparation of the new economic regulators for the next five-year plan (1976–1980) which will include both a revamping of the wage system (allowing wage increases to be separated from profits, in some areas) and the elimination of current restrictions on an enterprise's right to distribute income between its development and participation funds.

Although economic growth was satisfactory in 1973 (industrial production rose by 6–7 percent and agricultural production increased by 5–6 percent), Hungary still faced serious economic problems. For example, the large state subsidies to heavy industry continued to grow, while deflated prices still did not reflect the true value of consumer goods. One reason for the stable prices was the Government's wage policy. Fear of inflation and its economic and political consequences, as well as strong public pressure to increase already expanding social welfare benefits, caused Kadar's regime to allow modest annual increases in real wages in the state sector, which caused even greater inequities in income distribution. Owing to these factors, the Party felt constrained to decree another "one-time, extraordinary" wage raise at its Central Committee plenum held on November 28, 1973. This measure affected those industrial and construction workers not covered by the November 1972 increase, as well as a number of employees in state and local administrative, economic, and budgetary organs. The Party thus managed to avert another upsurge of discontent, but only temporarily; until it lifts all wage restrictions, the danger of recurring tension remains. Between 1972 and 1975, Hungary also had a persistent problem in the area of foreign trade. Hungary's balance of trade with the West was unfavorable, but at the same time the country accumulated large surpluses from trade with several socialist countries (e.g., Bulgaria, Czechoslovakia, Poland, the USSR, and Mongolia). Such "profits," however, were a quasi liability rather than an asset because they represented a drain on the country's supply of commodities.[52] For example, in the 21-month period ending 1974,

Hungary registered a 331,900,000 forint surplus in its trade with Bulgaria. The imbalance was serious enough to cause a meeting between the two country's top Party leaders, Janos Kadar and Todor Zhivkov, who discussed ways of reducing the disequilibrium.

There were still other problems the Party tried to cope with following the plenum of November 1972. Some were old or recurrent, as for example, the control of income differentiation and the imposition of socialist morality, and some were new, such as the need for family planning and the growing influence of the ideas of the New Left in the West.[53] None, however, were as serious as those faced before the November 1972 plenum. Thus, on November 28, 1973, when the plenum of the Central Committee of the HSWP convened in Budapest, it drew up a balance sheet of the preceding year which indicated that those 1972 plenum decisions whose deadline for implementation had passed had been carried out and that the implementation of those tasks requiring a longer period of time was proceeding at a satisfactory pace.[54]

The Eleventh Party Congress

However, when the Eleventh Congress of the HSWP met from March 17 to March 22, 1975, the economic, social, and political problems facing Hungary were as acute as they had been in 1972, and the Party leadership again raised the issue of ideological conformity. Indeed, restrictions on cultural expression had reached a new climax in 1973 and 1974 when the police and judiciary acted against the intellectual community on four different occasions. In late October 1974, for example, writer Gyorgy Konrad, sociologist Ivan Szelenyi, and poet Tamas Szentjoby were arrested and temporarily detained on trumped-up charges of conspiracy and espionage.[55] Although nothing has been heard of Szentjoby since then, both Konrad and Szelenyi were expelled from Hungary in the spring of 1975.

The Konrad-Szelenyi case provides a representative sample of recent official attitudes toward cultural affairs. Demands for greater ideological conformity and for the display of a more Marxist spirit in cultural and academic works have led to the creation of a restrictive atmosphere and the imposition of sanctions on alleged offenders. The sanctions have included expulsions from the Party, dismissals from jobs, police searches, the confiscation of manuscripts, arrest and detention, trial, and exile. In addition, it has become increasingly difficult to acquire exit visas for the purpose of attending cultural conferences in the West, and Party organs dealing with questions of cultural and ideological theory have assumed a rigidity of approach and hardness of tone unmatched since 1956. This hard-line policy was particularly evident at the Eleventh Party Congress.

Addressing the Congress as the only female member of the Politburo and as chairperson of the editorial staff of *Tarsadalmi Szemle* (the Party's monthly devoted to ideological issues), Valeria Benke condemned those scholars and researchers who had "drifted into the troubled waters of revisionism and ultraleftist or other turbid streams."[56] She cautioned that on the ideological front there cannot be any compromise. The messages of the Congress were clear and loud: greater ideological commitment and less cultural and academic freedom. As a result, literary and artistic life entered a new period of stagnation in which published creative output was at best mediocre.

The most pressing problems before the Congress, however, were economic and social ones: inflation, rapidly rising subsidies, insufficient funds for social benefits, the definition and implementation of workers' rights, and the future of the NEM.

Rampant inflation hit Hungary because of the impact of large increases in the prices of fuel and raw materials, both of which the country lacks. In 1975, for example, the average price of raw materials and sources of energy increased by 52 percent over the 1974 price level. The price for crude oil delivered to the Hungarian frontier jumped from 16 to 37 rubles a ton (at the prevailing exchange rate 37 rubles is worth $49.50), but the prices of Hungarian machinery exported in 1975 increased by only 15 percent and that of exported agricultural produce by only 28 percent.[57] Hungary derives 40 percent of its national income from foreign trade, but must import almost all of the basic materials and fuel used in producing goods for export. Price increases on imported products rendered the 1975 economic plans for industrial enterprises suddenly obsolete and caused the rapid accumulation of a considerable trade deficit with industrially developed countries. This deficit jumped from 1,300 million foreign exchange forints in 1972–1973 to over 6,300 million by the end of 1974.

Inflation also compelled the Government to augment its subsidies in order to stabilize the economy. Price supports on imports alone rose from 5,000 million forints in 1973 to 24,000 million in 1974, and the state budget for 1975 earmarked 36 percent of its total expenditures for subventions mainly to support prices. Although huge subsidies have thus far prevented panic among both producers and consumers alike, the subsidies have nevertheless created an artificial price system—a phenomenon that leads to irrational economic decisions, retardation of genuine economic growth, and a failure to keep pace with economic change. Indeed, the more that is given for subsidies, the less can be spent for investment and the achievement of social goals. Yet both of these areas have acquired increased importance in recent years.

Since 1972, the Kadar regime has curbed the import of Western machinery, restricted the granting of bank credit, examined enterprise investment proposals more critically, and reduced the number of large-scale state projects planned each year. At the same time, the higher cost of imports has hindered the completion of several projects considered vital to economic modernization. Higher prices have also resulted in the excessive stockpiling of working capital. In the metallurgical industry a recent decline of 255,000 tons in the export of processed goods to the profitable Western market meant a loss of valuable foreign currency.

The maintenance of price stability through subsidies has retarded the implementation of such social policies as improved family allowances, the unification of pension systems, the building of more state housing, the development of a health service network, et cetera. The intractability of Hungary's economic and social problems, the protests and dissatisfaction they have provoked from the state's industrial workers, and the anxiety they have induced among the public at large, have prompted the Party to reassert central control and national priorities. Consequently the further expansion of market forces scheduled under the New Economic Mechanism has been frozen, and a partial retrenchment of enterprise autonomy has been instituted. The guidelines adopted as well as the resolutions passed at the Eleventh Party Congress clearly indicate that this situation will continue and perhaps become even more pronounced.[58] Nevertheless, there is no indication that Hungary will return to a command economy with quantitative indicators and prescriptive planning. Far from it. What the present political elite actually desires is greater modernization, efficiency, profitability, and the application of more rational management, labor, production, and organizational procedures.

Of course, the issue is not as simple as it appears. The economic and social problems are closely interwoven with political ones. For example, the demands of blue-collar workers for higher wages are not merely demands for more money; they are also demands for increased social status, prestige, power, and preferential treatment. Since 1971, similar demands have resulted in the establishment of a free legal aid service, higher taxes on incomes in the private sector, centrally decreed wage increases for state workers, curbs on income-producing activities of agricultural cooperatives, increased educational opportunities and other privileges. Ever since the March 1974 Central Committee plenum, the principle of the workers' leading role in the implementation of Hungarian socialism has been expressed by the concept of "factory democracy," which has now been formally incorporated into the Party's new program. The development of democracy in factories and other commercial enterprises was given considerable emphasis at the Eleventh Congress; the delegates even passed a resolution spelling out the importance attributed to it by the Party's top leaders. Factory (or enterprise) democracy, according to the resolution, provides an opportunity for workers to play a genuine role in enterprise management by entitling them to hire and fire enterprise managers, evaluate managerial work, and control a large portion of an enterprise's funds. It also encourages creativity among workers and greater worker participation in local and higher-level public affairs. Factory democracy is thus a major tool in developing a socialist relationship between managers and workers.[59] As Kadar explained, the basic institutions affecting factory workers are the Party; the trade unions; the Communist Youth League organizations functioning in factories, enterprises, and state farms; the production conferences; and other workers' forums.[60] Factory democracy therefore means greater Party contact with workers everywhere and on a daily basis. While the Party elite hopes that enterprise democracy will enhance the workers' sense of responsibility, at the same time, the leadership runs the risk of creating an unwelcome constellation of power among newly politicized workers who could take their leading role at face value and feed on the success they have had since the November 1972 Central Committee plenum when the Party shifted its priorities from the further development of economic reform to the implementation of social policy and workers' rights. It is also conceivable, however, that the recent changes in the social structure caused by the institution of factory democracy could enhance the Party's power among factory workers and other enterprise employees. With the gradual recentralization of economic direction and the concomitant growth of specific functions for local party organizations, there are no indications that the strength of the Party will increase rather than decrease as a result of enterprise democracy.

Summary

With the inauguration of the Hungarian People's Republic, the Communist Party became the basic structure around which both state and society were shaped. Since 1949, the Party has not been challenged by any competing political organization; the Party's leading role in Hungarian society has thus remained constant. What has changed, however, is the composition, aim, and operation of the Party. Since Hungarian Communists are also members of the world Communist movement, under the direction of the Kremlin, all Hungarian policies—especially those concerned with foreign affairs—are either directed from or approved by the Kremlin.

Between 1949 and 1953, the Rakosi regime interpreted the principle of the vanguard role of the Party to mean that only the leadership of the Party was qualified to decide what was good or bad, right or wrong, for ten million Hungarians. Armed with the principles of Stalinism, which culminated in the development of the cult of personality, Rakosi excluded the Hungarian people from determining their own goals based on their own political, social, and economic needs. During this period of socialist construction, the Party created the machinery required to build an economic base of heavy industry, but the revolutionary changes resulting from the rapid implementation of the Stalinist prototype of industrialization had a negative effect on the standard of living of most Hungarians and thus alienated them. In its drive to socialize society, the Rakosi regime eliminated all remnants of a market economy and centralized the decision-making process; it also substituted quantity for quality in production and statistics for real output. Therefore, although postwar industrial production increased two- to threefold over prewar production, the Hungarian standard of living declined, rendering the economy a subsistence economy with a deficit.

When the Communist Party of the Soviet Union, under Georgi Malenkov, began to liberalize its policies in the process of de-Stalinization, the Central Committee of the HWPP, under Imre Nagy, condemned Rakosi's practices and worked for two years to decompress the overcentralized machinery of the Rakosi dictatorship. However, when Rakosi was restored to power in 1955, his sudden reversal of the trend toward de-Stalinization ended the decompression process (which had its own built-in dynamics), and in October 1956 Hungary exploded in open revolt. As the spontaneous support of the revolution revealed, the Hungarian people, including rank-and-file Communists, had lost confidence in the Party and its leaders. Thus, a new, Hungarian—rather than Soviet—model of development had to be created, which, of course, meant a drastic departure from the Party's previous line.

After 1956, the Party under Kadar introduced a more subtle and "democratic" mode of operation. Although the new regime abolished the independent organizations (such as the workers' councils) that had sprung up during the 1956 revolution, at the same time it co-opted their leaders by assigning them positions in similar Party organizations; it also flung open the doors of the Party to admit new members with no questions asked. The use of terror to silence opposition continued after 1956, but Kadar's methods were more tolerable (jail and expulsion from the Party or country, instead of execution) because the cult of personality was gone; therefore the relationship between the regime and the citizenry improved. As an emphasis on efficiency in production gradually replaced the emphasis on statistical output, the Party leaders became more flexible in their approach, and at times, they even compromised between ideological and pragmatic goals. The success of Kadar's conciliatory policies aimed at restoring national unity, however, could be assured only through continued liberalization and a struggle against Rakosi-type dogmatists and extreme reactionaries. In both of these efforts, Kadar received the personal endorse-

ment of Khrushchev as well as moral and material support from several socialist countries.

By 1962, the year of the Eighth Congress of the HSWP, Hungary was ready to begin its postmobilization (i.e., modernization) phase of development. That process, however, called for the abandonment of the revolution from above and the dismantling of the mobilization system even at the risk of generating new bureaucracies, institutions, and loyalties with dynamics of their own. Hence, Kadar introduced his alliance policy, which presupposed a modification in both the ideology and the criteria of social control. It created new roles for both Party and non-Party members and obligated the regime to coordinate the actions of diverse groups and develop legitimate institutions.

During the remainder of the 1960s, more or less severe criticism of the alliance policy continued to surface, varying with the occasion and the goal of the critics. In the mid-1960s, for example, Party officials in the provinces capitalized on the dissatisfaction of industrial workers, who complained of high prices and low wages, to criticize the economic impact of the policy. In 1970, at the Tenth Party Congress, the dogmatist opponents of alliance, many of whom occupied high positions in the Party, criticized the ideological impact of the policy on the grounds that it gave the more educated members of Hungarian society an advantage over the workers. It could be hypothesized, however, that as Hungary modernizes, functional differentiation and complexity force the leadership to relax controls which, of course, creates greater competition and therefore a potential for greater differentiation between working-class and managerial standards of living. Just because Kadar controls the party leadership, does not mean that he is always able to reconcile differences within the Party. Dogmatists in the lower and middle levels of the hierarchy are still opposed to modernization as such and are quite capable of blocking it or at least slowing it down. This became evident at the November 1972 plenary session of the Central Committee of the HSWP.

As a result of persistent pressures exerted by labor leaders and conservative Party dogmatists against proponents of the NEM, the 1972 Party plenum voted sizeable wage increases for a large number of workers. However, when the impact of this measure wore off, new pressures applied by the same groups resulted not only in the revamping of the entire wage system, but in a comprehensive set of measures designed to increase the status, role, and participation of the working class in socialist construction. Simultaneously, the government introduced significant changes in the country's economic regulators (e.g., in the norms governing the distribution of enterprise income). By the time the Eleventh Party Congress convened in 1975, the leadership of the HSWP had reversed the trend toward economic and political decentralization in an effort to enhance the status of blue-collar workers; it sanctioned its new policies under the rubric of adapting to new circumstances, solving new problems, making necessary corrections, eliminating the obsolete, and so on. The changes implemented between 1972 and 1975 were relatively substantial; however, they did not dismantle or destroy the post-1968 reform system qua system. The Party leadership utilized the Eleventh Congress as a forum to explain that further change would take place along the lines endorsed at the November 1972 Central Committee plenum. At the same time, it gave assurances that the system itself would remain intact and that an earnest attempt would be made to ensure that future modification would not be arbitrary or abrupt.

Further centralization was one of the policies most emphasized within this general framework. Various congressional speeches and documents stressed that national social and Governmental interests would take priority over group and individual interests. Speakers also underscored that control and supervision of the implementation of centrally made decisions had to be more energetic, consistent, and effective, a course of action necessitating more timely and more frequent ministerial intervention in the affairs of commercial enterprises. In addition, the Party emphasized that it was important to bring the plans of individual production units into harmony with the objectives of national economic policy. Given Hungary's particular economic problems, the envisaged recentralization of economic planning will most probably affect such areas as investment, credit, imports from the West, allocation of scarce raw materials and semifinished products, prices, and the transformation of the production structure of selected large enterprises. On the other hand, most firms will continue to enjoy the right of deciding upon their production profile, sources of supply, and customers, and they will have considerable leeway with respect to foreign trade. It is reasonable to assume that the more profitable and efficient an enterprise, the more independent it will be.

As a direct result of the Eleventh Party Congress, the National Assembly has enacted laws unifying the country's pension system, decreasing the retirement age for agricultural cooperative members, increasing the maximum allowable pension, and raising minimum old-age benefits as well as derivative pensions paid to war widows and orphans. Stress on the leading role of the working class and the special significance of workers in large industrial enterprises will probably result in further concessions to the demands of blue-collar workers for greater prestige and a higher, more secure standard of living. Finally, greater ideological commitment, less cultural and academic experimentation, and a more severe attitude toward nationalism, Maoism, and the "pseudoradical" leftist opinion were also among the basic messages of the Congress. Some opinions voiced at the Eleventh Party Congress indicated that conservative forces within the Party are bent on instituting a more rigid policy of literary control. In response to those opinions, however, several Hungarian authors and poets (e.g., Ferenc Juhasz, Ferenc Karinthy, and Gyula Fekete) came out strongly in defense of the most complete freedom possible for all types of artists and writers.[61] Apparently, there are limits beyond which many literati are not willing to accommodate the Party in its demand for cultural conformity.

4

Political Participation and the Problem of Legitimacy

Between 1949 and 1953, the Rakosi regime demanded the loyalty and cooperation of all Hungarian citizens without allowing any substantive citizen participation in the processes of government. The Party viewed the people as a resource to be exploited for achieving the two basic goals of industrialization and indoctrination. Any opposition to the Stalinist version of socialist construction was suppressed through police terror. Moreover, no Hungarian citizen could remain aloof from Rakosi's totalitarian mobilization because the regime compelled all citizens to "take part" in and show support for the political process by attending mass meetings and organized demonstrations. Citizens were supposed to express their views on all subjects in which the Party had a vested interest, but they were also supposed to apply dialectical reasoning creatively in order to realize that the Party's policies were indeed correct. In other words, under Rakosi, the Hungarian citizenry was programmed to provide only positive input to the decision-making process. Its specific role was to support the policies of the regime. This kind of controlled, compulsory political participation was vital to the maintenance of a system that utilized people for the top-down transmission of predetermined values as well as for the generation of support without critical feedback. Political participation during the totalitarian mobilization phase of socialist construction in Hungary was an empty form manipulated by the leadership of the Party to validate the output of the political apparatus. It thus served only an output function.

Prerevolutionary Participation

Participants in the frequent, exhilarating demonstrations and marches celebrating all sorts of achievements in the socialist transformation of society must have felt some sense of accomplishment, even though they were only performing the ceremonial function of a ritual staged by their despotic regime. The medals and pins given to those who fulfilled their tasks in more than satisfactory manner and the personal recognition extended to the "heroes of labor" were further manifestations of paying lip service to grass-roots democracy. The Rakosi regime also enhanced the image of participation by recruiting various mass organizations (such as the Patriotic People's Front, the Hungarian Women's Federation, and the Alliance of Working Youth) to help create "transmission belts" for implementing policy. The Party planted members to raise and analyze issues at the meetings of these mass organizations so that, contrary to the expectations of most of the people attending these assemblies, discussion always centered on the implementation of policy instead of its formulation. The signing of the Stockholm Peace Appeal in 1950 is a case in point. When the Soviet Union initiated a peace movement and branded the United States as a "warmongering country opposed to peace," the Hungarian government followed suit and launched a program to convince the population to participate in the "building of peace." In Budapest, pairs of agents went from apartment to apartment, making clear to the occupants what was expected of them. "The Party, the Government and the world need your signature so that we can force the imperialists to stop rearmament and the production of nuclear weapons." Another form of promoting the ostensible participation of the masses in the "output" of the regime was to agitate for 100-percent participation in elections. Before World War II, suffrage had been restricted to men above the age of 25 and women above the age of 34, who fulfilled a six-year residency requirement; universal suffrage for all citizens above the age of 17 therefore meant a great deal to many Hungarian voters, even if there was only one combined party list to vote for. Furthermore, many Hungarians probably participated in these rituals simply because participation provided a release of tension or a sense of power.

Following Stalin's death, the Nagy regime eliminated all but the most essential mass rallies, retaining only those commemorating socialist holidays. (Rakosi continued this policy when he regained power in 1955.) The mass meetings that had been used by the Party to establish contact with people at a grassroots level gradually began to disappear, and a new form of political participation evolved—group protest against the Party's Stalinist policies. For example, the farmers who had been forced into collectivization by the Rakosi regime sent delegates to Nagy, with a strong endorsement of his decollectivization policies. Dissatisfied intellectuals took advantage of the post-Stalin "thaw" and formed voluntary discussion groups, such as the Petofi Circle, or used the *Literary Journal* and other forums to exert indirect influence on the Party and the Government. Whether or not they succeeded is difficult to establish. However, one thing is certain: contrary to the wishes of some of the Party elite, the Government allowed groups critical of the role and methods of the Party to function in Hungary for the first time since 1949. The decision makers may have ignored this input, but they did not suppress the criticism. By contrast, during the brief second period of Rakosi's rule, the possibility of substantial, critical participation outside the formal decision-making channels was practically nil. Not until the turmoil of October 1956 did the political participation of the governed acquire a serious and meaningful function in Hungary.

Postrevolutionary Participation

When the spontaneous revolution broke out in Budapest, thousands of workers' councils were organized throughout the country. Following the example set in Yugoslavia, the councils were both democratic (i.e., open to all workers) and influential. During the revolution, the decisions of these groups had a feedback effect on the decision-making process of the Party and the Government. However, the revolt was short-lived, and in its effort to reestablish the authority of the Party, the Kadar regime officially banned the workers' councils as well as all the other independent organizations that had sprung up during the revolution.

The patterns of participation characteristic of the postrevolutionary period differed from those existing prior to November 1956 in both the nature and extent of the participation sanctioned. The Party, which was in great disarray during the Soviet invasion in November 1956, had to rebuild from scratch and elaborate new policies to avoid the mistakes of the past. The functional imbalance of the political apparatus under Rakosi (too much power concentrated at the apex of the pyramidal structure with too little potential for influencing decisions existing at the bottom) had been a major factor contributing to the revolution in 1956. To remedy this disequilibrium, the new Party leadership, under Janos Kadar, offered Party membership to "anyone past the age of 21 who agrees with the ideas of Marxism-Leninism, who accepts the Party's policy, works honestly for the building of a socialist society, and is ready to take an active part in the work of the Party's local organizations."[1] On the one hand, the Party encouraged Hungarians (especially the young) to join the ranks of the "vanguard of the proletariat," but on the other hand, it told them not to be concerned with policy making; the Party elite wanted the population to keep working hard for increased material rewards and to stay out of the affairs of state. New party policy stated explicitly that no one in Hungary would be *forced* to participate in any political activity. In June 1957, the Party further liberalized its policy to allow qualified non-Party people to participate in all political activities except Party functions.

In the late 1950s the Party gave the numerous mass organizations functioning as "transmission belts" between the Party and the masses a more meaningful role in the decision-making process. This was especially true of the several managerial and intellectual apparatuses. It seems, however, that a turning point in the regime's attitude toward democratic participation came in 1962 when leftist Party conservatives challenged the Kadar regime on the issue of the ideology of the alliance policy. By then, Kadar's policy of economic modernization and the rise in the people's living standard had produced tangible support for the regime. Hence, the regime wished to avoid a return to a primary dependence on coercion. The only alternative open to it was to solicit the positive and loyal cooperation of the Hungarian people.

Participation During the Postmobilization Period

Between 1962 and 1968, the regime made a strong effort to convince people by both word and deed that its alliance policy was not merely a tactical maneuver but a genuine, long-lasting change in the Party's approach to the creation and operation of a socialist system. The evidence was overwhelming. The Stalinists and supporters of Rakosi were purged from high positions in the Party and the Government. Once that had been accomplished, the number of political arrests began to taper off, dropping to zero by the

end of 1966. The regime also closed a large number of forced labor camps, and by 1964 it had discontinued the jamming of Western radio stations. More and more people were granted permission to travel to the West, and the populace seemed to be more relaxed. In October 1968, the Government adopted a new law to regulate the activities of the network of people's control commissions; the ordinance transformed the arbitrary and persecutive character of these state agencies by changing their avowed goal from the "defense of the socialist order" to the defense of the popular interest.

In the late 1960s the Kadar regime also liberalized its policies affecting the electoral process and the nature of the trade union movement. The reformed electoral code of 1966 granted single-candidate constituencies the right to establish multicandidate races; it also provided the opportunity for recall. (However, owing to the screening power of the Patriotic People's Front, this code proved to be a failure: in the 1967 parliamentary elections to fill 349 seats in the National Assembly, more than one candidate appeared in only 9 races). Finally, the labor code of 1967 transformed the role of the trade unions from that of a transmission belt to that of a protector of workers' rights.

The relaxation of Party control accruing from the above changes did not dramatically increase overall citizen participation in the processes of government. It was not until the early 1970s that a major breakthrough occurred in this area. The electoral law passed in October 1970 eliminated some of the obstacles to effective participation and gave electors a freer choice in the nomination process; people could now legally propose candidates of their own choice. The purpose of the new law was to stimulate greater grass-roots participation and foster greater responsibility of elected officials toward their constituencies. Another law enacted a year later increased the authority of local councils in both financial and legal matters. Similarly, the Uniform Cooperative Law of 1971 granted legal and economic independence to agricultural producers' cooperatives; it also gave these cooperatives the right to band together in associations to protect their own interests. Since the agricultural producers' cooperatives included only state employees engaged in agricultural work, the representation of nonmember employees and workers remained an open question. Then, in January 1975, the presidium of the National Trade

Union Council ruled that it is justifiable to create trade union organizations for such people. Consequently, local trade union groups began to organize all agricultural cooperative employees and workers. Finally, the Youth Law of October 1971 staked out a prominent place for the Communist Youth League in Hungarian Society. The intent of this legislation was to protect the existence and legitimacy of conflicting "socialist" interest groups within Hungarian society.

Between 1965 and 1975 the Kadar regime used the expansion of political participation as bait to entice the Hungarian populace to cooperate in economic matters. Because the regime needed the positive loyalty of the entire population to implement economic modernization and make the socialist system work, it made a strong effort to mobilize all the social forces capable of promoting the development of the system. Under the label of "expanding socialist democracy," this mobilization effort was even extended to people working in the humanities, the arts, and the sciences; after 1965, literature, the film industry, and the indigenous theatre began to flourish. In effect, Kadar won his battle against both left-wing dogmatists and right-wing revisionists because he succeeded in uniting both Party and non-Party people behind his program. Prior to the October 1956 revolt, the Communists in Hungary did not have the active support of important local elements. Only during Nagy's short rule and Kadar's postmobilization era did they muster some voluntary support for their policies.

Social Restratification

As a result of the totalitarian mobilization policies of both Rakosi and Kadar, by the early 1960s, when Hungary entered the postmobilization phase of socialist construction, Hungarian society had undergone a drastic social restratification.

Between 1949 and 1966 the number of persons employed in industry and construction doubled. In 1949, the countrywide ratio of manual agricultural laborers to nonagricultural employees was 54 percent to 46 percent; in 1966 it was 31 percent to 69 percent.[2] By 1965, only 14 percent of the country's total arable land area was divided into small private plots (which, incidentally, provided almost half of the national agricultural income); the rest of the land belonged to state farms or cooperatives, one-third

of which operated at a loss. The rapid rate of industrialization had a great impact on urbanization. Between 1949 and 1966, the overall population of Hungary increased by about 10 percent, but the population of cities with over 40,000 inhabitants rose by more than 30 percent.[3] One concomitant of urbanization was the diffusion of mass communication: practically every wage earner read one or more newspapers; most households were equipped with radios and about one-fourth of them had television sets. In other words, conditions favoring political socialization had improved to such an extent as a result of de-Stalinization that coercive measures had become almost obsolete.

The social mobility associated with industrialization affected different segments of the labor force differently. Between 1949 and 1962, 24 percent of the children of manual agricultural workers moved to urban areas and engaged in nonagricultural manual work; this intergenerational vocational discontinuity accounted for more than 50 percent of the social mobility in Hungary in that period. In addition, about 20 percent of the children of agricultural laborers took up nonmanual work.[4] Thus, more than 54 percent of the children of manual agricultural workers entered a different social stratum from that of their parents during the mobilization phase of socialist construction. In the same period, only 7 percent of the children of nonagricultural manual workers accepted any kind of agricultural employment; but the greatest postwar intergenerational vocational continuity was recorded among the children of white-collar fathers: roughly 67 percent remained in their father's social stratum, and the rest became nonagricultural manual workers.[5]

It is also interesting to note that, prior to 1966, the social mobility of women was much less than that of men. Only 36 percent of women workers accepted employment placing them in a different social stratum from that of their parents, whereas 43 percent of the same generation of men changed social stratum through their jobs.[6] Furthermore, during the early Rakosi period, 90 percent of men in agricultural employment who married still chose brides from their own social stratum; in the mid-1960s the proportion was only 45 percent.

Social mobility had a great impact on marriage, pregnancy, abortion, and reproduction rates in postwar Hungary. (See Figure 4.1.) The demographic transition induced by the socialist economic trans-

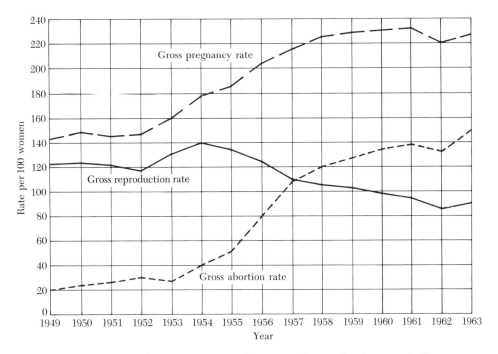

Figure 4.1. Estimated gross pregnancy, abortion, and reproduction rates in Hungary, 1949–1963.

Source: James L. Scott, *Projections of the Populations of the Communist Countries of Eastern Europe, by Age and Sex: 1965–1985* (Washington, D.C.: U.S. Bureau of the Census, 1965).

formation of Hungarian society included a large decline in the gross reproduction rate and an equally large increase in the gross pregnancy and the gross abortion rates: the gross reproduction rate in Hungary decreased from 124 per 100 women in 1950 to 88 per 100 women in 1963; in the same period the gross pregnancy rate per 100 women increased from 146 to 224. During the five-year period 1954–1959, the number of births dropped by 32 percent while the number of legal abortions rose by more than 900 percent. In 1963, the 174,000 legal abortions accounted for 51 percent of known pregnancies terminated during that year.[7] In 1965, Hungarian doctors performed 135.6 abortions for every 100 deliveries.[8] The new attitudes and values created by improved material conditions, decreased political pressures, and the diffusion of socialist ideology contributed to the large numbers of pregnancies terminated by abortion. In addition, the liberalized abortion laws enacted in 1956[9] enabled women to use abortion as a method of birth control. The inadequate income of

families having only one wage earner also contributed to the high rate of abortion.

Another striking aspect of the demographic transition in Hungary was a dramatic rise in the suicide rate. In 1965, 30 out of every 100,000 people took their own lives. Tight economic conditions as well as an increase in alcoholism and attendant social problems were the leading causes of this phenomenon.

Contrary to ideological expectations, social mobility in Hungary did not produce a classless, egalitarian society. Instead, by the mid-1960s the old "bourgeois" class distinctions had yielded to a socialist differentiation of classes based on occupation, income, education, prestige, and location of residence. The ruling elite was made up of high Party and Government officials as well as top level military and security officers. This group constituted about 3 percent of the population in both 1965 and 1975. The so-called middle class, which included managers, professionals, the technical intelligentsia and other nonmanual workers, comprised 15 percent of the population in 1965 and 24 percent in 1975. The working class of skilled, and unskilled manual workers encompassed about 51 percent of all wage earners in 1965, and 55 percent in 1975. Manual agricultural workers accounted for about 29 percent of active wage earners in 1965 and about 15 percent in 1975; independent farmers comprised about 2 percent of active wage earners in 1965 and about 3 percent in 1975.[10]

The highest-paid wage earners were the intellectuals and technical experts. Next came the skilled and trained workers, who earned about half as much as the highest-paid wage earners. Unskilled industrial workers and manual agricultural workers (who together constituted approximately 50 percent of salaried workers) received less than skilled industrial workers. About 10–15 percent of the population—many of whom were retired pensioners—earned or had pensions of less than 400–500 forints per capita a month, which placed them below the poverty line.

Similar differences existed in education. In 1963, about 12 percent of the middle class held a college degree and about 25 percent had graduated from high school. However, no worker held a college degree and only 3 percent had high school diplomas, while 30 percent had completed 8–11 years of schooling. The agrarian population fared even worse: none had attended college; only 1 percent had completed high school; 19 percent had 8–11 years of schooling, and 77 percent had only 1–7 years of education. In 1963, the probability that an unskilled worker's child would complete high school was five times less than it was for an upper-middle-class child, and the probability of attending college was ten times greater for an upper-middle-class student than for a student of unskilled-working-class origin.[11]

Thus, educational opportunities, like other opportunities in Hungary, differed according to the parents' social, economic, and political standing. Prestige was determined by Party status, income, occupation, education and material possessions. By the late sixties, a new *Zeitgeist* had emerged which, due to its pragmatism, has been nicknamed "livelihood realism," "frigidaire socialism," or simply, "what's in it for me?"[12] It is interesting to note, for example, that between 1950 and 1971, per capita personal consumption rose by nearly 250 percent. Taking the 1950 consumption level as 100, in 1971 the food consumption index was 172; for consumer goods, it was

294; for clothing, 1,106; for other industrial goods, 406; and for services 251.[13] It is clear that a new brand of pragmatism swept across Hungary after the abortive revolt of 1956.

In the 1960s and 1970s most Hungarians were still proud of their cultural heritage and nationalistic. However, the old feelings of chauvinism, racial prejudice, and religiosity were gone. They had been replaced by egocentrism, status consciousness, and materialism. Whether the new values were preferable to the old ones is difficult to determine. Indicators obtained through various official pollsters in Hungary show that a certain amount of frustration existed (and continues to exist) among Hungarians unable to influence their own destiny. It is perhaps for this reason that by the mid-sixties, Hungary had one of the highest suicide rates in the world combined with a low birth rate, a high abortion rate, and a high divorce rate[14] (fourth in world ranking).

Another attitude-related social problem in Hungary was the so-called generation gap between young people and the older generation. "The experiences of their elders who were threatened, uprooted, denounced, betrayed, robbed, beaten, corrupted, bombed, shot, starved, and misled, have little real meaning for the young; for them, these experiences are tales of heroism out of a past which has little significance in the world they now face."[15] According to a poll taken in 1968, the young valued honesty, truthfulness, helpfulness, love for a fellow human, and loyalty. Thirty-two percent of the youth interviewed believed in God; 66 percent considered themselves to be primarily materialists, but of that 66 percent only 14 percent professed Marxist and socialist values.[16]

The displacement of traditional values alienated the young from their elders. The espousal of new values that were often contradictory to socialist ideology increased the estrangement. For example, goal orientation for certain occupations was closely linked to status seeking rather than professionalism; the sharp differentiation in levels of income led to egocentrism and social alienation rather than incentive for improvement; a drastic slow-down in upward social mobility in the 1960s created a new animosity between urban and rural populations that undercut the campaign for national unity; and finally, under the slogan of egalitarianism, the regime created a distinct trend toward favoritism and stagnation in education—87 percent of college students were sons and daughters of the prestigious social stratum, which led to a further division between the rural and urban populations in Hungary.[17]

In order to alleviate some of the tensions created by social restratification, the Central Committee of the HSWP gave its final, official approval to the New Economic Mechanism (NEM) in May 1966. The NEM was designed to create new energizing forces in Hungarian society through an appropriate mixture of incentives and rewards that would gradually convert the apathy and hostility of the population into passive acceptance and ultimately into positive loyalty. It is important to keep in mind that by the time the HSWP adopted the NEM as official policy, the USSR had been experimenting with Libermanism (the application of economic reforms proposed by Yersei Liberman that established a profit motive and the semblance of a socialist market economy), which proved to be successful enough to induce Kremlin leaders to give their tacit approval for similar reforms elsewhere in the Soviet sphere of influence.

The Search for Legitimacy

Actually, the NEM did not become operational until Jaunary 1, 1968. The preparation for its successful launching required a series of new measures to condition the Hungarian people toward its positive acceptance. Consequently, the cadre officers of the Party were given specific instructions to permit any qualified person to fill positions of leadership in economic enterprises without regard to membership in the Party.[18] In November 1966, the Party began to train able propagandists whose task was to explain the new economic concepts to rank-and-file Party members in the cities and the countryside. The same year, the Party established a new Institute of Social Sciences whose members were to assist Party ideologists in their theoretical work.[19] The Institute also had another function: it served as a liaison between the party and the economic architects of the NEM. The immediate aim of the Party leadership, however, was to use the Institute as a base for organizing and training a number of experts in different fields of the social sciences; later the Party would assign these experts the task of troubleshooting any problems that developed in the process of implementing the NEM.

Such problems included the role and position of the Party and trade unions in the NEM; the role and position of the working class in Hungarian society; the relation between employment and manpower training; methods of control; socialist realism; nationalism; and so on. The Institute therefore became a buffer between liberal Party economists (supported by intellectuals and technocrats) who were demanding greater freedom from Party and Government control and conservative Party leaders (supported by staunch bureaucrats and trade union officials) who were trying to hold on to their positions of authority. This clash of interests was very strong at the Ninth as well as the Tenth Party Congresses. It is still very much alive today. On his visit to Budapest in November 1972, for example, Brezhnev had a specific mission: to pacify the two opposing groups in the interest of working toward national unity and economic efficiency.

Simultaneously with the preparation of the NEM, the Kadar regime began to liberalize its policies affecting cultural activities. In the July–August 1966 issue of *Tarsadalmi Szemle*, the Study Group for Culture endorsed the publication of "works that are ideologically debatable and more or less in opposition to Marxism or socialist realism, as long as they possess humanistic values and are not politically hostile."[20] By broadening the concept of socialist realism and narrowing the idea of hostile literature, the regime set the stage for a gradual decrease in the level and intensity of interference in cultural affairs. Consequently, it initiated a new period of cultural autonomy, within which the talent and criticism of the Hungarian intellectuals could grow, develop and serve the national interest with only a limited risk to the Party. Greater freedom of inquiry was also allowed in such disciplines as sociology, and the findings of social researchers were published and distributed throughout the country. For example, the study of *Social Stratification in Hungary*, which was completed in 1963 and published in 1966, dared to imply that the Marxist concept of "class" was not a useful analytical tool because it obscured the genuine differences that existed in Hungarian society.[21] The Party permitted similar challenges to be published in other books and scholarly articles because the regime had already embarked on a silent course of bargaining in which it was willing to trade concessions for cooperation.

In 1968, when the NEM became operational,[22] the number and extent of these concessions grew. Economic leadership in commercial enterprises was turned over to both non-Party and Party experts and managers empowered to determine how many workers each operation required and to cut staff, if necessary. Party decisions affecting the management of enterprises were guided by economists rather than ideologists. Decentralization also affected pricing. Under the pre-NEM, centralized system, the Government regulated prices according to the Marxian labor theory of value; under the NEM, prices were determined by a price-center type[23] instead of a strictly value type. (In October 1971 the regime introduced stricter price controls, which represented a retreat from the NEM.) The NEM likewise revised the method of determining profits. Under the command economy, profit was calculated as a specific percentage of cost, whereas under the NEM, profit was viewed as a nonsurplus equated with the excess of returns over expenditures. Furthermore, enterprise profits were divided into profit-sharing funds and thus belonged to the enterprises rather than to the state. The old egalitarian system of centrally determined wages was replaced with a more equitable wage system based more or less on real output. There was greater freedom of movement within the labor force once the NEM was functional. In sharp contrast to previous policy, if an employee desired to change employment voluntarily, under the NEM he could hand in notice and leave for another job without suffering any material loss (e.g., loss of benefits). Whereas management alone had the right to make social allotments, introduce incentive techniques, and enforce labor discipline, the trade unions now had sole jurisdiction over industrial safety.

To summarize, in 1968, central programming of production was replaced by direct bargaining between enterprises; central allocation of investment was replaced by self-financing; the rationing system was abolished and a market for the means of production established; enterprise incentives—based on the fulfillment of obligatory targets—were changed in favor of profit maximization; centrally fixed wages were replaced by a link between wages and enterprise profit; and the administrative price system was replaced by a market price system. The new economic program thus had a double purpose. On the one hand, it aimed to bypass the stubborn, unimaginative, and backward apparatchik whose doctrinaire interpretation of socialist economy could only mean rigid, self-defeating central planning. On the other hand, it aimed to provide new incentives for the unmotivated, unskilled, uneducated member of Hungarian society whose only interest in the socialist economy was equated with improved social benefits and no obligations. Hence, the NEM was supposed to equip the Hungarian Communists with new methods of economic know-how that would afford greater economic progress and a smoother control of the economy by the Party; most importantly, the successful implementation of the NEM would enable the Party, through what Janos Kadar called "cooperation," to maintain its leading position vis-à-vis working people and society as a whole. In other words, the Kadar regime realized that Communist success in Hungary was not solely a question of material success, but a question of legitimacy as well.

Problems of Legitimacy

The NEM was not a pat formula for achieving economic progress and socialist democracy in Hungary. It was the most liberal economic program ever introduced in the Soviet orbit of influence, and there were many problems connected with its implementation. Perhaps the most serious ones stemmed from Party-management-labor relations. Party experts admitted that the economic reforms would eventually necessitate political changes. Therefore, in early March 1969, while the virulent anti-Dubcek propaganda campaign was taking place in other socialist countries, Kadar announced a political reform program. He appealed to the Hungarian nation for support because, according to Kadar, gradual reform was the only way of building socialism in Hungary. In the six months that followed the announcement, Moscow took the Hungarian programs and intensions under close scrutiny. Although Kremlin leaders never explicitly stated their position on the reforms, they must have tacitly approved of them because in the fall of 1969, there was a sudden resumption of training in the Soviet Union for local Hungarian Party officials and, in April 1970, at ceremonies commemorating the twentieth anniversary of Hungarian liberation, Brezhnev praised Hungarian achievements. Meanwhile, the Hungarian press stepped up its attack on the West's allegations of liberal trends in Hungary. No doubt, the Hungarian reformers were anxious to improve their socialist image and show Moscow that Hungary was still a reliable ally.

The development of a practical mechanism for this scheme was very difficult. The Party leadership followed a very cautious approach in solving the problems generated by economic reform. It took certain concepts of decentralization and parliamentary reform from the Poles and borrowed others from the Czechoslovaks, East Germans, and other conservative neighbors who had resolved conflicts relevant to their problems, mixing them with some liberal formulas of their own. Whenever reforms were introduced in Hungary, the regime would always opt for a low-key approach. One of the regime's main problems was (and still is) to convince the public of the need for personal discipline during the sensitive period of reform. Because of political considerations, the regime held up the implementation of wage-differentiation and postponed closing down inefficient factories for more than three years after the enactment of laws sanctioning such actions. Worker opposition to changing the traditional socialist egalitarian pay system and to potential unemployment gave ammunition to Party dogmatists who disagreed (and still disagree) with the "concession to capitalism" inherent in the NEM. Consequently, at the Eleventh Party Congress in 1975, the Party elite emphasized the strengthening and institutionalization of what is known as "enterprise democracy." According to the congressional resolution: "It provides an opportunity for workers to play a genuine role in enterprise management, and in local and public affairs; it encourages creativity among workers and is a major tool in developing a socialist relationship between executives and subordinates; it increases the workers' sense of responsibility and serves as an incentive for greater effort on the job."[24] However, since the basic institutions of enterprise democracy are the Party, the trade unions, and the KISz organizations functioning in factories, nonfactory enterprises, state farms, and other workers' forums, the present Party elite also believes that enterprise democracy will in the final analysis result in greater incentives and increased production.[25]

Although enterprise democracy represents a step away from top-down economic administration, the recently adopted system of worker participation does not function perfectly. According to an in-depth analysis of Hungarian trade union membership, there are several disturbing phenomena in the practice of

enterprise democracy.[26] For example, of the approximately 175,000 trade union stewards who are supposed to confer regularly with the members of their locals, 20 percent fail to do so. The process whereby members of agricultural cooperatives participate in decisions concerning the management of their farms is also suffering from shortcomings. Following several successive waves of mergers, by the fall of 1974 there were 1,923 agricultural producers' cooperatives (APCs) with an average area of 2,900 hectares apiece —compared to 4,507 APCs with an average of 900 hectares each in 1961. These APCs now include several villages. Moreover, traditional, small-scale peasant farming methods have been replaced by modern scientific systems. In the new situation, an ordinary collective farm member is unable to form an overall view of work on the farm; he therefore has a completely new relationship with the president of his cooperative, who is often more highly educated than other workers on the farm. In fact, some managers of collective farms do not allow nonexpert members to interfere in questions of management. Yet, according to Party directives, a cooperative farm manager must possess social and political abilities as well as economic ones, because he needs the support as well as the criticism of the members of his collective.

The Kadar regime has made (and hopes to continue to make) the most noticeable gains in obtaining public participation in the parliamentary process. To make this form of involvement in the system attractive, the regime both ordered another facelifting for the largely rubber stamp National Assembly in 1971 and at the same time promulgated an electoral reform containing aspects of genuine democratization.[27] Although the National Assembly elected on June 15, 1975 included a higher percentage of young and women representatives and contained less dead wood than the previous Assembly, the promised changes in the real political role of Parliament have failed to materialize. There are still too many Party members in Parliament (71.0 percent compared to 73.72 percent in 1971) and no representatives of the private sector (which comprises about 45 percent of the citizenry); furthermore, the Council of Ministers and the Presidential Council (not Parliament) remain the supreme lawmakers. At the same time, there are indications that Parliament's authority to look into domestic consumption policies, corruption, and programs such as education, welfare, and medical services has been enhanced by the facelifting. Although the legislature still does not have the power to force the Government to comply with the will of Parliament, the urgency and seriousness of some of the issues under examination have served to complement the investigative authority of the National Assembly. For example, a 1974 inquiry by the National Assembly's Social and Health Committee into the shortage of physicians in rural areas led to the enactment of administrative measures designed to remedy the situation. The problem was how to prevent doctors from practicing in areas of their own choice rather than in the areas of great demand. In 1974, out of 24,000 doctors in the entire country, 10,000 worked in Budapest. In 1973, there were 2,500 vacant posts in rural areas for doctors, and several villages in Hungary had no doctor at all; in addition, a number of school-doctor jobs and enterprise-doctor posts remained vacant.

On November 19, 1974, the Social and Health Committee found the situation alarming and disclosed that almost half of all Hungarian villages did not have a single independent physician. During debate in the Assembly, deputies made several suggestions for improving the delivery of medical services, and some members of Parliament requested that the Ministry of Health introduce appropriate administrative measures to remedy the deplorable situation. Following their recommendations, the Ministry of Health issued a new set of rules according to which only those people who have received at least a two-year work contract or who have an indefinite appointment to a medical position will be included in the medical register. This should prevent young doctors needed in provincial hospitals or village districts from taking up temporary or occasional work in Budapest.[28] Parenthetically, the reason doctors prefer to practice in Budapest or other large cities is a monetary one. Since the official pay of doctors is not commensurate with the remuneration of engineers or highly skilled workers, most urban doctors receive gifts and gratuities that amount to more than their monthly pay. Doctors do not expect to receive gratuities in small towns and villages where the clientele is less sophisticated and less well off.

Despite the positive results of the investigations of the Social and Health Committee, the reform affecting legislative operations has not to date improved the effectiveness of the National Assembly as a whole.

A much more meaningful reform affecting the political scene in Hungary was the enactment of Electoral Law No. 3 on October 3, 1970. Under the new law, people continue to have the right to nominate candidates to run for seats in Parliament and local government units against the list drawn up by the Party, but the Patriotic People's Front no longer has a legal monopoly in screening opposition candidates. True, there are still prohibitions against the nomination of persons openly hostile to socialist principles, but now, at least, there appears to be no mechanism that assures the election of an official candidate. Individual electors can nominate prospective candidates from the floor of the nominating convention, provided that these candidates receive one-third of the votes in an open show of hands.

The Kadar regime decentralized other government functions in its campaign to augment public participation in the political system. In the Spring of 1971, the regime passed a new Local Council Law that was consistent with its pre-1973 political decentralization policies. The law stipulated that all tasks related solely to local interests or all issues capable of being resolved most effectively on the local level should be relegated to the jurisdiction of the local councils. In reality, however, the authority of the councils was restricted to matters of culture and education, social welfare, and local economics.

In that same year, the Government introduced a new Youth Law that detailed the responsibilities of the various units of society to young people, as well as outlining the duties and rights of the country's youth vis-à-vis society. Consequently, several of the old leaders of the Communist Youth League (KISz) were purged and the organization's monopoly authority in youth affairs was broken. The Party also promised young people that they would have more opportunities to rise to leading positions in the Party, the Government, and industry and as a gesture of sincerity, the Tenth Party Congress decreased from 21 to 18 the minimum age of admission to the Party. The regime also effected some changes in the administration of higher education, granting university administrators and students more authority to deal with campus problems. One example was the introduction of student parliaments; another was the codification in the state regulations pertaining to high schools and vocational schools of the rights of students and of KISz school organizations; a third example comprised the resolutions and directives issued by the KISz Central Committee. According to a recent survey, however, the right of students to decide questions concerning their own affairs exists only on paper in most schools.[29] Finally, the Party promised to remedy some of the social ills influencing young people's attitudes, although the two serious demonstrations of March 15 and 21, 1972, seem to indicate that the remedies have not yet provided a cure for the malaise that disturbs the youth.

Other areas receiving consideration in the political liberalization process are legality and police authority. The new Passport Law of 1970 enables unsuccessful applicants to obtain both a written statement of the reason for being refused a passport and an appeal of the initial decision. In 1971, the Hungarian Minister of Justice announced the abolition of the death penalty for economic crimes. Since then, the entire jurisdictional structure and overall legal procedure have been overhauled.

The June 1972 statute enacted by the National Assembly to amend the organization and function of Hungary's courts of law was an important link in the chain of political reform growing out of the March 1969 resolution of the HSWP Central Committee. Whereas the New Constitution of April 1972 spells out the general rules of reorganization, the new law fills in the framework. Although it retains a good many provisions of the 1954 law on the judiciary, the new statute introduces so many bold and sweeping changes that it amounts to a thorough reform of the judiciary system. The new law significantly extends the law courts' sphere of activity to the handling of both labor disputes and lawsuits between enterprises. It elaborates the essential points concerning spheres of jurisdiction, organization, and the functioning of the courts, along with details on the pattern of court organization, the extension of the possibility of appeal, the reintroduction of "single judges," and the significant role to be played by the court collegia in ensuring uniformity in the administration of justice. It is a particular merit of the new code that it lays down detailed rules on the election of judges, thereby putting an end to unconstitutional practices.[30] (For further details on the court and judicial reforms, see Chapters 6 and 7.)

Changes in the legal system include qualitative improvements in legal administration and the upgrading of the procedural rights of defense counsel. Furthermore, several old-fashioned "political crimes" are now considered misdemeanors punishable only by fine.

With regard to the role and authority of the secret police, the once autonomous and all-powerful instrument of terror had been losing ground ever since Kadar came into power in 1956, yet no one officially challenged its unrestrained jurisdiction with any seriousness until 1970. In January of that year, Interior Minister Andras Benkei complained that the police are often used as final arbiters of disputes in which no illegality is even suspected; in many cases these conflicts arise simply from the failures of officials to work out their own problems. He announced administrative decisions (arrived at within the ministry) aimed at checking such proceedings and asked for a clear codification of his ministry's duties vis-à-vis other government ministries. Four years later, on October 25, 1974, the Presidential Council issued a decree-law on state and public security that provides a legal framework for the uniform and systematic regulation of the activities of the Ministry of the Interior. This decree-law delimits the framework for the future activities of both state and public security agencies, and the Council of Ministries has issued a decree providing the appropriate regulators.

The goal of the Presidential Council decree-law is to define the tasks associated with protecting state and public security. The most important activities under this heading are preserving internal state order, combatting criminality, ensuring public order, enforcing traffic regulations, carrying out activities connected with state administration, providing uniform fire prevention safeguards throughout the country, and protecting state borders. The Council of Ministries' decree contains detailed regulations for the protection of internal state order and stresses the importance of uncovering and preventing the execution of plots that would jeopardize domestic peace or the human rights of Hungarian citizens.[31]

The main significance of these laws and regulations lies not in their substance but in the question of who issued them. It is surprising that the Council of Ministries and the Presidential Council chose to issue decrees rather than to place the matters before the Parliament for legislation, which would have been in harmony with both the letter and the spirit of the constitution. By issuing decrees, the Government avoided submitting these important matters to public discussion.

The new Local Council Law of 1971 is another example of the Hungarian political reform movement favoring increased political participation and popular representation in local government. County, municipal, and village councils play an important role in solving Hungary's economic, social, and cultural problems. The guiding principles approved by the Eleventh Party Congress in 1975 stated that the councils' sphere of authority must be enlarged and that their function as the people's representative must be developed. The councils are required to create and implement programs to satisfy the people's needs in the areas of culture, public health, social welfare and communal activities; the councils are also charged with ensuring an adequate supply of commodities and services to each community. Although the councils are in direct contact with the population and are therefore familiar with local problems and needs, citizen input to decision making is superficial. Means for measuring public needs, such as town-hall meetings or public hearings, are unknown in Hungary. Direct contact between council members and the population implies a chain of command through the local spokesmen of various mass organizations. Decision making is therefore slow and bureaucratic, and duties are often shunted onto other councils or the ministries. In many cases the division between the councils and the ministries is not clearly established. The treatment of clients is often unsatisfactory, and cold refusals of citizen requests or exaggerated adherence to procedures are frequent. Nevertheless, political participation by constituents in council decision making is much more democratic than it was before the 1971 enactment of Law No. I (the so-called Council Law).[32]

Probably the greatest achievement so far in the recent process of political reform in Hungary has been the modernization of the constitution. The old 1949 Constitution, a relic of the Stalinist period, was sadly lacking in any serious relationship to present-day realities. The conspiratorial, underground psychology of the drafters of the Old Constitution had obscured the Party's role in society and precluded a clear definition of the rights and duties of the citizenry. Thus, the Tenth Party Congress authorized the National Assembly to revise the 1949 Constitution. Accordingly a 25-member committee was established in June 1971 to prepare the new basic law. The New Constitution has a different purpose from that of the Old Constitution; it reflects all the social, political, and economic changes that occurred between 1949 and 1972. The new document is less a program than a mirror of cumulative achievement, and it therefore contains nothing that anticipates the future; it registers facts rather than hopes and confronts the reader with the realities of life. Those realities are first and foremost the reflections of Kadar's view of socialism. The New Constitution affirms that Hungary is in a transitional stage of development toward a socialist republic. It does not reveal, nor would the regime state, how long this interim period will last. This, too, is a reflection of the regime's pragmatic approach to the problems of Hungarian statecraft.[33]

Summary

Postwar politics in Hungary, like those in all other Eastern European countries in the Soviet bloc, provide a classic illustration of the erratic character of public participation; the magnitude of this critical indicator of legitimacy varies considerably with economic and political growth. The 1945 euphoria of revolutionary mobilization, which stimulated popular political involvement in Hungary, was dampened when Rakosi vanquished the old regime and turned his attention to building a new order in the Stalinist mold. The shrinkage of participation that followed served as output rather than a feedback function. The pageantry of frequent demonstrations and marches celebrating the victory of the workers were manifestations of participatory burlesque instead of participatory democracy. There was no distribution of power during the Rakosi era; there was no political competitiveness resulting from participatory activities; there were no political gains offered for political participation other than the accolade bestowed on obedient citizens through Party membership. Hungarians, under Rakosi, joined the Communist Party not as citizens interested in shaping policies and selecting candidates but as individuals seeking jobs and material rewards available through Party patronage.

Not until 1962, when the Kadar regime was challenged by conservatives on the issue of the alliance policy, did political participation acquire a more democratic character. By then, the regime had begun to relinquish the old policy of dependence on coercion and to solicit the positive and loyal cooperation of the Hungarian people. Kadar's slogan: "Whoever is not against us is with us," symbolized political opportunity for a new segment of Hungarian society. In the late 1960s, the Kadar regime was willing to allow a gradual increase in citizen participation in exchange for cooperation in economic modernization (i.e., in the implementation of the NEM). It was not until the early seventies, however, that a major breakthrough in political participation occurred. The electoral law of 1970 gave voters a freer choice in the nomination process and compelled elected deputies to be more responsive to the needs of their constituents. One year later, local councils were granted greater authority in educational, financial, and legal matters. Employees of cooperative farms were given the right to organize and have an input in the decision-making process. The National Assembly was given expanded investigative authority. Administrators and students at colleges and universities were permitted to assert their rights in the decision-making process. Adoption of the 1972 Revised Constitution considerably strengthened Hungarian civil liberties. The 1972 law on the organization and function of Hungary's courts of law had a similar positive impact on participatory democracy. In short, because of Janos Kadar's great dedication to the NEM, political participation became a legitimized attribute of the Hungarian political culture in the early 1970s.

Since the November 1972 plenary session, however, political participation in Hungary has shifted ground, and the net result of this process has been to weaken rather than strengthen the NEM. Through the combined lobby of the National Trade Union Council, the National Council of Agricultural Producers' Cooperatives, and the Enterprise Control Committees, the staunch dogmatists in the Party have once more succeeded in asserting their interests despite opposition from the managerial class; in 1975 the conservatives gained the support of the Eleventh Party Congress for strengthening and institutionalizing what has since become known as "enterprise democracy." The extent of worker participation that has resulted from enterprise democracy goes far beyond what the founders of the NEM considered sound and reasonable from the standpoint of economic efficiency, yet there are some Party leaders —Kadar included—who believe that enterprise democracy will strengthen the NEM by generating greater initiative and productivity among workers. Whether the present Party leadership will be successful in its attempt to steer worker participation in that direction remains to be seen.

PART II

The Conversion Functions

5

Policy Making, Interest Aggregation, and Rule Making

The 1972 Revised Constitution makes it perfectly clear that the Hungarian People's Republic is a socialist state (not yet a socialist republic) and that the Marxist-Leninist party of the working class (the HSWP) is the leading force in Hungarian society. An analysis of these two strictures in conjunction with postulates from the Party statutes (for example, that the Party is the only organization capable of leading and representing the workers) reveals that there is limited access to policy making in Hungary. The issue then becomes whether interest-group politics have any meaning at all in the Hungarian political process. Can organized groups compete for power and/or influence? What is the role of the Party in the decision-making process? Do organized groups play a role in the formulation of policy? What are the formal and informal processes of policy making?

The Organization of State Authority

The Rakosi regime had established socialist institutions in every aspect of Hungarian political, social,

and cultural life as early as 1953. Except for a few slight modifications, these institutions have remained the same. Political power in the Hungarian People's Republic still originates from four major sources: the executive and legislative organs of state power, the state administration, the judiciary, and the public prosecutor's office. Moreover, there is still no separation of legislative, executive, and judicial powers. The unity of these powers is justified on the ideological grounds that in a socialist state there is only one will, representing one interest, and therefore there can be only one public power. Competing interests would weaken and eventually destroy socialism. Hence, at least in theory, all institutions serve only one interest because, as Chapter 1 of the Revised Constitution states, "All power is exercised by the working people."

The legislative and executive organs of state power include the National Assembly and the Presidential Council as well as the local councils. Hungary is divided into nineteen counties, and each county is governed by a People's Council. The organs of state administration are, on the one hand, the government and the executive committees of local councils, which are elected bodies, and on the other hand, the organs of specialized administration, whose members receive their mandate by appointment (with the exception of the heads of departments, the ministers, who are also elected). The rights and duties of the administration are spelled out in statutes. Therefore, to abrogate, quash, or reverse an administrative decision handed down by a superior administrative organ, there must be evidence of statutory infringement. This restriction does not apply, however, to the Council of Ministers, which is the highest arbiter of administrative decision making.

The judiciary in Hungary, as in other socialist states, has a special position. Its function is to implement the "socialist rule of law," which in effect is synonymous with representing the interests of the Party as the ultimate defender and guarantor of the rights of the working people. The organs of state power elect all judges, who, in turn, have a general obligation to report back on their activities.[1] The responsibility of the courts to the organs of state power is thus assured. Hungary's highest court is the Supreme Court, whose president is elected by and responsible to Parliament. Below the Supreme Court are the county, district, labor affairs, and military courts. In Budapest, the Capital Court acts as a county court and the city district courts act as district courts. In other cities, the city courts also serve as district courts. Only the Presidential Council of the People's Republic has the authority to organize, merge, abolish, or determine the territorial jurisdiction of the courts.

The Office of the Public Prosecutor is an altogether separate entity. It is linked more closely to the Party than to the executive and legislative organs, the state administration or the judiciary. The public prosecutor's office has two basic functions: to ensure that the state's social and cooperative organs as well as its private citizens adhere to and enforce adherence to the law;[2] and to prosecute any act that violates or endangers the local order of society or the security and independence of the state.[3]

There are several administrative units that do not belong directly to the system of state organs described above, for example, the state economic units charged with production or with providing communal services, and the state enterprises that either produce goods directly or service various health, cultural and trade bodies. All of these units are under the jurisdiction of the organs of specialized administration and are governed by civil or labor laws rather than administrative statutes.

Although the organization of Hungary's political institutions is basically the same as it was under Rakosi's Stalinist rule, the mode of operation of these institutions has changed significantly since 1968. In this chapter we analyze the quasilegitimacy of the Kadar regime in terms of the dynamism (or pluralism) of the Hungarian political process.

The 1971 and 1975 Hungarian Elections

On April 25, 1971, 7,344,918 Hungarians (71.8 percent of the population) went to the polls to elect 352 members of the National Assembly and 68,946 members of the three types of local councils—village, town, and borough (found in Budapest only). Electoral Law No. 3, promulgated October 3, 1970, abolished direct elections to the 19 county councils and to the Budapest Municipal Council; the town and village councils of each county now elect the members of the county councils, and the borough councils of Budapest elect the members of the Budapest Municipal Council. The law states that 75 percent of the members of the county and Budapest councils must be elected from the membership of the lower-ranking councils, and the remainder is to be selected from the body of ordinary citizens who possess the right to vote. Because the 1970 law abolished the district councils,[4] there are now separate elections for the National Assembly and the local councils. The first independent elections for the local councils were held in 1973 and the first, separate elections for the National Assembly occurred in 1975; these elections must be held every five years thereafter. The new method of staggered elections seeks to build voter confidence and interest in the system.

In 1971, 49 out of 352 constituencies nominated multiple candidates; 36 of the "multiple-candidate" constituencies were in the provinces and 13 were in Budapest—in one Budapest electoral district there were 3 candidates running for one seat. However, all candidates supported the program of the Patriotic People's Front (PPF). Therefore, the National Assembly elections were in reality a plebiscite for or against candidates chosen by the PPF (i.e., the regime). Nevertheless, there were 3.5 times as many opposition votes cast in 1971 as in 1967; in fact, the

68,996 opposition votes cast in 1971 represented 0.9 percent of all valid votes. Furthermore, compared to the legislature elected in 1967, the 1971 National Assembly was a much more realistic cross section of Hungarian society. About 33 percent of the former parliament's membership had not been renominated; the new assembly thus had a younger average age, more women (23.9 percent as compared to 19.8 in 1967), and more non-Party members (100 as opposed to 80 in 1967). The number of seats held by members of the Party apparat was 44 (10 less than in 1967); only 9 of the 44 (2 less than in 1967) participated in the central apparatus responsible for Party policy. The lower-level apparat held 35 (8 fewer) seats. The largest single group included the 10 (in 1967 there had been 12) first secretaries of the Party's county committees and the 9 first secretaries of its district committees. The Budapest City Committee had only one first secretary in the assembly, whereas the Budapest districts had four and the Party's town committees five. Although the number of Party apparatchiks holding seats in Parliament had declined, there was no change in the number of legislators representing the lowest level of Party officials —there were still only three. Thus, "grass-roots" Party officials were virtually absent from the new assembly. However, 9 of the 13 members (70 percent) of the 1971 Politburo were elected to the National Assembly (the same number had served in the 1967 legislature), and 36 of the 105 members of the Party's Central Committee (34.2 percent) held seats in the same parliament.

The various mass organizations controlled 30 (5 fewer) seats in the 1971 assembly. Of these, the trade unions held 10 (1 less); the Communist Youth League (KISz) had 5 (2 more than in 1967); the PPF had 9 (1 less); the Hungarian Women's Organization had only 1 (4 fewer); and three other mass organizations together held 5.

Representatives of the state administration held 43 (an increase of 4) seats in the 1971 National Assembly. Within this group of deputies there were 5 ministers, 3 deputy ministers, 23 local council officials (including 9 presidents), and 5 members of the Presidential Council (including the chairman, his deputy, and the secretary).

According to the regime, Party and state officials held only 117 of the 352 seats in the new parliament; but if one discounts the 11 pensioners and 6 clergymen elected in 1971, only 218 seats were occupied by

representatives of the productive and creative sectors of society (industry, trade, agriculture, medicine, education, the arts, etc.), and there was not one representative of the private sector among them, in spite of the fact that in 1971 there were some 89,000 private artisans and about 10,000 private merchants in Hungary.[5] Nor was there a single scientist among the 352 members of the 1971 parliament.

The 1975 elections for the Hungarian National Assembly, held on June 15, resulted in the traditional victory for candidates of the Patriotic People's Front. (See Table 5.1.) In 318 of the 352 electoral districts

Table 5.1.   1975 Election Statistics

Category	Absolute Number	Percentage
Population	10,500,000	
Eligible Voters	7,760,464	
Votes Cast	7,574,213	97.6 of eligible voters
Abstained	186,251	2.4 of eligible voters
Valid Votes	7,527,169	99.4 of votes cast
Invalid	47,000	0.6 of votes cast
For PPF	7,497,060	99.6 of valid votes
Against PPF	30,109	0.4 of valid votes

Source: Nepszabadsag, June 17, 1975.

candidates ran unopposed, and the overwhelming majority of them—299—were elected by between 99.1 and 99.9 percent of the valid votes. It is interesting to note that there was a larger voter turnout in the countryside and in provincial towns, both for and against the PPF, than in the cities. The largest vote against an unopposed candidate—4.1 percent— was cast in a Coongrad County constituency, where Mrs. Aladar Vallyon, a teacher, had been nominated. In the municipal areas, the largest percentage of opposition votes was 1.8, cast in Budapest against Bela Boros, secretary of the capital's Communist Youth League Committee.

Whereas in 1971 there were 49 multiple candidacies, in 1975 there were only 34—all double candidacies. This amounted to only 9.6 percent of all candidacies, a decrease of 4.3 percentage points, or 30.6 percent, compared to 1971. Thus, past predictions that the number of multiple candidacies will

Table 5.2. Selected 1975 Election Results

Name	Position(s)	Percentage of Votes Won
Bela Biszku	Politburo Member° and Central Committee Secretary	99.9
Jeno Fock	Politburo Member (former Premier)	99.9
Pal Losonczi	Chairman, Presidential Council	99.9
Frigyes Puja	Foreign Minister	99.9
Arpad Pullai	Central Committee Secretary	99.9
Gyorgy Aczel	Politburo Member and Deputy Premier	99.8
Janos Kadar	HSWP First Secretary and Politburo Member	99.8
Gyorgy Lazar	Politburo Member and Premier	99.8
Rezso Nyers	Central Committee Member and Director, Economic Institute	99.8
Antal Apro	Politburo Member and Speaker of the House	99.7
Karoly Nemeth	Politburo Member and Central Committee Secretary	99.7
Sandor Gaspar	Politburo Member and Secretary-General of the National Trade Union Council	99.6
Imre Gyori	Central Committee Secretary	99.5
Istvan Sarlos	Politburo Member and Secretary-General of the Patriotic People's Front	99.5

°Only 9 of the 13 Politburo members ran for election.

Table 5.3. Breakdown of the 1975–1979 National Assembly by Term of Office and Sex

Occupational Category	Electoral Status		Sex		Total of Occupational Category
	Reelected	Newly Elected	Men	Women	
Party Apparat	26	14	35	5	40
Mass Organizations	16	6	16	6	22
State Apparat	27	10	33	4	37
Clergy	4	2	6	0	6
Industry	55	49	56	48	104
Nonagricultural Cooperatives	9	3	7	5	12
Agriculture	27	34	49	12	61
Teaching	20	12	17	15	32
Medicine (physicians)	7	5	7	5	12
Creative (writers, journalists, scholars)	11	2	12	1	13
Pensioners	13	0	13	0	13
Total	215	137	251	101	352

increase from election to election have failed to materialize. In 3 of the 34 constituencies with two opposing candidates, neither candidate received a majority; consequently, a second round of elections was scheduled in those three electoral districts. In 18 of the other double-candidate constituencies, the races were rather close, with the winners receiving between 50.6 and 58.6 percent of the vote. In the remaining 13 districts, the victors won by much more comfortable margins, obtaining between 60.4 and 72.9 percent of the votes cast.[6]

Among the county's highest-ranking Party and Government officials, neither Janos Kadar nor Karoly Nemeth received the highest number of votes in the 1975 election. (See Table 5.2.) In 1971, Kadar had won the highest share of votes in Budapest. Why not in 1975? Another interesting point concerns Jeno Fock's March 15, 1975 resignation as premier, for reasons of health. Established parliamentary practice requires that the prime minister under whom the state budget is placed before the National Assembly remain in office until the house votes to implement the budget. Was it absolutely necessary for Fock to resign just a few months before the new National Assembly was to take office? This question is especially appropriate since Fock continued to be in good health and because he was reelected to both the Politburo and the National Assembly.

As shown in Table 5.3, it is interesting to note that of the 352 deputies elected to the 1975–1979 National Assembly, 137 are new delegates, which represents a turnover rate of 38.9 percent (compared to about 30 percent in 1971). Of the total number of deputies serving in the 1975–1979 assembly, 101 (or 28.7 percent) are women, as opposed to 69 (19.7 percent) in the 1967–1971 assembly and 84 (23.8 percent) between 1971 and 1975. However, in June 1975, 42 percent of all active wage earners in Hungary were women, and in some professions (e.g., teaching, public health, and cooperative work), the number of female workers exceeded that of men. Exactly 31.2 percent of the deputies now serving in the National Assembly have been elected between three and five times: 61 deputies were reelected for a third term in 1975; 27 were elected for the fourth time, and 22 for a fifth term. Those who were elected for the second time number 91, or 25.8 percent of the total membership. There is one deputy, Laszlo Pesta, a pensioner, who has served in all postwar National Assemblies. Four delegates are serving

their ninth term; four members have begun their eighth term; and five representatives, including Janos Kadar, were reelected for the seventh time.

Table 5.4 indicates the occupational breakdown of the National Assembly elected in 1975 and compares it to that of the Assembly elected in 1971. Members of the Party apparat hold 40 (−4)° seats in the current National Assembly; of those 40 seats, members of the central apparat hold 9 (0) and 31 (−4) belong to members of the middle- and lower-level Party apparat. Out of the 125-member Central Committee, 34 are members of Parliament. Thus 9.6 percent of the deputies are Central Committee members, or to put it the other way around, 27.2 percent of the Central Committee are parliamentary deputies. (In 1971, the Central Committee had 105 members, 36 of whom held seats in the assembly.) Ten of the fifteen members of the Politburo were elected to the 1975 National Assembly. (In 1971 nine Politburo members were parliamentary deputies, but at that time the Politburo had only thirteen members.)

The various mass organizations control 22 (−8) seats in the new National Assembly. Of these the trade unions hold 8 (−2), with NTUC secretary-general Sandor Gaspar, a Politburo member, reelected for an eighth term. The Communist Youth League (KISz) has 3 (−2) representatives in the new assembly. KISz first secretary, Laszlo Marothy, who became a Central Committee member in November 1973 and a Politburo member in March 1975, was not nominated as a parliamentary candidate. The apparat of the Patriotic People's Front (PPF) has 6 (−3) members in the new National Assembly. As before, the Hungarian Women's Organization is represented by 1 member, Mrs. Laszlo Erdei, who was elected for the fifth time. Four other mass organizations have 5 (−1) seats in the new National Assembly. They are the Hungarian Partisans' Association, the National Office for Physical Education and Sports, and two national organizations for ethnic minorities (the South Slavs and the Germans).

Representatives of the state apparat hold 34 (−9) seats in the new National Assembly. The Presidential Council has 3 representatives, the presidium of the National Assembly 2, and the Council of Ministers 7 (+2). A state secretary and a deputy minister representing the political division of the Hungarian

---

°Numbers in parentheses indicate the net loss or gain of seats compared to the 1971 National Assembly.

Table 5.4. Occupational Breakdown of the 1975 National Assembly

Occupational Category	1971	1975	Change
Party Apparat	44	40	−4
Central Apparat	9	9	0
County and Lower Level	35	31	−4
County First Secretaries	10	10	0
Mass Organizations	30	22	−8
Trade Unions	10	8	−2
KISz	5	3	−2
PPF	9	6	−3
State Apparat	43	37	−6
Central Apparat	16	12	−4
Council of Ministers	5	7	+2
County and Lower Level	27	20	−7
County Council Presidents	9	8	−1
Pensioners	11	13	+2
Clergy	6	6	0
Industry	96	104	+8
Manual Workers	27	50	+23
Directors and General Managers	21	22	+1
Engineers	6	5	−1
Agriculture	55	61	+6
Producers' Cooperatives Chairmen	25	16	−9
Skilled Workers (producers' cooperatives)	5	14	+9
State Farm Managers	8	1	−7
Skilled Workers (state farms)	1	5	+4
Cooperatives (nonagricultural)	8	12	+4
Teaching	33	32	−1
Elementary School (teachers)	7	11	+4
Higher Education	12	11	−1
Elementary School (directors)	9	3	−6
Medicine (physicians)	16	12	−4
Law	0	1	+1
Creative (writers, journalists, scholars)	10	12	+2

armed forces also serve in the new assembly. (The armed forces have three more representatives in the 1975 National Assembly.) The remaining 20 (−7) delegates from the middle- and lower-level categories of the state apparat are representatives of various local councils.

Leaders of the Party apparat, the mass organizations, and the state (i.e., officialdom) hold 99 seats in the new assembly, or about 28 percent of the 352 seats. The remaining 253 seats, or about 72 percent, are occupied by the so-called "productive-creative sector," which includes 13 (+2) pensioners, 6 clergymen, 104 (+8) industrial employees, 61 (+6) agricultural employees, 12 (+4) nonagricultural cooperative employees, 32 (−1) teachers, 12 (−4) physicians, 1 (+1) lawyers, and 12 (+2) literary writers.

How effective was the 1971–1975 National Assembly? Its plenum met 17 times and was in session for a total of 34 days. An average plenum lasted two days. The assembly adopted 23 laws. The overwhelming majority of its 352 members participated in debates. Many of them took the floor several times. All in all, 493 speeches were delivered by members about the various items on the agenda, and there were 39 interpellations from the floor of the house—there had been only 33 in the preceding National Assembly. The female members of the house distinguished themselves in this latter area. In fact, 12 of the 87 female members of the assembly, which was proportionately more than the percentage they represented in the total membership of parliament, addressed questions to members of the Government and to leaders of central state offices.

Between 1971 and 1975, the standing committees of the National Assembly became the real workshops in which legislation was developed; they also assumed responsibility for directing and checking the Government's work. Thus, these standing committees accomplished the day-to-day work of the National Assembly. With the creation of a new committee for construction and communications in December 1972, the number of standing committees reached 11. More than half of the members of the 1971–1975 assembly had a seat on one of its standing committees. The committees held 240 sessions, some of them lasting more than one day, and discussed over 300 agenda items.[7] The standing committees were active not only within the confines of the National Assembly, but also in factories, offices, communities, and other places where they often held meetings.

Although not detailed in a Western sense, press coverage of the work of the standing committees made these meetings appear to be both democratic and in the public interest.[8] To promote both of these virtues, members of Parliament would frequently engage in grass-roots activities, arranging to meet electors, by attending meetings of factory committees, agricultural cooperatives, local councils, the PPF, etc. To understand the essence and importance of grass-roots politics in Hungary, it is necessary to examine the nature and role of interest groups in the Hungarian political process.

Interest Articulation and Aggregation

Before 1968 Hungary had a centralized economic system controlled by Government directives aimed at implementing predetermined 3- or 5-year plans; the system was based on the assumption that in a socialist society the economic interests of enterprises, social groups, and individuals automatically coincide. This attitude was reflected in the importance given to planning and in the emphasis placed on the plans themselves. In principle, these centrally prepared plans furthered the interests of diverse groups by serving the interest of the people's economy (i.e., the socialist state). The Government maintained that the centrally drawn up plans and tasks promoted equally the interests of the various fields and enterprises—and, indeed, those of the various groups of workers within a single enterprise.

Although it was never publicly acknowledged, it was privately known that the tasks laid down in the plans were not equally advantageous to every enterprise: a task useful to one enterprise could be detrimental to others. Moreover, the interests of various groups within a single enterprise did not always coincide: the interest of top management might not be the same as that of the foreman. Indeed, certain conflicts of interest were considered natural.

With the introduction of the NEM in 1968, the Party and Government revised their earlier, mistaken views concerning the relation between the interests of various groups. Under the new economic system, clashes of interests between or within enterprises were no longer taboo. In fact, the creators of the NEM assumed that such conflicts existed and would continue to exist. Therefore, with the aid of such means as flexible price, tax, income, and credit policies, they tried to foster new attitudes among the citizenry to ensure, for example, that workers and managers would seek to resolve conflicts of interest through consideration of a higher objective, the well-being of the Hungarian socialist community.

In 1970 Gyorgy Aczel argued that Hungarian society was in a stage of socialist development in which antagonistic and insoluble contradictions did not exist. He maintained that all social classes and strata were equally interested in strengthening the economic power of socialism, which was synonymous with the national interest. However, since 1970 and despite Aczel's assertions, the Kadar regime has acknowledged three types of legitimate interests: national, group, and individual. Acceptance of these three tiers of interests and of the necessity to strive for their optimal coordination and harmony may be regarded as the hub of the NEM. It is relatively easy to define national and individual interests, but it is difficult to delineate group interests in Hungary because there are so many different kinds of groups: a group may comprise an entire social class (such as workers or peasants), an entire sector of the national economy, a branch of industry, a number of enterprises, or a single enterprise. Faced with this bewildering array of multiple and closely interlocking interests, the Party becomes an umpire, making certain that national interests prevail over special interests. The delicate political task of trying to harmonize diverse, conflicting interests is entrusted to Party members and organizations; they are expected to accomplish it through political propaganda, persuasion, and personal example. Although Party organizations are instructed to refrain from interfering directly in enterprise activity, no one knows what arm-twisting may take place behind the scenes when arguments fail to convince opponents of the merits of Party policy. The problem is further complicated by the fact that Party organizations and members are frequently both participants and arbiters in the same conflict. For example, Party members (including local Party leaders) may also be members of enterprise groups; as a result, awkward situations often develop in which the personal interests of Party members clash with the interests of the Party.

Ever since the HSWP announced that the political goal of the economic reform was to create conditions more favorable for the further development of socialist democracy,[9] Party and Government officials, scholars, and experts have been searching for new methods of political control and supervision that would prevent the development of a "workers' state" in which the managerial class enjoyed a privileged and superior position. The crux of the problem for theoreticians and practitioners alike has been how to achieve democratic legitimacy (a Western concept) without destroying the leading role or supremacy of the Party (a Communist concept) in Hungarian society. This problem has become even more complex since the November 1972 Central Committee plenum, when the designers of various reform proposals discovered that the successful implementation of reform in any society requires the cooperation, initiative, and support of a very large segment of the populace. In a society that claims to be on the road to socialism, the support of the workers is imperative. However, the Kadar regime is only passively accepted by the Hungarian people at large and is viewed with suspicion and apprehension by the conservatives in the Party. The former group is apathetic because it is not convinced of the sincerity of the ruling elite, whereas the latter group mistrusts the Party leadership because of its liberal policies.

The discussion in Chapters 3 and 4 of the challenges to reform provides some of the reasons for conservative opposition to the Party leadership. The conservatives also opposed Kadar's interpretation of "socialist legality" (which imposed a greater degree of self-restraint on the collective Party leadership in the exercise of its decision-making power) and several of the changes in the organization of the Party. Immediately after the March 1974 Central Committee plenum and the demotion of Rezso Nyers, the conservatives scored an important point for their side when high-ranking Party officials began to talk of new forms and methods of factory democracy, a phrase that has since been formally incorporated into the new Party program.

During the Eighth Congress of the HSWP (convened in November 1962), the Party Control Commission was made independent of the Central Committee. From then on its members were elected by the Party Congress,, and they were not allowed to belong to the Central Committee. Whenever the Party Control Commission and the Central Committee held joint meetings, the members of both groups had equal voting rights. The authority of the Control Commission was further strengthened by the November 1966 Ninth Party Congress, which sanctioned the commission's assumption of the functions of the

Central Auditing Commission. It can be argued that these measures were designed to prevent any one Party leader or group from manipulating the Control Commission toward a possible coup. The Ninth Party Congress also voted a change in Party statutes that freed local Party organs from the domination of their leading personnel. Since 1966, all local Party leaders have been elected by a secret ballot of the local membership. In 1969, the Party streamlined its practice of democratic centralism by allowing Party members to present complaints, orally or in writing, to any superior Party organ, up to and including the Central Committee. In that same year it renewed its efforts to enhance intra-Party democracy and improve the habits of leadership. Instead of accepting a single, clear-cut draft of a proposed policy, the elected bodies of the Party can now request their respective apparats to submit alternative proposals. Since 1970, the Party has held membership meetings without a fixed agenda on a regular basis, and the accountability reports delivered by Party functionaries have been free of ideological rhetoric, revealing a pragmatic approach to implementing policy. (The average Party member is now more interested in how policy is translated into practice between congresses than in the formulation of general statements.) In several instances the secretaries of local Party organizations have relied on the help of leaders of basic Party organizations in preparing their periodic reports. The results of public opinion polls of the general public and of members of basic organizations have been (and will continue to be) used to guide the selection of candidates in local Party elections; and, of course, district nominating committees can propose more than one candidate for a given post. Moreover, rank-and-file members have the prerogative of writing in candidates. The Party has further strengthened the position of its rank-and-file membership through the 1970 elaboration of two new statutory clauses: the first stipulates that Party leaders must reply to comments made at a Party forum at that same forum; the second protects members against reprisals for criticism or the disclosure of mistakes. Both provisions enable the membership of the Party to keep a closer watch over the activities of its executive. Finally, members expelled from the Party may now appeal their expulsion.

There should be no doubt about the far-reaching significance of the above changes in the general rules of the game. Yet there are skeptics in Hungary who maintain they have "seen it all before" and who therefore reason that as the Party giveth, so the Party taketh away. Proof of this wisdom may lie in the 1975 provisions of the revised Party statutes,[10] which call on Party members to "display revolutionary vigilance against all antisocialist phenomena"; to serve and defend, under all circumstances, the interests of socialist society; not to reveal their divergent views in public; and to comply with similar restrictions which before the November 1972 Central Committee plenum were tacitly recognized but never enforced. The skeptics of Hungarian society include a large portion of the youth, who desire a brighter future and genuine guarantees against the reemergence of the practices of the Rakosi regime (e.g., of the cult of personality). In sum, both extremes of the Hungarian political spectrum seek security.

As matters now stand, everybody in Hungary knows that the state is not going to wither away, and that as long as a division of labor is necessary between government and society, the state will remain a separate organization with its own distinct interests. Hungarians also recognize that because the people's democratic system has abolished man's dependence on private property, the average citizen is now dependent on those who manage socialized property, i.e., on the economic and political mechanism of socialism. Since this new type of dependence has produced new loyalties that have generated a different set of organized interests from those generated by the loyalties arising out of a dependence on private property, the behavior of interest groups in Hungary (and other socialist states) is quite different from that of interest groups in states that encourage private ownership. The replacement of private property with socialized property has resulted in a drastic restratification of Hungarian society that has destroyed most of the old economic, social, and political values and created new ones around which today's interests are organized.

The Party elite sits at the top of the present political and social ladder, reaping the rewards of political power, social prestige, high-paying jobs, et cetera. By virtue of its status it exerts the greatest influence on making the policies aimed at implementing the socialist system of values. On the next rung are the leaders of the state apparatus; below them are the leaders of the trade union, the cooperatives, the PPF, and the youth and other auxiliary organizations. The rank-and-file members of the party and of other mass organizations occupy the lower rungs of the ladder. Citizens at every level seem to be competing, within the realm of possibility, for higher positions in a race to reach the top (i.e., the safety area) of the political and social structure. Since most Hungarians do not believe that such an opportunity is within their reach, they are apathetic or suspicious of the system; they lack both motivation for goal achievement and initiative for participation in the political system because they surmise that their rewards are not going to improve much in the near future.

Yet, if we compare the political style of the present, most powerful decision-making group, the Politburo-Secretariat, with that of the ruling clique existing in the early 1950s under Rakosi,[11] there is reason for cautious optimism. The 16 individuals who constitute the two, current, powerful Party units are a fairly cohesive group, united around the person and basic policies of Janos Kadar; they follow a pragmatic approach in determining the country's needs and capabilities. This practicality is reflected in the more evenhanded delegation and decentralization of authority. (See Table 5.5.) The most powerful organ in the HSWP is no longer the Secretariat, but the Politburo-Secretariat, which is essentially one body, since only 3 out of 7 Central Committee secretaries (Andras Gyenes, Imre Gyori, and Arpad Pullai) are not Politburo members. Although the Politburo-Secretariat still retains its position as the primary decision-making unit, the influence of the Central Committee has grown considerably since 1968; at the same time, the Party has relinquished substantial authority to the state administration, the trade union, the cooperatives, the enterprises, and the local councils. This is probably one reason why some talented economic specialists, technicians, and administrators work not for the Party itself, or among its leadership, but in the various state and nongovernmental hierarchies throughout the country as well as in subordinate Party organs. It has been a definite policy under Kadar to shift personnel not only within the Party leadership but also between the Party leadership and outside agencies, especially the Government. These lateral transfers are motivated both by the desire to entrust certain fields of endeavor to particularly able and reliable people, and by the wish to increase the experience and expertise of the affected individuals. One result of this policy has been a sizable decrease in the number of top Party leaders (i.e., of Politburo-Secretariat members)

serving multiple functions. As of this writing, only Gyorgy Lazar as Premier, Gyorgy Aczel and Istvan Huszar as Deputy Premiers, Antal Apro as Chairman of the National Assembly, and Pal Losonczi as Chairman of the Presidential Council concurrently hold leading positions in both the Party and the Government. This development is in line with Kadar's policy of respecting the functional division of labor among the various sectors of society. The policies and backgrounds of the current Party leaders[12] indicate that they are a very intelligent, competent, and dedicated group with considerable political and administrative talent. They are rational, pragmatic, and humane in their approach to resolving the political and social problems facing Hungary in the seventies.

This is not so, however, with the Party's parent organization, the Central Committee. As has been documented in Chapters 3 and 4, some members of the Central Committee have severely criticized, if not actively hindered, the reform program pursued under Kadar's initiative and direction. And if we consider that 31 percent of the pre-1975 Central Committee occupied high positions in the state apparatus (or to put it differently, that only 5 of the 23 members of the pre-1975 cabinet were not also members of the Central Committee), it becomes obvious that the influence of this organization as a whole is very strong indeed. However, unlike the 18 members of the Politburo-Secretariat, the 125 members of the Central Committee do not form a homogeneous group. Far from it. There is a wide range of differences in such variables as the age, education, occupation, background, and, of course, ideology of the Central Committee membership. These differences surface in the form of criticism of Party policy and personnel, and frequent voting to determine committee decisions. However the divisions are harmless because the committee only meets a few times a year, for relatively short periods of time. Thus the Politburo, the Secretariat, the chairmen of the permanent committees and collectives, as well as the department chiefs actually carry the weight of decision-making within the Party.

A detailed examination of the roles of the members of the Politburo and the Secretariat will enable us to discern the division of functions and the delicate balance of power through which the leaders are able to maintain their ruling positions. In 1976 Kadar served a pivotal function within the leadership of the Party; each of the 14 other members of the Politburo

Table 5.5. Party Leadership in 1975

First Secretary
Janos Kadar

Secretariat (6)
Bela Biszku
Andras Gyenes
Imre Gyroi
Karoly Nemeth
Miklos Ovari
Arpad Pullai

Politburo (15)
Janos Kadar, Chairman

Gyorgy Aczel   Gyorgy Lazar
Antal Apro   Pal Losonczi
Valeria Benke   Laszlo Marothy
Bela Biszku   Deszo Nemes
Jeno Fock   Karoly Nemeth
Sandor Gaspar   Miklos Ovari
Istvan Huszar   Istvan Sarlos

Central Control Committee (25)
Janos Brutyo, Chairman
Janos Veneczi, Secretary

Agitation and Propaganda Committee (14)
Miklos Ovari, Chairman

Economic Policy Committee (8)
Karoly Nemeth, Chairman

Youth Committee (15)
Arpad Pullai, Chairman

Cooperative Policy Collective (15)
Pal Romany, Chairman°

Cultural Policy Collective (27)
Miklos Ovari, Chairman

Economic Collective (35)
Karoly Nemeth, Chairman

Party Building Collective (15)
Bela Biszku, Chairman
*Industry, Agriculture, and
Transportation Collective* (15)
Sandor Borbely, Chairman

Central Committee Department Heads
Karoly Grosz, Agitation and Propaganda
Imre Pardi, Economic Policy
Janos Berencz, Foreign Affairs
Joszef Kozari, Party Finances
Sandor Jakab, Party and Mass Organizations
Sandor Racz, State Administration
Deszo Nemes, Party Academy
Henrik Vass, Institute of Party History
Sandor Lakos, Social Science Institute

Heads of Mass Organizations and Party Publications
Laszlo Marothy, Communist Youth League (KISz)
Istvan Sarlos, Patriotic People's Front (PPF)
Istvan Katona, *Nepszabadsag*
Vera Lajtai, *Partelet*
Valeria Benke, *Tarsadalmi Szemle*

Central Committee (125)°°

°On July 2, 1975, the Central Committee of the HSWP relieved Pal Romany of this post to allow him to assume the position of Minister of Agriculture.
°°Alternate membership abolished in 1970.

was responsible for a specific area of activity. Economic policy fell within the purview of Karoly Nemeth. Working with him were Gyorgy Lazar (who was also serving as prime minister), Istvan Huszar, Pal Losonczi, and Sandor Gaspar (the general secretary of the Trade Union Council). Although Kadar personally guided the overall handling of Party affairs, Biszku was in control of the day-to-day operations of the Party; he was assisted by Imre Katona (first secretary of the Budapest Municipal Committee and a newly elected deputy to the National Assembly) and the Budapest Party *aktiv*. Foreign affairs were under the direction of Fock and Lazar, while Apro, Sarlos, and Marothy were in charge of the mass organizations. Finally, the new chief of propaganda and education affairs was Miklos Ovari who was supported enthusiastically by Dezso Nemes and Valeria Benke, and unenthusiastically by Gyorgy Aczel.

The actual work performed by the secretaries also reveals their standing within the power structure. Aside from Kadar, who oversaw the whole operation of the Party secretariat, each secretary was assigned an area of competence. In 1976 these areas were: Ovari—propaganda, cultural policy; Biszku—party affairs; Gyenes—foreign affairs; Nemeth—economic affairs; Gyori—education, culture, sciences; Pullai—youth.

The actual powerholders then were Biszku, Kadar, Lazar, Nemeth, Ovari, and to some extent Pullai. Nemes and Benke had to be content with a seat on the Agitprop Committee operating under the chairmanship of the relative upstart, Miklos Ovari. Apro's demotion to the chairmanship of parliament deprived him of any real function within the Politburo; his former activities as liaison with Moscow has been completely taken over by Komocsin and Fock, who received some assistance from Ovari. However, since Komocsin had died in May 1974 and Fock had resigned from the premiership in March 1975, Ovari was the only one of the three to remain in the inner circle of the power structure. Although he had come to the Secretariat of the Central Committee four years after Pullai, the Eleventh Party Congress considered Ovari more valuable than Pullai and thus made him a member of the Politburo as well. With the removal of Aczel and Nyers from the Secretariat of the Central Committee in March 1974 and the removal of Nyers from the Politburo in March 1975, Nemeth and Gyenes moved up to these two

important policy-making bodies as replacements. Lajos Feher's resignation from the Politburo because of ill health and Gyula Kallai's involuntary retirement from the same body were the final moves in a shake-up that drastically altered the makeup of the "club of powerholders": Aczel, Feher, Fock, Komocsin, and Nyers—all loyal supporters of Kadar and the NEM—had been replaced by a new guard of younger Communists—Gyenes, Gyori, Huszar, Lazar, Marothy, Nemeth, Ovari, and Sarlos. Losonczi's unexpected co-option into the Politburo, in July 1975 was intended to increase the representation of the economically important agricultural sector.

The real threat to the stability of this arrangement (and thus to the power and position of Kadar) comes from those who are not within the inner core of Party activity. Aczel, Apro, Benke, Fock, Gaspar, and Nemes all experienced Party members and leaders, who are fully aware of the complexities of politics in Communist states. Kadar, of course, is well aware of the problem of "joblessness" and tries to offer these leaders some token functions. Yet, the fact remains that within the Politburo, consensus is not automatic; compromises are necessary to achieve a majority on many issues. Kadar is able to maintain control of the Politburo by virtue of two circumstances: his extraordinary abilities and the type of opposition he encounters.

Kadar is a man of great perception and intelligence. Basically a shy person, he tries to reason with and cajole his opponents, rather than insisting on compliance with his policies. Thus, many of the issues that are voted on in meetings of the Politburo have actually been settled through compromises worked out in advance. The threat of forced compliance remains in the background because compulsion is left out of discussions. Kadar's frequent reliance on the most intelligent men around him (in the past these have included Fock, Aczel, Nyers, and Ovari) has been of great value to him in treading a cautious course. At the same time his extraordinary politeness frequently helps to disarm his opponents. Kadar is also aided by the fact that his opponents on the Politburo do not and cannot jell into a cohesive group. They are opponents only on some issues; on others they are supporters. In short, Gaspar, Benke, Nemeth, and Lazar are issue-oriented and do not pose ideological opposition.

Aside from the Party and the Government, whose interests overlap, the third most influential interest group in Hungary today is organized labor. In no other socialist country, except Yugoslavia, is the function of trade unions recognized with such official tenacity as in Hungary; the Party and the Government both acknowledge that the union is necessary to defend the interests of the workers. According to a resolution passed at the 22nd Trade Union Congress (convened in 1971) the unions play a dual role: they defend and represent the workers' interests, and at the same time, they communicate and interpret Party policy to the working class.[13] Sandor Gaspar, secretary general of the Trade Union Congress, has interpreted this latter role to mean that the trade unions both transmit and actively participate in the creation of policy. Although in the past the transmission of policy consisted in relaying orders and commands as well as in giving instructions to workers regarding their duties and obligations to the socialist state, today the process is different. Information given to workers now includes an explanation of their legal and political rights as well as a description of opportunities for jobs and training. Similarly, trade union locals organized among enterprise workers are no longer required to be mere junior partners of management in fulfilling production plans. Since the Tenth Party Congress, when the National Trade Union Council (NTUC) seriously criticized the Party for several omissions concerning workers' rights from the Guidelines, a more detailed exposition of the principles and practice of worker participation in the decision-making process of enterprises has been worked out by the Party.

Although, by their own admission, the trade unions are still far from being an effective pressure group, their goal of becoming such a group is firmly supported by the Party, the Government, and the trade union leadership. The reason for this is obvious. Since the introduction of the NEM in 1968, a division of labor has emerged in Hungarian society. Sandor Gaspar has stated that this new division "institutionally serves the purpose of representing, coordinating, and solving the conflict of various interests."[14]

Probably for these (and other) reasons, since 1969 rank-and-file workers have become more responsive and demanding in their attitude toward both state authority and their trade union representatives. However, this attitude of the workers does not coincide with the attitude the regime would like to see develop. At the Tenth Party Congress in November

1970, Jeno Fock charged that Hungarian workers were still inner-oriented. Gyula Virizlai of the NTUC later repeated this charge. Both claimed that the working class was concerned primarily with its own welfare instead of that of the community as a whole, and that it held the regime responsible for whatever affected workers at home or on the job.[15] If these observations by Fock and Virizlai are accurate, then we may conclude that Kadar's reform movement, which sought to foster the growth of interest-group articulation among Hungarian workers, did not achieve this objective. Instead, the movement seems to have above all stimulated a desire for security among the working class. This desire is more in harmony with the basic tenets of proletarian ethics than with the principles of participatory democracy. It therefore appears that, in the name of the proletariat, Hungarian workers are now demanding egalitarianism instead of supporting a "merit system" whose objectives sometimes conflict with the interests of the workers.

In fact, between 1970 and 1974 the unions emerged increasingly as pressure rather than interest organizations. At times the pressures they exerted were so great that both Party and Government officials succumbed to them at the expense of pursuing other social interests.[16] For example, the NTUC's strong stand in favor of loosening or even eliminating the close link between wages and profits caused the regime to alter its wage policy and agree to implement periodic, independent wage increases for all workers employed by the state. On the question of the enterprise reorganization ordered by the Central Committee plenum in November 1972, the NTUC vigorously called for observing the principle of interest protection, which resulted in the elaboration of factory democracy. However, on the issues of wage differentiation and craft unions, the NTUC sided with the Party and the Government, who favored wage differentiation and opposed the formation of craft unions.

The demand for craft unions to safeguard professional interests within the union movement had grown out of intraunion criticism alleging shortcomings and neglect in the existent industrial-union system, Gyula Kovacs, secretary of the Union for Workers in the Hungarian Aluminum Industry Trust, for instance, once declared that the Hungarian Labor movement had no expressly professional trade unions, only branch unions, and that these did not satisfactorily represent professional interests. The same view had been echoed by Otto Juhasz, secretary of the Construction Workers Union, Dezso Lontai, secretary of the Enterprise Trade Union Council of the Municipal Taxicab Enterprise, Istvan Peter, secretary of the Hungarian Union of Municipal and Local Industries Workers, and other labor leaders who recommended that professional groups be represented in the various leading political organizations in proportion to their numerical importance, as was the case with enterprise trade union organizations. Although the Party has yet to authorize a reorganization of the trade union movement, the fact remains that under the NEM, trade unions have ceased to be mere conveyor belts for directives from above; they have to a certain extent taken on the more meaningful and responsible task of trying to protect workers' interests. These interests, according to Lajos Mehes, secretary-general of the Iron and Steel Metalworking and Electric Power Industry Workers' Trade Union can be safeguarded just as well by the existing industrial unions as by craft organizations. Mehes believes that craft differences (i.e., differences between the interests of various occupational groups within an enterprise unit) are less important than differences between factory units. What seems to be implicit in this reasoning is that the workers' demand for egalitarianism presupposes an egalitarianism within the trade union movement.[17] The present trend toward the diversification of groups into subinterest groups within the same enterprise, and the concomitant emergence of new special interests make the job of trade union locals much more difficult by compelling frequent readjustments of their interest-protection activities. Consequently, it is no longer in vogue to refer to the cliché: one enterprise—one interest; instead it is much more realistic to whisper: one enterprise—several interests.

In 1967, when the regime decided to legitimize interest-group activity, it enacted two important pieces of legislation that gave institutional guarantees to the two largest, non-Party, non-Government groups in Hungary. The new Labor Code granted trade unions the right of consent, the right of decision, the right of control, the right of veto, and the right of opinion. Similar rights were given to members of cooperatives. The Agricultural Producers' Cooperative Law established the legal and financial means for safeguarding cooperative interests. Executive authorities can no longer promulgate legally binding decrees concerning "issues of importance" to collectives without prior negotiation and consultation with either the National Council of Agricultural Cooperatives (NCAC) or the regional associations. Any ministry that intends to adopt measures "fundamentally" affecting the operation, organization, or business of the cooperatives or regional associations must obtain a written agreement from the NCAC or the regional associations. Moreover, if the interest-protection units of the cooperatives submit inquiries, proposals, or complaints to any state organ, the latter is legally obliged to answer within a reasonable period of time; if a ministry rejects a request made by or with the approval of the NCAC, it must submit the matter to the Council of Ministers, if that is the wish of the National Council.[18]

As a result of these liberalizing measures, the NCAC has been able to participate in drafting some of the laws, resolutions, and decrees affecting agriculture. Since 1968, the National Council has also been able to work out agreements with specific ministries on such problems as the repair of agricultural machinery, water conservation, and the procurement of fruits and vegetables. The regional associations have achieved similar though less important gains. Although there have been no known cases of arbitration or conciliation, the producers cooperatives have developed a self-assertive attitude that is recognized as legitimate throughout the country. The NCAC has systematically fought against state monopoly in certain agricultural sectors. For example, the President of the NCAC, Istvan Szabo, argued vehemently on the floor of the National Assembly and in the pages of the Party's theoretical journal, *Tarsadalmi Szemle*, for the free marketing of pork. He was able to muster support not only from lower-ranking NCAC officials, but also from several deputies in parliament as well as from radio and press commentators. Szabo campaigned for many other rights on behalf of the cooperatives;[19] some campaigns were successful, others were not. Probably the greatest achievement resulting from the political pressure exerted by the cooperative movement between 1971 and 1975 was the merger of the County Marketing Centers with the producer cooperatives, a move that enabled the cooperatives to utilize new facilities for the speedy sale of their produce at reasonable prices. The cooperatives also won the right to establish their own credit unions. These latter accomplishments signaled the end of marketing and credit monopolies in Hungary. Even so, the cooperatives have not obtained rights and privileges equal to those of their competitors, the trade unions.

The local councils constitute another group that benefited from the movement toward greater participation and democracy in Hungary in the late 1960s; they acquired greater independence and the power to protect their own interests. Until 1967, the local councils were organs of state administration that were completely controlled by various central authorities. Since October 1967, however, the councils have become independent units of local self-government; although they are still considered organs of state administration, they can now levy development fees and utilize other revenue-generating devices in addition to collecting the usual taxes on enterprise and cooperative profits and wages.[20] They also have a say in matters concerning regional industrial and economic development, communal services, guidance and education, housing, health, etc. To improve the efficiency of local government and eliminate unnecessary bureaucracy, groups of several smaller neighboring villages have been incorporated as towns; each community retains its own identity in a united, common council. These larger town councils can exert greater influence on their rivals in the hierarchy of administrative bureaucracy, the county councils, which have frequently refused to grant authority to the district councils and have turned down the demands of village and town councils. In such controversies, local council deputies have more often than not been denied adequate information, which made them dependent on the directors of their executive committees and administrative departments. The result was constraint, rivalry, and a lack of coordination and cooperation among the councils and other administrative agencies. The new Local Council Law enacted in the winter of 1971[21] tried to alleviate this friction by clearly delineating the spheres of responsibility of the councils and by guaranteeing the various components of local government protection against further encroachment by other governmental units. Since 1971, the local councils have been more autonomous not only in administrative matters but in economic and budgetary ones as well. The domination of the council plenum by the executive committee has practically disappeared: the law prohibits it and, in practice, the deputies are now much better

informed because they are doing their homework. Furthermore, the plenum can annul those decisions of the executive committee that have been made on the basis of the powers granted to it under the plenum's authority. The 1971 law also excludes the chairman of the executive committee from appointing the committee secretary or the members of the secretariat. The secretary is nominated by the executive committee of the superior council and elected by the plenum of the council concerned. The plenum also appoints the numerous department heads and determines their activities. Under the new law, the councils not only possess coercive powers, they also dispose of certain political, legal, and financial incentives. For example, through the establishment of permanent, ad hoc committees that have noncouncil members serving on them, the local councils are able to draw the local population into active participation in the governmental process. This power, when successfully executed, is recognized with some envy by other competing interest groups.

The foregoing discussion has centered primarily on the interest articulation and aggregation of five major groups, but there are many others, such as the Young Communist League, the Writers' Union, the Association of Journalists, and the National Council of Hungarian Women, that could be mentioned here. None of these groups however, carries the prestige or influence of the first five. Furthermore, the interests of these latter groups overlap to a great extent with those of the five already discussed. The interests of the Young Communist League, for example, overlap with those of the Party, and the interests of the National Council of Hungarian Women overlap with those of all five groups. Thus, a consideration of the numerous subordinate groups that take part in the Hungarian political process could blur rather than clarify the question of interest articulation and aggregation in Hungary.

Rule Making

At the outset of this chapter, we asked whether group politics have any real meaning in the Hungarian political process in view of the dominant role of the Party. It should be clear from the discussion so far that group politics in socialist Hungary are quite different from group politics in the United States, Canada, the United Kingdom, France, or, for that matter, Denmark, New Zealand, and other small nonsocialist countries; in Hungary the regime does not permit organized groups to compete for power *against* the HSWP. As Janos Gosztonyi, former editor-in-chief of *Nepszabadsag*, put it: "By socialist democracy we mean freedom of democracy for the people building socialism, not freedom to abate our enemies. It is precisely against them that we vigilantly defend the democracy of the working class."[22] However, it is also true that the Party wants to generate support by allowing increased participation in the decision-making process; to generate initiative by offering tangible rewards to citizens who actively build socialism; to use human skills and knowledge as a resource; to eliminate the red tape and procrastination of an inflated bureaucracy; and to place the control of this process of interest articulation and aggregation outside Party channels. Nevertheless, the Party remains the sole arbiter in this basically political process because, according to its leaders, the Party safeguards the common welfare and protects the interests of all. The question then arises of whether the various participants in the process below the Party level perceive the post-1966 reforms—economic as well as political—as an end in themselves or as just window dressing (i.e., the playing of the game for the game's sake). The answer to this question might tell us whether the inertia existing among lower-level Party leaders and the apathy found among Hungarian workers are reflections of these two opposing perceptions. The Party elite takes the position that the Party is doing and will continue to do everything in its power to prevent any one group from ever again monopolizing control of the Party and/or the socialist system. To this end, in March 1969, the Central Committee of the HSWP created seven commissions to study the most urgent political problems generated by the reform movement. Information available in 1975 did not indicate that these seven commissions had completed their work; if they had, then some of their proposals had not yet been published or enacted into law. Nevertheless, the following legislation and proposals resulted from their investigations: (1) a new law on the courts and court justices, enacted in 1972; (2) a new law on criminal proceedure, enacted in 1973; (3) a law on state attorneys, enacted in 1972; (4) a decree-law amending the 1968 law on state administrative procedure, issued in 1972 and (5) a Presidential Council resolution on the legal policies and principles regulating the application of the law (including

state administrative law), promulgated in 1973. Proposed but not yet enacted are: (1) a new criminal code; (2) a new civil code; (3) a new code of civil procedure; (4) a new law on state administration; (5) a new law on Party-state relations; and (6) a new law on the structure and functions of the government and the legislature. The first four of these were supposed to have been enacted as part of the 1971–1975 five-year legislative plan.

That these new and projected laws resulted from the investigations of Party-appointed commissions clearly indicates that legislative initiative emanates from the Party elite and not from the electoral constituents or their representatives. By implication, only the Party knows what is good for Hungarian society. It is conceivable and even probable, however, that the Party relies to some extent on public opinion in its decision-making process. The utilization of opinion surveys and various studies by Hungarian sociologists, for example, shows that this is indeed the case. Even so, the process of rule making should not be equated with any procedure operative in the West. There are no checks and balances, no lobbying, no legislative scrutiny through prolonged and controversial hearings, and no requisite legislative "process." The 352 members of the National Assembly meet only twice a year for 10 to 14 weekdays, and in this short period of time they enact a large number of measures. Consequently, the real work of developing legislation, which should be the responsibility of the National Assembly, is in fact accomplished by a handful of people organized in various committees under the control of the 21-member Presidential Council.

In exercising this "substitution" function, the Presidential Council implements a copious legislative program through "decree-laws" that have the force but not the form of normal laws. To remain operative, decree-laws must be presented for approval to the "next session of the National Assembly"; however, the National Assembly always rubber-stamps the decisions of the Presidential Council. What is even more disturbing to some students of constitutional law is that most of the 21 members of the council have important full-time jobs, and the drafts of the decrees are never discussed by the members of the permanent committees. In effect, since 1949 the Presidential Council has usurped a great deal more legislative power than the lawmakers ever intended it to possess. Thus, it is fair to generalize

Table 5.6. State and Government Leadership in 1975

Group and Position	Person Filling Position in 1975
Presidential Council (21)	
Chairman (nominal head of state)	Pal Losonczi
National Assembly (352)	
Chairman	Antal Apro
Council of Ministers (23)	
Prime Minister	Gyorgy Lazar
Deputies	Gyorgy Aczel
	Janos Borbandi
	Istvan Huszar
	Gyula Szeker
	Ferenc Havasi
Ministers:	
Agriculture and Food	Pal Romany
Culture	Laszlo Orban
Defense	Lajos Czinege
Education	Karoly Polinszky
Finance	Lajos Faluvegyi
Foreign Affairs	Frigyes Puja
Foreign Trade	Jozsef Biro
Heavy Industry	Pal Simon
Home Trade	Istvan Szurdi
Interior	Andras Benkei
Justice	Mihaly Korom
Labor	Laszlo Karakas
Light Industry	Mrs. Janos Keseru
Metallurgy and Machine Industry	Tivadar Nemeslaki
Public Construction and Urban Development	Jozsef Bondor
Public Education	Karoly Polinszky
Public Health	Emil Schulteisz
Transport and Telecommunications	Karoly Rodonyi
Chairman, National Planning Office	
(ministerial rank)	Istvan Huszar
Chairmen with State Secretarial Rank	
Central Control Commission	Gyula Dabronaki
Central Statistical Office	Jozsef Balint
Information Bureau	Peter Varkonyi
National Bank	Matyas Timar
National Material and Price Control	Bela Csikos-Nagy
National Water Conservation Office	Imre Degen
Office for Church Affairs	Imre Miklos
Office for Local Councils	Lajos Papp
National Physical Training and Sports	Sandor Beckl

that the Hungarian government governs by decree without explicit authorization from parliament; in most Western nations this practice would be considered a grave constitutional violation.

As matters now stand in Hungary, there is no clear delineation between the legislative prerogatives of the National Assembly and those of the Presidential Council or the Council of Ministers (i.e., there are no constitutional directives specifying which types of problems are to be settled by law and which are to be resolved by decree-law or government decree). It is true that the extraordinary powers of the Presidential Council are now being watched more closely than in the past, but it is also true that the restrictions imposed on the council by the Revised Constitution are vague. For example, the National Assembly (not the Presidential Council) now approves the implementation of the budget;[23] rules related to the fundamental rights and duties of the citizens are now established by law (i.e., by parliament);[24] and the National Assembly maintains control over how the constitution is respected (it can declare illegal any act by a state agency that violates the constitution or hurts the interests of society).[25] However, these constitutional guarantees are ineffective if the legislature does not invoke them. The National Assembly as a whole is too clumsy a body to judge its own laws and acts; to date, there has not been a single case of review. Whether there will be any in the future is too academic a question for us to answer.

Finally, it is worth considering the issue of legislative initiative. According to the 1972 Revised Constitution, the Presidential Council shares the right to initiate legislation with the Council of Ministers, the standing committees, and any member of the National Assembly.[26] However, the constitution also specifies that members of parliament must place proposals on the parliamentary agenda; this provision puts deputies at a disadvantage in initiating legislative bills vis-à-vis the Presidential Council and the Council of Ministers. If a proposal comes from the floor, the speaker of the house must inform the National Assembly about it and move that it be placed, or not placed, on the agenda. The author of the proposal is sometimes allowed to address the assembly. The plenum then decides on the fate of the proposal, without prior discussion.[27] It should be emphasized, however, that as of now there has never been a single proposal from the floor to initiate legislation, nor, for that matter, has any motion ever come from the floor.

In sum, the National Assembly has gained in stature and influence in the past few years, but its lawmaking powers are still inferior to those of the Presidential Council and the Council of Ministers. In 1970, for example, it was not the National Assembly but the Presidential Council that enacted most, if not all, of the laws of political significance, including the new travel and passport regulations. Again, the five-year legislative program mapping out the most significant measures to be enacted between 1971 and 1975 was prepared by the Ministry of Justice in cooperation with other ministries and not by the National Assembly. Finally, ministries carry too much weight with the standing committees, which, instead of scrutinizing potential legislation, simply sponsor drafts submitted by the various ministries. The result is a collusion between the executive and the legislature that hinders effective and constructive debate on the merits of each bill.

In a nutshell, Hungary's main problem at present is how to complete the reform program initiated in 1968. The Kadar regime instituted the liberalizing program to dismantle the mobilization system in favor of a modernization system. However, the successful implementation of the modernization system also requires some modification of both the ideology and the criteria of social control. There are three different approaches to this problem. First, Party conservatives at the lower level of the Party organization as well as low-income workers oppose any reforms; they would like to preserve the old mobilization system under the slogan of "egalitarianism." Secondly, among the Party elite, the state bureaucracy and the leaders of the mass organizations, there are people who would like to replace the mobilization system with the modernization system, but who are hesitant to do so because they are either afraid of purges or simply do not know how to proceed when it comes to revising ideology and social controls. Finally, some Party leaders, some managers, and the intelligentsia feel that the regime is neither proceeding fast enough nor going far enough in moving Hungary toward a modernized political culture.

6

Rule Adjudication

Well over a century ago Alexis de Tocqueville observed that mankind often respects "the mere formalities of justice long after the substance has evaporated," for the courts lend "bodily influence to even the mere shadow of law."[1] Between 1949 and 1960, the administration of justice in Hungary was at times no more than the enforcement of a "shadow of law," because in Communist political systems law, for the most part, serves the political ends of the regime. The form of justice instituted by the Communist regime in Hungary has been called "political justice" (by the late Professor Otto Kirchheimer),[2] "revolutionary justice" (by Andrei Y. Vishinsky), or "socialist law" (by contemporary Hungarian scholars). These political definitions are appropriate descriptions of the Hungarian Communist system of justice because since 1949 Party authorities have used the law for political ends. Under Rakosi, the law became above all an instrument of the state, serving the interests of the ruling elite.

In statist, dictatorial, or totalitarian societies the administration of justice is generally based not on abstract principles, but on the necessity of enforcing the political norms of the ruling elite. In such societies opposition to government policies (or the mere act of expressing a contrary opinion) is construed as an act against the state, punishable by the full weight of the law; anyone who strikes out against any element of what the state considers to be the law is a *hostis*, or an enemy of society, and as an enemy he must be punished.

Societies in which the law is administered according to the principles of political justice are not "lawless" states. Indeed, these states usually abide very strictly by the letter of the law. The substance of the law, however, differs from the principles of justice that have prevailed in Anglo-Saxon jurisprudence. In the purge trials held under Rakosi, for example, the prosecutors and judges followed strictly legal procedures: the evidence was clear; there were witnesses whose testimonies condemned the accused; and the sentences were meted out legally. That the evidence was fabricated; that the witnesses were coached and lying; that the testimonies were false and the depositions forged did not concern the judges. They abided by the letter of the law. They administered justice on the basis of what appeared to be airtight evidence, and they "legally" condemned the accused.

In the administration of political justice, the power elite is free to deem any action a political offense. At one time, as an old Hungarian joke holds, spitting on the sidewalk was considered to be a political comment. Today, even mild public criticism of the regime is permitted. In general, political justice implies inequality before the law. The worker who steals bread in a Communist state, for instance, is usually punished less severely than the former landlord who is apprehended for the same crime. Favoritism in the administration of justice is by no means limited to societies ruled by dictatorial regimes. A white American who runs over a black man while driving in the South is likely to receive a less severe punishment than a black man charged with the same offense. However, whereas racism is theoretically illegal and unconstitutional in America, in a Communist society the class bias is legal, deriving its legitimacy from the constitution. Political justice, thus, seldom implies more than procedural guarantees that cloak the embodiments of rule. For ultimately, as Pascal said, "*La justice est sujette à disputes; la force est très reconnaissables, et sans dispute.*"[3]

To understand the legal system of Communist Hungary, it is necessary to appreciate the differences between justice and political justice. Contemporary Hungarian law is not based on abstract concepts of justice; it is rooted in socialist concepts of justice, socialist rules of conduct, and socialist laws designed to protect the working class.[4]

The Concept of Justice During the Mobilization Era

Before August 20, 1949, when the present Hungarian constitution was ratified,[5] Hungarian law was based on codified Roman Law. By World War II, Hungary's laws and regulations had become outmoded both because they were based on ancient customs that favored the upper class and because they were abused by the various dictatorial regimes that manipulated them to serve particular interests. The enactment of Hungary's first constitution changed this tradition. The document was modeled after the Soviet Constitution of 1936, and like its predecessor, it was a state-

ment of accomplishment reflecting the "fundamental changes effected in the economic and social structure of the country."[6] Moreover, according to Matyas Rakosi, the constitution fulfilled "the workers' need to strengthen [a] social order which they support[ed] and which they regard[ed] as favoring their interests."[7] The 1949 Constitution embodied the concept of the dictatorship of the proletariat by granting a leading role in society to the working class. The ruling position accorded this class is clearly reflected in the principles governing the administration of justice and in the structure of the court system.

Following the Communist assumption of power in Hungary, justice was based not on the principle of equality under law, but on the concept of class rule. Article 41, Paragraph 1 of the 1949 Constitution calls upon the courts to "punish the enemies of working people; safeguard the state, the social and economic order, the institutions of the people's democracy, and the rights of the workers; and educate working people to observe the rules governing the life of a socialist commonwealth."[8] Although Article 49, Paragraph 1 declares that all citizens of Hungary are equal before the law, it also asserts that the judiciary must serve the cause of revolutionary, or socialist, justice. It instructs judges to utilize courts as instruments of class warfare and directs them to base awards and decisions on the class character of the accused instead of on the merits of each case or on the guilt or innocence of the accused. Advisory Opinion No. 214 of the Civil Division of the Supreme Court declares that

> justice administered in the interest of class warfare, of necessity, presupposes the clarification of the class character of the action and the class affiliation of the parties involved. This is a result of the observance of the basic norm of socialist legality by every judge, because the laws and other legal provisions are the tools which secure the class interest of our society's leading force.[9]

Since 1949 the Supreme Court has insisted on applying this form of justice in nearly all cases arising out of transgressions of the law. For instance, in one case the bourgeois class affiliation of the defendant caused an appellate court to raise his sentence to eight years from the original three-and-one-half year sentence.[10] In another case, because the defendant belonged to the working class, her sentence was reduced.[11]

The Rakosi regime regarded the law as an instrument of coercion to be used against enemies of the Party, enemies of the leadership, and personal enemies of Rakosi himself. Rakosi deliberately set out to destroy Laszlo Rajk and his codefendants in a clear application of the law for political ends.[12] Rakosi and his collaborators in the purge trials of the early 1950s accused Rajk and other members of the Communist Party of attempting to restore fascism.[13] It is now clear that the state's accusations against Rajk and his comrades were without foundation, and that their confessions were extracted by torture or in some cases by promises of leniency. Those who could not be sentenced legally because they failed to confess were murdered without trial.

Even though evidence for the Rajk trials and for many other miscarriages of justice was gathered by repugnant methods, the courts of Hungary participated in these trials and condemned "innocent people, revolutionaries, Communists, and veteran fighters in the workers' movement . . . on the basis of trumped-up charges. . . ."[14] These convictions were based on the principle of revolutionary justice that condemned all those opposed to the policies or activities of the leadership as enemies of the people.

Another basic premise of the Hungarian system of justice during the Rakosi era was that the law must serve an "educational" purpose. The courts were expected to "teach" defendants to obey the law and to work toward the creation of a moral society.[15] Using Soviet law as a precedent, the courts employed lectures and sentences of "correctional labor" to educate wayward citizens. Unpaid compulsory work days at newly established corrective labor camps were meted out to the guilty instead of prison sentences; convicted criminals were also required to attend seminars designed to teach them how to observe the laws of Hungary.

A third premise of the judicial system in this period was the presumption of the defendant's guilt. The burden of proof rested not with the prosecutor, but with the defendant. A man brought to trial was presumed guilty, and his innocence had to be established by his defense counsel or by himself. Yet, throughout this era, defense lawyers often sided with the prosecutors in demanding the conviction of the accused.

Crime by analogy was another principle of law applied during the Rakosi regime, but it was not applied as widely in Hungary as it was in the USSR. Contrary to the principle of *nulla poena, sine lege*,[16] the doctrine of crime by analogy sanctions the punishment of certain activities on the grounds that although they are not proscribed, they are socially dangerous and analogous to acts that are specifically prohibited. The Rakosi regime applied this doctrine to a large number of cases during the purge trials of 1949–1951.

The principles outlined above, which formed the basis of revolutionary law as practiced by the Hungarian Communist leadership under Rakosi, amounted to a justification of the Party's dictatorship over the entire society. The Party leaders employed legal procedures to justify terror. Law in the hands of the ruling elite became a "political category," to use one of Vishinsky's favorite phrases, and in this way, both law and justice became tools of Party politics.

Rakosi used the law to imprison a large portion of the Party leadership, including Imre Nagy, Janos Kadar, Gyula Kallai, and many other Communists. This "revolutionary lawlessness" of the Communist Party contributed in no small measure to the revolution of 1956. When in 1956 the people of Hungary rose and challenged a great many of the Stalinist conceptions of law and revolutionary justice, Nagy's prophecy that "the denial of human honor, of Communist morality, and of socialist legality . . . brings grim retribution" came to pass.[17]

Changing Concepts of Justice Since the Revolution

Although the revolution of 1956 failed to effect a change in Hungary's political system, a great many alterations have occurred in the Hungarian legal system since that date. Prompted partly by the genuine revulsion of Communist leaders who had themselves suffered dishonor, defamation, degradation, and torture, and partly by changes in the application of law in the Soviet Union, the Kadar regime abolished the most flagrant uses of terror. The changes effected since 1956 have been enormous, and although the law still serves political ends, it is now applied more impartially and without the utilization of blatant physical coercion.

Since the early 1960s, the regime has disallowed class bias in the administration of justice. It has instructed the judiciary not to consider class affiliation as a basis for the enforcement of justice. Although some Hungarian Stalinists still insist that in "a political case . . . class background is . . . important,"[18] in most cases the law is applied equitably.[19] According to the deputy chief of the prosecutor's office, "Today all enjoy the same rights before the law and only crime is prosecuted."[20] Thus, the abolition of the class basis of justice has taken place in practice if not in theory. In fact, during the summer of 1969 in discussions between the author and eleven judges of the Budapest court system, not one of the judges mentioned the class basis of justice. Most of them believed that Hungary no longer had a social structure based on the former division of classes, and most agreed that socialist justice must serve the development of the entire Hungarian society.

Since 1960 the Kadar regime has also clarified the distinction between political crimes and offenses that either have no relationship to the state or do not endanger the existence of the political system. The state has been consistent in cracking down on hostile political action, but it no longer views all violators of the law as enemies of the state. All but one of the eleven judges interviewed in 1969 carefully differentiated between antisocial and antistate activities. One estimated that only one or two percent of all cases concern political questions. This same judge stated that he spends 20 to 30 percent of his time with criminal cases and the remaining 70 to 80 percent on issues of inheritance, divorce, etc.

A third important change effected in the Hungarian system of justice has been the abolition of the wholesale use of terror against the citizenry to induce positive commitments to the regime. Kadar has attempted to alter the evaluative orientations of the people through pacific methods. For example, since 1959 recollectivization has progressed without the widespread physical coercion used during the early 1950s. Another evidence of the change in policy was the demotion of Imre Dogei, a minister of agriculture from 1958 to 1959. Dogei, who publicly advocated Stalinist and Maoist views, was expelled from the Party and assigned to a minor research post; he was not tried and condemned for antistate activity as he would have been under Rakosi.

The educative character of Hungarian socialist law has remained largely what it was in the 1950s, but the forms of corrective labor have changed. For example, convicted criminals are no longer deported to the mines for corrective work. The educative character of the law is evident, however, from the constant lecturing that guilty parties receive from judges and from the efforts to release minor criminals to the custody of their work community.

The concept of crime by analogy was one of the primary precepts of Stalinist law. Although it is difficult to ascertain from court records the extent to which this concept is still applied, official policy seems to have discarded this remnant of Stalinist "lawlessness." The eleven Hungarian judges interviewed by the author denied the validity of the principle of crime by analogy. They further rejected the claim that the courts automatically presume the guilt of the accused. Under Kadar, the judiciary has modeled its formulation of the presumption of guilt or innocence after the theoretical bases for the administration of justice elaborated in the post-Stalinist USSR; the basic premises concerning the guilt or innocence of the accused were taken from an article by Professor M. S. Strogovich, printed in the November 17, 1960 issue of *Literaturnaia Gazeta*. The article said, in part, that

> according to the law, the defendant has the right to question the accusation, but he cannot be asked to prove his innocence. It is not the defendant who must prove his guilt. . . . No sentence can be pronounced as long as any doubt remains concerning the defendant's guilt. This is a firm principle of our court process.[21]

When pressed about the fact that in the USSR this principle has not been applied with complete regularity, the judges interviewed in 1969 suggested that in Hungary the courts have been much more consistent in applying the Strogovich norms.

Abolishing the use of terror and diminishing the use of law for political ends has aided the Kadar regime considerably in its efforts to legitimize its rule. Law remains an instrument of political justice in Communist Hungary, but it is applied more equitably so that serving the political ends of the regime is no longer the major function of the judiciary.

The Legal System

The Hungarian legal system is based on constitutional provisions supplemented by a whole series of acts establishing codes of conduct for administrative, social, scientific, and military affairs. Penal law is based on the Criminal Code of 1961; civil law on the Civil Code of 1959; labor law on the 1951 Code of

Labor as amended by the new Labor Code of 1967;[22] laws concerning youth on the Youth Law of 1971; and family law on the Family Code of 1952. In addition, codes of civil, administrative, and criminal procedure were enacted in 1952, 1957, and 1962 respectively. These codes provide the bases for judicial procedure.

The Organization of the Judiciary

After World War II, the Hungarian court system was radically reorganized. The first step in this direction was taken as early as January 25, 1946, when people's courts were established to prosecute citizens who had supported the Germans and the Hungarian fascists. These original Hungarian people's courts were slightly reorganized several times before the present judicial system was finally established by the Constitution of 1949. Chapters 6 and 7 of that document treat the administration of justice. They also describe the composition and operation of the judicature and the offices of the public prosecution. Although there have been some alterations in the operation and function of these organs in the last twenty-five years (particularly in 1973), their essential structure has remained unchanged.

The lowest organs of the judiciary are the district (*kerulet*) and municipal (*jaras*) courts. These bodies are always courts of first instance, and their authority extends to all violations of law not specifically delegated to other courts. The county courts (*megyei birosagok*) and the Budapest Capital Court serve as both courts of original jurisdiction and appellate courts. They have jurisdiction over all cases concerning homicide, grave crimes against the state (such as treason or large-scale theft of state property), civil cases involving more than 20,000 forints worth of damage, and patent and copyright cases.[23]

The Supreme Court is the highest judicial body of Hungary. It has original jurisdiction in cases that have been specifically designated to fall within its field of competence and that have been referred to it by the chief public prosecutor of Hungary. It also serves as an appellate court for cases that have been decided by the county courts. It judges the constitutionality of laws and acts, as well as the constitutionality of decisions handed down by all lower courts. Finally, it establishes the theoretical principles of law and the legal guidelines that bind the courts (*iranyelv, elvi dontes*).

The Supreme Court has two main branches, the Civil Division and the Criminal Division; each of these divisions is subdivided into a number of benches (*tanacs*). The special Presidential Bench of the Supreme Court, composed of the president of the Supreme Court and ten justices appointed by him, is responsible exclusively for handling all cases concerned with principles of law.[24] The Presidential Bench has jurisdiction over both the civil and the criminal branches of the Supreme Court. The Military Tribunal (or Military Collegium) also nominally falls under the jurisdiction of the Supreme Court. This tribunal and its subordinate organs act in all cases arising out of military crimes of a serious nature. Although it is part of the Supreme Court, its activities are regulated by the Ministry of Defense.

For a limited time following the 1956 uprising, all courts contained "councils of the people's courts" to prosecute citizens charged with counterrevolutionary crimes. These councils, which resurrected the character of the postwar people's courts, were established in 1957 by Law No. XXXIV, but their operations had largely ceased by 1960.

The makeup of the courts reflects to a significant extent the organization of the Soviet court system. Each subdivision is headed by a president, or presiding judge. All lower courts comprise councils composed of three persons: one professional judge and two lay assessors. The opinions of the judges and of the lay assessors rank equally under the law; decisions are always reached by a simple majority. Courts acting as appellate bodies are composed of three professional judges. The official explanation for the difference in the composition of the courts is based on the diversity of their functions; the lower courts are responsible mainly for ascertaining the facts in a case, whereas the higher courts are concerned mainly with applying the law on the basis of legal principle.

Judges are selected for a term of three years by the competent organs of state power.[25] Thus, the president, judges, and lay assessors of the municipal and district courts are selected by the town or district council; the president and judges of the county courts and of the Capital Court are selected by the county or capital councils. The president, professional judges, and lay assessors of the Supreme Court are selected by the Parliament for a five-year period. The selection process, however, usually depends on recommendations submitted by the minister of justice.[26] Any person can be selected for the post of judge or lay assessor provided that he or she is older than 23 years of age and has never been convicted of a crime. Although there is no requirement for legal training for either judges or lay assessors, it is rare for a person without legal qualifications to be selected.[27]

Procedures to recall both judges and lay assessors have been established, but there is no record to date of such an action having taken place. The executive retains the authority to initiate recall—the minister of justice must recommend such an action.

Professional judges, unlike lay assessors, are officially employed by the Ministry of Justice and have full-time responsibilities. Lay assessors cannot be employed by the ministry for more than one month per year, and their place of employment must release them for this period with pay. In addition, they receive an income supplement from the Ministry of Justice while they are working on a case. A provision of the law protects judges and lay assessors by extending judicial immunity to them.[28] They can be prosecuted only with the consent of the Presidential Council and only upon the recommendation of the chief public prosecutor. Although this protection failed to extend immunity to judges and lay assessors during the Stalinist reign, today judicial immunity in Hungary is slowly becoming an important principle of law.

The Office of the Chief Public Prosecutor (*Ugyeszseg*)

The Office of the Public Prosecutor is charged with the following functions: ensuring the legality of all activities of the government; acting as a public defender; prosecuting those charged with committing a crime; and defending the state (i.e., trying all "enemies of the state"). The importance of the public prosecutor's office was reflected in the Constitution of 1949 by the inclusion of an entire section (Articles 42 through 44) devoted to describing its wide-ranging powers and organization.

Today, the Office of the Public Prosecutor exerts some type of control over every aspect of public life. Although this office performs functions related to law enforcement, it is not a part of the judiciary; it is a separate organ, subject only to the control of the highest political authority—the leadership of the Party and the state. According to one Hungarian source, the public prosecutor's office

is a specific, separate organ, entirely independent from the executive (branch) and subordinated only to the highest organ representing the authority of the state. Its position in the structure of the socialist state and its independence from the executive branch are determined primarily by its new function, namely its supervisory power, under which it supervises among other things the legality of the acts of cabinet members and ministers.[29]

The Office of the Public Prosecutor is headed by the chief public prosecutor (*Legfobb Ugyesz*), who "is elected by parliament for a period of six years."[30] He is legally responsible to parliament, which is empowered to recall him. In fact, however, he is a power unto himself because he is not subject to any executive or legislative control other than recall. He appoints all the public prosecutors who serve under him.

The Office of the Public Prosecutor is organized on the basis of hierarchical geographic principles. Each county has an office headed by a chief county public prosecutor (*Fougyesz*); the chief public prosecutor for Budapest also falls into this category. The lowest units, the district offices, are headed by district directors (*vezeto ugyeszek*). A separate branch of the Office of the Public Prosecutor is headed by the chief military prosecutor, who is directly subordinate to the chief public prosecutor of Hungary. The military branch is organized on a territorial basis and is in charge of investigating and prosecuting all crimes committed by members of the armed forces.

The functions of the chief public prosecutor's office are extremely broad. According to the constitution, its primary task is to guarantee observance of the law. Prosecutors basically supervise four separate types of legality: (1) general legality; (2) the legality of criminal investigations; (3) the legality of court procedures; and (4) the legality of punishment.[31] It is important to note, however, that "ensuring the observance of legality is primarily a *political* task which must be performed by understanding the *dialectic of legality*."[32]

The public prosecutor's office also prosecutes anyone suspected of endangering the social order or the security and independence of the country. The office is further charged with acting as the public defender; it is supposed to ensure consistent respect for those rights of citizens that are guaranteed in

Section 6 of the 1972 Constitution. However, this responsibility is circumscribed by the admonition that

> during the prosecution of a case the Office of the Public Prosecutor must keep in mind those *political* guidelines of the Party and state which, for each stage of development, give clear instructions for the utilization of the rules and laws that will further social progress.[33]

In other words, the prosecutor's office must ensure the observance of legality and protect the rights of the citizenry in accordance with the guidelines established by Party authorities for a particular stage of socialist development.

The public prosecutor is in charge of investigating all crimes and is responsible for bringing criminals to trial; however, the prosecutor's office itself actually conducts investigations only in cases concerning juveniles, occupational accidents, large-scale crimes against the state, and crimes against socialist property. Investigations of other types of offenses are accomplished by the competent agencies, such as the various organs of the Ministry of the Interior. In addition to investigating and prosecuting alleged offenders, the office of the prosecutor is charged with supervising the various institutions of incarceration and detention.

The prosecutor's office can influence any case at will. It can reopen a case or request a discontinu-ation at any time. It has the right not to enforce a decision or to enforce claims contrary to the wishes of the claimant. This office is also empowered, according to state Directive No. 31,[34] to undertake the preventive detention (*kozbiztonsagi orizet*) of any individual whom the regime deems a threat to the safety of the state. Although such detention is not to exceed six months, the very existence of this rule allows the office to function as an instrument of terror.

Between 1949 and 1956, Rakosi in fact utilized the prosecutor's office as an instrument of terror and coercion. Consequently, in 1959 the Kadar regime altered and amended the powers of this office through Law No. 9 (1959), which placed controls on the activities of the public prosecutors.[35] Since the mid-1960s there has been a distinct decline in the use of the public prosecutor's office as an instrument of terror and political justice, and the agency has gradually developed its role as public defender. Its vigorous handling of a case of corruption in a state catering firm—the so-called Onodi affair—was the first sign that the office no longer existed strictly to serve the interests of the Party. In fact, its investigations and the subsequent removal of several high-ranking officials caused serious discomfort to some leading Party functionaries. It is also worth observing that in 1969 the office handled a larger number of cases in the public interest than in previous years. Although the agency still does not function as an ombudsman or as a defender of individual rights, it

Table 6.1. Breakdown of Confirmed Convictions by Type of Crime and Year

Type of Crime	1968	1970	1972	1973
Willful Attack on Officials	1,114	1,471	1,385	1,270
Dangerous Parasitism	320	369	417	325
Brawling	2,848	5,846	6,421	6,744
Murder	122	394	384	324
Failure to Pay Alimony	1,408	1,211	1,627	1,856
Occupational Negligence	5,817	6,008	992	465
Libel	4,538	2,759	3,251	3,162
Theft	8,586	4,971	11,021	11,957
Embezzlement	2,850	1,521	3,371	3,380
Fraud	1,528	774	1,432	1,668
Total Number of Confirmed Convictions	29,131	25,324	30,301	31,151

Sources: Statistikai Zsebkonyv, 1970 [Statistical Pocket Book, 1970] (Budapest: Statisztikai Hivatal, 1970), p. 339; and *Statisztikai Evkonyv, 1973* [Statistical Yearbook, 1973] (Budapest: Statisztikai Hivatal, 1974), p. 505.

Table 6.2. Breakdown of Juvenile Convictions by Type of Crime and Year

Type of Crime	1968	1970	1971	1972	1973
Willful Attack on Officials	68	91	125	100	105
Assault and Battery	380	353	462	541	542
Libel	49	35	39	35	43
Theft	1,961	1,470	2,156	3,099	2,924
Embezzlement	48	32	61	81	76
Fraud	24	19	36	27	25
Total Number of Crimes Committed	4,553	4,942	6,801	7,171	6,506

Sources: *Statisztikai Zsebkonyv, 1970* [Statistical Pocket Book, 1970] (Budapest: Statisztikai Hivatal, 1970), p. 340; and *Statisztikai Evkonyv, 1973* [Statistical Yearbook, 1973] (Budapest: Statisztikai Hivatal, 1974), p. 504.

has taken significant steps toward insuring the observance of legality in Communist Hungary.

Crime and Law Enforcement in Hungary

In 1968, 54,854 Hungarians were convicted of some type of crime. Nearly 40,000 of those convicted were males between the ages of 18 and 60, which indicates that 1.2 to 1.3 percent of the total number of males in this age group sustained criminal convictions in 1968.[36] Table 6.1 indicates the breakdown of criminal activities resulting in conviction in 1968, 1970, 1972, and 1973.[37] Thievery and premeditated acts of bodily harm were the most frequently committed crimes. Crimes against property—including theft, embezzlement, and cheating the public—amounted to 15 percent of all convictions.

Between 1968 and 1973, juvenile delinquency was another serious problem in Hungary. Table 6.2 details the types of crimes committed by young people below age 18.[38] As can be seen from these data, theft was prevalent among young people; fully 43 percent of all juvenile convictions resulted from some type of thievery. In the late 1960s and early 1970s the Hungarian court system was also overwhelmed with civil cases. Table 6.3 indicates the extent of the problem.[39] The data show that 43 percent of all civil cases tried between 1967 and 1973 resulted from

Table 6.3 Breakdown of Civil Trials in District Courts by Type of Case and Year

Type of Case	1967	1968	1970	1972	1973
Divorce and Other Matrimonial Cases	30,005	30,905	33,663	36,303	35,790
Paternity Suits	3,175	3,403	3,257	3,672	3,683
Alimony	36,211	38,187	35,770	36,639	36,547
Property Claims	6,318	6,215	6,056	6,186	6,065
Noncontract Compensations	11,421	11,630	11,074	9,148	7,809
Evictions	5,614	5,866	5,905	5,223	4,872
Pension Suits	3,015	3,000	2,152	2,300	1,843
Suits Against Agrarian Cooperatives	995	1,485	1,726	2,125	1,861
Total Number of Civil Cases Tried in District Courts	161,826	165,171	170,664	179,775	180,896

Sources: *Statisztikai Zsebkonyv, 1970* [Statistical Pocket Book, 1970] (Budapest: Statisztikai Hivatal, 1970), p. 340; and *Statisztikai Evkonyv, 1973* [Statistical Yearbook, 1973] (Budapest: Statisztikai Hivatal, 1974), p. 494.

some type of family problem; most of these cases were divorce proceedings. These statistics suggest some weakening of the family structure, and there seems to be increasing evidence of a correlation between this weakening of family ties and the growing number of juvenile delinquency cases.

The maintenance of "law and order" has become a serious problem in Hungary. In recent years, the incidence of juvenile gang activities, rape, and assault and battery has increased. Judicial authorities have relied on educational measures to deal with these transgressions and have often handed down surprisingly light sentences, primarily because the Criminal Code prescribes relatively lenient punishments. The vast majority of Hungarians do not understand this leniency in meting out punishment.[40] Public demand for safety and court judgments often conflict.[41] Sentences such as the four-year detention meted out in 1969 to a gang leader who had raped a girl in Pesterzsebet bring increased public indignation. According to one legal specialist, "it makes no difference to the peaceful promenader or the young girl attacked by hooligans whether the attackers were seventeen-year-old juveniles or eighteen-year-old adults."[42] Preventive detention of recidivists is the hue and cry of the public, which has repeatedly demanded more aggressive prosecution and more severe punishments. The Party leadership has so far accepted the advice of those lawyers and public prosecutors who believe that most crimes have an underlying social cause;[43] however, the regime will sooner or later have to cope with public demand for stiffer penalties and stiffer sentences.

Summary

All political systems impose some form of political justice. The legal procedures employed for political ends in various types of societies differ from one another merely in degree and kind. In a rigidly dictatorial society, the law *always* and *only* serves the interests of political power; in such a society, justice is defined to protect the insular state. Before 1960 Hungarian justice was administered according to dictatorial principles, but since then, the tyranny of using legal procedures strictly to further the interests of political power has been disappearing. The principles of justice extending equal protection to all citizens and guaranteeing them greater personal freedom are slowly becoming accepted norms of the Kadar regime.

The administration of justice remains a political issue in Hungary. Laws and legal procedures are still used for political ends even though the present regime is trying to merge its political interests with those of the people as a whole. The Hungarian judiciary faces the immense task of administering justice to a people that for a long time did not receive just treatment under the law. The Hungarian Communist leadership must convince Hungarian citizens that they are no longer "disinherited children with neither a past nor a future,"[44] and the impartial application of justice seems to be a good way to begin this task.

7

Rule Application: A Case Study

During nearly three decades of Communist government, the application of rule in Hungary—the way in which laws and regulations are enforced—has evolved similarly to the principles governing the administration of justice; both aspects of the legal system have been modified to reflect changes in the political theory controlling the development of Hungarian society. As the regime has liberalized its policies, new, more humane, and more personal processes have replaced the rigorous, dictatorial application of rule that characterized Hungary's mobilization era.

A case study of two civil suits arising out of a conflict between the interests of three citizens and the interests of the state provides a unique opportunity to examine a specific example of rule application in Hungary at the beginning of the 1970s. The author selected these suits at random and no notification of the American observer's presence was given to the participants in the cases prior to the trials. The presiding judge, Dr. Arpad Faggyas, and the vice-president of the Budapest District Court, Dr.

Tibor Hardiczay, gave permission to the author to attend the trials and to conduct in-depth interviews with both the plaintiffs and representatives of the defendant.[1]

Pursuant to a decision reached in 1970 by the Executive Committee of Budapest's Fifth District Council, the Fovarosi Epitoipari Beruhazasi Vallalat (Capital Construction Investment Company)—known as FOBER—was instructed to build a school on land adjacent to an apartment complex. The land on which the school was to be built, however, was private property belonging to Mr. and Mrs. Lajos Ratter (Budapest, XX, Klapka u. 70) and Ms. Katalin Simon (Budapest, XX, Klapka u. 66). Since Hungarian law specifies that the state may claim the use of private land for public purposes if it offers proper remuneration,[2] FOBER asked the Executive Committee of the Fifth District Council to expropriate[3] the real estate on which the school was to be built. On February 15, 1971, the Administrative Directorate of the Council's Executive Committee sent out its order of expropriation (25.084/1971.) FOBER offered the owners of the land the following compensation (in forints):

Ratter

House	69,778
Tool shed	4,495
Open shed	630
Outhouse	1,380
Brick wall	864
Picket fence	558
Concrete walk	680
Land	18,830
Brick wall	250
Vegetable plot[4]	368
Total	97,833
Minus 40% of cost of a new apartment[5]	27,907
Net compensation offered	69,926

Simon

House	24,570
Tool shed	4,640
Brick wall	1,056
Picket fence	252
Outhouse	690
Land[6]	23,075
Vegetable plot	325
Total	54,608
Minus 40% of cost of a new apartment	9,828
Net compensation offered	44,780[7]

Both parties were offered new apartments that were not located in the immediate vicinity of the property being expropriated. The apartments were one-bedroom units roughly equivalent in size to the appropriated one-story detached houses. The new apartments were in prefabricated buildings typical of those between 1969 and 1970. They had central heating, warm water, and indoor plumbing, advantages not available in the expropriated private dwellings. The official cost of these apartments ran between 75,000 and 100,000 forints, but their real market value was at least 30 percent higher.

The plaintiffs, however, decided that the compensation offered by FOBER did not adequately offset their loss of real estate, and they hired a lawyer, Dr. Miklos Fulop, to file suit in district court. Dr. Fulop was one of the many attorneys working in the No. 50 Legal Work Cooperative, the legal cooperative nearest the plaintiffs' residences. On March 15, 1971 the plaintiffs sued FOBER in the Budapest Central District Court. The Ratters demanded 53,803 forints in excess of the amount offered by FOBER, and Simon asked for 77,968 forints in excess of the offered amount. Both plaintiffs, on advice from their lawyer, requested that the defendant pay court costs and that 5 percent annual interest be charged on all amounts adjudged by the courts and unpaid within 30 days of settlement.

On May 18, the court heard the cases and ordered the administrative division of the court to appoint an official appraiser. That same day, Mr. Ivan Szinessy (Budapest, VI, Bajza u. 54), certified engineer and legal appraiser for the Court, was appointed to survey and officially appraise the contested properties.

In certified letters posted June 4, 1971, the appraiser notified the lawyers of both the plaintiffs and the defendant that an official appraisal was scheduled for June 11, 1971. FOBER, which had appointed Dr. Ildiko Kovacs to defend its interests, did not send its attorney to the appraisal. The appraiser notified the court, the plaintiffs, and the defendant of his findings on June 18, 1971. His findings revealed that the official appraisals were low and indicated that Mr. and Mrs. Ratter were due 38,579 forints whereas Katalin Simon was due 61,885 forints in addition to the compensation offered by FOBER.

The cases were tried July 2, 1971 in the District Court of Budapest (Budapest, V, Marko u.). Present were the plaintiffs (Mr. and Mrs. Ratter and Katalin Simon), their attorney (Dr. Miklos Fulop), a witness for the plaintiffs (Laszlo Selymes), the attorney for the defendant (Dr. Ildiko Kovacs), members of the court, and the court stenographers. The court consisted of a presiding judge (Faggyas) and two lay assessors who desired to remain anonymous. Each trial lasted about one hour and was followed by five to ten minutes of official deliberations. Everyone except the judge and the two assessors was excluded from these deliberations. The court decided in favor of the plaintiffs, but it awarded them slightly less than they had asked for. The decision was not appealed by the defendant.

The court is located in a drab building that has housed courts and other offices of legal administration ever since its construction over 50 years ago. It now serves as the Central District Court of Budapest. Trial rooms are located on all sides of the several corridors on each floor and civil suits are almost always handled in one of the many courtrooms on the fourth floor. The courtrooms are small (15′ × 15′), badly lit cubicles. When a trial is in progress, the judge sits on an elevated dais, flanked by two assessors seated on a slightly lower level. The court reporter also sits on an elevated platform. (The reporter assigned to the two cases under discussion did not take verbatim transcripts; he wrote down a summary of the statements given as answers to specific questions and statements by the judge.) Observers and witnesses sit on benches and chairs whereas plaintiffs and defendants sit with their lawyers, facing one another at desks placed at lower than and at right angles to those of the judge and the assessors.

The judge in the Ratter and Simon cases was about 45 years old and wore a dark business suit. By profession he was a trained lawyer; he had been a judge for the past eight years.[8] The assessors were very different from one another.[9] One was a woman in her late fifties who worked on an assembly line in a textile factory. She was a high school graduate who had completed her secondary education through a night extension program. The second assessor was an accountant in his late forties. He appeared to be interested in the process but was unwilling to commit himself lest he make an error in judgement. Assessors are elected for a period of three years during which time they are called upon to hear at least one case.[10] This was the first case for both of these assessors. All three members of the court had studied the cases and were clearly familiar with them.[11]

The lawyers in the cases presented a sharp contrast. The plaintiffs were represented by Dr. Fulop, a competent lawyer in his mid-forties who clearly possessed the conviction that his case could not be lost; his salary as a member of Legal Cooperative No. 50 was around 2,600 forints per month, which put him in the middle bracket of officialdom. The lawyer for the defendant, Dr. Ildiko Kovacs, worked for the construction investment firm as one of four lawyers hired to defend the enterprise's interests. She was in her early thirties and seemed to lack the incentive to fight the cases very hard.

The plaintiffs were semiskilled manual laborers in their early fifties; they were of peasant background and had at best an eighth-grade education.

Their houses had been constructed by hand in the late 1920s, and over the years the owners had slowly added onto them, carefully whitewashing the structures to cover the imperfections. The buildings had both benefited from improvements and suffered from war damage. The small and by now dirt-gray houses were surrounded by small plots of land on which the plaintiffs grew a few flowers and a small amount of vegetables. The paths to the outhouses were visible and well-worn. With the construction of five-story, high-rise apartments in the next block, the plaintiffs believed that their lands had accumulated extra value, and they came to court to prove it.

The session began when the judge stood up and called on the audience to stand while he announced that "The Court of the Hungarian People's Republic is now in session." He then asked the plaintiff to call the first witness. Lajos Ratter came before the judge, who reminded him in simple layman's language of his duty to tell the truth and called his attention to the fact that perjury is a crime punishable by law. This process was repeated for all those appearing before the judge; there was no oath-taking ceremony.

In each instance, the judge also asked the plaintiff to state his or her address, occupation, and age. Following the initial questions in the Ratter case, the lawyer for the plaintiff questioned the plaintiff about his house and about the work he had put into it to repair war damage. The plaintiff, still standing before the court, answered all his lawyer's questions, which were directed largely to the financial aspects of the case. The judge interrupted at times to ask questions or rephrase some of the plaintiff's answers. For example, when the plaintiff said, "I just had to reconstruct the large room," the judge rephrased the reply and instructed the stenographer to record, "He meant, he rebuilt the large room, isn't that right?"

Dr. Kovacs then cross-examined Ratter; however, she concentrated her questions on the actual value of the land and the house. At no time did she ask questions concerned with principles or judgments.

After the cross-examination, a witness for the plaintiffs, Laszlo Selymes, related the story of the World War II artillery and bomb damage and told the court that he did not know how much it would cost to replace those houses, but his own house could be sold on the open market for about 150,000 forints; he added that some black marketeers had offered 200,000 forints for it. The judge asked if he had any ill-feelings, hatred, or hostility toward the plaintiffs or anyone else in that neighborhood. The witness gave a negative response.

The judge, who made copious notes on a financial ledger throughout the proceedings, asked the official appraiser a few questions. The appraiser stated that he considered the claims of the plaintiffs rather excessive, but that the original compensation offered by FOBER was not equitable either. He suggested that the following adjustments be made:

Ratter

Offered by FOBER	Officially appraised value	Sued for
69,926	69,926	69,926
	38,579	53,803
	108,505	123,729

Simon

Offered by FOBER	Officially appraised value	Sued for
44,780	44,780	44,780
	61,885	77,965
	106,665	122,745

Here, for the first time during the trial, serious conflict arose. The attorney for the defense indicated that the figures in the appraisal were unusually high. She noted that the law only obliged her company to offer compensation based on the best available state estimate and not on the "fair market value." She also called attention to the fact that a much-needed school would replace the "shacks" and stated that the first duty of the company was to build that school. The judge responded rather sharply to the defense lawyer, stating that the principle of fair compensation is laid down clearly in the laws. Although the state has the right of eminent domain,[12] it must always offer a fair compensation. He emphasized that the needs of society cannot be impersonally construed. The court must take into consideration that it is dealing with human beings and not just the need for a school. These honest working people were being evicted from their own environments, and even if they were to move into nicer places, the law must protect their right to fair compensation.

The defense raised no serious objections to any other point throughout the trial, but adopted a rather passive role, simply citing the reasons for the original valuation. During neither of the trials did either of the assessors ask a question nor, in contrast to the very thorough note-taking of the judge, did they take any notes at all. The hearings in each trial lasted approximately one hour, after which time the audience was excused. Most of those present congregated in the corridor for five to ten minutes before reentering the courtroom to hear the decision. As the people of the courtroom stood, the judge announced that he was awarding 116,233 forints to Mr. and Mrs. Lajos Ratter. This sum was 7,500 forints less than they had sued for, but nearly 8,000 forints more than the officially appraised value of the Ratter property. In the Simon case, the judge awarded 112,428 forints, repeating the previous pattern—more than 10,000 forints less than sued for, but 6,000 forints in excess of the official appraisal. In each case the judge gave a brief summation in which he called attention to the fact that FOBER did not offer realistic prices for properties, which "although they are a part of our state, have so clearly been guarded and taken care of through the hard work of our working classes." He ordered FOBER to pay both court costs and five percent interest, should the company not deliver the properly endorsed checks to the plaintiffs within 30 days of the judgment.[13] He then closed the case and sat down.

To discern the principles on which the court based its judgment, the author interviewed the judge and assessors separately at the conclusion of the trials. The judge offered the most comprehensive legal opinion. He revealed that it was difficult to decide most cases related to eminent domain and contended that the basic problem in all such cases was the conflict between private and state interests. He explained that during the Rakosi era, the same cases would have probably been decided in favor of the defendant without any regard to the actual justice of the case; even though the courts under Rakosi frequently took into consideration the working class origins of plaintiffs, unless the plaintiffs were influential people, the courts had to decide in favor of the state in cases concerning eminent domain. The judge expressed a personal opinion that the plaintiffs in the Ratter and Simon cases were probably too interested in their own financial welfare, but he also said that the inherent unfairness of the State Capital Investment Firm had obliged him to rule against it. He stated that in addition to bringing justice to the people, the most significant purposes of current law were to make citizens realize that the state was no longer to be feared and to convince them that they, too, had a stake in the system.

Previous negative experiences with the courts had apparently shaped the opinions of the woman assessor, whose view of the proceedings largely paralleled that of the judge. Anxious not to let the unfairness of the Rakosi era return, she too believed that the application of rule must be based on fairness. Although she did not articulate it in Latin, she several times rephrased the Roman principle of law, *ex aequo et bono*.[14] The male assessor had no opinion except that he thought the decision was just.

Summary

These views reveal several trends in the application of law in Communist Hungary today. First, there is an evident, conscious contrast between past and present practices. The courts now emphasize the "positive" aspects of the socialist legality in the administration of justice (e.g., equality before the law) in contrast with the "illegalities" of the past. The terror and inequities of the Rakosi era and Stalinism still cast such a dark shadow on the awareness of the citizenry that those in charge of the administration of justice bend over backward to assure fairness in the application of rule.

Second, the administration of justice nevertheless remains motivated by political considerations. Justice is an instrument designed to serve the state; it is a political and not an abstract construct. However, the present regime is primarily interested in legitimizing its rule and this goal affects the judicial process.

Third, when called upon to decide an issue, every judge in a Communist country faces a very real problem; he must resolve the question, "What is the State?" It is clear that the state is comprised of many separate, conflicting interests, and the judge must determine which of those conflicting interests have priority.

Fourth, the role of the lay assessors is changing. Although we do not have full documentation, Sandor Barna's generalization that "the role of the assessors is diminishing in importance in cases where greater technical competence is required" seems to hold true for nonspecialized cases as well.[15] In the Ratter and Simon cases, the participation of the assessors was minimal. The present trend is for assessors to receive less and less work[16] as more cases are settled before the judges out of court; the administration of justice is thus slowly passing into more highly trained hands.[17]

Finally, we may conclude that with the greater professionalization of the courts it is increasingly probable that the letter of the law will be enforced. Nonetheless, the law remains a social category. In addition to serving as an instrument of justice, law is used universally as an instrument of power, and in Hungary, as well as in other Communist states, the needs of power always take precedence over the needs of law.

PART III

System Maintenance and Adaptation

8

Political Socialization and Political Communication

Since 1949, the Hungarian Communist leadership has considered few system-maintenance functions as important as the political socialization and education of the citizenry. Whereas the survival of the Hungarian Communist political system has depended to a significant extent on the acquiescence of the population to the rule of the Party, the progression of the system to a more advanced stage of development has required the active support of the citizenry for the goals set by the Party. The present regime in Hungary has all but abandoned the use of coercion; to assure the acquiescence and support of the citizenry, it relies instead on its political socialization program.

"Political socialization" refers to the process whereby a person receives political knowledge and accepts or rejects the system(s) of political values and beliefs handed down to him. In the literature of political science, political socialization usually means the inculcation of values in children,[1] and the transmission of knowledge from the older generation to the younger one.[2] However, the term has a broader

significance in Communist states where the political socialization process includes not only the creation of desirable political attitudes in children who were born into the Communist system, but also the reeducation of adults who acquired their values under conflicting political systems.

In Communist societies the overt behavior of the population must conform to certain norms. These norms generally include participation in organized political activities, maximization of production efforts, and support for government policies. Moreover, members of a Communist society must profess belief in the values deemed desirable by the elite. The inculcation of these values and of the entire Marxist-Leninist ideology is the goal of the political education and socialization efforts of any Communist government.

The inculcation of the desired values may be accomplished through various means. A regime may, for example, coerce the populace into accepting its norms. One drawback of this method is that the regime can never be certain to what extent the population has accepted the norms. Citizens conform because they fear repression; they feign acceptance of the ideological precepts, but their beliefs have probably not changed. As a result of this contradiction, dysfunctional activity may occur.

Another tactic the regime may utilize to inculcate political values in the citizenry is the encouragement of apathy. A regime employing this technique allows people to accept or reject the claims of the regime and requires minimum participation, which assures the unchallenged supremacy of the Party. Citizens may choose their own sets of values provided that these values do not *openly* conflict with those of the regime.

A third method of inculcating norms is through the process of political socialization. In this process the regime uses various pacific means to educate and convert the citizenry. The media and the political socializing agencies attempt to inculcate the essential values of the system, but the citizenry is not coerced into accepting them. People are allowed to accept or reject the values according to the importance assigned each value by the regime (i.e., certain essential values must be accepted). The constant repetition of political themes, some more subtly elaborated than others, is expected to accomplish the desired inculcation of values.

Each of the above three strategies has been utilized at some time in the implementation of the various Communist systems developed since the turn of the twentieth century. As Professor Richard Fagen observed, "In some instances, widespread apathy is adequate to ensure system functioning, in fact at times it is essential. In other cases, only the most positive evaluative commitments will suffice."[3]

The most purposive agencies effecting the inculcation of values in Hungarian society are the Party, the youth organizations and the schools, the trade unions, the military, and the various cultural groups. Since 1949, the family, the independent peer groups, and the churches have played both positive and negative socializing roles, depending on their relationship with the regime.

If a political system is to function effectively in a society, most of the interest groups in that society must consider *some* of the values embraced by the elite basic to their own survival. Yet, the groups constituting the society need not work equally to implement the desired values. The percentage of the total system of values a group must accept as well as

the required degree of commitment to these values depend on the function of the group and its relation to the source of power. The more closely related a group is to the source of political authority, the greater is the number of values it must accept; similarly, the closer the group is to the ruling elite the greater must be the intensity of its commitment to the desired values. The range and intensity of ideological commitment required of the various groups in Hungarian society today conforms, in general, to the schematic representation in Figure 8.1.

The methods used to inculcate values differ for the various groups in society. Direct ideological training is effective for the Party and for some groups within the youth organizations. The value messages contained in this type of training, however, are less effective in socializing groups farther from the focus of power, and therefore, a multifaceted approach must

Figure 8.1. Range and intensity of ideological commitment required of various social groups in Communist Hungary.

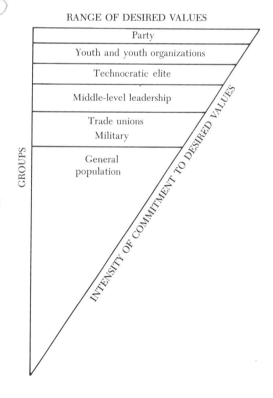

RANGE OF DESIRED VALUES

Party

Youth and youth organizations

Technocratic elite

Middle-level leadership

Trade unions
Military

General population

GROUPS

INTENSITY OF COMMITMENT TO DESIRED VALUES

be utilized to implant the desired values in these groups. The Hungarian Communist regime has relied increasingly on the media for political socialization at this level. As the number of socialization tools increases, the intensity of the regime's efforts to inculcate values decreases. With the increase in the quantity of socialization messages, the importance of each message decreases, and the Party is less capable of ensuring the internalization of each message. Furthermore, the more removed a group (or an individual) is from the center of power, the freer it (or he) is to reject the values espoused by the Party. Although the regime's allowance of rejection is not a license to espouse publicly a contrary set of values, it can still be considered an alternative. Consequently, in Hungary and other Communist states where the regime has chosen to employ the processes of political socialization rather than the strategy of coercion by political indoctrination and terror (i.e., the tactic of forcing the population to accept its values), a disparity can exist between the ideology and the norms accepted by the population. Hence, we may conclude that in Hungary the Party leadership and some members of the Party accept the ideology of Marxism-Leninism, but the general population only accepts some of the basic values of the system, rejecting the applicability of the entire ideology to their daily lives.

Development of Current Political Socialization Policies

Before merging with the Social Democratic Party in 1948, the Hungarian Communist Party sought to gain as many supporters as possible. The tactics employed during this period of "conversionary socialization" included the utilization of advertising to popularize the Party and the use of well-known speakers at mass meetings. In addition, anyone wishing to join the Party could become a member without submitting to careful screening; at the same time, the most vocal opponents of the Party were eliminated by force. During this period of power struggle, the Party's program emphasized the progressive role of the Hungarian Communist movement in the fight against fascism and Communist plans for the improvement of society.

With the initiation of state building in August 1949, the Hungarian Communist regime began to mobilize society. This mobilization phase of socialist construction lasted approximately 12 years—until 1961. During these years there was no political socialization in the proper sense of the term because the population was not given a chance to accept or reject the values and beliefs established by the regime. Indeed, during these years—except for the period from 1955 to 1957—the regime used force to coerce the citizenry into accepting and supporting Stalinist values. Mandatory attendance at seminars and compulsory participation in marches, as well as visitations by agitation and propaganda teams, ensured that the citizenry became politically educated according to the dictates of the Party.[4] Between 1949 and 1961, the regime sought to impose the values espoused by both the Soviet regime and the Hungarian Stalinist leadership. These values included: extending the class struggle; the adulation of Stalin and of Soviet accomplishments; total obedience to all decrees; unquestioning allegiance to the Party leadership; acceptance of the personal rule of Matyas Rakosi and of the Party elite; constant overfulfillment of work quotas; and an unceasing disapproval of Western democratic values.

The regime's campaigning in the mass media also characterized this period. Newspapers carried headlines advertising the success of a particular production drive to honor the birthday of Stalin or contained news items about the latest number of signatures gathered in support of the Stockholm Appeal (which was initiated to compel the United States to impose a moratorium on the manufacture of nuclear weapons, to stop nuclear tests, and to ban the atomic bomb). Radio stations broadcast interviews with workers who had invented new methods of production or with factory managers who had exceeded their monthly production quotients. Several books appeared detailing the crimes committed by enemies of the people and claiming that only the vigilance of the Party prevented the rebirth of fascism in Hungary. Posters and billboards assailed the populace from every wall and kiosk, from the insides of buses, and from fences. The posters repeated such themes as "Stop the Imperialist Aggression in Korea," "Free the Rosenbergs," "Ban the Bomb," "Long Live Stalin," "Tito Is the Chained Dog of American Imperialism," and "Fulfill Your Quota of Production by 200 Percent." Martial music and Soviet socialist songs blared from loudspeakers that also broadcast praises of Stalin and proclaimed the beauty of the Soviet fatherland.

In the early 1960s, the Kadar government realized that coercion was an expensive and inefficient method of achieving a consensus on values. Instead of using terror to force people to accept the values the ruling elite desired to impose, the leadership decided that the citizenry should be socialized into accepting the norms that are "good to obey." This decision undoubtedly reflected the discovery that

> . . . of all the mechanisms which might induce obligation, political socialization is the cheapest and most efficient. In general people obey because they fear the consequence of disobedience, or because they consider it worth their while to obey, or because they consider compliance the appropriate behavior. . . . Fear and expedience, the alternative methods of inducing compliance, are expensive in comparison. Police states must spend a great deal on institutions which keep the populace in line. Expedience can be nearly as expensive. Under such conditions, authorities must continually make it worthwhile for the citizens to obey, and the "worth" in "worthwhile" comes dear. But compliance based on the feeling that obedience is "good" or "appropriate" is cheap.[5]

The regime accomplished the changeover from coercive to persuasive methods of political socialization by depoliticizing public life and altering Party policies concerning which values must be inculcated in the citizenry. It abandoned the concept of extended class struggle, abolished the adulation of Stalin and of Soviet methods, replaced individual rule with collective leadership, ended the constant need to overfulfill production quotas, expanded its contacts with the West, and eased its restrictions on travel to the West. Furthermore, it encouraged patriotism and pride in Hungarian national accomplishments. Building a socialist society as a joint effort that would benefit everyone became the predominant value, replacing demands that the population support the USSR in its endeavors to implement Communism. Although no group or individual could challenge the authority of the Party leadership, and the Hungarian government still had to pursue a foreign policy prescribed by the USSR, the regime did begin to open the decision-making process to input from non-Party organs.

With the successful inauguration of the New Economic Mechanism in 1968, the Party effected further positive changes in the values adopted as the basis of its political socialization program.[6] Between 1968 and 1975, the values it wished to inculcate in the citizenry included approval of the regime's primary goal of building a socialist society and belief that this effort was the best way to extend the greatest number of benefits to the population and the nation. The present regime expects the population to accept all decisions made by the Party, but allows pluralism in the application of rule.[7] It places a premium on efforts to create a society characterized by socialist morality, but does not use terror to ensure the existence of such a morality. It advocates patriotic attitudes, but makes allowances for the individuality of members of the polity in nonpolitical spheres. It places a premium on independence in domestic decision making, although it follows the lead of the USSR in international affairs. It does not advocate the unquestioned adoption of socialist realism in the artistic realm, but allows experimentation to a far greater extent than ever before.[8] It encourages individual initiative and collective input to the decision-making process through the upgraded role of the local councils and the expansion of the importance of trade unions, the Parliament, the economic bodies, and even the judiciary. Finally, the regime places great emphasis on the value of Hungary as a European state and on maintaining the country's ties with Western Europe.

Between 1961 and the present, the Kadar regime adopted two approaches to the problem of political socialization. On the one hand, it subjected adults to techniques aimed at "negative consensus formation," emphasizing the mistakes of previous Party policies and encouraging the adult population to forget about politics and leave the political arena to the present Party leadership. On the other hand, it socialized children in a positive way, encouraging them to participate in the building of the ideal socialist society.[9]

To achieve negative consensus formation, the Party's political socialization program for adults emphasized the failures of the pre-1956 era, maintaining that they resulted from a "mistaken interpretation of Marxist theory" or from the "personality cult of Matyas Rakosi."[10] Examples of this approach can be found in such books as Ferenc Santa's *Twenty Hours*[11] or in such films as Istvan Szabo's *The Father.*[12] To develop the apathy of the citizenry, the leadership has discouraged active citizen participation in the governing process. The regime has also encouraged the depoliticization of public life; the only proof of support it requires from the politically passive population is a lack of antigovernment or antisystem activity.

The present government has also shifted the target of the socialization process. In contrast to earlier policies, it now considers the political education of children more important than the socialization of adults. By placing more and more emphasis on the political socialization of young people, the Party leadership hopes to create a future citizenry deeply committed to the values of socialism.

Current Party policy concerning political socialization was summed up in a 1968 Party directive specifying that the principal goal of the leadership is the creation of a new, socialist way of thinking for the entire population. The directive assigned the following tasks to all educational agencies:

> large-scale diffusion of up-to-date general knowledge among adults; extension of professional knowledge among industrial and agricultural workers, with a view toward encouraging production; education in literature and the fine arts; stimulation of the artistic sense; promotion of adequate forms of entertainment and leisure-time occupations; and *development of a socialist attitude through the activities listed above.*[13]

The Party considers the development of this new, socialist attitude in the Hungarian citizenry a necessary prerequisite to the continued progress of socialist Hungary.

Disparities Between Urban and Rural Political Socialization

The processes of political socialization applied to rural communities in Hungary differ significantly from those designed for urban areas.[14] Since adult-to-adult socialization is far less effective in rural areas, the regime has used this technique far less extensively there than in urban areas. The reasons for this difference are numerous. Before television became accessible to the rural population it was very difficult for the Party to reach the isolated peasantry. In most cases their traditional backwardness and basic distrust of the city placed them in opposition to the efforts of the Government. The Party could only hope to neutralize this opposition and change the attitudes of rural children through education. How-

ever, as a result of the collectivization policies implemented in the 1950s, the Party alienated a significant percentage of the peasantry. Consequently, not until the end of the 1960s did the peasantry give even tacit support to Government policies.

The adult-to-child socialization agencies in the villages are also distinguishable from their urban counterparts. Village schools are generally not well equipped and many of the rural teachers are not well trained. Few able, young teachers are willing to go to isolated villages, and the few who do go become disenchanted very fast. Urban prejudice against students from rural areas compounds the problem. The Party has been unable to influence local politics enough to resolve the difficulty.[15]

Furthermore, the Party has been at a disadvantage in rural communities because it has limited means through which it can reach the peasantry. Most residents of rural areas do not read journals, newspapers, magazines, or books; until television became popular and widely available there were few means through which the regime could transmit new themes of political socialization. The inaccessibility of the rural population has considerably hampered the Party's drive to inculcate a new socialist system of values in the peasantry.

Agencies of Political Socialization

The regime utilizes various agencies to implement its political socialization program. These agencies are either primary, informal social structures or secondary, formal organizations. Primary, informal agencies operate through face-to-face relationships, deep emotional attachments, and close social ties.[16] Secondary, formal agencies function through voluntary, but organized, citizen participation in activities that produce some desired social goal.[17] The family is a primary, informal political socialization agency, whereas the Party, the schools, the trade unions, the church, and the army are secondary, formal organizations. Peer groups are usually considered informal agents, but in Communist systems these groups, with the exception of friendship circles, generally participate in organized activities and therefore also function as formal, secondary agencies.

The Party.   In Hungary, the Party is the most important agency of political socialization. It operates both as an informal, primary structure and a formal, secondary organization: it politically socializes its own membership in local organs by acting as an informal peer group (especially in the close-knit units of small cells), and it exerts enormous formal influence on all groups and all other socializing agencies in Hungary. The Party determines the policies and themes of socialization; controls the operation of peer groups and of schools; and directly guides all other formal agencies of political socialization. Therefore, its importance overshadows that of all other agencies. In addition, the Hungarian Socialist Workers' Party wields some influence over all informal organizations and agencies, including the family. The amount of control the Party chooses to exert over these groups—which are outside the political system, but still perform political socialization functions—depends on the policies of the leadership and on the political situation. During the early 1970s the Party chose to exert a minimal influence over the family, the friendship circles, and most other primary agencies that did not threaten the system-maintenance functions of the regime.

The formal, adult-to-adult socializing functions of the Party include the political education of its members and the inculcation of the values espoused by the leadership. The Party provides political education for both Party members and interested citizens who do not belong to the Party. The educational program consists of courses held at the Evening Division of the University of Marxism-Leninism and of specialized political training at Party seminars or at the Party academy. The highest level of the Party's educational program includes study at the Political College (Politikai Foiskola) and training in Moscow.

The Evening Division of the University of Marxism-Leninism, first organized in 1952, reopened its gates after the revolution in October 1957.[18] It offers three different types of programs: a three-year general education course, a two-year special training course, and a special three-year course for "artistic workers" such as writers, graphic artists, actors, etc. In the three-year general education course, students study philosophy the first year, political economy the second year, and the history of the working-class movement the third year. In the special training course that lasts two years, students concentrate on the following subjects: philosophy, political economy, the history of the Hungarian and the international labor movement, comparative economics, sociology, computer sciences, and the building of socialism. In the specialized three-year course for those who make their living from the arts, such

courses as sociology, Marxist ethics, and dialectical materialism are offered in addition to the general education courses.[19]

All classes meet one evening a week for three hours. Rote memorization is required of first-year students, and their textbooks are quite dull; more sophisticated material is used in second- and third-year courses. After the successful completion of the general course a student earns the equivalent of a college degree (a B.A.); after the successful completion of the specialized training, a student has the right to write a doctoral thesis which, if accepted, becomes the basis for the award of a first-degree doctoral diploma (the equivalent of an M.A. from an American university).[20]

In 1960, less than 1,000 students enrolled in the Evening Division. As liberal benefits (such as an additional 28 days of annual vacation for purposes of studying) were slowly extended to students, the number of students grew. By 1969, in addition to the courses offered in the central offices of the college, courses were being taught in district and county seats, and in that same year there were 12,000 students enrolled in Evening Division courses in Budapest and 23,000 enrolled throughout the countryside.[21] By 1972, 38 special college centers had been established in the villages and provincial towns of Hungary to accommodate the increasing number of students.[22]

It is difficult to estimate how many students participate in each of the various programs of the Evening Division of Marxism-Leninism. Around 65% of the students attend the general education courses and approximately 7% attend the courses designed for "artistic workers"; there are no data concerning the number of students enrolled in either of the special programs.[23] We do know, however, that since 1971 the demand for Evening Division courses has exceeded the available places. Consequently, in 1974, the Evening High School of Marxism-Leninism was established to offer a preparatory course of study for workers who had not received enough formal education to enroll in college courses. The new Evening High School offers courses leading to a high school diploma acceptable in lieu of a regular secondary diploma; it also prepares students to enter the Evening Division of the University of Marxism-Leninism. One reason for the immediate popularity of the new system is that students enrolled in evening high school courses receive extra days of vacation to pursue their studies.

The political education of Party members usually takes place in courses organized by local cells, the Party's district committees, and the Central Committee. The Party's basic introductory educational program consists of short, ten-week courses. An intermediate program comprises courses lasting four to five months. The one- and two-year advanced courses are usually staffed by members of the Party's Agitation and Propaganda Division.[24] In 1974, the combined enrollment of the ten-week, four-to-five-month, and one-year courses was 20,000.[25] All Party courses, with the exception of the advanced two-year course, meet around one evening a week. The texts for the lower-level courses are taken almost entirely from Soviet Party education programs. Starting in 1961, students in the introductory Party seminars studied *The Foundations of Marxist Philosophy*,[26] translated from the Russian *Osnovy Marksistskoi Filosofii*.[27] In 1969, an updated version of the same book was introduced as the principal beginning text. In 1968–1969, the intermediate seminars concentrated on the Hungarian and international labor movements. The textbook used in these courses was *The History of the Hungarian and International Labor Movement, 1848–1945*.[28] Other works, including the speeches of Kadar and several other present-day Communist leaders, rounded out the intermediate curriculum. Only very small sections of the writings of Marx, Engels, and Lenin were read in the beginning and intermediate seminars or in the evening extension courses.

The Party has organized its advanced educational program under the auspices of the Political College. Established in 1955 as the Party College (*Partfoiskola*), it offers one- and two-year regular day-time courses taught on a full-time basis. Approximately 150 students attend the college annually, and each entering class consists of about 70–80 students.[29] The Political College has the following six academic faculties: philosophy, political economy, Party building, the history of the international labor movement, industrial economy, and sociology. The sociology department, however, was only instituted in 1970 and it did not begin full-time operation until the following year. Obtaining a "Party" education is one way citizens can insure their political and economic advancement.

Political College students were originally selected by the Party's district committees, but since 1968 would-be students may apply directly for admission without prior selection by the lower Party organs.

While attending school, students receive free tuition plus their entire normal salary; they are granted a leave of absence from their jobs for the duration of their studies, and they are encouraged to live in the high-rise dormitory of the College in Budapest. After completing the College program, students may take regular university final exams and prepare a doctoral thesis; upon the satisfactory completion of all requirements, they too may qualify for a Master of Arts degree in their own field.

The principal aim of the Party's advanced education program is no longer to socialize participants through the inculcation of accepted patterns of behavior. The primary goals of the Political College are to turn out ideologically advanced leaders and to introduce Party members to the problems and divergent perspectives within the international Communist movement.[30] Because of the elite status of the students receiving advanced political training, almost no concrete information is available concerning the methods utilized in Political College courses.

Youth Groups. Peer groups in Communist states constitute part of the Party's educational apparatus and are thus more important and more purposive agencies of socialization than their counterparts in non-Communist countries. The HSWP controls the activities of most Hungarian peer groups (except for the very small friendship circles),[31] making these groups formal, secondary agencies of political socialization. The two most important Hungarian peer groups operating on an adult-to-child basis are the *Uttorok* (the Young Pioneers) and the KISz (the Communist Youth League). The membership of both of these organizations is composed largely of students. The Young Pioneers includes girls and boys below age 14; membership in the Youth League is restricted to young people between 14 and 28 years of age. The League is officially described as a "political organization of youth functioning under the direct guidance of the Hungarian Socialist Workers' Party." Its task is to educate young people in the "Communist spirit."[32] The Young Pioneers' Association is directed by the League. It is less politically oriented than the League, although its members do receive some training in Communist ideology.

Each of these groups uses a variety of socializing techniques. The organizations publish weekly journals that are distributed nationally. The *Pajtas*

(Buddy) of the Young Pioneers has a weekly circulation of 230,000, and statistics indicate that most children in the Pioneer age group receive copies of the paper through their schools. As a matter of fact, subscribing to *Pajtas* seems to be mandatory in grammar schools. The weekly journal of the League, *Magyar Ifjusag* (Hungarian Youth) does not have as wide a circulation as *Pajtas*. It is aimed at the general reader between ages 14 and 22, but it is published in editions of only 220,000 copies, which indicates that *Magyar Ifjusag* only reaches a minority of the more than 750,000 Youth League members.

Locally, these organizations utilize a number of other political socialization techniques. Monthly meetings of Young Pioneers cells are organized by classroom teachers or KISz leaders assigned to the schools. Group activities may include anything from singing to taking trips together or playing games. The older children within the Young Pioneers receive an ideological training that is often quite sophisticated. To encourage members to do well in this type of instruction, the Party often offers free trips to the Soviet Union or summer camps and other rewards to those who achieve ideological competence.

Students are also socialized in a number of hobby groups connected with the Young Pioneers organization. The activities of these groups range from stamp collecting to sports or even the operation of a narrow gauge railroad on the picturesque hills overlooking Budapest. The political socialization activities undertaken in these groups are usually limited to participation in marches and public demonstrations on holidays.

One political socialization activity of each Young Pioneers cell is maintaining a bulletin board display or "wall newspaper" in the classroom. These displays are often relatively shabby and do not attract much interest. In a seventh grade class in Budapest, the wall newspaper for the last week of May 1969 contained articles with the following titles: "Death to the American Imperialists," "Socialist Construction Among Young Hungarian Soldiers," and an untitled handwritten essay on how to make a paper airplane. The first two articles were clipped from the daily papers. The person in charge of each cell's wall newspaper usually doubles as the secretary or treasurer of the unit. In 1974, a teacher in a Budapest grade school complained to the author that "frequently no one wants the jobs involved with Pioneer work. The students often take jabs at the (wall) newspaper editor and many students are reluctant

to make even minimal payments for Pioneer dues." A school principal in a rural school reported that the 13- to 14-year-old youngsters in her district consider the Pioneer secretary a *streber* (an apple-polisher), and since there are no volunteers for Pioneer positions, the principal must appoint students to fill these posts.

The membership of KISz groups is subjected to a much more serious political socialization effort. League activities range from ideological training in seminars to voluntary work in summer camps where members help with the farming and harvesting. The high school activities of the League include approximately 20 hours annually of national defense training;[33] however, sports, dances, and other recreational activities attract the largest numbers of participants. KISz also participates in adult-to-adult socialization programs through the trade unions. The League aids the trade unions in arranging "cultural rallies," selling tickets for films and theatre productions, promoting continuing education, and organizing trips or tours for young adults no longer in school. In all of these activities the League stresses the need to develop ideological competence as well as social responsibility.

The emphasis on political socialization within KISz groups was evident from the wall newspapers examined by the author in seven technical high schools and three *gymnasiums* in Budapest in 1969. Of the 212 articles, editorials, and pictures on display, 78 percent concerned some element of political socialization. The themes represented in these displays (in order of importance) were: the progress of socialism, American imperialism in Vietnam, Soviet progress, and success in sporting events. Only one article was found concerning pro-Arab policies, and it was a thinly disguised anti-Semitic tirade that someone had decorated with graffiti.

In addition to its political socialization function, the KISz recommends young people for membership in the Party. In evaluating applications, Party officials take into account the political education of the applicant; therefore, secretaries of the KISz cells are under great pressure from the Party to foster more "creative youth education programs." However, the membership of the KISz seems to be more interested in nonpolitical activities of the Youth League than in its political functions. This lack of interest in political activities can be ascertained from various sources. Party journals, for example, often contain articles critical of the insufficient ideological training of KISz members;[34] and in spite of the efforts of the KISz, only 1.1 percent of the university students in Budapest belong to the Party.[35]

Schools. The schools serve as exceedingly powerful agencies of political socialization affecting all children between the ages of 8 and 18. Although the techniques of incorporating the desired socialist values into the curriculum vary from class to class and from age group to age group, teachers generally use *all* subjects to illustrate certain political themes. Thus, they discuss the contributions of Mendeleiev, Pavlov, and Gagarin in science classes to emphasize the pro-Soviet bias of the regime, and in literature classes they analyze poems, short stories, and novels praising socialism to impress upon the children the values of the socialist system. The following excerpt from a fifth grade literature lesson shown on educational TV illustrates how teachers develop political themes in conjunction with the subject matter.

Teacher: The poets discussed today show Hungary as we see it, but when could these poets have seen Hungary as they have described it?

Student: After the liberation.

Teacher: How was the Hungarian landscape changed after 1945, and why can we say that now the people rule the land?

Student: People live comfortably; there are clothes available; there is plenty of food; and the people work for their own good. Through the changed countryside the people have changed as well.[36]

Educators can easily organize the study of historical events around various themes of political socialization. The eighth-grade curriculum for modern Hungarian history, for example, is structured according to these politically oriented topics:

Reapers' strikes at the beginning of the century

Hungarians in the Great October Socialist Revolution

The Hungarian Soviet Republic

A call to arms (The defense of the Soviet Republic)

Sandor Latinka (A Communist agrarian revolutionary)

Sallai and Furst

The Leipzig Trial

The empire of fear (Horthy's regime)

The Soviet Union's drive for collective security

Hungary's entry into World War II

March 15, 1942

March 19, 1944

October 15, 1944

The liberation of Hungary[37]

By integrating ideological material into the standard curriculum, the regime had hoped to inculcate a Marxist-Leninist *Weltanschauung* in the students; but, in spite of the strenuous efforts to transmit desired values in all areas of the curriculum, the Party has not been satisfied with the political training of a large number of high school graduates. To correct this problem, Hungarian educators recently inaugurated two new projects designed to improve the political socialization program in the schools. The goal of the first project was to encourage schools to provide a continuity of general ideological training through increased classroom use of centrally produced educational TV programs. As the result of a determined effort, approximately 40 percent of the schools now utilize educational television.[38] The second project introduced two new subjects into the curriculum, Citizenship Information and The Bases of Our Ideology. The first course was taught in sixth grade classes on an experimental basis in 1974–1975; the second course has been integrated into the senior level high school curriculum since 1972. The new courses provide "conscious political education and citizenship training for high school students."[39]

The regime has decided that students are the most receptive to the inculcation of ideology between the ages of 15 and 20, and it has therefore made The Bases of Our Ideology a compulsory subject for all high school seniors.[40] The course is usually taught three hours per week. Students in four Budapest high schools (N-231) queried informally by the author in 1971, maintained that the textbook used in the course is very poorly written and difficult to understand. They complained bitterly about the course because they thought it was extremely dull. Of these students, 55 percent believed they had learned "nothing new" and only two percent thought it was a good course; however, 38 percent felt that some type of course on this subject was necessary.

The Family.   The agencies of political socialization discussed above are all components of the political system of Communist Hungary. Agencies operating outside of the political system, however, can also carry out significant system-maintenance functions.[41] Thus, although the family is not subject to the control of the Party,[42] it can still inculcate either positive or dysfunctional values in the country's youth.

Many political scientists consider the family to be the most important of all political socialization agencies.[43] However, its importance as a primary agency of political socialization has diminished somewhat in societies where the family structure has been weakened by various factors. The average Hungarian family consists of 1.29 children,[44] and both adult members of the family usually work.[45] Consequently, Hungarian children spend much time during their formative years in nurseries or other environments away from the home and the influence of their parents. As a result, the primary role of the Hungarian family in the socialization process has decreased in the post-World-War-II era.[46]

Even though the family's impact on the process of political socialization is decreasing,[47] many Hungarian families still inculcate values antithetical to those prescribed by the regime. In rural areas where the family structure has changed less than in the urban areas affected by modernization, the family's role in inculcating negative political values is very significant. For example, many rural families practice religion, which is contrary to the regime's desire to eradicate religious practices. This conflict creates problems for the youth in many villages.[48] In both rural and urban areas, the determined anti-Russian attitude of many Hungarian adults provides a counterinfluence to the Party's pro-Soviet propaganda. Furthermore, parental behavior, including perhaps an unwillingness to work or a persistant heavy drinking problem, often counters the attempts of the formal agents of socialization to create a "new socialist man."[49] In sum, the Hungarian family remains an important primary agent of political socialization; it transmits attitudes and values to the youth, but the values it inculcates are not necessarily those advocated by the regime.

Other Agencies.   The churches, the army, and the intellectual and professional substrata of Hungarian society play limited, although in some instances important, roles in the inculcation of values in the populace.

The churches create troublesome problems for the present regime in Hungary because they, like many families, inculcate antiregime values in a significant percentage of the citizenry. This tendency is especially pronounced in the Catholic church which claims the religious allegiance of over 65 percent of Hungary's population. The regime's major objection to Catholicism is that since the authority of the Catholic church originates in Rome in the person of the Pope, Hungarian Catholics may develop extraterritorial loyalties that are a potential threat to the Party's hegemony. Approximately 50 percent of the people who belong to the Catholic church live in villages, and therefore, village priests are very powerful in shaping the values of young and old alike. In one village, for example, over 78 percent (N-148) of the women go to church on Sunday, and 43 percent usually go once a day. Of the total rural Catholic population, over 60 percent attend mass on Sunday. The religious ties are weaker in the city (specific data are not available), but most city churches are full for the Sunday morning services.[50]

The protestant churches pose less of a threat to the regime than the Roman Catholic church. The protestants are not a powerful, well organized, and efficiently directed group. Together the protestant churches account for only 28 percent of the population. Religious education among these faiths is weaker than among the Catholics, and only some minor religious cults encourage serious dysfunctional activity. Because the largest protestant denominations in no way undermine the Party's authority, they are more acceptable to the regime than the Catholic church.

Judaism is no longer a significant political socialization force in Hungary because of the wholesale destruction of the Hungarian Jews during World War II. Only 140,000 out of more than 500,000 Hungarian Jews survived the war, and only a limited number—perhaps 30,000—still practice their religion.[51] In 1969, the Jewish seminary in Budapest had only eight students. There are four seminaries in operation in the smaller Hungarian cities where the religious attachment of Jews appears to be stronger than in the capital.

The regime has attempted to control the negative political socialization functions of the churches by forbidding active religious opposition to the ideological foundations of the government, but the very affirmation of religious beliefs is in opposition to the concepts of Marxism. At the beginning of the 1970s, a stalemate had been reached between church and state: the churches preached religious doctrine but tacitly supported the policies of the present regime, and the party advocated the building of socialism while tacitly allowing many Hungarian citizens to participate in religious activities.

Several other secondary institutions contribute to the process of political socialization. These agencies provide positive reinforcement in adult-to-adult relationships, but they also instill values that may contradict those desired by the regime. The army and the apparat of the intelligentsia provide their own members with a separate *Bewusstein* that works against the Party's desire to integrate the various elements of society into a coherent whole. For example, army training programs inculcate in officers and soldiers alike a primitive nationalism that is contrary to Communist ideology. Nationalistic tendencies within the army in 1956 made it an unreliable tool of the Party, and even today, the nationalism of the army is a source of concern to the regime.

The intelligentsia's basically scornful attitudes toward the Party apparat act as a negative socializing agent in several meaningful ways. Although few intellectuals seem to be actively working against the regime, they are members of an elite and they are better off than the vast majority of the workers. In addition, they are able to travel in the West and accumulate material wealth. Through their knowledge of Western European and American living conditions, they recognize the relative backwardness of Hungary, and in their adult-to-child relationships, they pass on an admiration of the West and belittle the accomplishments of the USSR.[52] The fact that the intelligentsia exists as a separate social entity causes workers and peasants to be skeptical of the egalitarianism preached by the exponents of Communist ideology. It is very obvious to the working classes that well-known doctors and other professionals are able to afford fine new automobiles and ade-

quate housing; that famous sportsmen and musicians travel almost without restriction; and that scientists and factory directors live in a style far superior to that of the common industrial worker.

In 1970, all agencies of political socialization in Hungary, with the exception of the family, were under the direct or indirect control of the Party. The efforts of all these agencies were aimed at inculcating system-maintenance values in the citizenry. The fact that there has been no major dysfunctional activity in Hungary since 1956 indicates that the regime has been relatively successful in politically socializing the Hungarian population.

Summary

Since 1949, the Hungarian Communist regimes have sought to inculcate various values in the citizenry in order to make the leadership's task of ruling easier. Through the different agencies of political socialization the regimes have attempted to pass on the values desired by the Party. Although there have been significant discontinuities in the sets of values deemed important enough to inculcate in the citizenry, by and large, the regime's efforts to maintain control over the process have been consistently aimed at creating a citizenry that does not question the basic legitimacy of the system. The regime's efforts, however, have not been totally successful because such agencies as the family, churches, and peer groups transmit countervailing values that have proved strong enough to detract from the success of the officially sanctioned socialization program. In spite of the reality that several agencies continue to inculcate values that the Party does not officially approve of, the fact that system-maintenance values pervade Hungarian society testifies to the relative success of the political socialization efforts of the Party.

9

The Media as Instruments of Political Socialization

In Communist Hungary, the regime utilizes television, radio, newspapers, journals, books, film, theater, and music to reach the citizenry with political messages designed to inculcate socialist values. As the monopolist of power, the Government directly or indirectly owns all means of communication. It controls the media very carefully to prevent them from being used as negative agents of political socialization.

The regime exercises its power in a variety of ways. By staffing the various media organizations (publishing houses, radio stations, television networks, etc.) with trusted Party members, the Party is able to control the content of the messages relayed. By employing punitive measures against those authors whose works are antisocialist or otherwise not in accordance with the wishes of the Party, the regime wields a judicial weapon to control what is written and who writes. In addition, by empowering trusted Party editors to decide which plays will be performed or which books will be printed, the Party exercises financial as well as political control over the media, limiting the number and types of independent inputs to the communication process.

According to Professor Richard Fagen, however, this overwhelming control of communication "does not mean that the content of the media shapes political behavior in any direct and easily predictable manner, even in tightly controlled systems such as the Soviet polity. . . . However, the existence of a national mass media, with all that implies in increased message capacity, speed, and pervasiveness, changes in a basic way a system's potential for political communication.[1] The Hungarian Communist regime has had only limited success in orienting the behavior and values of the citizenry through the mass media.

The following examination of the various media of political communication in Hungary includes an analysis of the themes of political socialization emphasized in each of the media and an evaluation of the results of the Party's political socialization program.

Television

Television has had an enormous impact on Hungarian society. It has only recently become available to the majority of the population, and because of its novelty, it is much appreciated by an extremely large proportion of TV owners, who remain glued to the set every evening. It has become a sort of plastic household god and has created a situation similar to the one that existed in America in the 1950s when television was first introduced.

In 1956, there were practically no television sets in Hungary, but today television has become a major part of Hungarian life. In the early 1970s, there were nearly 2,000,000 TV sets in operation and almost every second family had one. The Hungarian government subsidizes the cost of television sets, but owners must still pay approximately 50 forints per month as a special "TV tax."

In 1968 and 1969, Hungarian national television transmitted 70 hours weekly on two channels in addition to the 25 hours per week of educational television programs.[2] During the week, regular TV transmission begins at 4:45 P.M. and ends around

Table 9.1. Hungarian Television Programming in 1969

Type of Program	Percentage of Total Broadcast Time
Political and Current Events	25.5
Drama and Literature	8.5
Classical Music	3.8
Cartoons	12.4
Entertainment, Including Sports	20.3
Documentary (informational), News	7.6
Educational TV	8.9
Children's, Evening Tales	8.4
Young Pioneers	4.0
Film Shorts	0.6

Source: Mrs. Tibor Erdesz and Istvan Fekete, "Tomeg-kommunikacios eszkozok szerepe a nepmuvelesben" [The Role of the Mass Communication Media in Education], *Statisztikai Szemle*, August–September 1969.

10:15 P.M.; on Sunday, transmission begins at 9 A.M. and ends at 10:30 P.M. Table 9.1 illustrates the types of programs shown in weekly broadcasts.[3] It is significant that the programming includes a number of non-Magyar productions. "Daktari" and "The Flintstones" are the favorite American shows. The British series, "The Saint," and "The Forsythe Saga" attract huge audiences, and viewers can choose from a wide variety of Western European movies and specials. Soviet and Polish spy series based on World War II events, such as "Captain Kloss" and "Stirlitz," are among the most popular shows produced in the Communist states.

Empirical evidence confirms the popularity of Hungarian television. In 1969, village residents considered possessing a television set more important than having indoor plumbing.[4] Television is popular in all age groups, but it is especially popular among people below age 24.[5] (See Table 9.2.) Furthermore,

Table 9.2. Popularity of Television in Hungary by Age Group in 1969

Age Group	Percentage Watching Television
Below 24	85
Between 24 and 59	76
People in Retirement: 60 and Older	43

Source: Mrs. Tibor Erdesz and Istvan Fekete, "Tomegkommunikacios eszkozok szerepe a nepmuvelesben" [The Role of the Mass Communication Media in Education], *Statisztikai Szemle*, August–September, 1969.

there is no correlation between a person's occupation and his or her propensity for watching TV. A large percentage of Hungarians in all occupational categories watch television.[6] (See Table 9.3.)

Television's effectiveness as a medium of communication and socialization is enhanced by the fact that those families who possess a set watch it nearly continuously. Only 10 percent of TV owners spend less than three hours per week watching programs; 50 percent spend 3 to 15 hours per week watching broadcasts; and fully 40 percent of families with television spend more than 15 hours per week in front of the TV set. Public interest in TV is also indicated by the fact that 90 percent of the people who do not own

Table 9.3. Popularity of Television in Hungary
by Occupation

Occupation of Viewers	Percentage Watching Television
Students (through college level)	88.5
Intellectuals (including managers)	88.0
Professionals	84.0
Clerical Employees	84.0
Skilled Laborers	81.0
Manual Laborers	74.0

Source: Mrs. Tibor Erdesz and Istvan Fekete, "Tomeg-kommunikacios eszkozok szerepe a nepmuvelesben" [The Role of the Mass Communication Media in Education], *Statistical Szemle,* August—September 1969.

a TV set spend nearly three hours weekly watching various programs.[7] As the data in Table 9.4 suggest, watching television is the most popular free-time occupation of most Hungarian village residents.[8]

The major reasons for watching television in Hungary in the 1960s are indicated in Table 9.5.[9] Based on a representative national survey of 1594 people, the data show that the vast majority of Hungarians watched television for entertainment. In addition, the less education the respondents had, the less likely they were to use television for strictly educational purposes. The differences, however, are minor, and all those queried viewed television primarily for entertainment.

Since television is such an excellent means of reaching the public, the regime utilizes it extensively for the transmission of certain themes and messages. The author examined two weeks of programs shown during the summer of 1969 and printed descriptions of another two weeks of scheduled programs (211 separate programs in all) to ascertain the themes and messages most frequently repeated in Hungarian television broadcasts. Table 9.6 and Figure 9.1 contain the findings of this study. The most frequently repeated theme—recent successes in the building of socialism—usually appeared in news programs. To convey this message, Hungarian television productions showed endless numbers of new machines at work and new buildings or factories under construction. Documentary films, studio dramas, and quiz shows also depicted the progress of socialist construction.

Anti-imperialist themes also appeared most frequently in television news broadcasts. The term "American aggressors," for example, was used seven times in a two-minute broadcast on July 18, 1969. Anti-imperialist themes were also evident in film shorts and comprehensive documentaries detailing the victories of various national liberation movements against the "lackeys of imperialism" or relating the success of Egypt against the "Israeli aggressors."

Programs addressing socialist morality were most often discussions, human-interest shorts, news broadcast, and television dramas. In fact, most discussion programs were directed toward the moral reeducation of the populace.

Table 9.4. Correlation Between Education and Use of Free Time of Village Residents°

Education	Percentage of Free Time Devoted to Various Activities							
	TV	Reading, Studying	Work-ing	Enter-tainment	Leisure, Rest	Others	Total	Number of Interviewees
Completed Less Than Eighth Grade	46.5	21.6	3.2	7.5	11.7	9.5	100.00	1,001
Completed Eighth Grade	39.8	27.0	4.5	11.7	6.5	10.5	100.00	1,051
Completed High School	30.4	37.4	4.4	13.7	4.1	10.0	100.00	342
Completed College or Other Higher Education	32.5	42.6	1.6	6.5	3.8	13.0	100.00	108
Average	40.9	26.9	3.8	10.1	8.1	10.2	100.00	

°Compiled from a random stratified sample.
Source: Laszlo Harangi and Zoltan Vitar, *Televizio falun* [Television in the Village] (Budapest: Nepmuvelesi Propaganda Iroda, 1967).

Table 9.5. Correlation Between Education and Why People Watched Television in the 1960s

| Education | Percentage of Group Watching Television for Various Reasons | | | | | | | |
	Education	Infor-mation	Enter-tainment	Rest	Com-fort	Lack of Other Cultural or Edu-cational Opportu-nity	Total	Number of Interviewees
Completed Less Than Eighth Grade	14.9	5.3	65.6	4.7	8.0	1.5	100.00	660
Completed Eighth Grade	19.3	5.2	57.9	6.5	6.7	4.4	100.00	675
Completed High School and College	18.9	8.9	51.0	5.4	7.3	8.5	100.00	259
Average	17.4	5.8	60.0	5.6	7.3	3.3	100.00	1594

Source: Laszlo Harangi and Zoltan Vitar, *Televizio falun* [Television in the Village] (Budapest: Nepmuvelesi Propaganda Iroda, 1967).

The theme of alliance with countries in the socialist commonwealth was stressed in both news broadcasts and documentary films. The aim of this propaganda theme is to inculcate in the citizenry admiration for the achievements of the Soviet Union and other socialist countries. Material utilized to present this theme included films taken from television broadcasts of other socialist states, news broadcasts on the new plans of the USSR, and interviews with visiting socialist dignitaries.

Table 9.6. Themes of Political Socialization Appearing Most Frequently on Hungarian Television°

Theme	Number of Times Repeated
Building of Socialism	65
Anti-Imperialism	59
Socialist Morality	51
Alliance with Nations in the Socialist Commonwealth	49
Socialist Patriotism	21
Antinationalism	20
Anti-Individualism	15
Negative Impact of Cult of Personality	14

°Based on four weeks of television programming in the Summer of 1969. While other themes were identifiable in the programs, none appeared more than five times during the two-week period examined.

Socialist patriotism was emphasized mainly in TV dramas dealing with historical subjects and in debates or discussion programs concerned with the problems of nationalism. This theme was frequently stressed in educational TV broadcasts, where it was interwoven with lectures on history and literature. These programs often pointed out the dangers of nationalism and attempted to distinguish the positive aspects of socialist patriotism from the harmful, negative elements of chauvinism and nationalism.

Anti-individualist themes showed up most frequently in television dramas depicting the necessity of subordinating individual needs to those of the community. Drama and discussion programs scored long-haired hippies who refused to give up their individuality, and interviews presented Party officials who decried "antisocialist behavior" as a survival of bourgeois morality.

The topic of anti-Stalinism was almost always discussed indirectly in various types of dramatic programs. During the four-week period examined in the survey, there was no direct mention of the faults of Rakosi or Stalin, but four television dramas and an editorial attack on Chinese policy served as vehicles for condemning dictatorial methods of rule.

No data are available concerning the population's desire to view programs not sponsored by the government. In the border areas, watching Vienna, Bratislava, or Novisad stations is a common practice among adults, but the younger generation in these

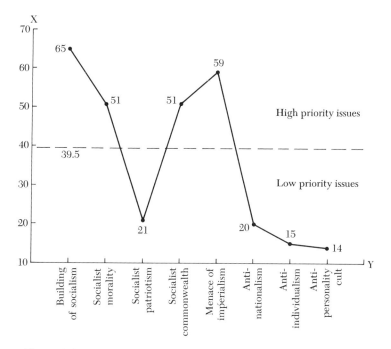

Figure 9.1. Importance attributed by the regime to eight themes of political socialization according to the number of times each theme was repeated on Hungarian television during a four-week period in the summer of 1969. X = number of times theme was mentioned; Y = themes; 39.5 = mean number of times all themes were mentioned.

areas seems to prefer Hungarian broadcasts. One reason for this difference in viewing habits may be that many young Hungarians do not know as many languages as their elders. It is also possible that the regime's televised political socialization program has been more effective in educating the youth than in altering the attitudes of adults.

The regime has used television successfully to influence and improve the education of the rural population. Many peasants have been willing to adopt attitudes advocated on TV. Although the peasantry has traditionally been slow to accept new ideas, its ready acceptance of values advocated on television is making it somewhat easier for the regime to influence political behavior in the villages.

Excellent educational programming has also made this medium an important instrument of political socialization. Educational television reaches nearly 50 percent of all schools, and it is extensively used to teach important subjects, including history, literature, languages, and science. TV courses are taught by good actors who present the material skillfully; reaction to the shows by administrators, teachers, and students has been uniformly favorable. The content of the lessons is well presented, but the regime's ideological orientation is easily observable in most subject matter, particularly history and literature.

To summarize, Hungarian television reaches a significant number of people, and the government uses this medium extensively to transmit political messages to the population. On the other hand, the government's monopoly over this means of communication makes certain types of television programs dysfunctional because the population, weary of constant repetition, fails to internalize the prescribed values. For example, the constant airing of programs about new victories in the building of the socialist society has helped to create a skeptical, "so what" attitude among viewers. The majority of the Hungarian people watch TV strictly for entertainment and are less interested in informational programs or in clearly political broadcasts than in comedy or dramatic productions.

Radio

Although television is the most popular mass medium, the regime still utilizes radio as an important means of political communication. No data are available to indicate how many Hungarians adopt behavioral patterns advocated in radio broadcasts, but a survey of 8,000 people in 1969 showed that 69 percent of the people listened to daily news broadcasts, whereas 62 percent read the daily newspapers and 42 percent watched the news on television.[10]

All radio stations are owned and operated by the state; programs are relayed via the three Hungarian radio networks. Kossuth radio operates about 20 hours a day, while Petofi radio broadcasts 17 hours daily. There does not seem to be any substantial difference between the programs broadcast by the two networks, but there is a great deal of variety in their daily programming, which includes classical and popular music, opera and drama, poetry and news, sports programs and travelogues, as well as children's tales and political commentary. In addition to Radio Kossuth and Radio Petofi, a third network, the Third Program, began transmitting in 1971. In the first six months of 1976, the Third Program broadcast mainly serious classical music and literary programs, sprinkled with jazz and stereophonic transmissions; the network was on the air for 9 hours on weekdays and 15 hours on Saturdays and Sundays.

The Communists have utilized radio very successfully since their ascension to power. Initially, the Party used radio to convince the Hungarian citizenry of the legitimacy of Rakosi's rule and the progress being made by the Hungarian state under Communist guidance. In the factories, loudspeakers broadcast the programs of the national stations, which were frequently interrupted by propaganda messages exhorting workers to greater production efforts. In the villages, loudspeakers placed on rooftops and power poles informed the provincial population of events outside its own world and facilitated transmission of government propaganda. The Kadar regime no longer relies on "loudspeaker education"; the popularity of transistor radios has made it unnecessary.

No program illustrates the successful use of radio as an instrument of political socialization better than the ten-year-old weekly series entitled "Szabo csalad" ("The Szabo Family").[11] Hungarian sources claim that the series has over 2 million listeners.[12] The impact of the program is evident from the thousands of letters the producers and author of the series purportedly receive. Public pressure has forced the author to change the plot of the series several times, and public reaction to the show has occasionally gotten out of hand. There have been several incidents in which the authors have been unable to stop the flow of people who came to the studio "to give blood or even skin grafts to save (an accident) victim" of the series. The success of the series can be gauged from other examples as well. Mention of an exhibition at the National Gallery resulted in a doubling of the number of visitors to that exhibit. Discussion on the program about a particularly bad product resulted in its boycott by a large segment of the populace.[13]

The aim of the series is to depict a microcosm of Hungarian life, and through this depiction to mold public opinion and public attitudes. The most familiar theme of the series is the importance of Communist morality. The theme is portrayed through the healthy, moral family life of Uncle and Mrs. Szabo. Szabo's daughter, who is a surgeon in a village hospital, exemplifies devotion to public service. The activities of Bandi Szabo, an engineer who manages a large firm, emphasize the importance of building socialism. The authors of the series utilize Bandi's trips to encourage the development of affection for other socialist countries and to illustrate the poor conditions faced by workers in capitalist states. The program portrays the antisocial aspects of opportunism through the character of Erno, who fails in his efforts to climb the ladder of success; and the problems of the U.S. are introduced through Freddie, an uncle who has returned from America. The author of "The Szabo Family" has admitted that although the series tries to raise moral problems, its main purpose is to "shape public opinion" and inculcate desired socialist attitudes in the listeners.[14] The series is certainly the most successful of the regime's efforts to utilize radio in the political socialization process.

Newspapers and Journals

In Hungary, newspapers and journals are the most widely utilized medium of adult-to-adult political socialization. Although most Hungarian newspapers and journals are technically published by independent social or economic organizations such as the trade unions, the women's associations, or the Csepel Iron Works, in reality the Party controls the content of this medium. It exercises strict control over each publication by naming responsible editors whose political allegiances are beyond question, and by invoking punitive measures for the publication of content contradictory to government policies. These measures do not insure complete control over the printed matter in periodical literature because of recurrent disagreements over the interpretation of the party's policy, but the dual method of control does minimize the danger of any periodical working actively against the Party.

More than 650 periodicals were published in Hungary during 1969. Twenty-seven of these periodicals were daily papers. The combined pressrun of the 22 local and 5 national newspapers printed in Hungary daily was nearly 2,200,000. The Party's own newspaper, *Nepszabadsag*, is the most widely read daily, with an average pressrun of over 800,000; each of the other four major dailies has a pressrun of less than 200,000. *Esti Hirlap* is a popular daily publication that features sensational news.[15] It reports robberies, murders and traffic accidents in gruesome detail. *Magyar Nemzet* and *Nepszava* are the official papers of the Government and the trade unions respectively, and *Nepsport* is the daily sports paper. In addition to these four dailies, there are magazines and newspapers published for various special interests groups (from women to stamp collectors). These publications include such magazines as the *Nok Lapja*, a family journal for women, and *Elet es Tudomany*, a popular scientific weekly.

The regime uses the daily papers for relaying information and developing themes of political socialization. A content analysis of 50 randomly selected issues of each of the four daily newspapers for the period of July 1, 1968 to July 1, 1969 (N = 4 × 50 = 200) revealed the following division of information: foreign news, 22 percent; domestic news, 78 percent.[16] Of the foreign news items printed, 13 percent were factual or neutral, 23 percent concerned the accomplishments of the Soviet Union, 11 percent contained news of the socialist democracies, 2.5 percent were devoted to thinly disguised anti-Chinese views, 27 percent enumerated problems encountered by imperialists, and 22.5 percent were devoted to other themes. The technique

most frequently utilized by writers of anti-West or anti-American (i.e. anti-imperialist) articles was the interspersion of value judgments among carefully selected facts about an event. Sixty-two percent of the factual reportage consisted of dispatches from UPI, AP, Reuters, AFP, TASS, and other news agencies. Of the items concerning domestic news, 26 percent concerned public, governmental, and Party activities; 12 percent discussed the economy; 12 percent presented information and analyses of art, popular culture, and literature; 5 percent reported sports events; 25 percent was devoted to advertisements; and the remaining 20 percent treated miscellaneous subjects. Table 9.7 shows the frequency with which the main identifiable themes of political socialization appeared in the four daily newspapers analyzed.

Table 9.7. Frequency Distribution of the Main Themes of Political Socialization Appearing in Four Hungarian Daily Newspapers Between July 1, 1968 and July 1, 1969

Theme	Percentage of Total Column Inches
Building of Socialism	23
Socialist Morality	16
Menace of Imperialism	11
Support of Socialist Commonwealth	8
Socialist Patriotism	3
Antinationalism	3
Anti-Individualism	3
Subtotal	67
Nonclassifiable, Nonidentifiable Themes	33
Total	100

Although the government expends great sums of money on newspapers and journals in order to instill Communist values in the readers, the effectiveness of this medium of political socialization is hard to determine. Unfortunately, only scant data are available. When asked what they read in the paper, Hungarian respondents often answer, "The standing of the National League, First Division, in soccer."[17] However, research conducted in the late 1950s through interviews with Hungarian refugees indicated that people fleeing Hungary were exaggerating when they stated that they never read the paper or that they didn't believe what they read in the official news. Furthermore, the findings of the project in which Hungarian refugees were interviewed suggest that Hungarian citizens were affected by the world view presented in the political socialization media, and most especially by that elaborated in the newspapers. Thus, some evidence indicates that newspapers and journals do significantly affect public opinion in Communist Hungary.

Books

The Hungarian Government was quick to grasp the importance of literature as a purposive instrument of political socialization. Following the period of socialist transformation in Hungary, the Government used both fiction and nonfiction as media of political communication. Soon after coming to power in 1949, the Rakosi regime reorganized the publishing houses, placed reliable apparatchiks in charge of them, and began subsidizing nearly all works published in book form. By lowering the price of books, the leadership hoped to encourage the population to purchase more works to read.

The Hungarian Stalinist regime also exerted pressure on writers, constraining them to produce proregime works whose style conformed to the socialist realism advocated by Soviet Communist leaders. Rakosi's government provided directives on the type of works that had to be written, offered large rewards for works that conformed to those directives, and forbade publication of nonsocialist works. Between 1949 and 1953, it used these means of censorship to shape the public's literary taste, that is, to develop "progressive reading habits" in the citizenry, and to impose the values and style of socialist realism (the realistic, didactic portrayal of an ideal socialist society) on all Hungarian literary publications. Works glorifying Rakosi or Stalin, hailing the successes of socialism, condemning imperialism, and heaping accolades on Soviet brothers appeared in large quantities.

After Stalin died, there was a renaissance of Hungarian literature in which writers began to explore themes more troublesome to the regime. Many works critical of the Government originally circulated from hand to hand, but eventually the "radicals" succeeded in taking control of *Irodalmi Ujsag*, the Hungarian equivalent of the Russian *Literaturnaia Gazeta*. On the pages of this newspaper and in the

tabloid, *Hetfoi Hirlep*, excellent literary pieces appeared showing the deep dissatisfaction of the Hungarian people. Peter Kuczka's "Nyirseg Diary"[18] was the first major, open criticism of the regime's policies. Kuczka described the deep dissatisfaction of the peasantry. Erno Urban's "Pickle Tree," a satire performed in 1954 by the National Theater, also expressed dissatisfaction with the tyranny of Rakosi's dictatorial rule. Packed houses burst into spontaneous applause night after night when the tyranny of the "chairman" ended. Other critical works that appeared and stirred much public debate during these years include Tibor Dery's superb novels, *The Unfinished Sentence* and *Niki*; Gyula Hay's play, *Justice for Gaspar Varro*; as well as many films, poems, novels, and plays concerned with the terror of Rakosi's rule.

When the Kadar government came to power after the 1956 revolution, it tried to silence the hostile writers by imprisonment. But the new leadership soon realized that it would not be able to coerce writers into producing great literary works in support of the regime. After 1957, the Party therefore decided to encourage literary mediocrity by publishing insignificant, badly written, but noncontroversial books. However, since the introduction of more liberal policies in the 1960s, the regime has eased restrictions and offered financial rewards to good writers.

Hungarian publishing houses have produced a staggering number of books since 1945. In 1966 alone, a combined total of 45,000,000 copies were printed of the 4,660 books published in that year. Table 9.8 lists the most popular authors in Hungary and the number of their works published between 1945 and 1956.[19] These figures make it clear that an impressive number of volumes has been published in post-World War II Hungary, but a survey of 12,000 people, undertaken in 1962 by the Central Statistical Office of Hungary, provides evidence that a surprisingly small number of Hungarian people read books.[20] Results of the survey show that 61.6 percent of the citizenry did not read books at that time, 6 percent read one volume per year, 12.6 percent read two to three books annually, 11.6 percent read four to six volumes each year, and only 8.2 percent of the people read more than six books per year. The additional statistics from this survey listed in Table 9.9 indicate the predictable fact that there is a direct correlation between reading habits and education.[21]

Table 9.8. Most Popular Authors in Hungary Between 1945 and 1956

Author	Number of Copies of Works Printed in Hungary
Mor Jokai	7,300,000
Zsigmond Moricz	4,700,000
Kalman Mikszath	4,000,000
Maxim Gorkii	1,300,000
Janos Arany	1,300,000
Honore de Balzac	1,300,000
Emile Zola	1,280,000
Leo Tolstoi	1,200,000
Mark Twain	1,100,000
William Shakespeare	1,000,000
Victor Hugo	900,000
Guy de Maupassant	870,000
Stendahl	870,000
Jack London	870,000

Source: Ferenc Erdei et al., eds., *Information Hungary* (New York, London, Budapest: Pergamon Press, 1968).

Vast differences exist between the reading habits of the city and the village populations. Less than 20 percent of the peasants read books and only 5 percent read more than six books a year as compared with the national averages of 38.4 percent and 8.2 percent respectively. A comparison of the turnover of books in village and in city libraries further supports this distinction between the reading habits of urban and rural populations. In village libraries the turnover rate in 1966 was 17.7 percent compared with 28.0 percent in city libraries.[22]

Although the reading habits of the intelligentsia differ considerably from those of the other strata of society, exact data analyzing the reading preferences of the populace by occupation are not available. The authoritative *Information Hungary* states that "as regards the purchase of books, there are naturally great differences between the professional and the working classes and the peasants," with the largest percentage of books being bought by the professional classes.[23] Thus, in the political socialization process the Government uses books largely to win the allegiance of the professional classes, whose support the Kadar regime considers essential.

It is important to consider what types of books appeal most to the reading public. In a survey taken during 1964 (N = 20,402), sociologists compiled a list of authors whose works were checked out most frequently from one of Budapest's main libraries. Table 9.10 presents their findings.[24] Similar data gathered in the same library in 1934 is detailed in Table 9.11.[25] The most significant difference between popular tastes in 1934 and 1964 appears in the selections of foreign authors. Preferences for Hungarian writers changed little during this time. Of the Hungarian writers, Jokai, Moricz, Mikszath, Mora and Gardonyi remained in the top ten. The major themes portrayed in the works of these authors are patriotism, support for moderate reforms, and a condemnation of the survival of the semi-feudal, undemocratic social system. Together with the children's books written by Elek Benedek, the works of these five authors account for 23.5 percent of the books read in Hungary today; the works of the six most popular contemporary authors constitute only 4.4 percent of the total.

Tables 9.12 and 9.13 describe the literary tastes of the more than 20,000 people who frequented the Ervin Szabo Library in 1964, analyzing the reading

Table 9.9. Correlation Between Education and Reading Habits of Hungarian Citizens

Education	Nonreaders	1	2–3	4–6	More Than 6
Completed Less Than Fourth Grade	87%	3%	5%	3%	2%
Completed Fifth Through Seventh Grade	77	5	8	6	4
Completed Eighth Grade	55	6	14	14	11
Completed High School	29	7	19	25	20
Completed College	17	8	20	26	29

Source: Mrs. Adam Horvath and Istvan Kemeny, "Kik olvasnak es mit?" [Who Reads and What?], *Valosag*, no. 6 (1965).

Table 9.10. Most Frequently Read Authors in the Ervin Szabo Library in 1964

Hungarian Authors	Number of Readers	Foreign Authors	Number of Readers
Mor Jokai	2,319	Jules Verne	630
Zsigmond Moricz	774	Alexandre Dumas	268
Kalman Mikszath	667	Leo Tolstoi	267
Geza Gardonyi	656	Emile Zola	192
Ferenc Mora	253	Victor Hugo	183
Istvan Fekete	208	James Fenimore Cooper	178
Zsuzsa Thury	162	Maxim Gorkii	145
Ferenc Molnar	143	Alexei Sholokhov	132
Marta Gergely	136	Honore de Balzac	127
Elek Benedek	134	Guy de Maupassant	126

Source: Mrs. Adam Horvath and Istvan Kemeny, "Kik olvasnak es mit?" [Who Reads and What?], *Valosag*, no. 6 (1965).

preferences of Hungarians according to the occupation and educational background of the readership.[26] These statistics indicate the relative popularity of two Soviet writers, Gorkii and Sholokhov, whose works accounted for 10 percent of the foreign authors read. Despite their popularity, however, the two Soviet writers together have only as large a readership as the fifth most popular Hungarian writer, Ferenc Mora. Although the works of some

Table 9.11. Most Frequently Read Authors in the Ervin Szabo Library in 1934 (in order of importance)

Hungarian Authors	Foreign Authors
Mor Jokai	Jack London
Ferenc Herczeg	John Galsworthy
Geza Gardonyi	Sinclair Lewis
Kalman Mikszath	Stefan Zweig
Kalman Csatho	Thomas Mann
Lajos Zilahy	H. G. Wells
Zsigmond Moricz	Jakob Wassermann
Janos Komaromi	Pierre Benoit
Ferenc Mora	Knut Hamsun
Renee Erdos	Franz Werfel

Source: Pal Drescher, "Mit olvas a Fovarosi Konyvtar kozmuvelodesi fiokjainak kozonsege?" [What do the Readers of the Capital Library's General Education Division Read?] *A Fovarosi Konyvtar Evkonyve, 1934* [Capital Library Yearbook, 1934] (Budapest, 1934), in Mrs. Adam Horvath and Istvan Kemeny, "Kik olvasnak es mit?" [Who Reads and What?], *Valosag*, no. 6 (1965), p. 53.

Soviet authors are published in relatively large numbers today, they have surprisingly few readers; only Sholokhov and Gorkii appear to be popular in Hungary. No other Soviet author can be found among the most frequently read writers.[27]

The dearth of interest in Soviet and socialist political literature extends to readers of all ages. Even the high school students who are required to read political literature for their courses do not take this type of reading seriously. In two, local public libraries in Budapest, only 9.5 and 10 percent of the volumes taken out by students in 1971 could be classified as political literature, and in several other branch libraries the figures were thought to be even lower.[28]

At the present time, the regime permits publication of some works that are quite critical of past and present methods of governing in Hungary. Notable among these works are Endre Fejes's *Scrapheap,*[29] Lajos Mesterhazi's *Manhood,*[30] and Ferenc Santa's *Twenty Hours.*[31] These books deal honestly with the terror used during Rakosi's reign and raise significant questions concerning the legitimacy of the Party's rule. Magda Szabo's *Moses One, Twenty-one*[32] contains a bitter complaint against the rigid doctrinaire attitudes of the older Communists. Andras Berkesi's best-seller, *The Trout and the Fish,* and his *Wailing Wall,* Gyorgy Konrad's *The Visitor,* Sandor Laszlo Bencsik's *History Viewed from Below* Akos Kertesz's *Makra,* and several works by Gyorgy Moldova[33] deride the false morality of the Hungarian Party and discuss the severe alienation generated by

Table 9.12. Authors Read by Hungarians in Each of Ten Occupational Categories in 1965

Leadership, Intelligentsia	Professionals, White-Collar Workers	Skilled Laborers	Unskilled Laborers	Co-operative Farmers	Retired Persons	Nonwage Earners	Grade School Students	High School Students, Apprentices	College Students
Jokai	Jokai	Jokai	Jokai	Jokai	Jokai	Jokai	Verne	Jokai	Jokai
Mikszath	Moricz	Moricz	Mikszath	Moricz	Mikszath	Moricz	Jokai	Moricz	Mann
Istvan Fekete	Mikszath	Mikszath	Moricz	Mikszath	Moricz	Mikszath	Gardonyi	Mikszath	Tolstoi
Thomas Mann	Tolstoi	Gardonyi	Gardonyi	Gardonyi	Gardonyi	Gardonyi	Moricz	Verne	Dumas
Nemeth	Zola	Verne	Verne	Verne	Verne	Verne	Benedek	Gardonyi	Mora
Tolstoi	Fekete	Dumas	Dumas	Sholokhov	Tolstoi	Dumas	Molnar	Tolstoi	Nemeth
Moricz	Dumas	Tolstoi	Tolstoi	Mora	Zola	Tolstoi	Cooper	Dumas	Hugo
Rath-Vegh	Hugo	Hugo	Gorkii	Dumas	Dumas	Zola	Mikszath	Fekete	Sholokhov
Sinclair	Passuth	Mora	Hugo	Tolstoi	Mann	Mora	Thury	Hugo	Maupassant
Zola	Mora	Zola	Sholokhov	Berkesi	Balzac	Fekete	Mora	Mora	Moricz

Source: Mrs. Adam Horvath and Istvan Kemeny, "Kik olvasnak es mit?" [Who Reads and What?], *Valosag*, no. 6 (1965).

Table 9.13.   Literary Preferences of Hungarians by Education and Occupation in 1965

| Education | Hungarian Literature | | World Literature | | | | | |
	Classical	Other	Classical	Soviet	Other	Detective; Sex Fiction	Youth Novels	Total
College Degree	8.9	28.0	18.8	5.7	22.9	7.9	7.8	100%
High School Diploma	12.9	25.0	19.2	6.6	17.7	9.9	8.7	100%
Completed Eighth Grade	22.3	21.5	15.5	6.0	9.7	8.2	16.8	100%
Completed Fifth Through Seventh Grade	24.0	24.0	12.0	6.2	6.7	7.3	19.2	100%
Completed First Through Fourth Grade	20.8	28.1	10.9	4.8	5.6	6.3	23.5	100%
Occupation								
Leadership, Intelligentsia	13.2	25.4	17.1	6.0	23.2	7.4	7.7	100%
Professionals (white-collar workers)	16.0	24.3	17.9	5.9	16.1	10.4	9.4	100%
Skilled Laborers	19.1	22.6	15.6	6.6	11.7	9.9	14.5	100%
Unskilled Laborers	18.5	23.4	13.5	8.0	9.8	9.4	17.4	100%
Co-op Farmers	25.2	27.4	9.5	7.2	4.5	5.0	21.2	100%

Source: Mrs. Adam Horvath and Istvan Kemeny, "Kik olvasnak es mit?" [Who Reads and What?], *Valosag*, no. 6 (1965).

the Hungarian socialist system. The Party allowed publication of these works because it decided that they would serve as safety valves for dissent. Current Government policy allows publication of any books that are not politically hostile to the regime; published authors may espouse "ideologically debatable, though humanistic values even if they are more or less in opposition to Marxism and to socialist realism."[34]

Although the publication of new, liberal works has sparked great interest and much debate in intellectual circles, the data presented in this section suggest that the vast majority of the Hungarian public prefers to read older, less controversial works; the most popular writers have been popular for the past 50 years.[35] Controversial contemporary works do seem to affect the behavior and values of the intellectuals who read these works, but the intellectuals make up only a fraction of the populace and they constitute a rather closed society. Therefore, books mildly critical of the Hungarian political system do not pose a real threat to the regime; they do not serve as significant negative socializers because the audience they reach is relatively small.[36]

One corollary of the fact that books have an insignificant dysfunctional effect on the general population is that books also have a limited positive effect

on the inculcation of desirable socialist values. Active public support for the Government, anti-imperialist attitudes, and willing endorsement of Soviet politics are not achieved through books.

Film

The motion picture industry in Hungary is owned and regulated by the Government. Until the 1960s, the Central Committee's Education Department made all decisions concerning both the content and the style of the approximately 20 feature films and 200 documentaries, newsreels, and short features produced each year. The Hungarian Communists have displayed a particularly strong interest in film production since the nationalization of that industry in 1948. Between 1945 and 1948, only one film of any consequence was produced in Hungary. It was entitled *Somewhere in Europe* (1947), and it conveyed a primitive antifascist sentiment, an endorsement of pacifism, and a condemnation of World War II. After the Communist Party seized power, films were used to enumerate the ills of the past and the crimes of the Horthy regime. *The Soil Under Foot* (1949), *Miska the Magnate* (1949), and *The Dress Uniform* (1948–1949) emphasized the snobbery and crimes of the nobility and depicted the peasants' struggle for land. Many insipid films produced in the style of socialist realism were released in the early 1950s, including *The Liberated Earth* (1950), *Full Speed Ahead* (1951), and *Baptism Under Fire* (1951). The life depicted in these films was so far removed from the reality and problems faced by Hungarians under Rakosi that the Party practically had to recruit film audiences. The production of banal films damaged the reputation of Hungarian filmmaking and created a negative attitude in the public toward Hungarian films. In 1952, for example, after seeing the movie, *Life is Enjoyable If You Sing*, a high school class, which had been compelled to see the movie, tore up the seats and assaulted the manager of the theater.

The cultural renaissance of 1954–1956 saw the production of a number of good films, such as *Spring in Budapest, Accident*, and *Professor Hannibal*. These movies called for reforms and advocated humanitarian goals, but the production of films with these themes ended after the failure of the revolution in 1956. The films produced between 1957 and 1960 were uninspired and badly made. Once again the familiar themes condemning the past became the steady diet of movie-goers. The productions of this era included *Sweet Anne* (1955), which depicted the ills of the presocialist era, *Iron Flower* (1957), which showed the oppression of the workers in the 1920s, *Smugglers* (1958), which dealt with the misery of the peasants during the Horthy era, and *The Thirty-ninth Brigade* (1959), a movie about Communist Hungary's historical predecessor, the Soviet Republic of 1919.

During the 1960s, new themes began to appear in movies that concentrated on the problems of contemporary Hungary. The films made in that decade were bolder in content and more experimental in style. The plots and messages were more closely attuned to reality. These films still portrayed themes intended to create support for the system, but they also discussed the shortcomings of the system. The films of younger directors, including Andras Kovacs, Ferenc Kardos, Miklos Jancso, Ferenc Kosa, Pal Sandor, Istvan Gaal, Sandor Sara, and Istvan Csurka, tackled the issues created by the revolution of 1956. Movies like *The Father, Twenty Hours, Yesterday*, and *The Thousand Suns*, criticize the Government's coercion of the people. Movies such as *The Thrown-up Stone, Forbidden Ground, Round-up, The Confrontation*, and *The Red and the White* condemn violence, whether in the service of the cause or for

its own sake. Bureaucratic obstructionism is scored in *Walls, Breakout, Difficult People, Sirokko*, and *Crazy Night*. In *Walls*, for example, an actor questions whether people who choose not to return from a vacation in the West are really defectors.

> What do you mean he defected? There is a certain flow of emigrants from every country of the world. That's quite normal. It's only we who make political refugees out of these unlucky emigrants. . . . In the West, he'll make a lot more (money). If we don't let people take part in public life, if we don't share responsibility with them, they'll feel like strangers in spite of the red-white-and-green phrases. They'll go where they are strangers, but at least they'll earn a lot more.[37]

Government control of the film medium extends to the import of foreign films. Movies depicting the negative features of capitalist societies, such as Antonioni's *Zabriskie Point*, are offered as evidence of the decay of bourgeois democratic states. Political content, however, is not the only determinant of whether a foreign movie can be shown; the Government also considers a film's commercial potential, because Hungary has to pay much-needed hard currency to film producers, including the Soviet Union, for the purchase of non-Magyar films. In spite of these political and economic limitations, Hungarian movie-goers can see a large selection of foreign films. During the week of February 19–25, 1970, for example, 41 foreign films were shown in Budapest. Of these 41 films, 27 originated in the West and only 14 came from Comecon countries.[38] Even more foreign films were shown in the summer of 1973. During the week of July 12–18, 1973, 57 foreign movies played in Budapest. (See Table 9.14.) Thirty-six of these films were produced in non-Communist European states and Japan (11 in the United States, 8 in France, 6 in the United Kingdom, 5 in Italy, and 6 in four other countries); only 21 films were imported from Communist states (the largest number—8—came from the USSR).

Attendance at foreign films is very uneven. Soviet films and productions from other socialist countries generally do not attract large audiences whereas even second-rate American movies draw huge crowds.[39] This preference for Western European and American productions is an urban phenomenon related to the number of choices open to city residents, whose movie-going habits reflect their artistic

Table 9.14.   Foreign Films Shown in Budapest, July 12–18, 1973

Origin of Film	Title°	Origin of Film	Title°
East Germany	Girl on the Team		
	Osceola	France	The Big Man
	Goya	(continued)	A Man Whom I Love
	Sons of the Great Bear	Italy	The Compromiser
	In the Tracks of the Falcon		Sabata Is Here
	The Killer of the Wilderness		The Tiger
Czechoslovakia	Oasis		All My Songs Are Yours
	Wedding Without a Ring		Indifference
	Morgiana, the Blue-Eyed Cat	Denmark	Olsen's Gang
Poland	Everything for Sale	Switzerland	Carmen
Soviet Union	Daring	Japan	The Banished Samurai
	Andrej Rubliov		The Devil's Inn
	In the Captivity of the Sultan	United Kingdom	Valerie
	The Curious License Plate		Mary, Queen of Scots
	The Knights of Success		Anne of a Thousand Days
	An Old Robber Is Not an		The Last Valley
	Ancient Robber		A Hard Day's Night
	Day of Vengeance		The Private Life of Sherlock
	Koma's Adventures		Holmes
Yugoslavia	The Firing Line	United States	The Last Picture Show
Rumania	The Sea Wolf		West Side Story
Bulgaria	The Last Gangster		The Andromeda Strain
West Germany	The Secret of the Silver Lake		Mackenna's Gold
	The Magician		Divorce American Style
France	The Great Catch		Goldenhead
	Modern Monte Cristo		Take the Money and Run
	The Spinster		The Phantom of the Opera
	The Pirate's Fiancee		Funny Girl
	The Cop and Those Ladies		Hello, Dolly
	Seemingly Without a Motive		Cold Turkey

°The titles of some of these films have been translated literally from the Hungarian because the original titles were not available.

Source: Nepszabadsag, July 11, 1973, p. 11.

and political preferences. The high attendance at Soviet and other Communist films in the villages results from a lack of such choices; few non-Communist films reach village theaters, and rural residents will go see *any* film to break the routine of village life. However, in spite of the regime's efforts to channel a great number of Soviet films to the villages, a strong anti-Soviet feeling prevails among the rural population and affects the response of the movie-going audience.[40]

The films shown in Hungary are viewed by the Party as effective instruments of political socialization, but the Party's efforts to guide public opinion toward support of the system through the utiliza-

tion of this medium have met with limited success.[41] Movie-goers in Hungary prefer either to ignore the political message or to see films with no political implications. The Party meets with resistance because most people who go to the movies are seeking entertainment, not political education.[42]

Theater

Theater is a much more selective medium of political socialization than film because theater productions reach considerably fewer people than movies; nevertheless theater can serve a very powerful political socialization function. Unlike the Horthy regime and the Dual Monarchy, the Hungarian Communist regime has encouraged workers and peasants to attend theatrical performances. Since 1946, the state has subsidized legitimate theater, and ticket prices have been within everyone's reach. Today, even the National Theater charges only 13 to 28 forints per performance. Furthermore, in factories and state offices, trade union representatives (audience organizers) distribute cut-rate tickets to the workers and offer free theater tickets as rewards for superior work or as inducements for workers to see a particular play.

Between 1949 and 1956, Hungarian theatrical productions adhered to the style and content of Soviet theater. Socialist realism dominated all plays. Bad, unimaginative Hungarian and Soviet plays composed the major portion of Hungarian theatrical offerings, and the population was pressured to attend. However, theater became important as a negative socializer in the two years preceding the revolution of 1956. Plays such as Laszlo Nemeth's *Galileo*, and Erno Urban's *Justice for Gaspar Varro* and *The Pickle Tree*, attacked the dictatorship of Rakosi in scathing terms. These plays represented the first free efforts of Hungarian dramatic writers since the mobilization of society had begun in 1948. For several years after the revolution, very few good plays by Hungarian authors were produced. It was not until the middle of the 1960s that first-rate Hungarian dramas again appeared on the stage. At the present time, the regime encourages the production of plays that are somewhat controversial, such as Istvan Orkeny's *The Toth Family*, which criticizes the arbitrary use of power. The Party sees these plays as intellectual safety valves for the release of discontentment.

The most popular of these dramatic "safety valves" are the productions of the Comedy Theater (*Vidam Szinpad*) and the Microscope (*Mikroszkop*); both groups specialize in political satire. During the 1972–73 theater season, their productions most critical of the politics of the regime were *Little Gate* of the Comedy Theater and *Clear Water into the Brain* of the Microscope. Perhaps the most popular and enjoyable production of the latter group was the 1969 offering of *Gentlemen and Comrades*. One example of the criticism allowed to appear in the show was a monologue in which the popular comedian Laszlo Kabos, declared: "Well, my wife always says, 'don't you worry, my boy, as long as Kadar is at his desk, everything is all right . . .' Well, I agree, but I would

like to find out where Kadar was on August 21, 1968" (the day of the invasion of Czechoslovakia). Other examples of political humor can also be found in the monologues of Geza Hofi, the excellent humorist of the Microscope, who takes frequent and well-prepared potshots at the most flagrant abuses of the system.

Although all major towns have at least one professional stage company, a preponderance of Hungary's legitimate theater groups perform in the capital, where they produce a very large number of plays each year. Table 9.15 lists the 55 plays presented in Budapest theaters during the 1969–1970 season; the offerings included works by only two modern Russian playwrights, and not one example of socialist realism was produced that season. Excellent performances at the Puppet Theater, satirical reviews, and the circus round out the fare of Budapest theater-goers. In addition to the shows mounted at major theaters, there are amateur theater productions in district houses of culture (found in all cities and villages) and in factories, and many Budapest repertory theaters send traveling companies to small towns and villages that do not have a permanent, professional theater group of their own.

The variety of plays produced in Hungary is astounding, and because tickets are cheap, productions are accessible to a cross-section of the population. Nevertheless, the Government does not consider this medium an essential means of political socialization. Only 25 percent of the plays produced in 1969 were written by contemporary writers, and only slightly more than 10 percent contained political messages. The regime mainly controls the escape-valve shows, clearly indicating tolerable limits and carefully supervising productions. The government has evidently accepted the fact that people go to the theater for cultural enrichment and entertainment.

Music

The Hungarian Communist Party has used music as an instrument of political socialization ever since the liberation of the country in 1945. It made its first direct attempt to inculcate new values in a reluctant citizenry through music in June 1946. With the aid of several able assistants, Andras Mihaly, head of the Cultural Affairs Department of the Hungarian Communist Party, developed a plan

Table 9.15.   Theatrical Productions in Budapest During the 1969–1970 Season

Author	Title	Author	Title
Chekhov	*Uncle Vanya*	Katona	*Bank Ban*
Fejes	*Good Evening Summer, Good Evening Love*	Goda	*The Man of the Planet*
		Moricz	*Be Good to the End*
Feydeau	*Flea in the Grass*	Weores	*The Rower from the Moon*
O'Neill	*The Iceman Cometh*	Shakespeare	*The Merchant of Venice*
Maugham	*Theater*	Hochhuth	*Soldiers*
Shakespeare	*Othello*	Frisch	*Biography*
Thurzo	*How Long Can One Be an Angel?*	Rozov	*On the Racetrack*
		Durrenmatt-	
Andras	*Naked Brain*	Shakespeare	*King John*
Albee	*A Delicate Balance*	Radoev	*Romeo, Juliette, and the Benzin*
Molnar	*Lilion*		
Shaw	*The House of Broken Hearts*	Galambos	*The Student*
Ibsen	*Solness the Builder*	Torin	*The Bill*
Kovasznai	*Blue-Haired Women*	Fo	*The Archangels Do Not Play Flipper*
Simon	*Plaza Suite*		
Bernstein	*West Side Story*	Wicherley	*A Wife from the Country*
Vujicsics-Kardos-Brand	*Luxembourg 14-55*	Plautus-Santelli	*The Ghost*
		Goldoni	*Servant of Two Gentlemen*
Fall	*Pompadour*	Gavault-Charvay	*Something Always Happens*
Johann Strauss	*One Night in Venice*	Christie	*Murder in the Park*
Lehar	*The Land of Smiles*	Illyes	*The Loss of Eden*
Loewe	*My Fair Lady*	Dery	*To Face the Truth*
Schiller	*Intrigue and Love*		*Travel in Buronia*
Karinthy	*Dreams of Budapest*	Weiss	*The Zero-Death Gentlemen*
Lorca	*The Love of Donna Rosita*	Zoltan	*Oratorio from the Underworld*
Szomory	*Mink*	Anouilh	*Medea*
Tennesee Williams	*Rose Tattoo*	Giraudoux	*The Apollo of Bellac*
		Veszi	*Fire in the Bukk*
Shakespeare	*Timon of Athens*	Szuts	*They Reared a Dove in Their Heart*
Urban	*Saint or Madmen?*		
Chekhov	*Ivanov*		

to enlist music with "new content" in the service of the cause. The Party first infiltrated the Association of the Friends of Children (*Gyermekbaratok Szovetsege*), the largest single Social Democratic youth group. It detailed Mrs. Zoltan Rev to serve with the Association, and under her direction, Istvan Raics wrote a new anthem for the children to a tune by Zoltan Kodaly; Raics' lyrics depict a positive view of the future. After the final Communist takeover in 1949, the anthem became the official song of the Young Pioneers:

> The Pioneer Youth
> Looks to a better future;
> It fights for a nicer world
> And it is willing to die for it.

The Party repeated this procedure of using music for the purposes of socialization when it commissioned a new march that some thought would eventually replace the "reactionary" National Anthem (it never did). This time, an important official of the Communist Party's Department of Cultural Affairs, Endre Szekely, asked Raics to produce a "Song of the Republic" aimed at popularizing the new form of government. The song, whose tune had originally been written by Etienne Mehul, an 18th century French composer, contrasted a negative image of the past with the bright present:

> Exploitation, servants' fate
> Was the rule in this country for a thousand years.
> The best part of the people suffered.

The state belonged to the lazy,
While the people carried the brunt of the burden.
He who gazes into the past can only see wounds,
Only blood, pain and tears.
The Republic calls us today to work and fight;
It gives a new meaning to our lives.
The lips of millions sound it hopefully:
Long Live the Republic!

The Communists also utilized music to foster pro-Soviet attitudes. Hungarians learned to sing both Russian folk songs and new Soviet songs that detailed the great accomplishments of the Soviet Union, heaped praises on Stalin, and emphasized the beauty of the Soviet countryside. In late 1949, the Party ordered the creation of the Hungarian-Soviet Friendship Society, whose tasks included organizing youth and adult choirs to acquaint the population with Soviet music. The choirs dressed in Russian *rubashkas*, and their repertoires contained such songs as "We Sing for Comrade Stalin," "From Countryside to Countryside," "Our Strength is in the Righteousness of the Cause," and "My Capital, Moscow," as well as old-time favorites such as "Katiusha," "Poliushka," and the Ukranian folk song, "Bandura." Another means of injecting pro-Soviet attitudes via music was the popular *chastushka* singing at factory or office cultural events. The Party adopted *chastushka* singing from the Soviet tradition in which satirical verses are set to popular tunes. The content of the Hungarian verses was nearly always political.

Still another method of popularizing Soviet culture was to sponsor performances of Soviet musical groups including the Georgian State Ensemble, the Moiseiev Ballet, the Alexandrov Ensemble, the Red Army Chorus, and the Piatnitskii and Beriozka Ensembles. Although the performances of these groups were well attended, Soviet music and Russian songs never became accepted as integral parts of Hungarian culture; the population was unwilling to learn to appreciate the new marching music or the songs praising Stalin.

Since 1957, the Government has abandoned the policy of using music to inculcate pro-Soviet attitudes in the citizenry, although some popular songs still convey political messages.[43] Hungarian composers who wish to have their works performed no longer have to write music praising Soviet society in the style of socialist realism. They may now compose works formulated according to contemporary musical aesthetics. Two of the best new works performed during the 1970–1971 season were Kalman Szokolyai's opera score for Federico Garcia Lorca's *Blood Wedding* and Emil Petrovics's *Crime and Punishment*; both are thoroughly modern, stylistically complex works. Most importantly, however, citizens no longer have to put up with the constant blare of thousands of loud speakers broadcasting marches and patriotic songs *ad nauseum*. Although the Kadar regime still uses music to encourage patriotism and to develop a sense of national identity among the citizenry, it no longer uses the medium extensively as a means of political socialization.

Themes of Political Socialization

Communist programs of political socialization seek to create a new man, a man of a special mold, as Stalin put it. This new Communist man is supposed to subordinate his own fortune and fate to the achievement of the socialist ideal. He is supposed to be an active person, a thoroughly honest and determined leader, a disciplined follower, and a conscious supporter of the class struggle and the revolutionary movement everywhere. He must be unprejudiced and love his fellow man regardless of race, religion, or nationality. In addition, the ideal Communist is expected to be an internationalist willing to work for the creation of a world community of Communist societies.

Communist regimes attempt to inculcate socialist values in both adults and youth through the processes of political socialization. In its campaign to reorient the values of its citizenry, the present Hungarian Communist regime relies on the following four positive and four negative themes of political socialization:

Achievements in the building of socialism	The menace of imperialism
Socialist morality	Antinationalism
Patriotism	Anti-individualism
Love for the socialist commonwealth	The negative impact of the cult of personality

The Government glorifies the progress of socialist construction through nearly all agencies of socialization and all media of political communication.

The Party, the KISz groups, and the schools constantly emphasize the importance of building socialism. Outstanding workers, youth groups that help with the construction of factories, and soldiers who serve by building roads all receive awards through the factories or the various trade unions. Radio, television, and newspapers continuously discuss the operation of new factories or the development of new production techniques and advertise the regime's successes in the economic realm. Many writers use the positive contributions people make to the building of socialism as thematic material for films and plays.

Those agencies that are under direct Party control bear the responsibility for inculcating socialist morality in both children and adults. Local Party organs, KISz groups, and trade unions harp on the subject of creating an upright, honest society in seminars and lectures designed to persuade people to accept a somewhat puritanical set of values. Vulgar language may not appear in print. The publication and sale of pornography is prohibited by law and houses of prostitution are also illegal. Books, newspapers, plays, and movies portray dishonesty and immorality as the remains of a bourgeois past expected to die out with the establishment of socialist society.

All formal agents of socialization try to instill socialist patriotism in children and adults alike through a variety of means, including a large number of patriotic books and historical novels; the comic strips in some of the newspapers; films based on historical events; and frequent television coverage of events and socialist accomplishments that are distinctly Hungarian. Because it excludes chauvinism and includes solidarity with the working classes of the world, "socialist patriotism" supposedly differs from "nationalism." In reality, the Government's efforts to inculcate this value merely reinforce a fierce Hungarian nationalism.

Newscasts and daily papers promote the idea of a socialist commonwealth through frequent mention of the common goals of all socialist countries. In addition, trade unions and youth groups sponsor inexpensive trips to socialist countries in an effort to develop greater understanding among the feuding nationalities in Eastern Europe. Furthermore, each year, foreign trade fairs and exhibitions bring the products of other socialist countries to Hungary, and movie theaters and television programs feature shorts about the accomplishments of the "fraternal states."

Party organs and trade unions constantly warn the citizenry that imperialism threatens the very existence of Hungary and the socialist commonwealth. Curricular materials, posters, radio, television, theater, and movies, as well as public lectures emphasize this theme. Soviet allies—the Arabs for example—are portrayed as peace-loving people, whereas enemies—including the Israelis—are depicted as lackeys in the pay of the United States. American activities are labeled imperialistic in all media; United States intervention in the Dominican Republic and in South Vietnam was publicized in television programs, newspapers, and film shorts.

Another major negative theme in the political socialization program is antinationalism.[44] Nationalist sloganeering or abuse of another socialist nation (such as Rumania) carry a 1,000-forint fine. National symbols cannot be displayed without Communist symbols. The Hungarian flag is always flown with a red flag, and a red star has been incorporated into the national seal. Newspapers and television broadcasts condemn the strong nationalism of certain segments of the population as a remnant of capitalism. Nationalism, of course, also implies an anti-Soviet viewpoint, and the Government has placed tremendous emphasis on the inculcation of pro-Soviet attitudes.

Individualism is a favorite target of the regime's political socialization program. The Party, the youth organizations, and the trade unions regard nonconformity, especially among young people, as a most unhealthy manifestation of antisocialist attitudes. The Government admonishes individualists for "aping the West;" long hair and hip clothing are considered symptoms of the influence of American decadence. The mass media even deride listening to rock music as a harmful activity. The evils of placing individual interests above community goals is a familiar theme in books and theater as well as in frequent lectures and seminars organized by the KISz to inculcate anti-individualist values in Hungarian youth.

Finally, the negative impact of the cult of personality and of the dictatorship of Matyas Rakosi is the theme of political socialization that has created the greatest number of problems for the Government. Since the revolutionary legitimacy of the Kadar regime is based partially on its claim to have deposed the former tyrant, the regime must allow criticism of Rakosi and blame the failures of the past on his mistakes. In Party and KISz seminars as well as in the schools, instructors emphasize the mistakes of

Rakosi and contrast his defective leadership with the enlightened leadership of the present Party elite. The fact, however, that the dictatorial methods of a tyrant are criticized makes it easy for some people to attack Kadar or the Soviet leadership through oblique criticism of the rule of the deceased Rakosi.

Evaluation of the Political Socialization Program

Our analysis of the political socialization program implemented by the Hungarian Communist regime shows that the Government places great emphasis on inculcating a new system of values in the citizenry and that it maintains strict control over the agencies capable of instilling dysfunctional ideas in the people. The success of the regime can be gauged most clearly from an examination of the degree to which its messages have been internalized by the population as a whole. In the absence of empirical data, it is impossible to calibrate the political socialization of the citizenry, but it is possible to discern, in general terms, the influence of the three most important themes of political socialization and to determine the dominant political values of the population.

In its campaign to inculcate in the citizenry acceptance of and support for a socialist system, the Party has given top priority to disseminating information about the victories achieved in the building of socialism. This element of its political socialization program has produced some positive results. Despite two antiregime youth demonstrations in March 1971, today in Hungary there seems to be little dysfunctional activity; the system-maintenance functions of the regime are not deliberately obstructed by the citizenry as a whole.

However, even though dysfunctional activities are not in evidence, few people take the idea of building socialism seriously; they are more interested in increasing their own nest eggs than in assuring the construction of a socialist society. Since the initiation of the reform era, the regime has indeed encouraged enrichissez-vous attitudes in the citizenry, but the selfish attitudes of the vast majority of citizens and their lack of commitment to socialism remain persistent problems for the leadership.

The theme of anti-imperialism is the second most-repeated message of political socialization. There is no doubt that the regime has been successful in inculcating a condemnation of various aspects of American policy in the people of Hungary. The military activities of the United States in Southeast Asia, Lebanon, and the Dominican Republic as well as the large number of American bases in Europe serve as clear examples of the "menace of imperialism." However, even though the regime has been reasonably successful in convincing the Hungarian citizenry of a potential U.S. threat, it has not succeeded in inculcating the attendant pro-Soviet values. On the contrary, in the era of detente, Hungarians tended to view both the United States and the Soviet Union as aggressive, superpowers whose foreign policies were a direct result of their relative military strength.

The regime's attempts to create a highly moral socialist society have been notably unsuccessful. In spite of the constant repetition of themes designed to create a new morality, Hungarian society is not the most upright in the world. For instance, such scandals as the notorious "Onodi affair" provide bad examples for most of the citizenry and infuriate Kadar and the more puritanical leaders of the Party. Many Hungarians in a less powerful position than Onodi also resort to corruption and bribery, thievery, moonlighting, semilegal maneuvering, and other types of dishonesty to supplement their incomes. The drive for a higher standard of living, for cars, and for apartments has contributed to the development of cynical attitudes about honesty. In their struggle for material benefits, a significant percentage of the population, especially in the capital, is willing to condone opportunism and excuse corruption. This weakening of personal moral standards has resulted in a decrease in social stability. Hungary has one of the highest rates of suicide[45] and divorce[46] in the world, and until new restrictive legislation was passed in 1974, it had one of the highest legal abortion rates in the world.[47] In addition, alcoholism and illegal prostitution remain serious problems in Hungary today. In fact, illegal prostitution had become such a problem that in 1972 the regime was forced to crack down on the most notorious prostitution ring, whose members made nearly a million forints yearly and possessed hard currency, gold, and foreign bank accounts, all of which are prohibited by law.[48] Thus, we may conclude that purposive political socialization has not yet succeeded in instilling the ideals of a socialist morality in the majority of the Hungarian population.

The regime also has encountered problems with the political socialization of today's youth. In general, the political education received by the youth through all the formal agencies of political socialization has left the majority of the young people with a large vocabulary of ideological justification but no real belief in anything except survival and personal advancement. Some estimates place 85 percent of the young people between ages 16 and 28 in this category.[49] In Hungary, there now exists what Ferenc Santa called a "consolidated generation," which does not understand the hardships that existed prior to World War II or the terror of Stalinism in Hungary; therefore, comparisons with the past that place the Kadar regime in a favorable light do not make a deep impression on most of Hungary's young people. They are present-oriented when compared to the older generations whose beliefs are oriented either toward the past or the future. The vast majority of today's youth have learned not to be concerned about ideology. With the exception of a few youngsters influenced by Mao and Che Guevara,[50] the present generation of young people do not want to change the socialist system. On the other hand, they only support the regime to reap the material benefits of the system. They regard the leadership as alienated from the majority of the population and have little real respect for the Party elite, most of whom they label as bureaucratic hacks. The positive and negative themes of political socialization that the regime has attempted to inculcate in the youth have been internalized as tools of communication rather than as deep beliefs and accepted values. Nonetheless, the youth are "quite loyal, rather than opportunistic. The only problem is that there can be nothing gained from this loyalty because it is based on the soil of indifference, of apathy and of [a desire to] live in privacy."[51]

Summary

In Hungary and other socialist states the Communist Party utilizes the media as instruments of political communication to transmit desired messages and inculcate socialist values in the population. The media through which this transmission takes place are radio, television, newspapers, journals, books, film, theater, and music. As the monopolist of power, the regime is free to transmit any message desired by the Party. All media present the eight major themes depicting the values the regime is most anxious to inculcate in the citizenry. Although these themes are most noticeable in television broadcasts, they are also communicated through the other media. These themes are the building of socialism, alliance with other nations of the socialist commonwealth, socialist morality, socialist patriotism, anti-imperialism, antinationalism, anti-individualism, and anti-Stalinism. The frequency with which each theme is repeated in relation to the total number of messages depends on the time frame of one's observation. Since the introduction of the reform era in the 1960s, the most-repeated messages have been the necessity of building socialism, the desirability of alliance with the Soviet Union and other members of the socialist bloc, and the importance of socialist patriotism.

The successes and failures of the regime are difficult to evaluate. There can be little doubt that the regime has been successful in instilling values in the citizenry that are different from those possessed by American and Western European societies. Some of these values are peculiarly collectivistic, others are clearly Hungarian with a thin veneer of socialism added as a disguise. The regime has achieved its greatest success in inculcating an acceptance of the system in the citizenry. Hungarians have even been convinced to grant the Kadar regime a measure of legitimacy. The failures of the regime are largely connected with its inability to improve human nature and to create a new, honest, hardworking, community-oriented, positive hero—the much-desired socialist man. The failure of the regime in this respect, however, is due not only to the faulty activities of the Party, but also to the failure of human nature, that is, the imperfection of man himself.

10

The Distribution
and Problems of Welfare

Since a major premise of Communist ideology is that the state should take care of the basic needs of all citizens, the provision of medical care, education, housing, and various other social services is a fundamental part of all Communist social welfare programs. In addition, the equitable distribution of welfare and a continuous improvement in the standard of living are key objectives of most Communist regimes. The legitimacy of the present Hungarian regime depends on the Government's ability to supply the population with goods and social services that were not available to nearly 70 percent of the citizenry before the Communists came to power. In fact, the very survival of the Kadar regime depends, in part, on the leadership's ability to both satisfy the demands of the population and raise the general standard of living through an equitable redistribution of the national wealth.

Contemporary political scientists define welfare as the "allocation of goods, services, honor, status, and opportunities of various kinds from the political system to individuals and groups in society."[1] The distributive capability and beneficiaries of a system are determined by the decision-making elite, which allocates goods and services in accordance with its own values and goals. Our examination of the allocation of welfare in Hungary will include a brief discussion of the background of current problems, a survey of the types of welfare provided, a description of the present standard of living, and an analysis of the impact of recent economic reforms.

Origins of Existing Welfare Problems

In 1945, a progressive democratic coalition, whose main goal was social reform, replaced the bankrupt social and economic system of the Horthy regime, which had failed to provide adequate benefits to the vast majority of the citizenry. Prior to the democratic revolution of 1945, Hungary still had a semifeudal social and economic structure. The vast Hungarian peasant population was for the most part barely literate and lived in rural isolation, alienated from urban ways and suspicious of any attempts to impose modernization on its primitive life style.

Since industrialization was not a priority of either the Dual Monarchy or the Horthy regime, Hungarian industry had developed slowly and haphazardly prior to World War II. During the first 50 years of the twentieth century, only 13.7 percent of the peasants left agriculture to make their living from industrial production.[2] Society was rigidly stratified, and there was a clear distinction between rich and poor. An outmoded aristocracy retained eighteenth century privileges while few economic benefits accrued to workers, poor peasants and the semiskilled office employees who made up the vast bureaucracy of the state. Although education was supposed to be free, few workers or peasants could send their children to school beyond the sixth grade. Medical care was extremely poor, and tuberculosis took a deadly toll. The lack of widespread medical and social services demoralized the citizenry.

Between 1945 and 1949, a number of changes were made in the system of welfare distribution. The platforms of all progressive parties active during this period called for basic reforms in the economy and the social welfare system. On March 15, 1945, the coalition government promulgated a land-reform law providing for the division of large estates and the distribution of former property of landowners among the peasants; the government also extended basic welfare benefits to workers hitherto not covered by social insurance, guaranteed a free education to all citizens, and established the present system of public schools.

The Communist Party's slow consolidation of power was accompanied by various reforms in the system of production and distribution of goods and services. Under Communist tutelage, the coalition government enacted legislation to expand medical and educational benefits; build day-care centers and hospitals; lower the prices of tickets to theatrical performances and other cultural events; and renovate the most notorious slum buildings. One aim of the Communists in sponsoring these reforms was to increase popular support for the Party, which was preparing to expel its partners from the coalition government. When the Communist Party finally assumed exclusive control in 1949, however, the rudimentary social reforms implemented by the postwar coalition government had only slightly mitigated the inequities inherited from the Horthy regime.

Between 1949 and 1956, the Government continued to expand the country's social welfare programs, but it failed to alleviate many of the inequities of the prewar era. In reality, the Party merely replaced the rule of one stratum of the population with the dictatorship of another, turning the society upside down. The Rakosi regime combined revolutionary rhetoric, which proclaimed the supremacy of the workers, with the primitive accumulation of capital by a state capitalist system. The desire of the leadership to modernize the country resulted in policies that were every bit as oppressive as those of any nineteenth century industrial state. The work week was extended, "socialist overtime" (forced unpaid work) was mandatory, production quotas were continually raised, and working conditions were frequently atrocious. Furthermore, under Rakosi, some of the negative features of the distributive functions of the Horthy era (e.g., the unequal distribution of goods and services, and the bestowal of extraordinary benefits on the elite) were retained and the standard of living stagnated or declined. The leadership, which became isolated from the population, jealously guarded its power and privileges. Before the revolution of 1956, the Communist ruling elite enjoyed educational, medical, and economic advantages that were not available to the citizenry. In 1955 and 1956, most Hungarians became aware of the fact that workers, peasants, the bourgeoisie, and small bureaucrats were paying for the pleasures of the leadership. Demands for an end to the most blatant abuses of power and a more equitable distribution of welfare were significant causes of the revolution.

The regime that came to power after the revolt was saddled with the task of reorganizing the country in such a way that Government could satisfactorily take care of the basic needs of the citizenry. The adequate distribution of welfare became a primary goal of the Party in its drive to correct the mistakes resulting from the cult of personality.

The Distribution of Welfare

Medicine.   Health services in Hungary are, for the most part, free and widely available.[3] Membership in any trade union entitles citizens and their dependents to free medical care which includes sick leave, hospitalization, maternity benefits, surgical care, out-patient treatment, dental care, x-rays, and laboratory work. Drugs, eyeglasses, and medical supplies are available at minimal, state-supported prices. In the 1960s, medical insurance was also extended to members of the agricultural producers' cooperatives, who, however, had to pay six forints per month for this coverage. Today, everyone in Hungary except those privately employed or self-employed are entitled to free medical care.

Even though health services are basically free, there are some hidden costs of medical care in Hungary. Doctors who visit patients at home, surgeons, nurses, x-ray technicians, and orderlies in hospitals all receive tips, or honoraria, for their services. These fees for doctors depend on the type of service rendered and range from 30 forints per home visit to 2,000 forints or more for complicated surgery. Hospital patients give nurses and orderlies small tokens that usually amount to 10 or 20 forints daily per patient. In the villages, doctors frequently reap other benefits as well. For example, a doctor who practices in a village of 4,000 people reported that he receives all his eggs, poultry, vegetables, meat, and dairy products from his patients. Payment of these hidden fees, however, is regarded as a courtesy; these costs do not prevent people from seeking medical care because it is customary for people living on a low income or experiencing extreme financial difficulties to pay little or nothing to the physician.

Medical services are organized under the direction of the Ministry of Health. The state accepts responsibility for training medical personnel and for operating all medical facilities; it also owns and controls the drug industry. The medical system includes 130 hospitals, 4 medical colleges, neighborhood outpatient clinics, district and town polyclinics, as well as rest homes, facilities at various hot springs, and a well-developed pharmaceutical industry.

There are 25.1 doctors in Hungary for every 10,000 patients; 30.6 percent of the physicians are family doctors, the remaining 69.4 percent are specialists. The family doctor is the most important component of the Hungarian medical system. Each family doctor is responsible for providing general health care for the approximately 2,500–3,000 people who live in the neighborhood where he himself usually resides.[4] He sees patients in a small clinic, makes house calls on a regular basis to bedfast patients, refers patients who need special treatment to polyclinics and hospitals, arranges consultations, and serves as the major contact of the people with the medical profession. The family physician is also responsible for placing a patient on sick leave so that

he or she may be legally absent from work, and for checking on absenteeism, which is a serious problem in Hungarian industry. Finally, the family doctor cares for the aged in the neighborhood, assigning them to a geriatric nursing home when necessary.

Every small town and each district in the cities has one or more polyclinics—out-patient medical centers—administered by local, district, or village councils. These clinics provide services to ambulatory patients in need of specialized treatment not available through the neighborhood doctor. The staff of most of these facilities include eye, ear, nose, and throat specialists; ophthalmologists; cardiologists; urologists; gynecologists; dentists; pediatricians; internists; and surgeons.

Hospital services are provided for patients who cannot be adequately cared for at the polyclinics, but overcrowding in these facilities has become a very serious problem. In Budapest, for example, no new hospitals have been built since 1945, but the population of the capital has more than doubled since then, and the new system of free, universal medical care brings in tremendous numbers of patients who did not previously seek medical care because they could not afford it. In spite of the crowding, the care provided in Hungarian hospitals is generally adequate, although many of the facilities are extremely old and shabby, and waiting periods for admission can be very lengthy. Conspicuously absent from these hospitals is the sophisticated, modern equipment (e.g., kidney dilation and cardiac intensive-care units) widely used in hospitals in more-advanced countries. Most facilities lack a whole spectrum of basic, modern hospital equipment, and the multitude of drugs and devices that increase the safety and comfort of American patients are unknown to Hungarians. Much of Hungary's hospital equipment dates back to the early decades of this century, when some of the hospitals were built. In at least one Budapest hospital, there are only two toilets per 34 to 40 patients; in this same hospital, only one shower is available for each group of about 40 women. Patients are expected to provide their own towels, plates, cups, and silverware, and to tip all members of the hospital staff with whom they come in contact, from department heads to orderlies. In addition, the patient's family must bring some food to supplement the very basic diet provided by the hospital. Nurses are very scarce and, for the most part, badly trained. Family members or other patients help care for extremely ill, bed-ridden people. Mortality rates, however, are low, and the minimal hospital-care needs of the population seem to be reasonably well taken care of.

Industrial health services also constitute part of the national medical program. In 1975, 72 percent of all workers in the construction, and mining industries had a factory doctor available to them. Factory health services consist of first aid stations, sick rooms, accident treatment stations, and rescue services. Present regulations stipulate that one full-time doctor must be employed for every 2,000 workers. Doctors employed in the industrial health program are responsible for general health care, as well as for enforcing industrial hygiene and preventing industrial injuries.

Sick leave is available to all workers whose disabilities are certified by a doctor. Leave with full pay is guaranteed to all employees for up to six months, and 75 percent of the monthy salary is paid to anyone who is ill or disabled for six months to two years. People who are sick or disabled for two years to life, and patients who are unable to work as a result of negligence on the part of the factory are entitled to 66 percent of their full salaries. In cases of negligence on the part of the worker resulting in permanent disability, 50 percent of the full pay at the time of the accident is guaranteed for the lifetime of the worker.

Maternity benefits are another component of the state medical program. No expectant mother can be employed in potentially harmful physical labor after her sixth month of pregnancy, and pregnant women are entitled to 20 weeks of sick leave with full pay. Four weeks of this leave may be taken before delivery and 16 weeks after the birth of the child. For two months after the expiration of the paid leave, the place of employment must give the mother an hour off per day to feed her child, and for three months thereafter, a half hour per day for the same purpose. If the child is sick and there is no one to care for it, the mother must be given sick leave.

Mothers also get pregnancy and postpartum allowances from the state, maternity grants from their trade unions, and even free baby clothes. Furthermore, if a new mother prefers to remain at home to care for her child, she is entitled to unpaid leave from her job for up to three years after delivery, during which time the state pays 800 forints per month for the first child, 900 forints for the second, and 1,000 forints for every additional child, to replace lost income. As a result of these provisions, Hungary's lagging birthrate, which during the 1960s was among the lowest in the world, has begun to increase.

The regime has encountered serious difficulties in providing such extensive health care to the entire population. Since medical care is free to all but the 2 percent of Hungarians who are self- or privately employed, people seek professional advice for a multitude of ills (major and minor) that went untreated during the era in which the people had to pay for medical services. Hungarian medical facilities are therefore overcrowded and their staffs are overworked. Even though Hungary has 25.1 physicians per 10,000 people, there still are not enough doctors to meet the needs of the citizenry. Estimates based on the size of each doctor's minimal case load indicate that polyclinic doctors can spend six minutes or less with each patient, and neighborhood doctors, with patient loads over 2,000, have even less time to spend with each person seeking care. In addition, physicians do not have access to modern equipment or sophisticated diagnostic aids, and many of the new drugs developed in multi-million dollar research projects in Western European countries and the U.S. are not available to the Hungarian population because of a lack of hard currency. Although Hungary's drug industry is well respected, the Government does not have tremendous financial resources to pour into medical research. The shabby, badly equipped hospitals with a woefully inadequate number of hospital beds (e.g., 84,818 beds for more than 10 million people) further complicate the problem of providing adequate care.

Education.   Free education through high school is available to all Hungarians, and competent students are eligible to apply for virtually free university training. In addition, adults who did not complete high school or people who simply wish to pursue some type of training may take advantage of a number of high school programs, correspondence courses, and factory training programs. Education in Hungary is compulsory between the ages of six and sixteen. According to the statutes, "The first eight years are to be spent in general school on the completion of which the pupils who do not go to secondary schools [must] continue their studies in trade schools, and become skilled workers, or attend day classes in continuation schools."[5] Those wishing to continue their studies beyond the first eight years can either enroll in technical-vocational schools (*technikums*) or in general secondary schools (*gymnasiums*). Students in the *technikums* receive intensive training in one particular technical subject, such as architecture or engineering, in addition to a general education. Graduates of these schools are qualified paraprofessionals in their chosen field, who may choose to apply for further professional training at a university. Graduates of the four-year *gymnasiums* have received a general education aimed at preparing them for the university. Fifty-nine percent of Hungary's young people study in *gymnasiums*; 19 percent attend *technikums*; and 22 percent attend trade schools in lieu of formal secondary institutions.[6]

Upon completion of high school, qualified students may apply for admission to colleges and universities. In the 1966–1967 academic year, there were 52,300 students studying at the 91 institutions of higher learning in Hungary. In that same year, 17,400 students, or nearly 35 percent of the graduating class of the *gymnasiums*, were admitted to the universities. It must be borne in mind, however, that only 4.3 percent of all those in the 18–25 age group attend institutions of higher learning.

Although elementary and secondary education is free, colleges and universities charge a tuition ranging from 100 to 500 forints per semester. University students having superior grades or facing financial difficulties are eligible for scholarships of between 100 and 1,250 forints per month; they may also qualify for "social aid" totaling as much as 500 forints per month.[7] The free or extremely cheap meals provided in college cafeterias are another form of aid to those enrolled in university courses. Students who do not reside in the vicinity of the institution they are attending may stay in one of Hungary's 142 university

dormitories; the state also operates 288 youth hostels for nonlocal secondary students.

In theory, all Hungarians have equal access to educational opportunities, but certain dysfunctions occur in the actual operation of the system. There is a strong correlation between educational opportunities and social stratum: a disproportionate number of students enrolled in institutions of higher learning come from highly educated, professional and white-collar families.[8] In 1967 and 1968, for example, 57 percent of all students attending Hungarian universities were children of white-collar workers and professionals, whereas these groups constituted only 23 percent of the population.[9] Inequities even exist in the type of education obtained by high school students: the children of workers and peasants do not receive as solid a secondary education as the children of professional and white-collar workers.[10] Table 10.1, which analyzes the composition of the student population of Hungarian high schools and universities according to the occupation of the students' parents, shows what a pronounced advantage professional families have in the educational system. The data in Table 10.2 confirm the overwhelming importance of family background in determining who receives a higher education.[11] These data also indicate that students select a direction and reject certain educational possibilities even before they enter secondary school. In addition, Table 10.2 suggests that workers and peasants do not inculcate in their children an intense desire for higher education. It may be, however, that these children desire less education because their families cannot provide the

Table 10.1. Social Composition of Student Bodies by Parental Occupation

Occupation of Parents	Number of Children Enrolled per Thousand Families		
	Gymnasiums, Technikums	Trade Schools	Universities
Managerial	24	142	31
Professional, Clerical	32	108	25
Skilled Labor	55	59	9
Semiskilled Labor	52	44	7
Manual Labor	47	33	5

Source: Laszlo Jaki, "A palyavalasztas nehany problemaja" [Some Problems Concerning the Choosing of a Vocation], *Valosag*, no. 5 (1968).

Table 10.2. Type of Post-Grammar-School Education Desired by Elementary Students of Various Social Strata (in percentages)

Type of Education Desired	Occupation of Parents					
	Laborer	Peasant	Profes-sional	Clerical	Other	Total Sample
Gymnasium	20.1	11.5	63.0	24.3	23.5	22.6
Technikum	22.3	13.1	30.4	36.1	19.1	25.1
Other Secondary	1.7	1.6	4.4	2.6	2.1	2.0
Secretarial School	3.0	3.3	—	1.7	—	2.4
Vocational School	49.2	54.1	2.2	34.3	48.9	44.1
No Further Schooling	3.7	16.4	—	11.0	6.4	3.8
Total	100.0	100.0	100.0	100.0	100.0	100.0

Source: Laszlo Farkas and Tibor Kovacs, "A Komarom megyei altalanos iskolai tanulok tovabbtanulasi szandeka, illetve lehetosege" [The Desire and Possibility for Continuing Education among the Students of the General Schools in Komarom County], *Megyei es Varosi Statisztikai Ertesito*, no. 6 (1960).

necessary cultural and educational background to enable them to do well in their studies,[12] and the schools do not compensate for this lack. The problem appears to be similar to the one faced by ghetto children in the slums of large United States cities.

There are far fewer high school dropouts in the city than in the countryside.[13] In urban areas only 1.4 percent of the youngsters do not complete secondary school, but in the villages 8.1 percent of the youth drop out of high school.[14] A lack of secondary schools in the immediate vicinity of many isolated villages, urban prejudice against the children of peasants, and the inferior facilities and teachers at many rural schools are foremost among the factors that account for this disparity.[15]

In Hungary, a college degree is usually the key to a respected social position and financial security. Consequently, a considerably larger number of students compete for admission to the 91 institutions of higher learning than these institutions can accommodate. Theoretically, admission to the universities is open to anyone below 35 years of age. Selection is based upon four criteria: high school records, grades on examinations administered to graduating high school seniors, written and oral university entrance examinations, and recommendations from local KISz organs.[16]

During the mobilization era, the children of Party members, peasants, and laborers were given preferential treatment in the selection process regardless of academic achievement. Since the mid-1960s, how-

ever, children from working-class, peasant, and Party-member families have won admission to colleges and universities over students from families belonging to the intelligentsia only if their scholastic qualifications were equal. There were two basic reasons for this change in policy. First, there were not enough qualified university applicants from worker and peasant families to fill a quota equivalent to their percentage among the Hungarian citizenry. Second, the regime decided that the interests of a modern, industrialized nation required the universities to train specialists who, regardless of their social origin, could best contribute to the development of the country. Although the Ministries of Education and Labor attempted to reintroduce discriminatory practices on December 4, 1975, when they issued an order to classify all kindergarten, primary, and secondary students according to their social origin, public pressure and a direct order from the Party's Central Committee forced these ministries to rescind their mandate and reinstate the nondiscriminatory system that had been in use since the mid-1960s.

In conclusion, Government policies affecting the distribution of education did not serve the specific needs of working-class and peasant families in the 1960s and early 1970s because the regime determined its educational priorities through an evaluation of the needs of the country as a whole. Implementation of these policies caused certain dysfunctions in the purportedly egalitarian educational system by sharpening the distinction between the richer and the poorer social strata. The children of the vast majority of the citizenry, in contrast to those of the intellectual elite, were not adequately encouraged to achieve upward mobility through advanced education. The equalization of educational opportunities for all classes is not likely to occur in the near future, however, because of the regime's need for highly educated specialists.

Housing. When the Communist regime came to power in 1949, it nationalized all housing except single-family dwellings, and assumed responsibility for maintaining the nationalized structures as well as for building new living units. In its effort to provide sufficient housing for the population, the government has faced tremendous problems. During World War II, the majority of Hungary's residences were destroyed; in Budapest alone, nearly 85 percent of all living units were uninhabitable at the end of the war. The urbanization concomitant to the mobilization period brought large numbers of people from the countryside into cities that had not yet been rebuilt. In addition, Soviet exploitation of Hungary's scarce natural resources and industrial capabilities retarded construction and repair efforts. The general poverty of the country, the lack of raw materials and trained workers, and the scarcity of modern construction equipment made it impossible to keep up with the housing needs of the populace. Furthermore, the damages suffered in Budapest during the revolution of 1956 and the decay of buildings caused by poor maintenance and the slipshod construction common in the Stalinist era aggravated the problem. Even today, the provision of adequate housing is a critical problem; in fact, Hungary's housing program is the weakest link in the state's welfare system.

In 1968, there were 4,338,700 people living in apartments and small houses in Hungarian cities.[17] An average of 3.19 people lived in each one-to-two-room unit. The housing shortage has been most acute in Budapest. Between 1959 and 1966, the population of the capital grew by approximately 160,000 people, but the availability of housing failed to keep pace with this increase in population. In 1966, for example, there were at least 300,000 people in Budapest who did not have their own apartments. The plight of the thousands of people without apartments who are forced to sublet a room or a bed in order to have a roof over their head[18] reveals the seriousness of the housing shortage. In 1960 alone, there were 55,364

people who sublet 35,971 living quarters; of these, 26,761 rented beds only.[19] Among the people who sublet, 30 percent were below 25 years of age and 52 percent were married.[20] In violation of the law, which stipulates that no more than 250 forints per month can be charged for each sublet room, many landlords charged exorbitant rents of as much as 1,200 forints per month.[21]

The housing shortage has not been restricted to Budapest and other Hungarian cities. All investigations have shown that even in the villages, extremely crowded conditions exist.[22] Although most village homes are single-family units, subletting portions of these houses is a common practice. Frequently several generations share a rural residence that lacks all modern conveniences.

Theoretically, an apartment can be allocated to any resident who applies to the appropriate city, district, or village council. In Budapest, however, people are required to work in the city five years before they may apply for state housing. Decisions regarding the allocation of apartments must be based solely on the need of the applicant and the seniority of the application. In 1968, there were more than 100,000 applications for apartments in Budapest, and authorities anticipated a yearly increment of 100,000 requests.[23] In 1975, people who applied for an apartment in the large cities faced a five-to-ten-year waiting period.

Since 1971, state apartment rents in Hungary—unlike in most other socialist states—have been based on a complex system of evaluation; legislation passed in that year stipulates that such variables as the amount of space available, the location of the apartment, and the luxuries included in it (e.g., gas heat and hot water) must be taken into account in determining the rent. The new laws were enacted to decrease the enormous state subsidies required for housing. The regime expects to reduce its financial support of rental units as the salaries and incomes of the citizenry rise; by 1980 it plans to commit a minimum of state funds to rent subsidies. At the present time apartment rents fluctuate widely, but gas, electricity, water, and telephone costs are state-subsidized and therefore quite reasonable.

A number of factors limit Hungary's ability to build at a faster rate. The country still lacks capital, raw materials, an adequate pool of highly trained workers and modern construction equipment, which defeats even the most ambitious efforts of the Government. Since the inception of the New Economic Mechanism, however, the regime has begun to relinquish its monopoly over housing. It has initiated various measures to stimulate the investment of private capital in the housing construction industry and to ease the maintenance burden of the Government. One such measure allows the sale of older apartments in buildings containing less than twelve units.[24] In addition, the state is building new apartments for sale in perpetuity and encouraging groups and individuals to undertake building projects. It is also offering low-interest mortgage loans to those who desire to build or buy apartments.

Of the 88,000 apartments and other dwellings built in 1973 only 31,000 or 35.2 percent were constructed by state or cooperative enterprises. The remainder were projects undertaken by private groups. Most of these projects received financing from the state bank, but 13.2 percent were built without any investment whatsoever.[25] Of the nearly 31,000 apartments built by the state, almost half were sold to the general public at high prices. For example, in one of the luxury apartment houses completed in 1969 on Budakeszi Street in Budapest, the price of apartments varied from 150,000 forints for an efficiency to 320,000 for a three-bedroom unit, but the state had no difficulty selling the units.[26]

Another Government policy implemented in 1969 to stimulate construction allows cooperatives to build their own residences. In a venture of this kind, a number of families form a cooperative and either construct their own apartment house or have it built by a state-owned or private construction firm. These buildings usually contain five to eight 2–3 room units costing between 300,000 and 500,000 forints each.

The construction of private, single-family dwellings has been almost entirely restricted to rural areas. Since the early 1960s, a large number of new homes (including many modern, multistoried buildings) have been built in the villages, particularly in those areas where the new farm reforms have increased the revenue of the collectives. Most of the new peasant dwellings seem to be well constructed and comfortable, with garages instead of the traditional stables, although some of them do not have indoor plumbing or running water. Electricity and a large television antenna are standard items, however, even when there is no plumbing in the house. Of the new dwellings completed in 1966, all but 2 percent had electricity; 55 percent had indoor water; and more than 60 percent had bathrooms.[27] Another type of single-family dwelling beginning to make its appearance in Hungary is the small vacation cottage. Literally tens of thousands of these cottages have been built since 1968 along the Danube and near Lake Balaton; some are elaborate, extremely expensive structures.

To encourage construction and the purchase of real estate, state banks offer mortgage loans at very reasonable interest rates. A bank can lend up to 100,000 forints per living unit to families buying apartments built for sale by the state; the usual interest rate for this type of mortgage is 6 percent. In financing cooperative dwellings, banks can lend 40,000 forints at a minimal 2-percent interest rate while offering the balance of the loan at 6 percent. For single-family units, the maximum loanable to the builder-owners is 50,000 forints of which 20,000 can be lent at 2-percent interest and the remainder at 6 percent. These mortgages, which are usually 20- to 30-year loans, are extremely popular; between 1966 and 1968, state banks received 25,000 to 30,000 applications for mortgages.[28]

Although the new policies and increased Government support in financing have somewhat relieved Hungary's housing shortage, they have not affected the options of the average citizen. The wealthier segments of the population can now obtain pleasant, adequate housing, but manual laborers, skilled workers, and small bureaucrats cannot. Because of its need for capital and for relief from the tremendous burden of being landlord to the entire population, the regime has given preferential treatment to the ruling elite, the managerial leadership, and professionals—in a theoretically classless society.

The social repercussions of the housing problem are serious. Large numbers of people are jammed into housing units designed for single families. Young people do not marry because they cannot find a place to live, and marriages often break up because of the severe crowding. The cost of new apartments continues to rise, pricing those who do not make high salaries out of the housing market. This major failure in the distribution of welfare continues to be a primary concern of the regime as it attempts to base its legitimacy on broad popular support.

Government Subsidies. Provision of at least the bare necessities to the whole of society has been one of the Hungarian regime's much acclaimed achievements. To accomplish this task, the Government has

initiated large-scale price supports; the nationalization act and the reorganization of the price system in
1949 and 1950 were the first steps in that direction.
Although the New Economic Mechanism freed a
great many prices from official control and allowed
them to fluctuate, it did not affect the prices of basic
necessities, which still receive support.

Today, the Government subsidizes a wide variety
of goods and services including most heating fuels,
meat, domestic beer, milk, and bread. Price supports
also hold down the cost of some apartment rents,
lunches in factories and state offices, food in second-
and third-class restaurants, cultural events, and public transportation. The Government continues to
subsidize essential goods and services for political
reasons. Bearing in mind the disaffection of Polish
workers in 1970 and 1971 when bread riots occurred,
the present regime is unwilling to risk responsibility
for a similar series of events.

Social Security.   An extensive social security program is another important feature of the Hungarian
welfare system. Both families with children and the
aged receive financial assistance from the state under
this program. In addition to the maternity benefits
discussed earlier, the Hungarian Government extends aid in the form of "family increments" to families with one or more children. This welfare measure
was modeled after the Soviet income-maintenance
system. In 1970, the Hungarian family-maintenance
program offered 130 forints per year to families with
one child, 250 forints to those with two children, 435
forints to those with three, and 1,450 forints per year
to families having ten or more children.[29] (Statistics
were not available on assistance to families with four
to nine children.)

In 1971, 704,000 families out of the more than
2,909,000 Hungarian families received financial
assistance; in 1974, 796,000 families received state
support.[30] Because the families of peasants and workers are usually larger than those of office employees
and professionals, low-income families benefit significantly more from the family-increment program
than those in the upper income brackets; however,
women employed by collective farms receive only
50 percent of the family assistance offered to women
employed by the state.[31]

Retirement pensions are another social security
benefit paid by the Hungarian Government. In a
country that has traditionally neglected the needs of
its old people, this benefit has been most successful

in gaining popular support for the regime. Today,
approximately 1,747,900 out of a total of 1,900,000
people above 60 years of age live on retirement
income.[32] In 1975, the average retirement pension
was 1,430 forints per month per beneficiary, but an
estimated 800,000 pensioners still receive less than
1,000 forints per month. Women are eligible to receive a pension at age 55, men at age 60, but retirement at these ages is not compulsory. Employees may
continue to work and receive full salary if their place
of employment requests a continuation of their
services. When employees do retire, they may still
work, but only part-time; the law does not permit
pensioners to work more than 72 hours per month.
Although some enterprising pensioners succeed in
getting around these provisions of the law, many of
the older people who work part-time jobs are exploited and underpaid. Their employers often require them to work more than the allowable number
of hours, but they accept these conditions because
they need the money to survive.

Pensioners who retired prior to 1960 receive far
from adequate compensation. Before the 1970 and
1974 reforms of the retirement system went into effect, it was not unusual to find older people struggling
to survive on incomes of 360 forints per month, an
amount insufficient to cover living expenses. Even
with increased benefits, however, people who have
retired must resort to a variety of means to keep
body and soul together. They are often forced to
sublet or sell their apartments, depend on their children, work, or find other sources of income. For example, some pensioners rent a room to subletters;
others sign a maintenance contract in which they will
their apartment to a person who agrees to pay a
monthly fee to the pensioner until the latter dies. The
deplorable plight of pensioners is considerably mitigated by the availability of rest homes, sanatoriums,
and free medical care. Unfortunately, however, the
retired are unable to pay the honoraria that people
on full employment can afford, and consequently,
pensioners often receive inferior treatment.

The Government has instituted several reforms
to correct some of the deficiencies in the retirement
system. One of the most significant measures introduced in the 1960s extended benefits to retired collective farm workers,[33] who now receive 315 forints
per month from the state. They also receive 260
forints per month in old-age assistance plus some
additional aid (e.g., extra corn) from their cooperative
or state farm.[34] These benefits, however, are seldom

adequate, and peasants must rely on their own savings and resources to make ends meet. The 1970 and 1974 reforms of the retirement system equalized somewhat the large differential between the pensions of recently retired workers and those of employees who retired prior to 1960; it also increased the average pension by about 140 to 160 forints per month, and provided for an automatic two-percent annual increase in benefits to keep retirement pensions more in line with the rising cost of living.[35] Even with these reforms, older people in Hungary face a difficult struggle requiring sacrifice and dependency, but at least pensioners now receive some help, which—as many of them are quick to point out—was not the case in the past.

Recreation. Another social benefit enjoyed by many Hungarians is the state-sponsored recreational system, comprising a large number of recreational facilities—vacation homes, camps, sports clubs, mountain retreats, etc.—that are made available to the public for a nominal fee. They are sponsored and operated by the various Government agencies, large enterprises, and the trade unions, and all members of a union have access to the facilities of that organization. In 1966, the trade unions owned more than 4,000 libraries and sponsored 2,100 amateur theatrical and other cultural groups, providing programs for 44,000 union members. In addition, the unions sponsored and equipped 1,700 sports clubs which were utilized by nearly 400,000 members. All trade unions also maintain recreation and vacation homes, sanatoriums and health resorts. On Sundays and holidays these facilities are utilized free by the members of the unions. In some cases, a factory, a ministry, or a specialized branch of a union operates facilities exclusively for its own membership.

One typical facility, a boat house on the Danube near Budapest, is available to workers in one of the large wholesale hardware outlets. In addition to a very impressive collection of row boats, kayaks, and racing shells, the club has ping-pong tables, basketball courts, a card room, and a large terrace overlooking the river. It also has a restaurant where members can enjoy inexpensive food and drinks. On Saturday night, a dance band plays for the younger members of the union. The same organization has a vacation home on Lake Balaton where members can sail and water ski. It also maintains smaller units in the mountains of Hungary and a camp on the Danube north of Budapest.

All workers are entitled to 7 days of vacation after the first year of work and 14 days after the second. After this initial 2-year period, each succeeding year's labor entitles a worker to one additional day of paid vacation, up to a maximum of 28 days. Workers may spend their vacation in one of the union vacation homes located on the Danube, in the mountains, or near Lake Balaton. Each trade union allots the bedroom space in the facilities it operates to its locals; the representatives of each local respond to the vacation requests of members, sometimes after consultation with the Party secretary. Good workers are rewarded with choice assignments; unproductive workers and those out of favor with the Party or the union management receive the least desirable assignments at the least desirable times of year.

The cost of a vacation in these homes is minimal. For a two-week vacation, workers pay 5 to 25 percent of their monthly salary, depending on the type of accommodations provided at the rest home. Inexpensive meals are available at these facilities, and vacationers may use a wide variety of sporting equipment (from volley balls to boats) free of charge.

Like many other welfare benefits, recreational facilities are not equally available to all groups in society. In 1969, for example, only 9 percent of the peasantry belonged to trade unions; the other 91 percent—or more than 3,500,000 people—were ineligible for the union-sponsored recreational benefits. During the winter, peasants living in the villages are extremely isolated; only television breaks the monotony of their lives. The lack of recreational opportunities and vacation facilities hinders both the educational development and the social welfare of the peasantry, making their integration into the system much more difficult. The inequitable distribution of welfare benefits also contributes to the desire of much-needed agrarian workers to move to the city where industrial jobs with ample benefits are available.

The Real Standard of Living

A major goal of the Hungarian regime in elaborating the welfare distribution functions of the state has been the creation of conditions that would enable citizens to enjoy a reasonably comfortable standard of living. Until the end of the 1960s, the Hungarian regime effectively failed to achieve this goal. Salaries remained pitifully low, and the Hungarian people

Table 10.3.   Per Capita Income in Hungary in 1968 and 1973 (in forints per year)

	Blue-Collar Workers	Professional and White-Collar Workers	Co-op Peasants	Dual-Income Peasants
1968	12,999	17,162	13,336	13,168
1973	19,550	25,034	19,939	20,424

Sources: *Magyar Statisztikai Zsebkonyv* [Statistical Pocket Book of Hungary] (Budapest: Statisztikai Kiado Vallalat, 1970), p. 241; and *Statistical Pocket Book of Hungary* (Budapest: Statisztikai Kiado Vallalat, 1975), pp. 263, 265, 266.

were engaged in a constant struggle to provide for their basic needs.

In 1974, 5,100,000 Hungarians were gainfully employed.[36] Of these more than five million people, 56.0 percent were men and 44.0 percent were women.[37] Forty-four percent of all active earners worked in industry and construction,[38] 22.7 percent received their incomes from agriculture,[39] and 20 percent received dual incomes (from both agriculture and wages earned elsewhere).[40] The remaining 13.3 percent received reimbursements of some kind, lived on charity or patent royalties, or were not accounted for by the Hungarian Statistical Office.

Table 10.3 details the 1968 and 1973 per capita wages of Hungarian workers in four categories.[41] An analysis of the yearly living expenditures of these wage earners appears in Table 10.4.[42] Considered in terms of buying power, these expenditures indicate the real standard of living of each group of workers. Thus, for example, the entire food, drink, and tobacco budget of the white-collar and professional class amounted to only 171 forints weekly, or not quite 25 forints per day. For 25 forints one can purchase either two pounds of low-quality meat or four packs of cheap cigarettes, one liter of cheap wine or four liters of milk. Furthermore, the largest clothing expense listed in Table 10.4 is 3,341 forints per year, enough to buy only two new, inexpensive ready-made men's suits with nothing left over for small items. A mass produced winter coat of poor quality costs about

Table 10.4.   Expenditures of Wage Earners in 1973 (in forints and percentages of total expenses)°

Items and Services Purchased	Expenditures			
	Blue-Collar Workers	Professionals, White-Collar Workers	Peasants	Dual-Income Peasants
Net Income	19,550 = 100	25,034 = 100	19,939 = 100	20,424 = 100
Food, Drinks, Tobacco	7,950 = 40.66%	8,888 = 35.50%	8,598 = 43.12%	8,238 = 40.33%
Rent and Utilities	2,750 = 14.07	3,687 = 14.72	2,895 = 14.51	2,852 = 13.96
Clothing	2,655 = 13.58	3,341 = 13.35	2,241 = 11.24	2,837 = 13.89
Furnishings, Appliances	1,624 = 8.30	2,138 = 8.54	1,652 = 8.28	1,877 = 9.19
Health, Cleaning Supplies	466 = 2.40	775 = 3.01	307 = 1.54	298 = 1.46
Transportation	1,191 = 6.09	2,334 = 9.32	807 = 4.05	1,034 = 5.06
Culture, Sports, Education, Entertainment	979 = 5.00	1,579 = 6.31	664 = 3.33	763 = 3.73
Other Expenditures	1,141 = 5.84	1,921 = 7.67	1,243 = 6.23	1,088 = 5.32
Total Spending°	18,756 = 95.93	24,664 = 98.52	18,407 = 92.32	18,987 = 92.96
Net Savings	794 = 4.07	370 = 1.48	1,532 = 7.68	1,437 = 7.04

°Total percentages may not equal 100, since percentages have been rounded off to the nearest hundredth.
Source: *Magyar Statisztikai Zsebkonyv* [Statistical Pocket Book of Hungary] (Budapest: Statisztikai Kiado Vallalat, 1975), p. 263.

2,000 forints, and the least expensive custom-made garments cost 3,000 forints.

The figures in Table 10.4, however, must be interpreted with great caution. Although they indicate that professional and white-collar workers save the least money, these figures represent the average expenditures and savings of people with widely divergent incomes; about 16.4 percent of white-collar workers receive very low salaries (around 1,500 forints per month), whereas the salaries of 6.6 percent of this group are very high (over 15,000 forints per month).[43] Furthermore, salaries account for only a portion of the income of this latter group; translation and consulting fees, royalties, honoraria, and bonuses frequently triple or quadruple the earnings of professionals.

Distinctions between the standard of living of various occupational groups reflect the economic and social stratification that exists in Hungary.[44] Official Hungarian sources acknowledge three social strata: (I) mental laborers, (II) manual laborers, and (III) the peasantry. The first category includes Party leaders, doctors, teachers, collective farm managers, writers and artists, or in short, all those who are not employed in some type of physical labor. Table 10.5 details the official division of Hungarian society into its three component strata and indicates what percentage of the population falls within each stratum.[45] The economic distinctions that divide Hungarian society into these classes are shown in Table 10.6, which compares the salaries of employees in category I with those of workers performing nonagricultural physical labor (category II).[46]

Derived from the data presented in Tables 10.5 and 10.6, Figure 10.1 depicts the class structure of Hungarian society. Class distinctions are based pri-

Table 10.5. The Three Social Classes in Hungary

Composition of Each Social Stratum	Percentage of Population in Each Category
I. Mental Laborers (professionals and white-collar workers)	
A. Leaders and Intelligentsia	
1. Government, Party, and Economic Leadership	1.61
2. Technical and Top Cultural Intelligentsia	1.92
3. Teachers, Doctors, Artists	3.09
B. Other Office Employees	
1. Middle-Level Technocrats	7.86
2. Bureaucrats, Office Workers, Clerks	8.52
Subtotal	23.04 (2,100,000)
II. Nonagricultural Physical Laborers (blue-collar workers)	
A. Skilled Laborers	17.52
B. Semiskilled Laborers	18.76
C. Unskilled Manual Laborers	11.91
D. Janitors, Guards, etc.	2.78
Subtotal	50.62 (4,800,000)
III. Agricultural Workers	°
A. State Farm Workers in Physical Labor	
B. Collective Farm Workers	
C. Independent Peasantry	
D. Seasonal Workers	
Subtotal	26.34 (2,400,000)

°Breakdown for agricultural workers not available.

Source: Mrs. Sandor Ferge, "A tarsadalmi retegezodes Magyarorszagon" [Social Stratification in Hungary], Valosag, no. 10 (1966).

Table 10.6. A Comparison of the Average Salaries of Mental Laborers and Nonagricultural Physical Laborers with Different Educational Backgrounds (in forints per month)

Occupation	College	High School	Eighth Through Eleventh Grade	Seventh Grade or Less	No Schooling
			Educational Background		
Mental Labor					
Men	2,805	2,280	2,174	2,122	—
Women	2,053	1,485	1,383	840	—
Physical Labor					
Men	1,776	1,819	1,770	1,710	1,241
Women	586°	1,238	1,155	1,106	806

°Applies only to part-time work.

Source: R. A. "A munkasok es alkalmazottak keresete" [The Income of Workers and Employees], *Valosag*, no. 9 (1966).

marily on differences in income rather than in background. This conclusion is supported by studies indicating that children, regardless of the social origins of their families, tend to possess the same values as other children whose families are in similar financial circumstances.[47] Technocrats, managers, white-collar workers in positions of leadership, directors of prosperous cooperative farms, owners of small private stores, and the cultural and intellectual elite all live comfortably in Hungary; their standard of living is comparable to that of the middle class in the United States. People in the upper stratum of Hungarian society are able to take extended trips abroad, send their children to college, and buy apartments, vacation homes, or automobiles. However, only 15 to 20 percent of the population can afford these luxuries. At the same time, over 60 percent of the population belong to families earning less than 3,000 forints per month that have, at best, an acceptable standard of living, with little hope for significant improvement in the near future.

Despite its theoretical goal of building a classless society, the Hungarian Communist regime has fostered a socioeconomic system that places a premium on performance, knowledge, and efficiency. The New Economic Mechanism has only served to aggravate the differentiation between the various strata of society. To implement its plan, the Government offers rewards and incentives to those citizens who contribute most to the economic advancement of the state. Unless disaffected workers—who realize that in spite of the revolutionary rhetoric of the Party, their economic and social positions are in jeopardy—

can force the regime to alter its policies, the income differential between the upper and lower classes of Hungarian society will probably increase.

Although the New Economic Mechanism has contributed to the stratification of society, it has also succeeded in stimulating the channeling of additional welfare benefits to the Hungarian citizenry. The expansion of medical, educational, and social benefits is likely to continue throughout the 1970s, but housing problems will remain acute and the economic development of the country will create inflationary trends and some unemployment. Within these limits, however, the present system of welfare distribution appears to be the most equitable Hungarian society has ever witnessed.

How Hungarians View the Standard of Living

In May 1972, *Nepszabadsag* initiated a series of articles entitled: "How Do We Live Today and How Shall We Live Tomorrow?" At the same time, the paper took a public opinion poll, asking its readers to express their views on the subject.

The standard of living described by the respondents was at great variance with that presented in official statistics and reports. The key issue raised by readers concerned the inequality of wages and incomes. Most people who criticized the regime were of egalitarian persuasion (i.e., advocated a system that does not take individual performance into account in distributing social and economic privileges).[48] They objected to the excessively high

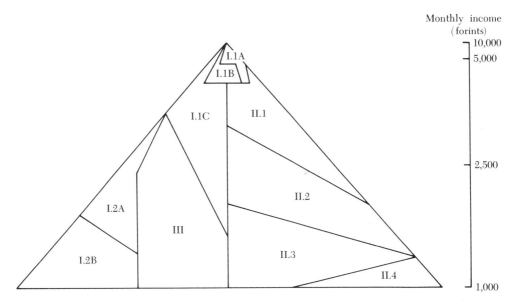

Figure 10.1. The class structure in Communist Hungary in the late 1960s (as derived from the data in Tables 10.5 and 10.6).

Sources: R.A., "A munkasok es alkalmazottak keresete" [The Income of Workers and Employees], *Valosag,* no. 9 (1966); and Mrs. Sandor Ferge, "A tarasadalmi retegezodes Magyarorszagon" [Social Stratification in Hungary], *Valosag,* no. 10 (1966).

earnings of enterprise managers, which some attributed to favorable circumstances rather than good performance. As one respondent put it: "If it goes on like this, profit sharing will cease to encourage people to be efficient and diligent, since remuneration depends not on the work performed, but on the position occupied."[49] Hungarians who share the above views are convinced that some managers give much less to society than they receive from it; in other words, they get much more than can be acquired by "honest work." This line of reasoning originates in the Marxist theory of labor value, which maintains that the value of an item is determined by the quantity of labor required to produce it. According to this theory, the working class creates most of the wealth in the world. Of course, in its drive to modernize the economic bases of the society, the Hungarian regime, as well as the leadership in most other Communist states, has considered the fruits of intellectual work more valuable than the products of physical labor and has thus rewarded brainpower more than brawn. That is why the "specialist" has a much better position in Hungarian society than the proletarian.

The readers of *Nepszabadsag* discussed one other fundamental problem that affects their standard of living: inflated prices. Many respondents complained about the high and constantly rising prices of consumer goods and indicated that they distrust statistics because the presentation of data can be deceptive to the average consumer. They condemned statistical reports that present the average increase of all prices, arguing that such statistics are useless because specific price increases affect families with dissimilar incomes in different ways. For example, families that cannot afford a refrigerator do not benefit from a 10-percent reduction in the price of these appliances, but such a reduction lowers the average of all prices. As pointed out earlier, families with low incomes can usually afford to purchase only a limited range of cheaper goods, which unfortunately are of poor quality. "Cheap goods are in terrible taste," wrote a respondent, "while tasteful ones (clothes, pots, furniture) are extremely expensive. And what should someone who has taste but no money do? Visit museums?"[50]

These opinions represent the views of the majority of the large number of respondents to the *Nep-*

szabadsag poll, most of whom were dissatisfied with the various social benefits (allowances, vacations, etc.) they received. They were also critical of the general distribution of welfare benefits, maintaining that people with substantial incomes receive more than necessary while more deserving citizens do not receive enough. They all urged the Government to implement stricter and broader social controls.

The Impact of the NEM
on the Standard of Living

If we bear in mind that since 1968 Hungary has been operating under the New Economic Mechanism, which, among other things, was designed to (and in fact did) raise the standard of living of most Hungarians, then even these criticisms reflect the success of the Hungarian reform movement, because the NEM decentralized economic planning and control, and rewarded individual initiative. Many Party officials and economic specialists claim that the NEM has been a great success. However, some economists have expressed concern about Hungary's rate of economic growth, which has been diminishing since 1972; if this trend continues, the NEM may not be as successful in the future as it was in the first eight years of its operation. Nevertheless, compared to the command economy it replaced, the NEM has been a brilliant achievement. Not only has the reform ensured that the interests of individuals, groups, and the citizenry as a whole can compete more equally in the formulation of economic policy, it has also caused a sizable increase in Hungary's GNP and real per capita income. The population's consumption went up by 30 percent between 1968 and 1975. Today, there are more durable consumer goods in Hungary than ever before. Unfortunately, as has already been pointed out, the NEM has also sharpened the class distinctions in Hungarian society.

In addition to overcoming persistent, old socioeconomic problems through the NEM, the Kadar regime has had to combat new ones created by the reform, many of which are corollaries of a particular phase of the NEM. Examples of problems specifically related to the NEM are the dilution of consumer buying power (rapidly rising prices have outstripped wage increases) and the threat of unemployment. Whereas the threat of unemployment has been tempered by fluctuating economic reports, price-wage disequilibrium has been chronic throughout

the existence of the NEM. Both union leaders and workers have been disturbed by insufficient increases in basic wages. When in 1971 and 1972 the Hungarian regime modified its wage system, it also decreed a general wage hike. Workers expected to receive higher wages as soon as the decree took effect. In reality, however, enterprises had 18 months to implement the decree; a lack of communication not only caused misunderstanding between management and workers, but also created frustration among the latter. The fear of unemployment was occasioned by official threats to close down several uneconomical enterprises that required particularly high subsidies. The regime's severe criticism of these uneconomical enterprises was also motivated by the exorbitant investment projects designed and implemented by district branches of various ministries as well as by enterprise managers and local councils. Ambitious projects initiated by these authorities required financing beyond that allocated in the economic plan. To ensure completion of these projects, the government had to appropriate additional funds and thus create an imbalance in the investment market. Until November 1972, the symptoms of this imbalance were multiplying, and the regime considered investment difficulties one of its most delicate problems.[51] In 1971, 80 percent of the Government's investments went to projects that were not completed with the alloted funds. For the fourth Five-Year Plan (1971–1975) investment demand was 50,000 million forints in excess of the maximum approved.[52] In fact, investment demand exceeded building capacity, resulting in both delays and an increase in building and labor costs. Unfortunately, Government intervention has only partially solved this problem and created several new problems; by centralizing the project selection process, the regime has contravened some of the stated principles of the NEM.

Another problem causing headaches for the regime is the friction between town and countryside. What is peculiar about the current manifestation of this persistent problem is that complaints about a drain of manpower are coming from enterprise managers, and not from the chairmen of the agricultural producers' cooperatives. The incomes of the peasants in many of these cooperatives are higher than those of workers in the state sector, which has irritated quite a few workers.

In 1971, to curtail the development of practices that might cause further differentiation between incomes in the private and state sectors, the regime introduced a new set of income tax regulations limiting the potential net income of employees in the private sector. It imposed a new, progressive tax that makes it hard for private artisans or retailers to earn more than 100,000 forints a year, and it delivered another blow to people labeled as "greedy and money-grubbing" by enacting a decree that outlaws land speculation and prohibits any family from owning more than two pieces of real estate—one for a permanent residence and the other for a holiday cottage. Still other measures (particularly those promulgated on January 31, 1976) limit the right of individuals to pursue secondary employment and new edicts also restrict the right of the agricultural producers' cooperatives to engage in ancillary activities that would have significant negative effects on the earnings of industrial workers. Many Hungarians interpret these Government actions as a political move to appease Party dogmatists and trade union egalitarians. Implemented to diminish the friction between workers in different sectors of the economy, the measures restrain competition and motivation—both of which are basic to the success of the NEM. However, if one recalls the consequences of the popular discontent that surfaced in Hungary in 1956, then the sacrifices the nation must make to appease the dissatisfaction of workers and ensure the success of the NEM do not seem so great. The Kadar leadership recognizes that compromise is necessary to achieve the regime's three main goals of implementing economic reform, obtaining legitimacy through popular support, and pursuing the foreign policies prescribed by the Soviet Union. Since the proreform critics of the Government policy are less numerous and less vocal than the antireform critics, the Government pays more attention to the latter. While the proponents of the NEM emphasize the need for economic efficiency, modernization, and rational management, the opponents of the plan stress the need for equality, full employment, and a complete range of welfare benefits. The question is, can the regime satisfy the demands of the value-oriented critics without first achieving the economic goals of proponents of reform? If a higher standard of living depends on a comparatively fast rate of economic growth, the answer is

no. The regime is simultaneously trying to generate reasonably rapid development, maintain economic stability, and satisfy the growing demand for social equality. In performing this delicate balancing act, the Kadar regime has encountered several new difficulties since 1973, not so much because of domestic factors and variables, but because of external ones. These external variables include the enormous rise in the cost of imported raw materials and the economic crises experienced in the capitalist states of the West. Since the NEM depends on close economic ties between Hungary and the West, the recession that occurred in the West between 1973 and 1976 endangered the very existence of the Hungarian economic reform.

Production Efficiency—A Balance Sheet

Among the fundamental problems facing Hungary today and in the forseeable future is the need to improve production efficiency and economize on the use of raw materials and energy. The Tenth Congress of the HSWP, held in November 1970, adopted a special resolution condemning inefficient industrial enterprises and suggesting ways to correct the inefficiencies; the same subject was discussed again during the February 1972 budget debate in the National Assembly. In August 1972, the Council of Ministries finally received reports from various ministries on the progress made toward achieving more efficient production.[53] Between 1970 and 1975, the Hungarian economy as a whole increased its productive capacity. The ratio of agricultural production to total production dropped, although the former increased in absolute value, which indicated a more effective utilization of manpower. The output of the processing and building industries also increased. The output of the chemical, pharmaceutical, and machine industries was up, but the output of the food processing and light industries was not progressing according to previous expectations. The aluminum processing and vehicle industries developed considerably, as did the knitwear and textile industries. Finally, power output increased because more oil was being processed and modern methods of power generation had replaced obsolete coal power generators.

On the enterprise level, however, the picture remained bleak. Technology was obsolete and restricted the productive capacity of both manpower and machinery. Equipment was being modernized neither fast enough nor sufficiently. The structural composition of output was imbalanced; many items were inefficiently produced; and the range of production was too wide. There were several reasons for these inefficiences. The financial and developmental resources of enterprises were used to increase capacity instead of to foster modernization. Further, the Hungarian economy was not competitive enough; some enterprises still enjoyed a monopoly on the domestic market, which enabled them to sell inferior products at inflated prices. State subsidies supplemented losses of income caused by inefficient production, and the regime preferred subsidies to unemployment. Finally, international cooperation was inadequate to relieve domestic financial difficulties. The import of more and more goods created a growing deficit in Hungary's balance of trade. In 1972 the Government took steps to correct the imbalance; it established a new licensing system (which resulted in a 20-percent decrease in the volume of consumer goods imported from the West in 1972) and increased production of Hungarian goods for export (e.g., light electrical ma-

chinery, wine, food products, and drugs.) (See Table 10.7).

In 1972, the regime also introduced a number of new measures to improve the production efficiency of Hungarian enterprises. For example, the minister of finance received authorization to withdraw development funds from enterprises that are to be reduced in size, and to use these funds to promote a greater efficiency in underproductive companies that would benefit from investment. In enterprises operating inefficiently, financial rehabilitation committees were set up to make recommendations for either the improvement or the suspension of operations. However, these new measures did not substantially revitalize enterprise production. On the contrary. Therefore, after the November 1972 plenum of the HSWP, about 180 enterprises were subjected to new state intervention because it was argued that their financial rehabilitation committees had failed to restore fiscal balance or eliminate some acute nonfinancial problem. Hand in hand with this centralized method of "modernization," the Party recentralized economic planning somewhat by creating a

Table 10.7. Hungarian Foreign Trade, 1968–1973 (in millions of foreign-exchange forints)°

	1968	1969	1970	1971	1972	1973°°
Imports	21,162.5	22,631.1	29,410	35,098	34,093	37,313
Exports	21,004.2	24,462.2	27,197	29,355	35,583	42,052
Total Turnover	42,166.7	47,093.3	56,607	64,453	69,676	79,365
Balance	− 158.3	+ 1,831.1	−2,213	-5,743	+ 1,490	+4,739
Imports from Socialist States	14,495.6	15,331.1	18,984	23,421	22,438	23,560
Exports to Socialist States	15,093.0	16,642.5	17,839	20,480	24,843	28,722
Turnover	29,588.6	31,973.6	36,823	43,901	47,281	52,282
Balance	+ 597.4	+ 1,311.4	−1,145†	−2,941	+2,405	+5,162
Imports from Nonsocialist Countries	6,666.9	7,300.0	10,426	11,677	11,655	13,753
Exports to Nonsocialist Countries	5,911.2	7,819.7	9,358	8,875	10,740	13,330
Turnover	12,578.1	15,119.7	19,784	20,552	22,395	27,083
Balance	− 755.7	+ 519.7	−1,068	−2,802	−915	−423

°Free-on-board (FOB) prices.

°°Estimates.

†Much of this deficit was deliberately incurred owing to the very large surpluses in rubles accumulated in the preceding five years. Because of the inconvertibility of currency within the socialist sector, the rigid insistence on a bilateral clearing of accounts, and additional restrictions on the use of surpluses even within the debtor country itself, a favorable balance of trade presents serious problems for Hungary.

Sources: *Statisztikai Havi Kozlemenyek* [Statistical Monthly Bulletin], no. 1(1974); and *Statistical Pocket Book of Hungary* (Budapest: Statistical Publishing House, 1973), p. 202.

State Planning Committee (headed by Gyorgy Lazar), which is a carbon copy of a similar institution in the Soviet Union. One may ask why it was necessary to create such an agency when there were (and still are) a host of institutions charged with the task of economic planning. The Party. Central Committee, the Council of Ministers, the Economic Committee (abolished upon the creation of the new agency), and, of course, the National Planning Office all supervise the various aspects of planning the state economy. However, if we keep in mind that the CPSU had openly criticized some of Hungary's NEM policies,[54] it is easier to understand why the Kadar leadership decided in 1972 to exclude further "dangerous" economic experimentation and revert to more stringent socialist planning in both industry and agriculture.

As a result of the regime's new economic policies, the investment front has cooled off and rampant overspending has ceased; in 1972, investment spending increased by only 2.5 percent, and in 1973, by a mere 2 percent.[55] But, in bringing the economy under control, the leadership has sacrificed technological innovation and modernization, curbed the decision-making prerogatives of the enterprises, and alienated (as well as removed from Government and Party positions) some of the supporters of the NEM. Between 1972 and 1973, national income, and industrial and agricultural production increased by about 6 percent, and although Hungary's balance of trade with the West deteriorated by 12 percent per annum between 1972 and 1974, in the same period the country maintained a very large surplus in its balance of trade with Comecon nations (a meaningless achievement because the forint is not convertible).

Hungary's standard of living did not change much in the early 1970s. Real wages increased by 3.2 percent between 1971 and 1974. However, because of the extra wage increases allotted in March 1973 to workers employed in state industries, workers paid by the state (30 percent of all workers) enjoyed a 5.8 percent increase in real wages, which means that the real wages of the rest of the nation's wage-earners (70 percent) increased by only 0.8 percent in three years. Since, in 1973, the national income increased three times faster than real wages, the Fifth Five-Year Plan (1976–1980) calls for a 2.8–3.2-percent increase in real wages and a 6.0–6.4-percent increase

in national income. Critics of the NEM have had an impact on this area of economic policy. The NEM has not produced a real differentiation in wages both because restrictions have been imposed by a new system of economic regulators instituted in 1975 and because real wages have remained too low. The regime's forced egalitarian wage policy outlined in 1975 consists of arbitrary adjustments from above carried out, not by the NEM, but by state intervention. All previous talk about the gradual extension of the free-price category has by now been forgotten, especially since inflationary pressure has forced the state to subsidize most of its basic industries in order to keep consumer prices at a fairly steady level. The Government even subsidizes import prices to keep domestic prices low. Although the regime's unspoken goal is to bring the West's prices into equilibrium with domestic prices, the necessity of maintaining a cushion of subsidies creates an artificial system isolated from economic reality. In the 1973 budget, it took 27.3 percent of gross expenditures, or 63,000 million forints to fill this cushion; in 1975, it took 36.1 percent of gross expenditures or 116,642 million forints. The fact that in 1968 (the year the NEM was introduced) only 35,000 million forints were needed to fill this same cushion leads us to question the effectiveness of the NEM in achieving a market-type economy.

Summary

Hungarians do not consider their reform complete. According to the architect of the NEM, former Politburo member Rezso Nyers, "recent measures—[the establishment of quotas, allocations, prohibitions, etc.]—do not mean a deviation from the current system of economic management. . . . practice has justified the principles of the reform."[56] Similar words were spoken by Janos Kadar at the Eleventh Party Congress: "The NEM has been proven right and necessary by the experience of more than seven years."[57] However, the HSWP guidelines issued for the Eleventh Party Congress emphasized that "we shall make even better use of the socialist planned economy as a means of achieving our present and future objectives and tasks, and shall improve the efficiency of its operations."[58] This change in policy will no doubt result in further restrictions and a pruning of independent enterprise management. Although a tightening of the reins of central direction is justified—at least temporarily—by the many objective economic problems facing Hungary today, the question is: Can the regime solve these problems (inflation, the outstripping of real wages by rapidly rising prices, lagging productivity, etc.) by this tactic?

According to the new premier, Gyorgy Lazar, several factors have had an adverse effect on the Hungarian economic situation despite the successes of the NEM.[59] For example, the growth in domestic consumption has been greater than that in domestic production, resulting in a considerable deficit in both the state budget and the foreign trade balance. A deterioration in the terms of trade with industrially developed countries has exacerbated these problems. Since the fall of 1973, inflation has rapidly accelerated in the West, and the prices of imported raw materials and energy have increased faster than the prices of exported finished and semifinished products. In 1974 and 1975, this imbalance, in effect, cost Hungary 14 and 12 percent respectively of its foreign trade earnings, the equivalent of several thousand million forints.

The 1974 decline in state revenues from economic activities coupled with expanded enterprise profits also had an adverse effect on the economy; the combination of factors distorted the incentive system used to orient enterprise activities and hindered efforts to increase labor productivity. In the same year, enterprises stockpiled excessive amounts of supplies and the production of goods requiring large amounts of raw materials increased at an above-average rate, creating an even stronger demand for imports. Although the Government spent more on investments in 1974 than planned, it still had to delay or drop the implementation of some important capital projects. Moreover, Government economy measures were not extensive enough, the modernization of the production structure progressed too slowly, and Hungarian industry did not respond rapidly enough to the fast-changing requirements of the world market. Between 1974 and 1976, Hungary proved unable to adjust its trade structure to changing world prices in order to permit a reduction of losses resulting from disadvantageous terms of trade. According to Lazar, the country's economic problems could probably be solved not by changing existing policies, but by implementing them more

determinedly. However, that would require a more rapid increase in labor productivity than occurred in the mid-1970s, as well as farsighted planning and responsible central direction.

Two goals of the present Five-Year Plan (1976–1980) that are central to the success of Hungary's entire economic policy are (1) economy in the use of raw materials and energy; and (2) increased productivity. However, the need for economy naturally extends into the field of investment, where it militates against a rise in productivity. The essential element in any increase in productivity and efficiency is better and more modern production technology, which can hardly be obtained without adequate investment. Centralization, however, limits the enterprise's already low investment funds and makes flexible adjustment to a fast-changing world market impossible. Since the Soviet Union, whose exports are sold at world market prices, is Hungary's most important supplier of raw materials, the fluctuation of these world prices (especially of that of oil) creates an element of uncertainty that makes it impossible to plan for a five-year period. Between January 1, 1975 and January 1, 1976, for instance, the prices of raw materials imported from the Soviet Union increased by approximately 52 percent, while those for machinery and equipment went up by 3.3 percent. At the same time, the prices of Hungarian machinery and equipment produced for export rose by only 15 percent, the export price of Ikarusz buses increased by 23 percent, the export prices of the products of light industry rose by 19 percent, and those of agricultural products by 28 percent. However, if we bear in mind that sources of energy, raw materials, and semifinished goods constitute 69 percent of all Hungarian imports from the Soviet Union (which represents 33 percent of the total of Hungarian imports), then it is fairly easy to calculate that Hungary suffered a 10-percent loss in 1975 in the terms of her trade with the USSR—a high price to pay for economic dependency. The negative impact of Hungary's new centralized price system on the country's economy can best be seen from the balance sheet of foreign trade with socialist countries: whereas by 1973, Hungary had already built up a surplus of 7,507 million foreign-exchange forints during the first quarter of 1975, the foreign trade balance showed a deficit of 120,000,000 foreign-exchange forints.[60]

Among the fundamental questions raised at the Eleventh Party Congress was: Can the reform of economic management introduced in 1968 survive without change? The answers provided in the resolutions and speeches of the Congress suggest that the reform policy will remain—with certain essential modifications—but at the same time, central direction must be made more effective. Actually, the recentralization of economic management can be construed as a double-edged sword. On the one hand, it will enable central Government and Party authorities to direct the transformation of the production structure of several large-scale industrial firms and control the allocation of foundry products, gasoline, diesel oil, fuel oil, copper, zinc, lead, tin and paper. On the other hand, it will also probably enable the regime to resolve some of Hungary's intractable economic and social problems and thus relieve the discontent they have provoked from the state's industrial workers and the anxiety they have produced among the public at large. Open worker dissatisfaction with certain "ideological deformations" of the New Economic Mechanism has contributed to the political and economic difficulties that have arisen in Hungary since the Tenth Party Congress, and the concessions made to the workers by the HSWP since 1972 have already helped to dampen this discontent. Consideration of workers' demands has also caused Hungarian Party policy to conform more closely with the politics and ideology of the CPSU.

11

The Political Culture

To believe in God when there is no God. That's great, that's East European.[1]

Perhaps no greater difficulty exists for a political scientist than that of delineating the political culture of a society without empirical evidence.[2] Yet, for those political scientists who study closed societies, the gathering of hard data remains an almost impossible task. They have to rely on published information, literary evidence, personal experiences, and impressions; they must measure and analyze the orientations of the citizenry through the old—and not very scientific—method of *fingerspitzengefuhl*. The difficulties of generalizing about the political culture of a Communist state are compounded by the tenuous relation between published evidence and reality. The conclusions of this chapter are based upon published data, literary evidence, and the personal experiences of the author, together with empirical data from 300 interviews conducted by the author in 1970–1971 and in 1974–1975. The evidence thus obtained should provide a reasonably accurate composite picture of the Hungarian citizenry's "modal patterns of orientations toward specific political objects."[3] In all political cultures, citizens manifest a variety of attitudes toward the political system, but in Hungary, because of the relative homogeneity of the population as well as the small size of the country and the common historical experience of the people, an identifiable composite sociopolitical orientation does exist. By and large, the Magyar population still accepts various stereotypes of itself—a tendency decried by Akos Kertesz in his novel *Makra*, one of the most significant works of the late 1960s.

> He who is black is a GYPSY. And what kind of [a man] is a gypsy? He steals, lies, knows how to play music, [is] subservient and underhanded. He who talks in a dialect is a PEASANT. The peasant is stupid, but cunning, and always complains. He whose grandfather is a Jew is a JEW. Erger-Berger-Sosberger, every Jew is a gangster. He whose hands are calloused is a WORKER. He who lives in Lorinc is a PROLI from the OUTSKIRTS.

He who lives in Vaci street is a downtown BOUR-GEOIS.[4]°

Although a Hungarian modality of orientations toward many objects is discernable, there are two distinct political subcultures in Hungary that deviate from the general models of political orientation. These two groups comprise (1) dedicated, ideologically motivated leftists, and (2) the few, strong, anti-Communist proponents of national independence. No one has been able to determine exactly what percentage of the population belongs to both these groups, but a reasonable estimate is that the two groups together include no more than five percent of all Hungarians. Thus, these subcultures are quite small, but they do exhibit clearly divergent patterns of political orientation.

In Chapters 8 and 9, we examined the transmission of political knowledge; in this chapter, we concentrate on the results of the transmission process—the orientations of the citizenry toward certain political objects. For the purposes of discussion, we categorize these objects as follows:

1. The state and nation
2. The political system
3. Incumbents
4. Political processes
5. The Communist Party
6. The international socialist system.[5]

We will discuss Hungary's political culture in terms of the cognitive, affective, and evaluative orientations of the citizenry toward these objects.

Cognitive Orientations

The cognitive political orientation of a society denotes the knowledge the citizenry possesses concerning the political system under which it lives and the political processes governing that system. Citizens generally acquire such knowledge through the schools and the other primary agencies of political socialization. The political knowledge of the citizenry varies with time and the intensity with which a regime desires to inculcate specific cognition in the population. The cognitive orientations of Hungarians living in the 1970s are based on their experiences during both the highly politicized period of Rakosi's rule and the generally depoliticized Kadar era. The political knowledge of the citizenry, thus, depends on the citizens' experiences with the political system as much as on their age, education, social class, and occupation.

The State and Nation.   The cognitive orientation of the citizenry toward the state and nation is perhaps the strongest of all orientations. Hungarians are determined Hungarophiles, and their patriotic attitude, expressed in the proverb *"extra Hungariam non est vita, si est vita non est ita,"*[6] is founded on their perception and knowledge of the state. That Hungary is a small state is now clearly recognized by the people; that it is dependent is well-known. The knowledge that "Hungary has no army, has no strategically defensible space, [that] the West merely shits on us, [that] the West is merely interested in Middle Eastern oil, [that] the UN is a useless organ, and [that] all you have to do is look at the numbers—there are 9 million Magyars and 240 million Russians,"[7] is accepted as a given of the Hungarian political culture of the 1970s. Similarly, Hungarians know that they are Europeans; they cherish and maintain close ties to Europe.

Hungarians, however, do not have a strictly realistic knowledge of their country's size and present situation. Their conception of the state includes a somewhat idealized picture of an "historic Hungary." Only the highly educated strata of the population realize that today Hungary is one of the smallest countries in the world. In the minds of most Hungarians, the real Hungarian state still includes territories that have belonged to other states for more than 50 years. In this persistent popular conception of historic Hungary, Transylvania, Slovakia, and the northern part of Yugoslavia are still Hungarian territory. Cluj is still called Kolozsvar; Osijek is referred to as Eszek; and Kosice remains Kassa. It is interesting that, literally translated, the Hungarian word for abroad (*kulfold*) means outside the earth. Likewise, a foreigner (*kulfoldi*) is one from outside

---

°The seemingly incomprehensible allusions in this quotation make sense in the specific circumstances of Hungary. "Erger-Berger-Sosberger" was one of the songs of the Hungarian fascists. The Hungarian text refers to the worker through the term *melos*, which implies a non-class-conscious worker. The "proli"—a shortened and pejorative term for "proletarian"—is a poverty-stricken worker. "Lorinc" refers to Pestszentlorinic, a district on the outskirts of Budapest where poor workers and peasants live; it is contrasted with the area where rich people live—downtown in the heart of the city, on fashionable Vaci Street.

the earth. The population's pride in recognizing people and things as Hungarian is enormous. Nobel-prize-winning scholars who have become citizens of other states are known as "Magyars living abroad." Even second-generation Hungarians like Mark Spitz are revered, and because of their Hungarian origin they are popularly regarded as proof of the extraordinary talents of the nation. Hungarians are proud of the distinctiveness of their culture, which is clearly distinguishable from the sea of Slavic customs and traditions surrounding it; knowledge of that distinctiveness is a key element in the cognitive political orientations of the entire citizenry.

The Political System.   Little evidence is available concerning the exact knowledge citizens possess about the political structure of the Hungarian People's Republic. To determine what the citizenry knows about the organization of political power, we asked 300 Hungarians the following questions: "What is the highest organ of state power in Hungary?" and "Who elects the members of the Council of Ministers?"[8] The responses to these questions were as follows:

What is the highest organ of state power in Hungary?

Parliament	23%
The Council of Ministers	19%
The Party	16%
The Presidential Council (*correct answer*)	12%
The Premier	11%
The Council (*sic*)	10%
Other incorrect answers or do not know	9%

Who elects the members of the Council of Ministers?

The Party	34%
Parliament (*correct answer*)	23%
The Presidential Council	17%
The electors or the people	12%
Other incorrect answers or do not know	14%

Such variables as age, income, education, and class did not significantly affect the answers to these questions, although citizens in intellectual occupations and elected officials were more likely to be knowledgeable about the system than was the rest of the population.

Until 1973, state-established school curricula contained no courses on the constitutional framework of the Hungarian political system. Although school children could identify the date of the promulgation of the new constitution, they had no specific knowledge of its contents or of the governmental organizations specified in it.[9] Until 1975, the constitution of the country was not included in any of the textbooks used in Hungary's secondary schools; it was not even included in the sourcebook used for the study of Marxism-Leninism at the College of Liberal Arts (*Bolcsesztudomanyi kar*) of the Eotvos Lorand University of Sciences in Budapest.[10] Only in 1975 did the sixth-grade text *Allampolgarsagi ismeretek* [Citizenship Information] begin to present parts of the constitution.

The citizenry's knowledge of local political structures is, perhaps of necessity, greater than its familiarity with the national governmental bureaucracy. Indeed, there are very few people who do not know which office in the local council they should turn to with their grievances. The local organs of power perform daily contact functions, and therefore the cognitive orientations of the citizenry are *ipso facto* more positive toward them than toward statewide political objects. Even so, the rural population often turns to the police for solutions to administrative grievances.

The general lack of knowledge about both the structure and the function of government is coupled with a lack of interest in politics. Although both the "Russian language [and] Marxism-Leninism [are] mandatory subject[s] at all universities and colleges" throughout the four years of university study,[11] only 15 percent of all college students living in communal dormitories (where the pressure to participate in politics is probably very strong) were extremely interested in politics, and over 55 percent did not exhibit any interest beyond a cursory glance at occasional articles in political newspapers.[12] This lack of interest in politics is prevalent also among industrial workers; only 5.3 percent of those interviewed in 1970 (N = 532) had strong opinions based on a knowledge of the political situation, whereas 62 percent of that same sample had no opinion or knowledge of political events.[13]

Incumbents.   Most citizens also know very little about the political leadership of the Hungarian republic. In our survey we asked two questions to measure the cognitive orientation of the citizenry toward incumbents: "Who is the President of Hungary?" and "Who is your elected Parliamentary representative?" The responses were:

Who is the president of Hungary?

Janos Kadar	43%
Jeno Fock	23%
Pal Losonczi (*correct answer*)	17%
Gyula Kallai	8%
Other incorrect responses or do not know	9%

Who is your elected parliamentary representative?

Correct answer	21%
Incorrect answer	34%
Do not know	46%

Although Kadar's popularity and predominant role in Hungarian politics might account for why 43 percent of the interviewees named him as president of Hungary, the fact that only 17 percent of the 300 people queried were able to identify Losonczi as the head of state indicates a lack of knowledge about both the constitutional framework of the system and the role of the incumbents in it. At the same time, the fact that fully 79 percent of those queried did not know who their parliamentary representatives were indicates both a lack of cognition and a lack of close communication between the elected and the electors.[14]

Hungarian surveys support these findings. According to interviews conducted in 1966 by the Mass Communication Research Center of the Hungarian Radio and Television Networks, 25 percent of an interviewed panel identified De Gaulle (out of the three names given) as the general secretary of the French Communist Party, and over 50 percent of those queried were unable to name the prime minister of Hungary.[15]

Political Processes.   The citizenry's knowledge concerning most of the input and output processes of the political structure is minimal. However, it is essential to distinguish between these processes and the policies resulting from them. By and large the population is aware of the more significant policies arrived at by the decision makers, provided that those policies are effectively publicized and that their implementation intimately affects the citizenry. Thus, for example, in 1970–1971 when the new laws con-

cerning the allocation of apartments were made public, very few people were unaware of either the existence of the new laws or their implications because they were well publicized in all the communication media.

At the same time, most Hungarians do not know how laws and executive decisions are made. Terms like "interest groups," "interest aggregation," and "lobbying" are neither commonly used nor understood. Moreover, the modal patterns of cognitive orientation in Hungary do not recognize a positive role for the masses in the input processes. Citizen participation in the political process is limited to the implementation and enforcement of policy determined from above. The polity accepts the decisions of the leadership for what they are: manifestations of the power of the Government, not the result of pressures articulated in the upward flow of meaningful political participation.[16]

The Communist Party.   In Hungary the Party fulfills such an important role in the system that the citizenry cannot avoid acquiring some knowledge of its existence. The reality of Party power is known to the vast majority of the citizenry. Through its enforcement of labor discipline (the Party secretary in local units of production frequently acts as the director of personnel) and its constant propaganda about the "leaders of the Party and the Government," the Party makes citizens well aware of its omnipotence.

The citizenry knows that the Government is expected to implement Party decisions. Indeed, even the Party debates of 1969–1971 concerning "socialist democracy" made it clear that the importance of the Party would not diminish, because the Party intends to hold onto the reins of power. The citizenry recognizes that, although there is a separation between the Party's administrative and rule-making functions, the ruling position of the HSWP cannot be challenged.

The International Socialist System.   Hungarians are keenly aware of the fact that Hungary is a part of the Soviet bloc, a member of the Communist political and economic alliance. A popular saying compares Budapest to Jerusalem at the time of the Roman occupation when Roman soldiers guarded the gates of the city. The presence of 50,000 to 60,000 Soviet soldiers in Hungary insures that the gates are well guarded, and Hungarians know this very well. On the basis of their own experiences in 1956 and their knowledge of what happened in Czechoslovakia in 1968, they recognize that, given the present international balance of power, Hungary of necessity falls within the Soviet sphere of influence.

Although evidence indicates that Hungarians possess some knowledge of the history of the Hungarian state and the Magyar people, and that they genuinely recognize the rule of the Communist Party and the Communist international system, most Hungarians are apolitical. In sum, the cognitive orientations of the Hungarian citizenry toward the six objects we have delineated seem to be minimal; they are much weaker than those of the citizenry of Western Europe or the United States toward these same objects. The Hungarian leadership does not take meaningful steps to inform the people of the processes governing their political system, and the citizenry as a whole does not appear to be interested in becoming more knowledgeable about the political objects that constitute that system. The reasons for this lack of interest can be found in the affective and evaluative orientations of the Hungarian polity.

Evaluative and Affective Orientations

It is difficult to differentiate between the evaluative and the affective orientations of citizens through a simple description of people's attitudes toward the specific political objects that make up their political system. The conceptual problem arises from the interrelation of the two types of orientations. We propose to equate the subjective, evaluative orientations of Hungarians with the "personal calculations"[17] of the citizenry. (How do people view the benefits they derive from the system's political objects? Are they satisfied with their—i.e., the citizenry's—role in the performance of the system?)[18] By comparison, we propose that the affective orientations of the citizenry correspond to the value judgments people make in relation to specific norms. (How do citizens think certain political objects *ought* to function? What expectations do people have of selected political objects?) Based on both their value judgments and their subjective evaluations of the effectiveness of the system, citizens either develop a positive feeling of attachment toward the political objects in that system or become alienated from them. It must be emphasized, however, that affective and evaluative orientations are seldom separable. For example, citizens may support an incumbent based on their positive personal evaluation of how well that incumbent has performed his official duties. At the same time, they probably also evaluate the type of job the incumbent has done in terms of an abstract norm of how that job *ought* to be accomplished to ensure that the system operates as it *should*. Furthermore, value judgments—affective orientations—are not always based on an objective, normative examination of events; sometimes they result from inconsistent visceral reactions to political phenomena. To use a simplistic example, a person may hate the Communist Party and at the same time he may be satisfied with life under Communist rule.

State and Nation. The Hungarian people have a strong positive attachment to the state. They recognize that the state expects little of them and that, at present, it does not require them to give up their lives for its survival. At the same time, they realize that they derive from its existence the benefit of remaining Hungarian citizens who are patriotic and proud of being Magyars. The intense patriotism and pride in Hungary as a distinct political and cultural entity, which have developed over the past thousand years, have not diminished in more than 25 years of Communist rule. Sandor Petofi, who died fighting against the Russians in 1849, remains the poet most esteemed by the people. The emotional attachment of the people to "Hungarianism"—the provincial concept that the Magyars are a special, martyred people, alone in the world—remains very strong, and the negative manifestations of Hungarian nationalism (i.e., prejudice against Gypsies and Slovaks and Rumanians) are still prevalent.[19]

Nonetheless, some segments of the population have begun to recognize the drawbacks of a blind attachment to the state. Thirty-nine percent of a panel of young Hungarians (N=317) interviewed in 1970 indicated a willingness not only to marry a foreigner, but also to emigrate from Hungary.[20] Proponents of the view that "people should be allowed to live anywhere on earth" can be found among the ever-growing number of young Hungarian women who marry men from other countries. Nearly everyone interviewed, however, identified the concept of "anywhere on earth" as the West.[21] The value judgment inherent in this identification is obvious. In Kertesz's *Makra*, one character makes a bitter comment on this subject: "No one can help [the fact] that

[Hungary] is what it is. That's the way it's always been and will always be . . . that is why one must leave it. . . ."[22] This remark sums up the disillusionment and disappointment of those citizens who have given up their loyalty to the state as it now exists. Political and economic motivations rather than a rejection of real patriotism account for this change, but the fact remains that the nineteenth-century concept of patriotism ("Here you must live and die") is no longer as prevalent as it used to be.[23]

Although the vast majority of Hungarians manifest a positive affective orientation toward their state and nation, the determinants of this orientation have begun to change as political and economic factors have acquired precedence over the question of national survival. Defections to the West, an exceedingly low rate of natural increase, and one of the highest suicide rates in the world have, in fact, contributed to a slow, but steady, decrease in Hungary's population.[24] The traditionally high rate of suicide is the most puzzling phenomenon because the social causes of suicide do not seem to be more prevalent in Hungary than in other countries in a similar socio-economic situation. The defections, the relatively low birthrate, and the high rate of suicide must be interpreted as political comments that form part of the fiber of the Hungarian political culture.

The Political System.   Perhaps no evaluative orientations contain more contradictions than those of the population toward the political system. Hungarians believe that they have a better life now than they had in the past; however, although they realize that they are less subject to pressure from the police state than citizens of other states in the Soviet sphere (i.e., they live better and travel to the West more freely than the citizenry in neighboring socialist states), they also recognize that *political* life is less free in Hungary than in the West. Nevertheless, in evaluating their own personal freedom and the relative benefits that the system provides for them, they primarily contrast their lot with that of people living in other socialist states or with what existed in Hungary during the Rakosi era. They appreciate the benefits the system provides for them, but they also recognize that these benefits are greater in theory than in practice; they have, for example, free medical and dental care, but tipping is mandatory for most doctors and everyone "must learn by himself that nearly all patients pay— not telling about it to other patients [in order] to pre-

serve an advantage for themselves—and that one must give a thousand forints to the doctor [even] if one receives a meager paycheck."[25] Hungarians understand that they have access to a free education through high school, but they also know that the acquisition of knowledge is less of a guarantee for advancement or success than good connections with the ruling elite.[26]

The Hungarian people also recognize that their standard of living has not increased rapidly enough. They are aware of the fact that in the 1960s there were less apartments built in Budapest for a vastly greater and more deprived population than were built in the capital city in the 1890s.[27] They know that the Eastern European economies, in spite of all official claims to the contrary, have progressed more slowly than the economies of Western Europe,[28] and that the Hungarian economy has suffered from the recession experienced in the West. Their personal calculations also take into consideration their desire for cars and the slow pace at which individual demands for automobiles can be satisfied.[29]

The affective orientations of the people include the realization that the political situation and Communist rule are unalterable. Whether they are loyal or disloyal to the system makes little difference, for all Hungarians recognize that the Communist system cannot be changed by peaceful means or by force of arms. A frequently told Hungarian joke describes this attitude more succinctly than survey data. According to this cynical joke, one male worker asks the other, "What is the difference between socialism and your wife?" The other answers, "Nothing. That's what there is, that is what you have to love." The revolution of 1956 failed to change the situation, and Hungarians seem to have adopted the attitude that their only hope is to assure themselves of what, under the circumstances, is the most tolerable life.

A large percentage of the citizenry has adapted to the inalterability of the situation by becoming apolitical in their orientations toward the system. Kertesz, in his *Makra*, described one citizen's view:

I just wanted to be the same type of animal as anyone else. Like everyone, a grey, happy spot in the crowd. [One] who is unnoticed; who can sleep soundly; who vegetates peacefully, gets increasingly bald and grows a round beer belly; whom the janitor respects; whom the foodstore clerk greets *first*; who buys his cigarettes and razor blades in the same *tabak*; who takes his child for a walk every Sunday afternoon while his wife fixes golden meat broth and who—along with Mr. Nagy, Mr. Kovacs and Mr. Perempovics—drinks his beer in the corner pub and engages in passionate debates on whether the draught beer or the bottled beer is better.[30]

Hungarians understand that the system retains an economic hold over them that is more powerful than the terror they lived through in the 1950s,

> . . . because the man whose hungry kids are awaiting him at home is not going to raise hell, buddy boy. He is going to watch what he is talking about; he does not risk being thrown in the can; he can't even afford to be kicked out of his job, nor can he take a 100 spot less home, because the child needs a roof; the child needs milk and fruit and shoes and a winter coat. . . .[31]

Thus, the average citizen "does not wish to have power . . . he merely wants slop and he doesn't give a damn about politics, and he doesn't want to save the world, nor does he want to create some kind of classless society."[32] It appears that most Hungarians merely want to be left alone to live as well as they can. These apolitical attitudes, clearly no threat to the system, afford the regime a sort of legitimacy by default and even provide it with a kind of support; however, this support is forthcoming only if the citizenry is left alone to search for the material paradise. Citizens do not want to be "prophets with their bare bottoms hanging out of their pants," rather they wish to be left alone, and "having already once [been] run aground by the radical denial of money" they now wish to make the most of the opposite extreme.[33]

The affective orientations of a small group of people, whom we can best classify as "true believers," are radically different in kind and causality from those of the majority of the citizenry. The believers are loyal to the symbols of Communist rule. They are immensely interested in politics, even though they do not generally participate in the meaningful determination of rule. They are people who invested the ideology of their youth, and their desire to change the world in the system and particularly in the early battles fought to establish Communist hegemony in Hungary.

Although [they] reject the presence of the movement [the system], they passionately cling to its past. They populate their lives with its songs, jargon, and customs, which are slowly losing their meaning, because only by clinging to the magic of a beautiful past can they resist passively so that by their actions they will not fall in the same camp as the believers in the old system, who are hated as much as the rulers of the new regime.[34]

Surprisingly enough, some true believers still cling to the ideals of the postwar (1945–1956) revolutionary phase of development. In an age of pragmatic decision-making, they seem to be an anacronism. Several of these old believers are former NEKOSzists (members of the Nepi Kollegistak Orszagos Szovetsege, the National Alliance of People's Colleges), if not in fact, at least in spirit.[35] Others are idealistic Communists, former apparatchiks whom the Party used to help build the system during the mobilization era. These people were active ". . . in the youth movements and in the trade union movements, in the schools and in the people's colleges, and in cultural circles. Everywhere [their purpose was] the complete capture of power—whether by democratic means or otherwise."[36] Many of the believers helped the Communists seize power, but were squeezed out of positions of leadership by new apparatchiks.[37] They were cast aside and frequently sent to prison, but neither of these experiences undermined their belief in the movement. They are the people who "helped [to create] state power, but are not now part,"[38] though are still enamored of it (the ideal of Communism). At a conference of intellectuals held in Keszthely, Hungary in 1971, many of these Communist idealists, in their forties at the time, sang the old movement songs to the somewhat embarrassed silence of the younger generation, who watched but neither understood nor desired to share in a past that was not theirs. Although the true believers do not question the regime and, in fact, accord legitimacy to it, the real allegiance of this group is not to the system, but to an ideal that had been corrupted "by people who serve every system of rule, because if they own two sets of underpants they would even screw their own mothers for the third."[39]

Some of the educated youth whose affective orientations have been colored by what they perceive as the hopelessness of their situation share the beliefs of the ideologues. These young intellectuals are dissatisfied with the fact that it would take perhaps twenty years of scrimping and saving to be able to afford an apartment, and they blame the system for deserting the true Communist ideology. There is also a faction of leftist young people who decry the materialism of their fathers.[40] These young people feel that "it would be easy to fight, or even to live in poverty in that damned capitalism, but what should [the young] do here where socialism has arrived? The new world is here, and there is nothing to expect anymore."[41] They realize that their ideal of socialism does not exist, but they do not wish to participate in the present political system.

This small group of older, disillusioned Communists and the naive, young leftists believe in a faith that has been compromised by the pragmatism of the Hungarian leadership. The necessities of system maintenance have rendered the faith healers and true believers anathemas to the Kadar regime, and yet these people still cling to their outmoded revolutionary zeal.

In contrast to both the believers and the majority of the population, a small group of people from a wide variety of backgrounds possess well-articulated, cynical attitudes toward the system. The cynics, some of whom are in the system-maintenance *apparat*, view the system as a sham. They are concerned primarily with their own survival and are willing to acquiesce to the requirements of the system. They know "the weathervane always shows the direction of the wind,"[42] and they are willing to bend with the prevailing wind. Those who are part of the decision-making *apparat* usually carry out their assignments with enthusiasm, for "if by fulfilling this task, a good point is marked [on the ledgers] at the Party bureau, it may come in handy."[43] Most citizens regard the cynics as real professionals. Kertesz summarizes the popular view of the cynic-opportunist as follows:

> This guy, he works his own workweek at Party headquarters or wherever he is sent, picks up the dough for it, then goes home to his family, like you or I. He drinks his daily ration of wine, plays his game of *ulti* [a Hungarian card game played by three people using special cards], sits in a restaurant or in a cafe, goes to the movies, takes the children to the beach on Sunday, buys a curtain or a vase for his apartment, picks up his pocket money from his wife (or perhaps he gives it to her, however, he has arranged it). So, when he is not on call, he is an ordinary human being. . . . And today

even the world saviours live damned well from the fact they are world saviours.[44]

What these political opportunists need most to survive in the system is not revolutionary zeal, but a healthy dose of cynicism that makes it possible for them to adjust to the zigs and zags of Party life without too much difficulty. As Hungarians sarcastically explain, the symbols "ς" and "|" have a special meaning for the cynics; "ς" represents the permanent, never-changing Party line, whereas "|" stands for the ideological deviations from that line. In the estimation of the cynics, the key to success is "not to dream of changing the world, but to live with the existing opportunities."[45]

Incumbents. The evaluative and affective orientations of the citizenry toward incumbents are even more blurred than the orientations of the population toward the state and the political system. In Hungary, as elsewhere, political power clearly separates those who possess it from those who don't. However, Hungarians who manage to obtain transitory positions of power adopt a more authoritarian self-image and more rigorous bureaucratic behavior than their counterparts in states where democratic traditions have prevailed for a long time. The power of the desk or the power of the uniform seems to transform the meekest Hungarian into a power-hungry tyrant. The population regards both small officials and the ministers of the state with contempt and fear. The distinction between "them" (the holders of power) and "us" (the helpless population) is very real. "They" order and command people, telling them what to do and what not to do. In fact, to a visitor, the whole of Hungary appears to be a giant kindergarten with a whole spectrum of officials acting as the teachers who constantly instruct their captive pupils. The population as a whole has no real recourse; like the pupils in a kindergarten, they have to accept the teachers' orders. Hungarian office-holders, state-employed clerks, bus drivers, doctors, and even secretaries are often brusque and rude. "Stand here, not there," "Don't you know you have to get a ticket first?" "Take this, comrade, and be happy you got it. . . ." Orders and discourtesy characterize the daily intercourse between officeholders and the population at large. Citizens often complain

> that the way the streetcar conductor spoke this morning with the passengers was just like [the

way] the guard talks to prisoners, because here anyone garbed in a silver-buttoned suit becomes A HOLDER OF POWER. The rest are only second-class citizens, a mob that has to be herded. The conductor [made us feel] that he would rather give the commuter a kick in the ass with the transfer so that the commuter would remember where the Lord lives.[46]

Of course, this personalized conception of tyrannical authority is not new; it has been common in Hungary throughout the centuries. Helplessness thrusts people into a blind rage or ominous despair, and daily existence becomes a *bellum omnium contra omnis*, a fight of "us" against "them."[47] Today, Hungarians regard most incumbents as "them," and passively accept "their" continued existence. The need to fight for everything and against all the small, unimportant unjustices has worn down the citizenry so that petty injustices no longer seem so terrible, and rudeness is endured as just one more effect of the political system. The predominant position of the political elite, like the authority of petty officials, is accepted without challenge, but citizens have little respect for the power structure. The concept of omnipotent rulers who constitute an unrespected, impersonal "them" is very much a part of Hungarian political culture.

In spite of the puritanical and modest life-styles of such Politburo members as First Secretary Janos Kadar, Bela Biszku and Gyorgy Aczel, Hungarians recognize that many administrators of rule are corrupt. The citizenry hears of such allegations that the minister of defense "kept" his girl friends in beautiful villas on Lake Balaton. It also knows that a member of the Politburo had his apartment paneled with walnut at a cost of 200,000 forints—the equivalent of the combined monthly salaries of 100 workers (at the time of the remodeling). It recognizes that members of the power elite travel in luxurious, black Mercedes, and that the concerns of the leaders have no relation to the desires and aspirations of the people. Citizens know all this, and yet, as long as they are left alone to live as well as they can, they grudgingly accord legitimacy to the power elite.

This legitimacy is granted to the regime because the citizenry generally has a positive orientation toward Janos Kadar. Kadar is a consummate politician whose popularity reached a pinnacle in the early 1970s. If there had been free elections in Hungary at that time, he could probably have been elected President on his own popular strength. For Janos Kadar was able to unify a split, occupied, and socially, politically, and economically ruined country, and he succeeded in achieving a far greater degree of domestic freedom and prosperity than exists in any other Eastern European state. Hungarians attribute their relative political freedom, the relaxed restrictions on travel to the West, and their comparatively high standard of living to Kadar. Kadar, in turn, has been smart enough to identify himself as both a leader in power and a leader opposed to conservative trends within the Party. On the one hand, he directs the Party, and on the other, he makes it clear that there are conservative forces in it which hold him back. His popularity helps to legitimize the authority of other incumbents because the Hungarian population realizes that without Kadar's leadership the situation would very likely be much worse.

Political Processes. Almond and Verba have posited that if citizens believe they can influence the political processes affecting their lives, they develop extremely positive attitudes toward themselves, the system under which they live, and their relation to that system. Their orientations are much more positive than those of citizens who have little or no access to the decision-making process but who are nevertheless affected by the decisions handed down.[48] In Communist Hungary, highly positive orientations toward the political processes of the state do not exist. The orientations of the Hungarian citizenry are influenced by conflicting demands, namely, the ideological requirement for all citizens to participate, the official discouragement of meaningful citizen participation, the general apathy of citizens toward input through the channels provided for public participation in the system, and the citizenry's acceptance of the status quo.

In accordance with Communist ideology, the official policy of the Hungarian Government stipulates that the citizenry must participate in the political activities of the system. Citizens are not supposed to just accept the regime's output functions; they are supposed "to participate in the [actual] formation of decisions."[49] According to this view, citizens must vote in order to express their interest in the political processes must participate in endless political meetings, and must demonstrate against the injustices existing *elsewhere* in the world. During the early years of Communist rule in Hungary, these ideological demands were coupled with actual enforcement activities (which were only abandoned in the late 1960s). However, throughout the Rakosi era and the first decade of the Kadar regime, the Hungarian Communist government was careful not to allow people to actually participate in the input processes; the principle of democratic centralism and the Communist domination of all mass activities insured that no *meaningful* participation ever occurred.[50]

Since the end of the 1960s, while paying lip service to increased democratic participation, the Government has in fact actively encouraged the population to withdraw from the political arena. To implement its policy of the depoliticization of public life, the Kadar regime has treated issues hitherto regarded as political as merely of topical interest, and has allowed the political decision-making apparatus to function without public participation in any but the most superficial forms of activities.[51] Thus, while encouraging people to take part in the nomination of locally selected candidates and in the election of representatives to positions of power, the Government has more than ever frowned upon citizen participation in the resolution of political, social, and economic issues. The meaning of the new policy seems to be: *"enrichissez vous"* without experimenting with dangerous ideas about real participation, such as those that brought about the August 1968 downfall of the Dubcek regime in Czechoslovakia.

The Government's demand for depoliticization could not have fallen onto more fertile soil. The citizenry's general disgust with the forced participation of the 1950s and the lack of meaningful alternatives to Communist rule caused it to become apathetic about its participation in the political processes of the system. In their cost-benefit analysis, citizens have carefully weighed the pros and cons of their role in the system and concluded that there is no benefit to be gained from attempting to alter the present situation. Left alone to pursue their own material interest, they are by and large satisfied with the present system.

And yet, Communist regimes are formally participatory regimes because they comprise the mechanism of suffrage and interest aggregation. The fact that in the last few years there have frequently been more than one candidate on the ballot in Hungary gives the appearance that the populace has some choice in political contests, but when all is said and done, the choice between two people who both operate within the same parameters of ideology is not really a choice.[52] The citizenry accepts this as a given of the political system. As the popular Hungarian riddle asks: "Where was the first, free, democratic election?" The answer: "In the Garden of Eden when God, pointing to Eve, told Adam, 'Choose yourself a wife.' "[53]

In spite of this cynical appraisal of their lack of alternatives, most Hungarian citizens have a sense of loyalty to the system and a guardedly positive affective orientation toward its political processes. They grumble about their own output-oriented role and about the fact that they are not able to change decisions which they know affect their lives, but as long as the system makes few unbearable demands on them, they accept it as legitimate and tolerate its processes.

There are two main reasons for the relatively easy acceptance of the existing processes. First, the notion of the self as an active participant able to influence the policies of the government is conspicuously absent from the Hungarian political tradition. Even during the late 1930s and the immediate post-World-War-II period, when there was some active citizen participation in the processes of government, civic competence was minimal. The view that individual initiative and group action is able to gain redress for grievances, which is so common in the United Kingdom and the United States, does not apply in Hungary. A feeling of helplessness and the acceptance of manipulation by the government causes the Hungarian population to act as "subjects" rather than participants. Second, although the Kadar government has made plenty of decisions that could affect the people intimately and negatively, it has failed to enforce many of those decisions. A predictable element of Central European *schlamperei* mitigates the residue of political terror left over from the highly coercive phase of Hungarian Communist rule. Citizens prefer the present situation to the uncertainty of an unknown regime that could reimpose a Stalinist type of rule.

The Communist Party.   The evaluative orientations of Hungarians toward the Party revolve around the question of joining the Party. Currently, the HSWP is composed of two disparate groups: the believers and the nonbelievers. The believers are scattered throughout all levels of the Party hierarchy; they conscientiously carry out their assignments, striving to become better Communists, but their ranks are small and not representative of the majority of Party members.[54] Most people who join the Party base their decision to become a member on considerations of personal gain; even today, if two people with equal professional qualifications compete for a position, Communist party membership can be the determining credential. Moreover, Party membership is mandatory for political advancement, including appointment to major professional or political posts.[55] Therefore, personal calculation aimed at promoting self-interest is an essential ingredient in the evaluative orientations of the Hungarian citizenry toward the object of the Communist Party.

Yet, in spite of the benefits to be derived from Party membership, most eligible Hungarians do not join. The reasons for their reluctance lie in both the evaluative and the affective orientations of the citizenry. Citizens generally agree that there are benefits to be gained from joining the Party, but these benefits do not loom large enough. Furthermore, most people do not wish to be part of the ruling Party elite; some reject Party membership because they realize that they do not qualify, and others refuse to join because they know that in their occupation as, say, clerk-typists, it really makes no difference whether they are Party members or not. Moreover, the need to conform to a continually shifting, ideologically reinforced Party line, as well as the bother of the permanent reeducation process, fill a large portion of the citizenry with a feeling of revulsion. Once more it is the attitude of the "them" versus "us." Most Hungarians believe that "we" should not become embroiled in Party affairs, for membership creates only problems. Citizens who do not belong to the HSWP acknowledge that the Party is the ruling force in Hungarian society, but even though they do not openly challenge its control, they do not feel compelled to prove their loyalty to it.

The International Socialist System. The evaluative and affective orientations of Hungarian citizens toward the international socialist system are more negative than their orientations toward any other object in the Hungarian political culture. To the Magyar people, the phrase "the international socialist system" and the euphemisms associated with it (such as socialist internationalism and socialist patriotism) mean simply alliance with the USSR. The vast majority of the citizenry regard this alliance as a distinct drawback weighing heavily on the Hungarian

nation. Most citizens believe, to some extent incorrectly, that they pay too much for the products they receive from the Soviet Union; whereas Hungary charges less than the going world price for all domestically produced goods that are exported to the USSR and other socialist countries, Hungary must pay world prices for all imports from the Soviet Union. Furthermore, although Soviet troops are hidden from conspicuous public view, their presence is a well-known and widely detested fact of life; some citizens even suspect that the Hungarian Government and people pay all the costs of this occupation.

The affective orientations of the people toward the object of a Soviet-dominated alliance system are also extremely negative. The most obvious expressions of these negative attitudes are the countless jokes dealing with Soviet exploitation of the Hungarian state, wishful thinking about Chinese domination of the USSR, and a curious and fervent support of an Israel that is "beating them." Hungarians also manifest negative orientations toward other members of the socialist commonwealth. Specifically, East Germans, Czechoslovaks, and Rumanians are the objects of Hungarian ire and distrust. These negative orientations are partly responsible for the failure of Comecon to function as an effective Eastern European common market; and yet, the possibility that Hungarians might alter their negative attitudes toward the international socialist system is very slim. On the contrary, most Hungarian citizens would have liked the Helsinki European security conference to force the removal of all Soviet forces from the Warsaw Pact states. Even if such an agreement could be negotiated, however, Hungary still would remain in the Soviet sphere of influence, and, therefore, Hungarians feel that they have to accept the present international balance of power. They tried to alter this situation by force in 1956, but it did not work. The popular expression, "that's what there is, that's what you must love," also sums up the attitudes of the Hungarian citizenry toward the international socialist community.

Summary

The Hungarian political culture includes a large component of cynicism that affects the orientations of the citizenry toward every political object. Nothing in the political spectrum is sacred. Nevertheless, Hungarians do share the positive belief that Hungary is an historic state, a once great nation, a distinct culture worthy of preservation. Petofi's motto (expressed in a verse he wrote in 1847), "My homeland is the most beautiful state in the territory of the five continents,"[56] still dominates the attitudes of the Hungarian citizenry. Despite the relaxation of travel restrictions and the influx of Western styles and ideas, a stubborn and quite parochial Hungarian nationalism persists. Efforts to preserve a culture and a language that are isolated in an alien sea of Slavic customs and traditions have given the Magyars a sense of purpose, a goal, and an orientation. That which is aimed at preserving Hungarian culture is "good," that which is opposed to its preservation is "bad."

Beneath the surface of this unifying nationalism, differences between the older and younger generations abound. The young are angry at the old for believing "that [the older generation has] created the new world for [the young], fought for it, starved for it, sweated for it, so that all the youth would have to do is enjoy life, singing and . . . not starting all kinds of new stupidities."[57] And the young are impatient and apprehensive because they believe that there is no place for them in the new socialist order and that only when the older generation dies out will the youth have a chance to rule in accordance with their ideals. But even these discontented young people are nationalists and in that respect, they are not divided along class, religious, financial, or educational lines. Indeed, a fervent belief in Hungary's future is the core of the population's common political culture. Citizens will grudgingly accord a qualified legitimacy to their leaders as long as those leaders protect Hungary and Hungarians from being swallowed up by forces from the East; Hungarians will accept the existence of Communist rule as long as that rule does not conflict too seriously with their basic sense of national pride. In spite of all their cynicism, contemporary Hungarians accept the warnings of the poet Miklos Radnoti who in 1944 (in the midst of World War II) wrote:

Man, listen, observe your world well:
this was the past, this is the wild present—
keep it in your heart, live in this world that's bad
and always know what you have to do to make it
    different.[58]

12

Conclusions

Nearly thirty years, the life of one generation, have passed since the Communist Party took over the reins of power in Hungary. For all these years, the people of Hungary have been living under a socialist system controlled by a single party that has attempted to transform the state from a semi-feudal, underdeveloped country to a nation of intermediate socioeconomic development. The first thirty years of Communist rule have undoubtedly brought about tremendous changes in the life of the country. Today,

Hungary is a people's republic; its social system is socialism. Among the most well-known features of socialism one can count the fact that the means of production are in the hands of the state and thus the exploitation of man by man has ceased to exist. The dictatorship of the proletariat is the dictatorship of the majority, of the working classes over the minority of former oppressors. This classic thesis in its practical functions, however, has been altered considerably as the former ruling class has disappeared. The remainder of the former "ex-

ploiters" have found a place in the society and the [new money makers like the] sweater-makers on Kigyo street [in Budapest] cannot be regarded as exploiters. The [Party's] politics of unity [are] an important step [in] the evolution of an all-people's state. Today in Hungary there are no bankers . . . , landlords . . . starving pariahs . . . , or worker-peasants possessing only one robe. . . . At the same time . . . , there are trust directors and soccer-players famous throughout Europe, engineer deputy ministers and small shopkeepers . . . , Party-secretaries and co-operative farm directors, Catholic priests who are active in the People's Front, American businessmen . . . , and camouflaged prostitutes active . . . around the most famous hotels, girls working at heavy construction and existing in barracks and hovels at Tiszaszederkeny, and students of acting who have just returned from a study tour in France . . . , workers from the Angyalfold district who own the brand new apartments they live in, and workers from Angyalfold who live in damp basement hovels. There are crowded dormitory rooms and parties in half-lit rooms, construction camps of the Young Communist League and trips abroad, workers holding down two and three jobs and schools in isolated farmsteads, world famous research institutes, bad cooperatives and good cooperatives, and many other images. . . .[1]

Although in the first thirty years of socialism the Communists have altered the foundations of Hungarian society, they have not yet achieved their goal of building a stable, economically developed, classless society. The vision of reaching socialism—that relatively unchanging, unrevolutionary, and blissful utopia—therefore remains a strong goal of the polity, and it is the force of change, not stability, that dominates Hungarian political life in the 1970s.

The regime that came to power in 1948 held that power through the creation and perpetuation of the myth of its own revolutionary legitimacy, which it attempted to infuse in the population; the Party pursued its leading role in society by working to radically transform the political, social, and economic life of the country. Its purpose was to modernize a backward polity and drag it into the twentieth century. The Rakosi regime attempted to accomplish this task by duplicating the Soviet model; later, when the Soviet model was no longer applicable, the Kadar regime set out on a course of its own, introducing the New Economic Mechanism in 1968.

The Hungary of the 1970s bears little resemblance to the Hungary of thirty years ago. Today the state is more industrial than agrarian, more urban than rural, and more modernized than backward. The process of economic modernization has been as successful in Hungary as anywhere in Eastern Europe. The Hungarian citizenry of the 1970s is more satisfied than ever before with the standard of living achieved under socialism. Today, Hungarians are demanding not an alternative to their present system but rather an improvement in its performance.[2]

The post-1956 Party has achieved this relative success in three stages. For nearly a decade following the crushed revolution, the Party and the state floundered, trying to find an alternative to the bankrupt system of Stalinist rule. Then, between 1968 and 1973, the Kadar regime sought to depoliticize public life and discourage citizen input to the processes of government. It no longer required the population's enthusiastic and active participation in the daily life of the regime; it began to interpret most issues from a pragmatic, nonpolitical point of view; and it no longer required that citizens openly demonstrate their support of the system. In the course of those five years the regime imposed stringent measures to concentrate the political direction of the state in the hands of a circumscribed Party leadership, guiding the policies of the Government and brooking no objections even from within its own ranks, but it no longer dominated the domestic life of the populace. Members of the state apparatus, intellectuals, managers, and all other groups constituting the social elite not immediately associated with rule-making were encouraged to go about their daily lives, to work efficiently, to make profit, or merely to administer the rule. The Party leadership, however, made sure that the citizenry got the message: "Leave the driving to us." Finally, in the mid-1970s, the regime attempted to alter its bases of legitimacy. It no longer claimed to derive its power from the possession of ideological truths or the ability to carry out the revolutionary transformation of a backward state; rather it based its claim to legitimate authority on its ability to provide the citizenry with the maximum of benefits generated by the international system of socialist states in an era of stability (as opposed to one of revolutionary change).[3]

Although it is true that Hungarians possess greater rights than ever before and that their domestic rights—to passports, to electoral choice, and to equal treatment under the law—have never been more liberal, the fact remains that the Party carefully delineates the parameters of their action: no citizen may challenge the policies decided by the Party elite, and the political leadership, in turn, must elaborate policies that express enthusiastic support for the USSR vis-à-vis its position in the international political arena.

The Hungarian leadership's intention of enforcing an unquestioning acceptance of its policies was made explicitly clear in the Party's ruthless dealings with the Lukacs school of philosophers and sociologists in 1973. When the leading Marxist intellectuals of the group demanded that the Party leadership liberalize and democratize its policies, the Party elite reacted by expelling three of the rebellious leaders from the Party, evicting them from their jobs, and prohibiting them and several of their followers from engaging in any further publication and research activities.[4]

Party compliance with Soviet-imposed constraints on the Hungarian political system and its leadership is necessitated by Hungary's geopolitical setting. Proximity to the USSR compels the HSWP to accept Soviet dictates in the determination of Hungary's foreign policy, even though Hungarian policymakers often disagree with the objectives of the Soviet leadership. In the 1970s, there has been serious disagreement over the following four crucial aspects of foreign policy: Hungary's role in the Conference on Mutual and Balanced Force Reduction, Hungary's foreign sources of energy, Hungary's foreign trade activities, and finally, the question of fiscal convertibility.

On the first issue, Hungary's position as a sovereign state was severely damaged by its relegation to "observer" status at the beginning of the conference. By undermining Hungary's ability to negotiate, the USSR showed that it intends to continue maintaining Soviet troops on Hungarian territory. Hungarians bitterly resent the presence of the Soviet military, but the Hungarian leadership is unable to force the withdrawal of Soviet troops because of predetermined policies resulting from Soviet domination.

The problem of Hungary's energy sources is extremely severe. The country satisfies 45 percent of its energy needs through imports of oil, natural gas, and electricity from Comecon states, and, more specifically, the Soviet Union provides nearly 92 percent of Hungary's imported energy.[5] In 1969, the Hungarian Government increased its heavy reliance on these imports when it began a determined effort to close down inefficient coal mines producing low-calorie fuels. It projected that increased gas and oil imports would replace these energy sources, but in 1971, the USSR began to use its fuel exports to Hungary as a political and economic weapon to hinder Hungary's economic liberalization. The heavy reliance on energy from the USSR forced the Hungarian Government to slow the tempo of economic reform and reopen some of the already closed mines. The Kadar regime is dissatisfied with the present trade relations between the USSR and Hungary, particularly with the fact that the price of oil imported from the Soviet Union climbed 120 percent in 1975. Further increases in the prices of oil and energy are expected to occur yearly between 1975 and 1980.

Hungary's foreign trade goals are also a cause of friction between the two states. Hungarian policymakers would prefer to trade a great deal more with the West and a great deal less with Eastern Europe and the USSR. (Hungary receives less for products exported to the Soviet bloc than for similar exports to the West.) However, before the Hungarian Government can translate its aspirations into reality, it

must overcome the following obstacles: forced specialization of production in fields such as textile and clothing manufacture—as prescribed by Comecon decisions, inefficient and unprofitable production activities, the necessity to purchase Comecon equipment which frequently is inferior to Western products, and the potential loss of Soviet sources of energy. Although there are several advantages to trading with Comecon countries—guaranteed markets, availability of Soviet raw materials, short transportation lines, no competition, the possibility of selling products of poor quality, and bloc-controlled currencies—Hungary's foreign trade specialists would prefer to trade with the West more than is currently possible, but the external constraints placed on the Hungarian leadership prevent it from pursuing an independent foreign trade policy.

Finally, the inconvertibility of the Hungarian forint remains a hotly debated issue. Because of Hungary's semiadvanced level of economic development, fiscal experts feel that the closed monetary system has outlived its protectionist usefulness; they surmise that the Hungarian economy would benefit more from participating in the open international monetary system than from continuing as a member of the closed monetary system of Comecon nations. They would like the forint to be convertible on open international money markets through a controlled, but floating, international exchange rate. Needless to say, the leaders of the USSR remain unconvinced of Hungary's perceived need for an open currency and will adamantly oppose any steps toward that end until the convertibility of the ruble on the international market has been established.

The Hungarian polity has managed to survive within this system of constraints. Citizens continue to vote, and the elite of the Party continues to determine the rules governing the operation of the nation's political life. The citizenry by and large observes the limits established by the Government and abides by its laws, causing little dysfunction in the system. It is not the best political system ever devised, nor the worst, and the people who live in Hungary recognize this fact and accept the system as legitimate. However, they would like to effect some changes within the system (such as a more equitable distribution of resources and goods) that would lead to stable and prosperous lives for the citizenry.

The imprint that nearly thirty years of Communist rule has left on Hungarian society is mirrored in the country's political culture. In building a socialist society, the Hungarian leadership has superimposed a set of values that has altered or abolished those values the ruling elite considered dysfunctional and reinforced those values considered compatible with socialism.

The basic values toward which the Party has tried to inculcate positive orientations in the citizenry are: (1) hard work for the benefit of society ("socialist construction"); (2) moral and ethical behavior ("socialist consciousness and socialist morality"); (3) political stability based on unchallenged Party rule and a single prevailing ideology ("the rule of the workers and peasants"); and (4) patriotism, tempered by alliance with the USSR and other members of the Warsaw Treaty Organization ("socialist patriotism and the fraternal alliance system").

The Party has also tried to infuse certain negative orientations into the political culture, that is, to create an acceptance of the "don'ts" of the system. Thus it has insisted that the population disapprove of any anti-Party activity, regardless of whether that activity comes from revisionist or Maoist sources. By examining the success of the Party in reaching these objectives, we can discern the emerging political culture of socialist Hungary.[6]

The orientation of Hungarians toward the construction of the material bases of socialism remains ambivalent. On the one hand, in cases where the regime has offered material rewards as incentives, those given the chance for significant material advancement have been willing to work relatively hard. On the other hand, in spite of the recent minor reorganization of the Hungarian economy that occurred in 1973,[7] the Party has not been able to generate a general enthusiasm for its goal of socialist construction; even today, the vast majority of Hungarian workers work inefficiently and slowly, and their productivity is far from the optimum. As one Hungarian economist bitterly summed it up: "They sort of pay us and we sort of work." The fact remains, however, that in spite of the slipshod manner in which many members of Hungary's labor force work, Hungarians have achieved a remarkably high standard of living. The attitude of the Hungarian population toward work, in spite of the Party's consistant criticism,[8] is likely to remain the same during the life of the present generation of workers. This relatively negative orientation toward work that would benefit society as a whole more than it would benefit individual members of society is unlikely to change because the rewards for such work are relatively

small and are distributed unevenly; the Party favors those segments of society that contribute most effectively to the country's general economic progress, and it rejects the demands for a higher standard of living and equal treatment that come from industrial workers, who constitute the most politically significant interest group in Hungarian society.[9] As a result, the regime has fostered an ever-increasing socioeconomic stratification as well as a feeling of futility among a majority of Hungarians. The perception of the futility of unprofitable labor translates into a persistent negative orientation toward the object of socialist construction.

The creation of a socialist morality has been one of the main, stated goals of the regime, which has tried to infuse positive orientations toward this political object in citizens of all ages. Although, here again, the leadership has had some success in achieving this goal (as noted in Chapter 9 of this volume), it is not likely that the socialization programs of the Government will induce people to act more ethically in the near future. Corruption, tipping, and the payment of unauthorized honoraria are extremely widespread. Most doctors still receive honoraria from patients who expect a little better treatment in return; and the embezzlement of funds, unauthorized price-hikes by food store managers on items purchased at cheaper rates, and theft of community property remain prevalent throughout Hungarian society. A biting satirical Hungarian *bon mot* analyzes the problem from a political perspective: Q.—"Why are the workers the steel on which the pillars of socialist society are built?" A.—"Because they don't make enough money and they are forced to steal."

There is very little the Party can do to eradicate corruption. The rapid development of the economy, which has afforded the possibility of upward mobility to individuals with professional skills, has made the task of implementing socialist morality doubly difficult. Furthermore, the misconduct of several Hungarian leaders, ministers of state, enterprize directors, and the like, has diminished the effectiveness of the efforts undertaken by a determined party leadership to remedy the lack of morality. Socialism has not cured the curse of corruption and it is not likely to create an ethical society for a long time to come.

The Party has been remarkably successful in creating political stability based on the unchallenged rule of the Party. However, although there can be little doubt that the Party has successfully isolated political power among a restricted elite and excluded the population from meaningful participation in the political processes, it has not been nearly as successful in legitimizing its rule. Most Hungarians accept the rule of the Party, but are unwilling to join it, and accord it little positive support. Their attitude is best expressed in the apocryphal remark of a Hungarian courtesan, who upon being asked to join the Party as a result of her excellent, masterful work, expressed her refusal with the innocent explanation: "My mother has even opposed my working in this line of work; you don't think that she will allow me to join the party!!!" Many people have obviously joined the Party for careerist purposes only. As Gyorgy Moldova, one of Hungary's controversial writers, explained, "If a man lives in a country as small as Hungary, he can never tell what the future will bring; it is better to prepare for it, so that [he can make] ready without undue haste. . . ."[10]

This lack of desire to commit oneself in the interest of the "cause" is not unique to socialist societies and certainly not unique to Hungary. In any society where political cynicism is rampant, apathy and a lack of involvement in the system inevitably accompany it. The desire to remain "uninvolved" was epitomized by one of Moldova's characters in the "Personal identification card of nonmembership" (Tagtalansagi igazolvany) he designed for himself:

In gold letters the checkered black and white covering bore the sign "Personal identification of nonmembership"; below [this sign, the following objects] were drawn: a cancelled swastika, a . . . cancelled five-pointed red star, a star of David and a cross, while on the other side the following lines [were found at the bottom of the card]:
"No! No! Never!
Yes! Yes! Always!
Without Good Friday there is no Resurrection!
Even without Good Friday there is Resurrection!
If you want: It's just a tale!
If you want: It's not just a tale!
Workers of the world, unite!
Workers of the world, leave me alone!"[11]

These orientations toward the Party and its shifting ideology are not likely to be altered during the life of the present political generation, which is steeped in the tradition of political cynicism.

Patriotism, whether it is called socialist patriotism or just plain nationalism, is the one area where the Party's desire to inculcate a positive orientation in the citizenry reinforced previously existing values. However, in contrast to the halfhearted, passive acceptance of other political objects, Hungarian patriotism is often excessive; it includes a strong anti-Rumanian and anti-Russian sentiment and a domestic brand of anti-Semitism that is only mitigated by a strong dislike for Arabs and pro-Arab causes. Manifestations of patriotism have resulted in several dysfunctional activities. For example, there were patriotic, anti-Russian demonstrations on the March 15 national holiday in both 1971 and 1973.

The Kadar regime has had no success at all in altering the negative orientation of Hungarian citizens toward alliance with the USSR; their negative attitude persists despite the economic rationale for Hungarian-Soviet trade and the political rationale for cooperation with the strongest power in the region. No population willingly accepts the presence of an occupying force and the Soviet army is regarded and will continue to be regarded as an occupying force. Hungarians have no illusions about their ability to expel the Soviet military, but they fervently desire to be free, at least from the visible forms of occupation. The following very popular Hungarian joke illustrates this point more clearly than any official explanation. A Hungarian peasant asks a teller at the National Savings Bank how the bank would insure a deposit of 10,000 forints, and the clerk informs him that the bank is insured by the Government, the Party, the strength of the Warsaw Pact, and finally by the presence of the victorious Soviet forces. "Well," the peasant continues, "but what happens if the Soviet forces decide to leave Hungary?" The clerk's response is characteristic of the population's attitude: "Uncle, wouldn't it be worth 10,000 forints to you to have them leave our country?"

The anti-Semitism that has been traditional in Hungarian society has abated a bit in the last five to ten years; however, within the lower-level, "populist," Party leadership, some signs of a renewed official anti-Semitism appeared in 1973; at the January meeting of the Party's aktiv (paid professional members and leaders) where cultural policy was discussed, Ferenc Suto, who worked in the Cultural Policy Division of the Party Central Offices, leveled a strong attack against the unwarranted Jewish influence in Hungarian cultural life, citing the theatrical performances of strictly "Jewish" plays such as

Joseph Stein's adaptation of Scholom Aleichem's *Fiddler on the Roof* and Imre Madach's *Mozes* as examples. Although he couched his attack in pro-Arab rhetoric (declaring that Hungary supports the fraternal Arab nations, condemns Israeli aggression, and condones kidnapping, guerrilla warfare, and hijacking as legitimate methods of the struggle against imperialism), his message of domestic anti-Semitism was clear.[12]

Suto's attitude reflects to a great extent the suspicion of many middle-lower-level officials and many workers that the Government contains too many Jews. In spite of the falseness of this allegation, a joke that has circulated in Csepel (Budapest's most highly industrialized district) between 1971 and 1973 shows that a strain of anti-Semitism is still common among workers. *Question*: "What is the difference between the new Gierek government in Poland and the Hungarian government?" *Answer*: "Since 1971, in the name of the new Gierek policy of equality, 50 percent of the Polish Government is Polish and 50 percent is Jewish, whereas in Hungary, 50 percent of the Government is *not* Polish."

However, the anti-Semitism associated with Hungarian patriotism is counteracted by a disapprobation of Arab policy in the Middle East. No segment of Hungarian society supported the Arabs during the wars of 1948, 1956, and 1973, and Hungarians continue to regard Arab intellectual and military ability with suspicion, despite the pro-Arab policies of the Warsaw Treaty Organization.

In addition to its efforts to inculcate the "desired values" in the Hungarian citizenry, the Kadar leadership has also tried to infuse some negative values in the population, that is, to teach the citizenry the "don'ts" of political life. The Party leadership decided at the November 1972 meeting of the Central Committee to take a strong stand against citizens who threaten the stability of the political system through the expression of views contrary to those dictated by Party. In the formal statements outlining a new set of proscribed activities, the Party made it clear that it would not tolerate any opinions it considered dysfunctional,[13] including support of the pluralism of Marxism-Leninism, criticism that socialist societies lack greater dynamism and humanism than capitalist ones, the notion that in reality in Eastern Europe there exists a hierarchical, bureaucratic, statist system of rule, and most significantly, theories that deny the primacy of the rule of the working class. Maintaining that "those engaged in

[conducting research into] society must always accept that their medium of experiment is society itself and that the incorrect solution could affect all of society and even endanger it,"[14] the leadership began to attack Party members holding these negative opinions, and on May 14, 1973, it expelled three "revisionist opponents": Andras Hegedus, Janos Kis, and Mihaly Vajda.[15] Several other sociologists of the Lukacs school of philosophy who held views similar to the three expelled ex-Party members also lost their research jobs at the Academy and have not been able to find suitable employment since that time. Those who were fired included the prominent sociologists Agnes Heller, Gyorgy Markus, and Maria Markus.

As part of its crackdown on political opposition, the Party launched a counterattack against Hungarian Maoists by arresting a young writer, Miklos Haraszti; in his book entitled *Piecework* (*Darabber*), he criticized the way in which the regime treats the workers in a factory in the Pesterzsebet district of Budapest. The charge against Haraszti was that he had tried to smuggle his manuscript out of the country to Yugoslavia. However, because public opinion was mobilized against the arrest, Haraszti's sentencing was postponed due to "the illness of the judge."[16]

In addition to harassing Haraszti, the Party moved swiftly against other leftist critics. In October, 1974 the police arrested the sociologist-writer Gyorgy Konrad, sociologist Ivan Szelenyi who was Konrad's coauthor on a number of studies dealing with urban problems, and a young poet named Tamas Szentjoby. They were accused of illegally circulating a copy of Konrad's new book, *The City Founder*. Although their complicity in breaking any law could not be proven, they were given a choice of leaving the country or facing trial. Szelenyi and Szentjoby left Hungary; Konrad remained and negotiated an agreement with the regime that was mutually acceptable to both parties.

Through these expulsions, arrests, and trials, the regime has made its point; it condemns anti-Party activity from both the right and the left, because it allows no one to challenge either official ideology or the political decisions of the Party. Most Hungarians now realize that the Party has reverted to the inspiration of fear as a means of controlling society, and the prevailing political culture reflects this realization. Consequently, in spite of the much-touted executive measure adopted in 1974 to regulate the activities of the police, there is only a very slight probability that, in the near future, government by fear and the suppression of all opposition will be replaced by the predictability of the law in the sphere of political activity and the allowance of moderate criticism aimed at altering the course of the leadership. The Party has thus succeeded in circumscribing the political participation of the population; by and large citizens accept the absolute authority of the Party because they recognize that the Party possesses the power to implement its policies.

The cost of the Party's successes and failures has been the creation of one of the most cynical political cultures that ever existed. People recognize that Hungary is located in Central Europe, "a bit in the direction of the left,"[17] and that even the reincarnation of Hitler brought to life by the writer Moldova can ask in a state of shock: "Aren't there any people in this country with a clean past?"[18] Citizens know that force rules the polity and that they cannot challenge that force, but they are not willing to legitimize the rule of the Party through voluntary supportive activity. They recognize that graft and corruption are prevalent but they only condemn it in the abstract because they know that these remains of the "bourgeois past" help mitigate the abusive power of the system.

And yet, the political culture of the Hungarian people does not include a total rejection of the sys-

tem. Hungarians learned long ago not to believe in the "perfectibility of man," "progress" and a "better future." Betrayed by history's false promises, and hopes held in vain, Hungarians have learned to accept what exists not as the best system, but as the best system possible within the framework of the existing balance of international power. Having learned the futility of expecting any external attempts to create internal change and recognizing their own limitations to change from within, they have entered their own very private depoliticized shells. This decision to turn away from political activity, to turn inward, to be interested but not involved in politics, however, was a conscious and very meaningful political act.

Since 1968, the small windows in the houses of the villages, and the balconies of the huge, prefabricated apartment houses of the cities have begun to bloom once again with flowers. Hungarians have thus symbolically begun to tend their own gardens—for their own enjoyment and for that of their children. Perhaps this turning inward represents the greatest step the population could take toward self-preservation, a happiness outside the political sphere in the relative tranquility and safety of the small material conveniences that the past few years of progress have enabled them to attain.

Notes

Preface

1. For a roundtable discussion on "Comparing East European Political Systems," see *Studies in Comparative Communism* 2 (1971), pp. 30–78.
2. See Peter A. Toma, "The Case of Hungary," *Studies in Comparative Communism* 2 (1971), pp. 43–46.

Chapter 1

1. For comparative figures, see Franz Borkenau, *World Communism: A History of the Communist International* (New York: Norton, 1939), p. 130.
2. For the aggregate cited data, see Karoly Nagy, "The Impact of Communism in Hungary," *East Europe* 18 (March 1969), 11–17.
3. M. Simai and L. Szucs, *Horthy Miklos titkos iratai* [Nicholas Horthy's Secret Documents] (Budapest: Kossuth Konyvkiado, 1962); and M. Adam, G. Juhasz, and L. Kerekes, *Magyarorszag es a masodik vilaghaboru* [Hungary and the Second World War] (Budapest: Kossuth Konyvkiado, 1961). According to Vincent J. Esposito, *A Concise History of World War II* (New York: Praeger, 1964), p. 400, 140,000 Hungarian soldiers were killed during the war.
4. Hugh Seton-Watson, *The East European Revolution* (New York: Praeger, 1961), p. 105.
5. See Ernst C. Helmreich, ed., *Hungary* (New York: Praeger, 1957), pp. 125–126.
6. Ferenc Erdei et al., eds., *Information Hungary* (New York, London, Budapest: Pergamon Press, 1968), p. 289.
7. Jeno Levai, "The War Crime Trials Relating to Hungary," in Randolph L. Braham, ed., *Hungarian Jewish Studies*, Vol. 2 (New York: World Federation of Hungarian Jews, 1969), pp. 253–296.
8. Erdei, *Information Hungary*, p. 297.
9. R. R. Betts, ed., *Central and South East Europe* (London: Royal Institute of International Affairs, 1950), p. 291.
10. Erdei, *Information Hungary*, p. 291.
11. *Ibid.*, p. 193.
12. H. Seton-Watson, *The East European Revolution*, p. 193.
13. "The transference of German assets in Hungary to the USSR (see Article 28 of the Hungarian Peace Treaty) meant that the latter also acquired a dominant interest in the development of Hungarian bauxite mining. Hungarian-Soviet companies were founded to monopolize all river and air transport, and the country's oil development. . . ." Betts, *Central and South East Europe*, p. 109.

14. Erdei, *Information Hungary*, pp. 293–297.
15. Betts, *Central and South East Europe*, p. 106. See also *The Truth About the Nagy Affair* (New York: Praeger, 1959); and H. Seton-Watson, *The East European Revolution*, p. 199. Seton-Watson erroneously claims that Kovacs died in prison.
16. Erdei, *Information Hungary*, p. 297. Cf. Gyorgy Ranki, *Magyarorszag gazdasaga az elso 3 eves terv idoszakaban* [Hungary's Economy During the First Three-Year Plan] (Budapest: Kozgazdasagi es Jogi Konyvkiado, 1963).
17. Erdei, *Information Hungary*, pp. 297–298. See also Betts, *Central and South East Europe*, p. 110.
18. Erdei, *Information Hungary*, p. 298.
19. See Miklos Lacko, *Ipari munkassagunk osszetetelenek alakulasa 1867–1949* [The Formation of Our Industrial Workers' Movement, 1867–1949] (Budapest: Akademiai Kiado, 1961); and C. A. Macartney, *October Fifteenth: A History of Modern Hungary, 1929–1945*, 2 vols. (Edinburgh: Edinburgh University Press, 1957 and 1961).
20. Erdei, *Information Hungary*, p. 298. See also Stephen D. Kertesz, "The Methods of Communist Conquest: Hungary 1944–47," *World Politics* 3 (October 1950), 20–54; Jozsef Revai, "The Character of a People's Democracy," *Foreign Affairs* 28 (October 1949), 143–152; U.S. House of Representatives, 80th Congress, Select Committee on Communist Aggression, Special Report No. 10, *Communist Takeover and Occupation of Hungary* (Washington, D.C.: GPO, 1948).
21. *Magyar Nemzet*, May 18, 1949.
22. Erdei, *Information Hungary, passim.*
23. As quoted in H. Seton-Watson, *The East European Revolution*, pp. 167–168.

Chapter 2

1. For an interesting analysis of this argument, see Charles Gati, "Modernization and Communist Power in Hungary," *East European Quarterly* 5, no. 3 (1971), 325–359.
2. Ferenc Erdei et al., eds., *Information Hungary* (New York, London, Budapest: Pergamon Press, 1968), p. 301.
3. Central Statistical Office, *Statistical Pocket Book of Hungary* (Budapest: Statisztikai Kiado Vallalat, 1968), p. 46.
4. Erdei, *Information Hungary*, p. 300. See also the pledges of the 1951 Second Congress of the Hungarian Working People's Party.
5. Erdei, *Information Hungary*, p. 300.
6. See, for example, Samuel S. Sharp, *New Constitutions in the Soviet Sphere* (Washington, D.C.: Foundation for Foreign Affairs, 1950); Paul E. Zinner, *Revolution in Hungary* (New York: Columbia University Press, 1962); and Stephen D. Kertesz, *Diplomacy in a Whirlpool: Hungary Between Nazi Germany and Soviet Russia*

(Notre Dame, Ind.: University of Notre Dame Press, 1953).
7. Ivan T. Berend, *Gazdasag politika az elso oteves terv meginditasakor (1948–1953)* [Economic Policy at the Start of the First Five-Year Plan (1948–1953)] (Budapest: Kozgazdasagi es Jogi Konyvkiado, 1964).
8. See, for example, Ferenc A. Vali, *Rift and Revolt in Hungary—Nationalism versus Communism* (Cambridge, Mass.: Harvard University Press, 1961); Paul E. Zinner, *Revolution in Hungary*; Tamas Aczel, ed., *Ten Years After: The Hungarian Revolution in the Perspective of History* (New York: Holt, Rinehart & Winston, 1966); Paul Kecskemeti, *The Unexpected Revolution* (Palo Alto, Calif.: Stanford University Press, 1961); Tibor Meray, *Thirteen Days that Shook the Kremlin* (New York: Praeger, 1959); *The Revolt in Hungary: A Documentary Chronology of Events* (New York: Free Europe Committee, 1956); and Janos Molnar, *Ellenforradalom Magyarorszagon 1956–ban* [The Counterrevolution in Hungary in 1956] (Budapest: Akademiai Kiado, 1967).
9. See Peter A. Toma, "Revival of a Communist Party in Hungary," *Western Political Quarterly* 14, no. 1 (March 1961), 87–103.
10. See Zoltan Roman's analysis in *Tarsadalmi Szemle* 22, no. 10 (1967), 16–21; and Karoly Nagy, "The Impact of Communism in Hungary," *East Europe* 18 (March 1969), 12.
11. *New York Times*, April 2, 1964.
12. Erdei, *Information Hungary*, p. 308.
13. *M. Sz. M. P. hatarozatai es dokumentumai* [Resolutions and Documents of the HSWP] (Budapest: Kossuth, 1964), pp. 528–536.

Chapter 3

1. Paragraph 3 of the Revised Constitution. For a summary, see Hungarian Special Report No. 14 (SR/14), *Radio Free Europe Research* (referred to below as *RFER*), July 28, 1972.
2. For an English text, see Jan F. Triska, *Constitutions of the Communist Party States* (Stanford, Calif.: Hoover Institution, 1968), p. 192.
3. Ferenc Erdei, et al., eds., *Information Hungary* (New York, London, Budapest: Pergamon Press, 1968), p. 344.
4. For a concise study of this period, see Rudolf L. Tokes, *Bela Kun and the Hungarian Soviet Republic* (New York: Praeger, 1967); and Ivan Volgyes, ed., *Hungary in Revolution: 1918–1919* (Lincoln, Neb.: University of Nebraska Press, 1971).
5. See Peter A. Toma, "Successful vs. Unsuccessful Revolutions," in Andrew Gyorgy, ed., *Issues of World Communism* (Princeton, N.J.: Van Nostrand, 1966), pp. 222–243.
6. *Nepszabadsag*, December 31, 1956.
7. *Nepszabadsag*, February 28, 1957. Cf. *Izvestiia* (Moscow), March 1, 1957.

8. For information concerning data included in this chapter, consult *A Magyar Szocialista Munkaspart X. Kongresszusanak Jegyzokonyve* [Minutes of the Xth Congress of the Hungarian Socialist Workers' Party] (Budapest: Kossuth, 1971), cited in subsequent notes as *Tenth Congress*.

9. "A parttagfelvetel alakulasa" [The Development of Acceptance of New Party Members], *Partelet* 13, no. 6 (1968), 9–11. See also *Nepszabadsag*, March 15, 1975.

10. *Nepszabadsag*, March 18, 1975.

11. Ferenc Nemeth, "Falusi partmunkank tapasztalataibol es feladatairol" [The Experiences and Tasks of Our Party Work in the Villages], *Partelet* 12, no. 12 (1967), 38–43.

12. I. R., "A jarasi partbizottsagok megnovekedett feladatairol" [The Increased Tasks of the District Party Committees], *Partelet* 12, no. 9 (1967), 22–29, esp. 24; and Istvan Markus, *Ezt lattam falun* [That's What I Saw in the Village] (Budapest: Markus, 1970), chap. 1.

13. Drs. Imre Kurucz and Mihaly Kornidesz, "As egyetemi-foiskolai partmunka" [Party Work at the Universities and the High Schools], *Partelet* 13, no. 2 (1968), 17–18; and Dr. Pal Miklos, "Diakok eszmei politikai nevelesenek nehany tapasztalata" [Some Experiences Concerning the Political Ideological Education of Students], *Partelet* 13, no. 1 (1968), 80.

14. "A parttagfelvetal alakulasa," 11; and Iren Nemeti, "A nok es a tarsadalom" [Women and Society], *Partelet* 13, no. 2 (1968), 7.

15. Kurucz and Kornidesz, "Az egyetemi-foiskolai partmunka," 17; and *Partepites* (Budapest: Kossuth, 1971) p. 264. The latter work is the official textbook of the Advanced School of the Party.

16. Judit Kovacs, *Utazas a noi egyenjogusag korul* [Travel Around the Equality of Women] (Budapest: Kossuth, 1966), pp. 123–128. There are no reliable official figures on the exact percentage of women Party members. Even Kadar's report, which lists most other figures, merely alludes to the fact "that women are proportionately represented" (*Tenth Congress*, p. 102). He does not say in proportion to what. That the lack of women members is a problem for the Party is made clear on pp. 268–272 of *Partepites* (Budapest: Kossuth, 1971).

17. *Nepszabadsag*, March 18, 1975.

18. For the role the Party plays in rule aggregation, see Chapter 5 of this book.

19. See *Beke es Socializmus*, July 1975.

20. See Ivan T. Berend, *Gazdasag politika az elso oteves terv meginditasakor* (1948–1950) [Economic Policy at the Start of the First Five-Year Plan (1948–1953)] (Budapest: Kozgazdasagi es Jogi Konyvkiado, 1964).

21. See the valuable study "Postwar Economic Growth in Eastern Europe" by Maurice Ernst in U.S. Congress, 89th Congress, 2nd Session, Joint Economic Committee, Subcommittee on Foreign Economic Policy, *New Directions in the Soviet Economy*, (Washington, D.C.: GPO, 1966), pt. 4, p. 887.

22. Erdei, *Information Hungary*, p. 303.

23. For a study on the reorganization of the Hungarian Communist Party, see Peter A. Toma, "Revival of a Communist Party in Hungary," *Western Political Quarterly* 14, no. 1 (March 1961), 87–103.

24. Cf. Gyula Kallai, "A magyarorszagi ellenforradalom a marxizmus-leninizmus fenyeben" [The Hungarian Counterrevolution in the Light of Marxism-Leninism], *Tarsadalmi Szemle* 12, no.1 (1957), 12–39.

25. *Nepszabadsag*, November 15, 1956.

26. *Ibid.*, December 31, 1956.

27. *Corriere della Sera* (Milan), January 16, 1957.

28. *Nepszabadsag*, January 25, 1959.

29. Figures published at the Ninth Congress of the HSWP held in 1966. Cf. *A Magyar Szocialista Munkaspart IX. Kongresszusanak Jegyzokonyve* [Minutes of the IXth Congress of the Hungarian Socialist Workers' Party] (Budapest: Kossuth Konyvkiado, 1966).

30. *Nepszabadsag*, February 12, 1964.

31. See Kadar's speeches delivered at the Third Congress of the Patriotic People's Front on March 20, 1964 and on March 21, 1964.

32. Magyar Tavirati Iroda (MTI) [Hungarian Press Office] October 18, 1964, as cited in J. F. Brown, "Hungary's Relations with the Soviet Union Since the Fall of Khrushchev," Hungarian Bureau of Research (BR), *RFER*, August 8, 1966.

33. Radio Budapest, October 25, 1964, 0800 hours as reported in *RFER*, October 26, 1964.

34. *Nepszabadsag*, April 17, 1966.

35. "Kadar Janos es Nyers Rezso elvtars felszolalasa a gazdasagiranyitas reformjat elokeszito bizottsag zaroertekezleten" [Reports by Comrades Janos Kadar and Rezso Nyers at the Final Evaluation of the Preparedness Committee for Economic Reforms], *Tarsadalmi Szemle* 21, nos. 7–8 (1966), 17–28.

36. See William F. Robinson, "The Hungarian Party Congress: A Wrap-Up," Hungarian BR, *RFER*, December 19, 1966.

37. See Ferenc Pataki, "A marxista szocialpszichologia tajekozodasi iranyai" [Marxist Directives for Sociopsychological Orientation] *Tarsadalmi Szemle* 22, no. 3 (1967), 77–96.

38. *Nepszabadsag*, November 7, 1970.

39. See Kadar's speech to the Tenth Party Congress, *Nepszabadsag*, November 24, 1970.

40. See Kozponti Statisztikai Hivatal [Central Statistical Office], *A lakossag jovedelme es fogyasztasa 1968–1969* [Income and Consumption of the Population 1968–1969] (Budapest: Kozponti Statisztikai Kiado, September 1970). It is interesting to note that, according to Rezso Nyers, about 25 percent of the Hungarian population was earning 800 forints per month, which is just

above the poverty level of 750 forints per month. See his "Problems of Profitability and Income Distribution," *New Hungarian Quarterly* 12, no. 41 (1971), 24–41.

41. *Nepszabadsag*, November 24, 1970.

42. See the report by Janos Bruttyo, Chairman of the HSWP Central Control Committee, *Nepszabadsag*, November 24, 1970.

43. *Nepszava*, September 27, 1970.

44. *Ibid.*, October 6, 1970.

45. *Nepszabadsag*, October 11, 1970.

46. *Ibid.*, November 24, 1970.

47. *Ibid.*

48. For an analysis of the November 1972 plenum, see KK, "Internal Party Problems and the NEM," Hungarian BR, *RFER*, April 24, 1973.

49. For the text of the resolution of the plenum, see *Nepszabadsag*, November 17, 1972.

50. See *Partelet* 18, no. 6 (1973).

51. See *Nepszabadsag*, March 22 and March 23, 1973.

52. See Table 10.7 in this book.

53. For an explanation of the last problem, see Chapter 5 of this book.

54. For the resolution of the November 1973 plenum see, *Nepszabadsag*, November 30, 1973.

55. For a detailed account of the Konrad-Szelenyi-Szentjoby case, see the Italian Communist Party daily *l'Unita* of October 29, 1974.

56. See *Nepszabadsag*, March 20, 1975.

57. See *Nepszabadsag*, February 23, 1975.

58. For the Party guidelines and resolutions, see *Ibid.*, December 8, 1974 and March 23, 1975, respectively.

59. See Hungarian SR/17, *RFER*, April 9, 1975, p. 6.

60. *Nepszabadsag*, March 18, 1975.

61. See *Vigilia*, March 1975; *Kritika*, May 1975; and *Irodalomtortenet*, no. 2 (1975).

Chapter 4

1. Zoltan Halasz, ed., *Hungary* (Budapest: Corvina, 1968), p. 145.

2. See Egon Szabady, "Social Mobility and the 'Openness' of Society," *New Hungarian Quarterly* 12, no. 43 (1971), 41–55.

3. Karoly Nagy, "The Impact of Communism in Hungary," *East Europe* 18 (March 1969), 13.

4. Szabady, "Social Mobility and the 'Openness' of Society," 47.

5. *Ibid.*, 49.

6. Andras Klinger and Egon Szabady, "A tarsadalmi atretegzodes es demografiai hatasai I" [Social Mobility and its Impact on Demography, Part I], *Kozponti Statisztikai Hivatal Nepessegtudomanyi Kutato Intezetenek Kozlemenyei* [Reports of the Institute of Population Research, Central Statistical Office], no. 7 (1965), pp. 1–325.

7. See James L. Scott, *Projections of the Population of the Communist Countries of Eastern Europe, by Age and Sex: 1965–1985* (Washington D.C.: U.S. Department of Commerce, Bureau of the Census, 1965), p. 5.

8. *Parade*, December 6, 1970.

9. On January 1, 1974 new rules on legally induced abortion went into effect. Under the new regulations the abortion committees have far-reaching powers to deny as well as grant permission for induced abortions. Thus the liberal 1956 laws have been drastically revised.

10. Szabady, "Social Mobility and the 'Openness' of Society," 44; Nagy, "Impact of Communism," 14; and supplement to *Nepszabadsag*, December 8, 1974.

11. Nagy, "Impact of Communism," 14. See also Susan Fergeova [Zsuzsa Fergel], "Socialni stratifikace v Madarsku" [Social Stratification in Hungary], *Sociologicky casopis* (Prague) 4, no. 6 (1968), 690.

12. *Nepszabadsag*, October 15, 1967.

13. *Ibid.*, April 4, 1973.

14. In 1972, 23,960 marriages were dissolved—a 1.7 percent increase over 1971. *Nepszava*, May 3, 1973.

15. Nagy, "Impact of Communism," 16.

16. Reported in *Ibid.*, 17.

17. Fergeova, "Socialni stratifikace," 682–963.

18. Jozsef Bolyas, "Uj igenyek a szemelyzeti munkaban" [New Developments in the Labor Force], *Tarsadalmi Szemle* 23, no. 5 (1968), 15.

19. Peter A. Toma, "New Economic Reforms in Hungary," paper delivered at the Far Western Slavic Conference, University of British Columbia, Vancouver, Canada, May 4–5, 1968.

20. "Az irodalom es a muveszetek hivatasa tarsadalmunkban" [The Influence of Literature and Art on Our Society], *Tarsadalmi Szemle* 21, nos. 7–8 (1966), 29–58.

21. Mrs. Aladar Mod, Mrs. Sandor Ferge, Mr. Istvan Kemeny, and Mrs. Gyorgy Lang, "Tarsadalmi retegzodes magyarorszagon" [Social Stratification in Hungary], *Statisztikai Idoszaki Kozlemenyek*, Vol. 90 (Budapest: Kosponti Statisztakai Hivatal, 1966).

22. For the strengths and weaknesses of the NEM, see Chapter 10 of this book.

23. See Bela Csikos-Nagy, *Pricing in Hungary* (London: Institute of Economic Affairs, 1968), and Bela Csikos-Nagy, *Szocialista arelmelet es arpolitika* [Socialist Pricing and Pricing Policy] (Budapest: Kossuth Konyvkiado, 1966).

24. See *Nepszabadsag*, March 23, 1975.

25. See, for example, the Report to Congress delivered by Janos Kadar, reprinted in *Ibid.*, March 18, 1975.

26. Izabella Jantsky, "Korulbelul 4 milio szervezett munkas" [About 4 Million Unionized Workers], *Munka*, November 1974.

27. See KK, "The Hungarian Elections and the New National Assembly," Hungarian Special Report (SR), *Radio Free Europe Research*, (*RFER*), May 24, 1971.

28. See Hungarian SR, *RFER*, November 26, 1974.

29. *Nepszabadsag*, April 20, 1975.

30. For further details of the new law, see Law No. IV, published in *Ibid.*, July 8, 1972.

31. See *Magyar Kozlony*, November 1, 1974.

32. See D. Hatvani, "Popular Representation in the Village," *New Hungarian Quarterly* 16, no. 58 (1975), 25–36.

33. For a concise analysis of the 1972 Constitution, see KK, "Hungary's 1949 Constitution Revised," Hungarian SR/14, *RFER*, July 28, 1972.

Chapter 5

1. Ferenc Erdei et al., eds., *Information Hungary* (New York, London, Budapest: Pergamon Press, 1968), p. 321.

2. See Chap. IV, Para. 51, point 3 of the 1972 Revised Constitution.

3. Chap. IV, Para. 42, point 3 of the 1972 Revised Constitution.

4. See *Magyar Kozlony*, October 14, 1970; and KK, "The Hungarian Elections and the New National Assembly," Hungarian Special Report No. 14 (SR/14), Radio Free Europe Research (*RFER*), May 24, 1971.

5. *Nepszabadsag*, October 28, 1972.

6. *Ibid.*, June 17, 1975.

7. *Magyarorszag*, May 25, 1975.

8. *Magyar Nemzet*, May 21–25, 1975.

9. "Resolution of the Hungarian Socialist Workers' Party Central Committee Concerning the Reform of the Economic Mechanism," Supplement to *MTI Weekly Bulletin*, no. 23, June 9, 1966.

10. For the draft of the revised Party statutes, see *Partelet* 19, no. 12 (1974).

11. See Carl Beck's, "Leadership Attributes in Eastern Europe: The Effect of Country and Time" in Carl Beck et al., *Comparative Communist Political Leadership* (New York: David McKay, 1973), pp. 113–118.

12. See Unity Evans, "The Hungarian Party Leadership," Hungarian SR/16, *RFER*, September 11, 1972; and Hungarian SR/16, *RFER*, March 25, 1975.

13. *Nepszava*, May 5, 1971.

14. *Ibid.*

15. *Nepszabadsag*, November 25, 1970 and February 28, 1971. See also William F. Robinson, "What is a Socialist Society?" Hungarian SR/13 *RFER*, June 11, 1971.

16. See K. Szamosi's article on "Policy and Implementation" in Hungarian SR, *RFER*, April 14, 1974.

17. See *Szakszervezeti Szemle*, no. 4 (1972); and *Munka*, no. 6 (1973).

18. *Magyar Kozlony*, October 11, 1967. See also KK, "A New Era in Hungarian Agriculture," Bureau of Research No. 3 (BR/3), *RFER*, March 15, 1968.

19. See William F. Robinson, *The Pattern of Reform in Hungary* (New York: Praeger, 1973), pp. 236–237.

20. *Figyelo*, February 7, 1968.

21. *Magyar Kozlony*, February 19, 1971.

22. *Pravda* (Moscow), June 1, 1969.

23. See KK, "Steps Toward Meaningful Parliamentary Activity in Hungary," *RFER*, December 22, 1969.

24. See chap. VII, para. 54, point 3 of the 1972 Revised Constitution.

25. See chap. II, para. 19, point 3 of the 1972 Revised Constitution.

26. See chap. II, para. 25, point 1 of the 1972 Revised Constitution.

27. See Antal Adam, "Some Problems of Socialist Constitutionality," *Jogtudomanyi Kozlony*, September 1969, 434–435.

Chapter 6

1. Alexis de Tocqueville, *Democracy in America*, trans. Phillips Bradley (New York: Knopf, 1946; originally published 1835–1840), p. 140.

2. In this chapter, we use Professor Kirchheimer's definition of "political justice": the use of legal means and procedures to attain political ends. See his *Political Justice* (Princeton, N.J.: Princeton University Press, 1961).

3. *Pensées de Pascal* (Edition Variorum par Charles Louandri, Paris: G. Charpentier et Cie., n.d.) chap. VII, no. 10, p. 184.

4. Janos Beer, Istvan Kovacs, Lajos Szamel, *Magyar allamjog* [Hungarian State Law] (Budapest: Tankonyvkiado, 1969), pp. 5–6.

5. For an English translation of the 1949 Constitution, see Jan F. Triska, *Constitutions of the Communist Party States* (Stanford, Calif.: Hoover Institution, 1968), pp. 182–195.

6. *Ibid.*, p. 182.

7. Matyas Rakosi, "A dolgozo nep alkotmanya" [The Constitution of the Working People] in Rakosi, *A bekeert es a szocializmus epiteseert* [For Peace and the Building of Socialism] (Budapest: Szikra, 1951), p. 117.

8. Triska, *Constitutions*, p. 190.

9. "A Magyar Nepkoztarsasag Legfelsobb Birosaga" [The Supreme Court of the Hungarian People's Republic], *Birosagi Hatarozatok* [Court Decisions] (Budapest: 1956), p. 61.

10. These cases have been printed in *Jogtudomanyi Kozlony* (1953), pp. 352–353.

11. *Ibid.*

12. *Rajk Laszlo es tarsai a nepbirosag elott* [Laszlo Rajk and his Accomplices Before the People's Court] (Budapest: 1949); and Andras Gyorgy, "Hogyan torzittotta el a dogmatizmus a tarsadalmi torvenyek marxista felfogasat" [How Dogmatism Distorted the Marxist Concepts of Social Laws], *Tarsadalmi Szemle* 19, no. 12 (1964), 89–102.

13. Rakosi, "A Rajk bandarol" [Concerning the Rajk Gang], in Rakosi, *A bekeert*, p. 170.

14. *Szabad Nep*, July 23, 1956.

15. Advisory Opinion No. 214, *Birosagi Hatarozatok*, p. 61.
16. No punishment without a previous law.
17. Imre Nagy, *On Communism* (New York: Praeger, 1957), p. 297.
18. Tibor Vago, in *Magyar Jog*, January 6, 1962.
19. Lajos Szamel, "A lakossag reszvetele a kozugyekben es a szocialista demokracia" [The Participation of the People in Public Affairs and Socialist Democracy], *Tarsadalmi Szemle* 22, no. 3 (1967), 37.
20. Quoted in George R. Urban, "Hungary," in Walter Laquer and Leopold Labedz, eds., *Polycentrism* (New York: Praeger, 1962), p. 76.
21. M. S. Strogovich, as quoted in *Literaturnaia Gazeta*, November 17, 1960, p. 2.
22. Laszlo Kahulitz, "A munkahoz valo jog es a munkakotelezettseg a szocializmusban" [The Rights and Obligations of Labor in Socialism], *Partelet* 12, no. 10 (1967), 74–81; and Ede Harangozo, "As uj Munka Torvenykonyve" [The New Labor Code], *Partelet* 12, no. 12 (1967), 44–48.
23. Law No. VIII, 1962; and Ferenc Erdei et al., eds., *Information Hungary* (Budapest: Pergamon Press, 1968), p. 331.
24. Law No. II (1954).
25. There is some confusion over the meaning of the term *valasztani*. In Hungarian the term can mean either choice, selection, or election. The usage of the term in college textbooks makes it clear that judges are selected, not elected. Beer, et al., *Magyar Allamjog.* p. 408.
26. Law. No. II (1954), Section 50.
27. Lay assessors are usually given legal training prior to serving on the courts. For the law enabling lay assessors to get a legal education, see *Igazsagugyi Kozlony* 2 (1958), 236.
28. Law No. II (1954), Section 16.
29. Laszlo Nevai, "Az ugyeszi altalanos felugyelet elvi alapjai" [The General Ideological Bases of Supervision by the Public Prosecutor], *Jogtudomanyi Kozlony* 12 (1955), 718.
30. Triska, *Constitutions*, p. 190.
31. Nevai, "Az ugyeszi," 735–738.
32. *Ibid.*, 720 (italics in original text).
33. Beer, *Magyar allamjog*, p. 426 (italics added).
34. (December 13, 1956).
35. Law No. IX (1959).
36. Central Statistical Office, *Magyar Statisztikai Zsebkonyv* (Budapest: Statisztikai Kiado, 1970), p. 221. (This is the Hungarian version of the *Statistical Pocket Book of Hungary*; it contains more information than its English counterpart.)
37. *Ibid.*
38. *Ibid.*, p. 222.
39. *Ibid.*
40. Zoltan Fulei Szanto, "Megegyszer a bunozesrol" [Once More Concerning Crimes], *Tarsadalmi Szemle* 24, no. 3

(1969), 106–107.
41. Mihaly Korom, "Az igazsagszolgaltatas a kozrend vedelmeben" [The Administration of Justice in the Defense of Public Order], *Nepszabadsag*, November 17, 1968.
42. Fülei Szanto, "Megegyszer," 107.
43. Odon Szakacs, "A bunozesrol oszinten, higgadtan" [Concerning Crime—With Honesty and Objectivity], *Tarsadalmi Szemle* 24, no. 1 (1969).
44. The phrase comes from Rainer Maria Rilke's *Seventh Elegie* "solche Enterbte, denen das Frühere nicht und noch nicht das Nachste gehort."

Chapter 7

1. Ratter v. FOBER (PKKB 18 P. 86,871); and Simon v. FOBER (PKKB, 18 P. 86,873) (FOBER: Fovarosi Epitoipari Beruhazo Vallalat [Capital Building Construction Investment Firm]; PKKB: Pesti Kozponti Keruleti Birosag [Pest Central District Court]).
2. Law No. 15 (1965), paras. 14–15. In Hungary a distinction is made between Laws passed by Parliament and Executive Orders having the force of laws. Law No. 15 (1965) falls in the latter category. Laws passed by Parliament are identified by Roman numerals whereas Executive Orders are classified by Arabic numerals.
3. The term used in Hungarian is *kisajatitas*, which means taking possession of and implies forcible eviction of the owner by the state. Dr. Gyorgy Kempis and Dr. Jozsef Varga wrote the best Hungarian book on this subject: *Kisajatitas* [Expropriation] (Budapest: Kozgazdasagi es Jogi Konyvkiado, 1971).
4. *Zoldkar* in Hungarian means the loss of the flowers, gardening areas, planted greens. It does not mean the loss of income that would result from the sale of potentially grown vegetables, only the loss of those plants actually growing on the plot.
5. Calculated as 40% of the actual cost of the apartment offered to the plaintiffs.
6. Difference from compensation offered to the Ratters is based on the difference in the size of the property.
7. In 1971, the value of the forint was officially about 12 to a U.S. dollar, but the government exchange rate was nearly 27 forints per dollar, and the purchasing power of the forint was approximately 45 forints to a dollar; the average per capita wage in Hungary was ca. 2,000 forints per month. In 1975, the government exchange rate dropped to 20 forints/dollar and the purchasing power fell to 32 forints/dollar, but the per capita monthly wage rose to almost 3,000 forints.
8. Contrary to Article 39, Paragraph 1 of the 1949 Hungarian Constitution, which specifies that all judges must be elected, as recently as 1971 judges in Hungary were still appointed. This practice also violates the provisions of Law No. II (1954) entitled the Judicial Rule for Judges. There is a very low turnover rate in Hungarian judge-

ships, aside from that generated by retirement because of age. According to the presiding judge of the Budapest District Court, 78 percent of the judges serving in Budapest in 1970 had been judges for more than the prescribed five years. This practice parallels that followed in the USSR where in 1965 76 percent of all judges had served previously in that capacity. *Bulletin Verkhovnogo Suda SSR* 1 (1966), p. 5.

9. There are 20,000 assessors in Hungary, which means that about one out of every 500 people is an assessor. About 30 percent of the 20,000 are workers, 15 percent are peasants, and the remainder are white-collar workers. Ferenc Nezval, "Az igazsagszolgaltatas fejlodese a felszabadulas ota" [The Development of the Administration of Justice Since the Liberation], *Allam es Igazgatas* 4 (1965), 39.

10. Law No. VI (1960), chap. 19, sec. 27, para. 40.

11. "Assessors must receive factual and legal information from the professional judge [acting in his capacity] as the president of the court on the day before the trial, or if there is no such opportunity, [they must receive information concerning] the social and economic implications of the case right before the beginning of the proceedings." Tibor Revai, *A dolgozok reszvetele az igazsagszolgaltatasban* [The Participation of the Working People in the Administration of Justice] (Budapest: Kozgazdasagi es Jogi Konyvkiado, 1970), p. 220n.

12. *Kisajatitasi jog*, Law No. 15 (1965), chap. 3. It is interesting to note that between 1868 and 1919 expropriation cases in Hungary were tried in front of sworn juries, much like in the United States. The law governing these proceedings was Law No. LXI (1868), para. 40, which stipulated that only the owners of houses could qualify as jury members. For the best survey of the law cf. Drs. Gyorgy Varga and Jozsef Kempis, *Kisajatitas*.

13. Law No. 15 (1965), chap. 3.

14. In equity and fairness.

15. Sandor Barna, *A Munka Torvenykonyvenek ertelmezese* (The Interpretation of the Work Code. No. II (1967) (Budapest: Kozgazdasagi es Jogi Konyvkiado, 1969), pp. 29–30 and 129.

16. Kalman Kulcsar, *A nepi ulnok a birosagon* [The Lay Assessor in Court] (Budapest: Akademiai Kiado, 1971), pp. 109ff.

17. On the increasing professionalization of even the assessors and on their legal training, see Revai, *A dolgozok*, pp. 201–203.

Chapter 8

1. David F. Aberle, "Culture and Socialization," in Francis L. K. Hsu, ed., *Psychology and Anthropology* (Homewood, Ill.: Dorsey Press, 1961); and Paul F. Lazarsfeld, "The Process of Opinion and Attitude Formation," in Paul F. Lazarsfeld and Morris Rosenberg, eds., *The Language of Social Research* (Glencoe, Ill.: Free Press, 1955).

2. Herbert H. Hymann, *Political Socialization* (New York: Free Press, 1961), chap. 4.

3. Richard R. Fagen, *Politics and Communication* (Boston: Little, Brown, 1966), p. 97.

4. The Government has not completely given up using administrative machinery to insure attendance at celebrations and national holidays. See, for example, Mihaly Gergely, "Hajnaltol ejfelig" [From Dawn to Midnight], *Uj Iras*, no. 8 (1967), 95.

5. Richard E. Dawson and Kenneth Prewitt, *Political Socialization* (Boston: Little, Brown, 1969), p. 211.

6. Ferenc Erdei et al., eds., *Information Hungary* (New York, London, Budapest: Pergamon Press, 1968), p. 301.

7. *Ibid.*

8. *Ibid.*, pp. 956–959.

9. *Ibid.*

10. *Ibid.*

11. Ferenc Santa, *Husz Ora* [Twenty Hours] (Budapest: Magveto, 1964).

12. Yvette Biro, "A *Nouvelle Vague* of Hungarian Films?" *New Hungarian Quarterly* 8, no. 27 (1967), 194.

13. Erdei, *Information Hungary*, p. 580 (italics added).

14. Agnes Havas, "Nacionalista hatasok gyermekeinkre" [Nationalist Influences on Our Children], *Tarsadalmi Szemle* 22, no. 3 (1967), 108–110.

15. On village life, see Andras Hegedus, "A mai falu es a szociologiai kutatas" [Today's Village and Sociological Research], *Tarsadalmi Szemle* 18, no. 4 (1963); and Istvan Markus, *Ezt lattam falun* [This I Saw in the Village] (Budapest: Markus, 1969).

16. Dawson and Prewitt, *Political Socialization*, p. 105.

17. *Ibid.*

18. *Nepszava*, October 8, 1957.

19. *Nepszabadsag*, September 15, 1965.

20. *Ibid.*

21. *Nepszabadsag*, January 8, 1969.

22. *Nepszava*, July 9, 1973.

23. *Nepszabadsag*, September 15, 1965.

24. *Nepszava*, December 1, 1959; and *Nepszabadsag*, October 17, 1963.

25. *Nepszabadsag*, May 25, 1974.

26. *A Marxista filozofia alapjai* [The Foundations of Marxist Philosophy] (Budapest: Kossuth, 1961).

27. (Moscow: Gospolitizdat, 1959)

28. *A magyar es a nemzetkozi munkasmozgalom tortenete, 1848–1945* [The History of the Hungarian and International Labor Movement, 1848–1945] (Budapest: Kossuth, 1967–1968).

29. *Nepszabadsag*, June 6, 1968, p. 5.

30. "A Politikai Bizottsag 1968 januar 9-i hatarozata a MSZMPKB Politikai Foiskolajanak feladatairol" [The January 9, 1968 Decision of the Political Committee Concerning the Tasks of the Political College of the

HSWP Central Committee], *Partelet*, 13, no. 2 (1968), 9–12.

31. Andras Hegedus, "Barati csoportok" [Peer Groups], *Valosag*, no. 8 (1964), 89–90.

32. Erdei, *Information Hungary*, p. 339.

33. For further material on defense training, see *Nepszabadsag*, August 2, 1968; and Laszlo Rozsa, "Elkotelezett tarsadalom" [Committed Society], *Nepszabadsag*, September 11, 1974.

34. Young people, however, are justified in criticizing the bureaucracy, the everyday tedium, the lackluster hacks, and the Party itself, whose structure is outmoded. For a thoughtful article, see Pal Salamon, "Vazlatok az illedelmes ifjusagrol" [Sketches Concerning Well-Behaved Youth], *Valosag*, no. 3 (1965), 46–54.

35. Dr. Imre Kurucz and Dr. Mihaly Kornidesz, "Az egyetemi-foiskolai partmunka" [Party Work at the University and at other Institutions of Higher Education], *Partelet* 13, no. 2 (1968), 17.

36. Jakab Ervin, "Reszlet egy magyar szakos tanarjelolt szakdolgozatabol" [Part of the Graduating Essay of a Teacher of Hungarian Language and Literature], *Tevepedagogia* 4 (1969), 150.

37. Mrs. Lajos Gyorgy, "Az iskolaradio tortenelmi musorai a tanoran" [The Historical Program of the School Radio during Classroom Hours], *Iskolaradio az oran*: *Modszertani tanulmanyok* [School Radio in the Classroom: Methodological Essays] (Budapest: Magyar Radio es Televizio Kiadvanyai, 1968), p. 25.

38. *Iskolatelevizio* [Educational TV], 15058, p. 1.

39. *Ibid.*, 498, p. 8.

40. Vera Volgyi, "Holnapra megtanulom a vilagnezetemet" [By Tomorrow I Will Have Learned My *Weltanschauung*], *Nepszabadsag*, February 24, 1974.

41. Fagen, *Politics and Communications*, p. 37.

42. *Ibid.*, pp. 41–42.

43. Kenneth P. Langton, *Political Socialization* (New York: Oxford University Press, 1969), pp. 150–160.

44. Central Statistical Office, *Magyar Statisztikai Zsebkonyv* [Hungarian Statistical Pocket Book] (Budapest: Kozponti Statisztikai Hivatal, 1969), pp. 11–12. Cf. *Haztartasstatisztika, 1966* [Family Unit Statistical Observations, 1966] (Budapest: Kozponti Statisztikai Hivatal, 1965, 1966, 1967, 1969). Cited in the following note as *Haztartasstatisztika*, 1967, p. 8.

45. 50.2 percent of Hungarian women have full-time jobs. *Ibid.*

46. Pal Santha, "A dolgozo szulok es a gyermek" [The Working Parents and the Child], *Valosag*, No. 5 (1965), 58.

47. Dr. Miklos Pal, "Diakok eszmei politikai nevelesenek tapasztalatai" [Experiences with the Ideological and Political Education of Students], *Partelet* 13, no. 1 (1968), 80.

48. *Ibid.*, 81.

49. Jozsef Foldesi and L. Tamas Puskas, "How Checkers Lives," *New Hungarian Quarterly* 10, no. 35 (1969), 219.

50. "Only 3 to 5 percent of the children (N = 260) go to church in the city." Laszlo Jaki and Laszlo N. Sandor, "Vasarnap, szabad ido, neveles" [Sunday, Free-Time Education], *Valosag* 8 (1966), 89.

51. Paul Lendvai, *Anti-Semitism Without Jews* (Garden City, N.Y.: Doubleday, 1971), p. 372. This figure was confirmed by the author in independent interviews with leaders of the Hungarian Jewish community in April 1971.

52. Havas, "Nacionalista hatasok," 108–110.

Chapter 9

1. Richard R. Fagen, *Politics and Communication* (Boston: Little, Brown, 1969), pp. 44–45.

2. Mrs. Tibor Erdesz and Istvan Fekete, "Tomegkommunikacios eszkozok szerepe a nepmuvelesben" [The Role of the Mass Communication Media in Education], *Statisztikai Szemle*, August–September 1969.

3. *Ibid.*

4. *Ibid.*

5. *Ibid.*

6. *Ibid.*

7. Laszlo Harangi and Zoltan Vitar, *Televizio falun* [Television in the Village] (Budapest: Nepmuvelesi Propaganda Iroda, 1967), p. 66.

8. *Ibid.*, Table A, p. 49. On the uses of free or leisure time in the city, see Laszlo Jaki and Laszlo N. Sandor, "Vasarnap" [Sunday] and Mrs. Sandor Ferge, "Munkanapok es pihenonapok" [Workdays and Leisure Days], both in *Valosag*, no. 9 (1965), 58–67.

9. Harangi and Vitar, *Televizio falun*, p. 62. Cf. Erzsebet Galgoczy, "Outdated Image of the Village," *New Hungarian Quarterly* 9, no. 20 (1968), 144.

10. There were 2.5 million radios in addition to the transistor sets in Hungary in 1968. Ferenc Bekes, "Telekommunkiacios kozvelemenykutatas" [Telecommunication and Public Opinion Research], *Nepszabadsag*, July 5, 1969.

11. For an interesting article in English see Istvan Forgacs, "Ten Years with the Szabo Family," *New Hungarian Quarterly* 10, no. 35 (1969), 166–170. See also Istvan Forgacs, "A Szabo csalad—otszazszor" [The Szabo Family—500 times], *A Magyar Hirek Kincses Kalendariuma* [Treasured Calendar of *Magyar Hirek*] (Budapest: Magyarok Vilagszovetsege, 1970), pp. 272–276.

12. Forgacs, "A Szabo csalad," p. 169.

13. *Ibid.*

14. *Ibid.*

15. "A popular socialist newspaper" according to Ferenc Erdei et al., eds., *Information Hungary* (New York, London, Budapest: Pergamon Press, 1968), p. 640.

16. The author utilized the following means to analyze the

content of the publications. The four daily papers were numbered by day, and 50 issues were selected according to a random selection table. After separating foreign news items from domestic news, the author categorized the articles by subject, and coded them according to column inches of print. The research included reliability tests in which 20 percent of the sample was recoded by a second observer. The issues tested to assure the reliability of the classifications were selected completely at random, an equal number from each of the fifty papers; the second coder classified 78.3 percent of the sample in the same categories as those chosen by the first coder. That percentage of agreement is statistically significant, but future researchers may desire to conduct their work on a different basis to attain a higher percentage of reliability.

17. Jozesef Foldesi and L. Tamas Puskas, "How Checkers Lives," *New Hungarian Quarterly* 10, no. 35 (1969), 219.

18. Peter Kuczka, "Nyirsegi Naplo," *Irodalmi Ujsag*, November 7, 1953.

19. Erdei, *Information Hungary*, p. 626.

20. Mrs. Adam Horvath and Istvan Kemeny, "Kik olvasnak es mit?" [Who Reads and What?], *Valosag*, no. 6 (1965), 48–56.

21. *Ibid.*, 51.

22. *Ibid.*, 50.

23. Erdei, *Information Hungary*, p. 626.

24. Horvath and Kemeny, "Kik olvasnak," 51.

25. Pal Drescher, "Mit olvas a Fovarosi Konyvtar kozmuvelodesi fiokjainak kozonsege?" [What do the Readers of the Capital Library's General Education Division Read?] *A Fovarosi Konyvtar Evkonyve, 1934* [Capital Library Yearbook, 1934] (Budapest, 1934), pp. 735–772 in Horvath and Kemeny, "Kik olvasnak," 53.

26. Horvath and Kemeny, "Kik olvasnak," 54–55.

27. For children's attitudes toward Russian books, see Agnes Havas, "Nacionalista hatasok gyermekeinkre" [Nationalist Influences on our Children], *Tarsadalmi Szemle* 22, no. 3 (1967), p. 110.

28. Vera Volgyi, "Holnapra megtanulom a vilagnezetemet" [By Tomorrow I Will Have Learned My *Weltanschauung*], *Nepszabadsag*, February 24, 1974.

29. Endre Fejes, *Rozsdatemeto* [Scrapheap] (Budapest: Magveto, 1965).

30. Lajos Mesterhazi, *Ferfikor* [Manhood] (Budapest: Szepirodalmi, 1967).

31. Ferenc Santa, *Husz Ora* [Twenty Hours] (Budapest: Magveto, 1964).

32. Magda Szabo, *Mozes Egy, Huszonegy* [Moses One, Twenty-One] (Budapest: Magveto, 1967).

33. Gyorgy Konrad, *A latogato* [The Visitor] (Budapest: Magveto, 1970); Sandor Laszlo Bencsik, *Tortenelem alulnezetben* [History Viewed from Below] (Budapest: Szepirodalmi, 1974); Akos Kertesz, *Makra* (Budapest: Szepirodalmi, 1971); Gyorgy Moldova, *Titkos zaradek* [Secret Addenda] (Budapest: Magveto, 1974); Andras Berkesi, *A pisztrang es a hal* [The Trout and the Fish] (Budapest: Magveto, 1967) and his *Siratofal* [Wailing Wall] (Budapest: Magveto, 1974).

34. In *Tarsadalmi Szemle*, 21, no. 7–8 (1966), 53. On the Party's cultural policy, cf. Gyorgy Aczel, *Eloadas a MSZMP Politikai Akademia hallgatoinak* [Lecture to the Students of the Political Academy of the Hungarian Workers Party] (Budapest: Kossuth, 1968) and by the same author, "Valaszok a *Literaturnaia Gazeta* kerdeseire" [Answers to the Questions Posed by the *Literaturnaia Gazeta*], *Tarsadalmi Szemle* 24, no. 10 (1969); Pal Pandi, "Beszelgetesek" [Conversations], *Nepszabadsag*, November 29, 1969; and David Binder, "Kadar Promotes Freedom in Arts," *New York Times*, June 20, 1968.

35. Piroska Dabos, *A munkasolvasok irodalmi izlese a Fovarosi Szabo Ervin Konyvtarban* [The Literary Taste of Workers in the Capital's Ervin Szabo Library] (Budapest: Szabo Ervin Konyvtar, 1964).

36. It is interesting to note that with the initiation of the New Economic Mechanism, commercial considerations became very important in the publication of Hungarian works. Cf. Geza Molnar, "As iro es a mechanizmus" [The Writer and the Mechanism], *Elet es Irodalom*, December 9, 1967. In 1967 and 1968 the bestsellers were Jeno Rejto's (alias P. Howard) funny, semidetective stories and the volumes of Andras Berkesi. The latter's spy and detective novels, written in the style of the best American thrillers, sold more than 100,000 copies each, netting millions of forints for the publishers as well as the author.

37. Andras Kovacs, "Walls," *New Hungarian Quarterly* 9, no. 32 (1968), 37; also by the same author "Kormanypartisag, ellenzekiseg" [Government Support and Opposition], *Nepszabadsag*, January 20, 1968, p. 9.

38. "Musorok" [Programs], *Films, Szinhaz, Muzsika* [Films, Theater, Music], February 15, 1970, p. 20.

39. When the author repeatedly tried to explain to several well-educated Hungarians how good some of the Czech and Polish films were, they could not accept it. The consensus of a great many people was that the American films were better and more relevant than any films produced in the socialist democracies.

40. "V. T., a schoolboy in the seventh grade (age 13) declares that he does not like the Soviet films. 'Why?' 'Because they are bad.' 'But why are they bad?' 'Because they are about war.' He had no more reason for holding his opinions." Havas, "Nacionalista hatasok," 109.

41. Yvette Biro, "A *Nouvelle Vague* of Hungarian Films?" *New Hungarian Quarterly* 8, no. 27 (1967), 5.

42. *Ibid.*

43. The Government even today tries to combine modern music with political content. See Janos Marothy, "Pol beat es kult pol" [Political Beat and Cultural Policies], *Uj Iras*, no. 5 (1968), 94–97.

44. A great many articles and books have appeared concerning the debate over the issue of nationalism. Some of the most significant publications are: Sandor Farkas, "Hazafisagot, de milyent?" [Patriotism, But What Kind?], *Uj Iras*, no. 9 (1967), 98–109; Imre Dobozy, "A korszeru hazafisagrol," [Concerning the Modern Concept of Patriotism], *Kortars* 12, no. 12 (1967), 1949–1958; Geza Perjes, "A hazafisag es a tortenelemszemlelet erzelmi es ertelmi osszetevoi" [The Spiritual and Intellectual Components of Patriotism and Historical Philosophy], *Kortars* 12, no. 12 (1967), 1959–1966; and Janos Kadar, *Hazafisag es internacionalizmus* [Patriotism and Internationalism] (Budapest: Kossuth, 1968).

45. In 1969, the suicide rate was 3.1 per 10,000 people, which is a significant increase from 1900 when it was 2.2 per 10,000. Central Statistical Office, *Magyar Statisztikai Zsebkonyv* [Hungarian Statistical Pocket Book] (Budapest: Kozponti Statisztikai Hivatal, 1969), p. 32; and "Hungarian Anxiety at Suicide Rate," *London Times*, August 8, 1968.

46. The 1969 divorce rate was 2191 per 10,000 marriages. *Zsebkonyv*, p. 19.

47. According to a Hungarian survey undertaken at the request of the Ministry of Education and the Ministry of Health in 1969, 11 percent of the girls in high school had undergone at least one abortion. This data was confirmed in a group discussion on Hungarian television in July, 1969.

48. "Milliomos prostitualtak a birosag elott" [Millionaire Prostitutes before the Court], *Magyar Nemzet*, February 18, 1972, p. 6. The case of Annamaria Szekely attracted international attention because the ring had an international clientele.

49. For an interesting article, see Mihaly Sukosd, "Az intellektualis ifjusag" [The Intellectual Youth], *Magyar Ifjusag*, January 30, 1970, p. 3; or Ferenc Tokei, "Reflexiok a leninizmusrol" [Reflections on Leninism], *Uj Iras*, no. 4 (1970), 13.

50. On the debate between the Maoists and the moderates, see the exchange between Rafis Hajdu and Miklos Haraszti published in *Nepszabadsag*, and *Uj Iras*. For Hajdu's two articles critical of the Maoists' views, see *Nepszabadsag*, January 10 and 24, 1970; and for Haraszti's rejoinder see the January 24, 1970 issue of the same. The original poem of Miklos Haraszti that prompted the debate is entitled "The Faults of Che"; it was published in *Uj Iras*, no. 12 (1969), 63.

51. Sukosd, "Intellektualis ifjusag," p. 3.

Chapter 10

1. Gabriel A. Almond and G. Bingham Powell, Jr., *Comparative Politics: A Developmental Approach* (Boston: Little, Brown, 1966), p. 198.

2. Jozsef Kovacsics, ed., *Magyarorszag torteneti demogra-*

fiaja [The Historical Demography of Hungary] (Budapest: Kozgazdasagi es Jogi Konyvkiado, 1963), Table 18, p. 260; and *Kozponti Statisztikai Hivatali Kozlemenyek* [Central Statistical Office Publications], February 7, 1970.

3. Primitive forms of health insurance have been in existence in Hungary since 1805, but the first substantial general fund, the Workers' General Fund for Sickness and Disability, was not organized until 1870. During the interwar years there were more than thirty medical insurance organizations operating in Hungary. Ferenc Erdei, et al., eds., *Information Hungary* (New York, London, Budapest: Pergamon Press, 1968), p. 505.

4. *Ibid.*, pp 506–507; Central Statistical Office, *Statistical Pocket Book of Hungary* (Budapest: Statisztikai Kiado Vallalat, 1975), pp. 282–283, referred to below as *Pocket Book* (1975).

5. Erdei, *Information Hungary*, p. 563. Cf. Gabor Mocsar, "Az elso es az utolso" [The First and the Last], *Valosag*, no. 8 (1966), 72.

6. Erdei, *Information Hungary*, p. 563.

7. Interview with Mrs. Gyula Barna in *Nepszabadsag*, August 12, 1969.

8. Mrs. Sandor Ferge, "A gyermekkel kapcsolatos nehany kerdes a statisztika tukreben" [Some Questions Concerning Children in the Mirror of Statistics], *Statisztikai Szemle*, October 1962, 967–992

9. Mihaly Sukosd, "Ertelmiseg a kuszobon" [Intellectuals at the Doorstep], *Valosag*, no. 3 (1965), 38.

10. Laszlo Jaki, "A palyavalasztas nehany problemaja" [Some Problems Concerning the Choosing of a Vocation], *Valosag*, no. 5 (1968), 68; cf. Ferenc Gazso, "Palyak vonzasaban" [The Attraction of Professions], *Valosag*, no. 9 (1968), 21–33; and Gyorgy Varhegyi, "Palyak vonzasaban" [The Attraction of Professions], *Valosag*, no. 6 (1968), 25–36.

11. Laszlo Farkas and Tibor Kovacs, "A Komarom megyei altalanos iskolai tanulok tovabbtanulasi szandeka, illetve lehetosege" [The Desire and Possibility for Continuing Education among the Students of the General Schools in Komarom County], *Megyei es Varosi Statisztikai Ertesito*, no. 6 (1960), 24.

12. Julia Sos (Mrs. Keri), "Akik a gimnaziumbol kimaradtak" [Those Who Dropped Out of the Gymnasium], *Valosag*, no. 6 (1965), 39.

13. Cf. Katalin Hanak, "Talalkozas a nagyvarossal" [Meeting the Metropolis], *Valosag*, no. 7 (1966), 63–74; Mrs. Aladar Mod, "A belso vandorlas es a tarsadalmi retegezodes vizsgalata Magyarorszagon" [Research into the Internal Migration and Stratification of Society in Hungary] (Budapest: Demografia, 1964); Tamas Szecsko, *Ember es nagyvaros* [Man and Metropolis] (Budapest: Gondolattar, 1966); and the magnificent literary treatment by Gyula Illyes, *Falusi kislany* [A Little Girl from the Village] (Budapest, 1957). (The figures cited in the

text have not changed significantly under the Kadar regime.)

14. Sandor Balogh and Mrs. Kalman Janki, "Az uj egyetemi foiskolai felveteli rendszer elso tapasztalatai" [The First Observations Concerning the New Admission Method of the Universities and Colleges], *Valosag*, no. 6 (1963), 55; and Farkas and Kovacs, "Komarom," 24.

15. For an interesting article on rural education, see Laszlo Jaki and Laszlo N. Sandor, "Allami altalanos iskola, Lesencetomaj" [General State School, Lesencetomaj], *Kozneveles*, no. 11, June 5, 1964, 411–415. In Szabolcs–Szatmar County the situation is even worse: fully 36 percent of the students do not finish the eighth grade. Mocsar, "Az elso," 72.

16. Cf. Laszlo Nagy and Miklos Nagy, "Az egyetemi es foiskolai felvetelek utan" [After Admission to the Universities and Colleges], *Partelet* 14, no. 11 (1969), 23–32.

17. Central Statistical Office, *Magyar Statisztikai Zsebkonyv* [Statistical Pocket Book of Hungary] (Budapest: Statisztikai Kiado Vallalat, 1970), p. 143, cited below as *Zsebkonyv* plus date.

18. Official data indicate that the law deems one half room per person adequate space. Gabor Czako, "Alberlok" [Subletters], *Kortars* 13, no. 1 (1968), 75. Cf. the literary treatment of subletters in Lajos Szilvasi, *Alberlet a Sip utcaban* [Sublet in Sip Street] (Budapest: Szepirodalmi Kiado, 1968).

19. Sukosd, "Ertelmiseg," 34.

20. Czako, "Alberlok," 76.

21. A revealing short story on the exploitation of those who sublet by Endre Veszi is "Alberlok" [Subletters], *Uj Iras* 10 (1967), 5–12.

22. For some extremely interesting material concerning housing conditions in Hungarian villages, see Miklos Volgyes, *A falusi lakossag tartos javakkal valo ellatottsaga* [The Supply of People in the Villages with Durable Consumer Goods] (Budapest: Szovetkezeti Kutato es Uzemszervezesi Iroda, 1963); and by the same author, *A falusi lakasviszonyok* [Apartments in the Villages] (Budapest: Szovetkezeti Kutato es Uzemszervezesi Iroda, 1963). The latter study concludes that "the housing conditions prevalent in the villages are far from the desirable and indeed far from acceptable" (p. 5). This study shows clearly that more than 40 percent of the people in the villages lived in one-room apartments (*Ibid.*, p. 12) and that renters and subletters were just as badly off in the villages as in the city (*Ibid.*, p. 24). In towns and cities other than Budapest, the housing conditions are equally bad. For a literary treatment of this problem see Ferenc Baranyi's reflections in *Uj Iras*, no. 6 (1964).

23. Czako, "Alberlok," 75.

24. The person renting these units at the time they come up for sale may buy them with a 10-percent down payment, the balance to be paid over a period of 25 years. For the decree see *Magyar Kozlony*, September 30, 1969, Decree No. 32/1969.

25. *Pocket Book* (1975), p. 239.

26. One indication of the rampant inflation in housing costs is the fact that the same units were offered for sale by their owners in 1975 at 450,000 and 850,000 forints respectively.

27. Volgyes, *A falusi lakasviszonyok*, p. 25.

28. Dr. Laszlo Gordon, "A lakohazepitesi kolcsonok uj kamatfeltetelei" [The Conditions of New Mortgage Loans for Apartment Buildings], *Partelet* 13, no. 1 (1968), p. 60. Between 1970 and 1975, 84,000 housing units were built annually. *Pocket Book* (1975), p. 239. These figures, however, do not represent an absolute increase of 338,000 as the statistics indicate, because during the same period, 75,000 dwellings were demolished. *Ibid.*, p. 238. Between 1976 and 1980, the regime expects to build 420,000–440,000 new apartments.

29. *Zsebkonyv* (1975), p. 249.

30. *Zsebkonyv* (1972), pp. 13, 152d; also *Pocket Book* (1975), p. 273.

31. Erno Csizmadia and Sandor Zsarnoczai, "A munkasparaszt szovetseg nehany mai problemaja" [Some Current Problems of the Labor-Peasant Alliance], *Tarsadalmi Szemle* 21, no. 12 (1966), 34.

32. *Pocket Book* (1975), pp. 272, 7.

33. Csizmadia and Zsarnoczai, "A munkas-paraszt szovetseg," 34.

34. Erdei, *Information Hungary*, p. 338.

35. *Magyar Nemzet*, February 15, 1970.

36. *Pocket Book* (1975), p. 7.

37. *Ibid.*

38. *Ibid.*

39. *Ibid.*

40. On people deriving dual incomes, see *Pocket Book* (1975), p. 251.

41. *Zsebkonyv* (1970), p. 150; and *Pocket Book* (1975), pp. 263, 265, and 266.

42. *Pocket Book* (1975), p. 263.

43. R. A., "A munkasok es alkalmazottak keresete" [The Income of Workers and Employees], *Valosag*, no. 9 (1966), 71–72.

44. For some Hungarian analyses of the developing social stratification cf. Andras Hegedus, "A szocialista tarsadalom strukturalis modellje es a tarsadalmi retegezodes" [The Structural Model of a Socialist Society and Social Stratification], *Valosag*, no. 5 (1964), pp. 1–15; and by the same author, "Tarsadalmi struktura es a munkamegosztas" [Social Structure and the Division of Labor], *Valosag*, no. 8 (1966), pp. 20–31. The statistical data are derived from a survey of 15,000 households that was undertaken in 1964 by the Central Statistical Office.

45. Mrs. Sandor Ferge, "A tarsadalmi retegezodes Magyarorszagon" [Social Stratification in Hungary], *Valosag*, no. 10 (1966), 26–27; and Mrs. Aladar Mod, "A tarsa-

dalmi retegezodes Magyarorszagon," *Tarsadalmi Szemle* 22, no. 5 (1967), 15–33.

46. R. A., "A munkasok," 71. Of all the Eastern European countries, Hungary has the lowest percentage of the female population participating in the labor force. Only 65 percent of Hungarian women between 20 and 54 years of age work, placing Hungary just ahead of Austria (56.3 percent), the United States (50.1 percent) and West Germany (48.8 percent) in this respect. *Economic Survey of Europe* (New York: United Nations, 1969), p. 249; and *A nok a statisztika tukreben* [Women in the Mirror of Statistics] (Budapest: Kossuth, 1974), p. 14; *1970 Census of Population* (Census Bureau: Washington, D.C., 1973), v. 1, p. 1635. Women's wages in Hungary, as elsewhere, are still seven to seventeen percent lower than those of males in corresponding positions. *A nok a statisztika tukreben*, p. 24.

47. Sukosd, "Ertelmiseg," 38.

48. For an analysis of the Party's position on egalitarianism, see Chapters 4 and 5 of this book.

49. *Nepszabadsag*, August 20, 1972.

50. *Ibid.*, and Hungarian Special Report Number 34 (SR/34), Radio Free Europe Research (*RFER*), September 12, 1972. For an interesting survey on this subject, see Miklos Szabolcsi, "Socialist Taste and the Socialist Mind," *New Hungarian Quarterly* 12, no. 43 (1971), 110–122.

51. See Premier Jeno Fock's speech on the country's most serious economic problems published in *Nepszabadsag*, October 24, 1971.

52. See *Nepszabadsag*, December 3, 1971.

53. See *Nepszabadsag*, August 27, 1972; and Hungarian SR/34, *RFER*, September 12, 1972.

54. V. Gerasimov, "Radnosti i trudnosti poiska" [The Joys and Difficulties of Searching], *Pravda*, August 31, 1972, p. 4.

55. For the entire period of the Fifth Five-Year Plan (1976–1980), the regime plans to increase investment spending by only 18–20 percent.

56. See interview of Rezso Nyers by Gyorgy Varga, editor-in-chief, in *Gazdasag*, no. 1, 1975.

57. *Nepszabadsag*, March 18, 1975.

58. See the Supplement to *Ibid.*, December 8, 1974.

59. See Hungarian SR/24, *RFER*, May 27, 1975.

60. *Statisztikai Havi Kozlemenyek* [Monthly Statistical Bulletin], 1975, I–IV.

Chapter 11

1. Imre Szasz, "The Covered Wagon," *New Hungarian Quarterly* 12, no. 43 (1971), 130.

2. In our examination of the political culture of Hungary in the 1970s, we define political culture as "specifically political orientations—attitudes toward the political system and its various parts, and attitudes toward the self in the system." Gabriel Almond and Sidney Verba, *The Civic Culture* (Boston: Little, Brown, 1965), p. 12. For the sake of consistency and comparability, we retain the three categories of orientation (cognitive, evaluative, and effective) proposed by Almond and Verba.

3. Lawrence C. Mayer, *Comparative Political Inquiry* (Homewood, Ill.: Dorsey Press, 1972), p. 163.

4. Akos Kertesz, *Makra* (Budapest: Szepirodalmi, 1971), p. 81.

5. Almond and Verba, *The Civic Culture*, p. 14. Our addition of "the state and nation, the Communist Party, and the international socialist system" as separate categories is warranted by the importance of these objects and their determining effect on the body politic of Communist Hungary.

6. "There is no life outside of Hungary, but even if there were, it would not be like ours (i.e., it would not be worth living)."

7. Kertesz, *Makra*, p. 215.

8. "Mi az allamhatalom legfelsobb szerve Magyarorszagon?" and "Ki valasztja a Minisztertanacs tagjait?" Our sample was representative in terms of age, education, income, and present social class.

9. August 20, formerly St. Stephen's Day, is now Constitution Day.

10. Emma Benedek, ed., *Szoveggyujtemeny a tudomanyos kommunizmus tanulmanyozasahoz* [Sourcebook for the Study of Scientific Socialism], 2 vols. (Budapest: Tankonyvkiado, 1970).

11. *A kozoktatasugy Europa szocialista orszagaiban* [Public Education in the Socialist States of Europe] (Budapest: Tankonyvkiado, 1965), p. 305.

12. Dr. Sandor Daroczy, *Kozvelemenyvizsgalat a kollegiumban* [Public Opinion Survey in the Dormitories] (Budapest: Tankonyvkiado, 1970), p. 43.

13. Laszlo Molnar, Ferenc Nemes, and Mrs. Bela Szalai, *Ipari munkasok politikai aktivitasa* [The Political Activity of Industrial Workers] (Budapest: Kossuth, 1970), p. 109.

14. Our sample was not representative enough of the geographical distribution of the population as a whole to enable us to distinguish between the cognitive orientations of village and city residents.

15. Ferenc Bekes and Balint Suranyi, "A politikai tenyismeretek szintjenek tarsadalmi osszefuggeseirol" [Concerning the Relationship Between Social Level and Factual Political Knowledge], *Valosag*, no. 8 (1970), 53. Cf. by the same authors, *Politikai ismeretszint es tarsadalmi retegezodes* [The Level of Political Knowledge and Social Stratification] (Budapest: Akademiai Kiado, 1968), especially pp. 487–491.

16. 'A KB titkarsag 1968 februar 26-i hatarozata az 1968–1969-es oktatasi ev feladatairol" [The February 26, 1968 Decisions of the Secretariat of the Central Committee Concerning the Tasks of the 1968–1969 Academic Year],

Partelet 13, no. 4 (1968), 20.

17. The term "personal calculation" was suggested by Professor Peter Shockett of The University of Cincinnati. The author gratefully acknowledges his permission to use this term.

18. Gabriel Almond and G. Bingham Powell, Jr., *Comparative Politics: A Developmental Approach* (Boston and Toronto: Little, Brown, 1966), p. 50.

19. Racial prejudice against Gypsies, Negroes, and Rumanians is widespread in Hungary even among the 10–14 year age group, according to a nationwide survey taken in 1968 throughout the Hungarian school system. Laszlo Halasz and Kornel Sipos, *Muveszeti kommunikacio hatasa faji eloiteletre* [The Effect of Artistic Communication on Racial Prejudice] (Budapest: Akademiai Kiado, 1969), p. 59.

20. Gabor Czako, "Orokkon orokke?" [Till Death Do Us Part?], *Valosag*, no. 9 (1970), 71.

21. *Ibid.*, 73.

22. Kertesz, *Makra*, p. 189.

23. The nineteenth-century Hungarian exhortative poem, "Szozat," by Mihaly Vorosmarty, states: "Outside of this land, there is no place for you, . . . here you must live and die." From 1867 to the present, every Hungarian school child has had to memorize this poem.

24. Central Statistical Office, *Magyar Statisztikai Zsebkonyv 1971* [Statistical Pocket Book of Hungary] (Budapest: Statisztikai Kiado, 1971), p. 68; and Mihaly Gergely, "Ropirat az ongyilkossagrol" [A Flier Concerning Suicide], *Kortars* 14, no. 11 (1969), 1774–1795 and *Kortars* 14, no. 12 (1969), 1977–1994.

25. Kertesz, *Makra*, p. 186.

26. Istvan Csaszar, "Utazas" [Journey], *Uj Iras*, no. 3 (1972), 10.

27. Gyorgy Konrad and Ivan Szelenyi, "A kesleltetett varosfejlodes tarsadalmi konfliktusai" [The Social Conflicts of Retarded Urban Development], *Valosag*, no. 12 (1971), 22.

28. Ivan T. Berend, "A termeloerok fejlodese: novekedes es strukturavaltozas Magyarorszagon a szocialista atalakulas negyedszazadaban" [The Development of Productive Forces: Growth and Structural Change in Hungary during the Quarter Century of Socialist Alteration], *Szazadok*, no. 4 (1970), 827–865, esp. 848, 855, 864.

29. Based on the number of new licenses, Hungary's stock of private automobiles increased by about 30,000 cars per year between 1968 and 1971 and by about 45,000 cars a year between 1971 and 1975, reaching nearly 500,000 by mid-1975.

30. Kertesz, *Makra*, p. 295.

31. *Ibid.*, 119–120.

32. *Ibid.*, p. 121

33. Ivan Vitanyi, "Ideologiai vallomasok" [Ideological Confessions], *Valosag*, no. 7 (1970), 38.

34. Kertesz, *Makra*, pp. 70–71.

35. On NEKOSZ, cf. Jozsef Bernath, *Fenyes szellok* [Bright Winds] (Budapest: Tankonyvkiado, 1970) and by the same author, "Fokusz" [Focus], *Valosag*, no. 3 (1969), 74–78; Bela Szalai, "Fordulat eve az egyetemeken" [The Year of the Turning point at the Universities], *Kortars* 15, no. 9 (1970), 1463–1472; and Gergely Szabo, "Nepi kollegiumok" [People's Colleges], *Valosag*, no. 1 (1967), 63.

36. Vitanyi, "Ideologiai vallomasok," 39.

37. *Ibid.*, 40.

38. Ferenc Santa, *Husz Ora* [Twenty Hours] (Budapest: Magveto, 1964), pp. 80–82.

39. Kertesz, *Makra*, p. 40.

40. Vitanyi, "Ideologiai vallomasok," 38.

41. Kertesz, *Makra*, p. 49. The alienated young can strike out at the system in only one way: by openly disobeying its orders and rejecting its goals. The only open opposition to the system comes from young Maoists who continually challenge Government policy. In spite of the arrest and sentencing of two young Maoists, Gyorgy Por and Sandor Bencze, to two-and-a-half and two-year sentences respectively, on June 8, 1968, 50–100 young Maoists demonstrated against the regime in Budapest on March 21, 1971.

42. Andras Kovacs, "Stafeta" [Relay], *Valosag*, no. 12 (1970), 32.

43. Erno Gondos, *Jonas es a cet Obudan* [Jonah and the Whale in Obuda] (Budapest: Magveto, 1968), p. 103.

44. Kertesz, *Makra*, pp. 82–83.

45. *Ibid.*, p. 85.

46. *Ibid.*, p. 89–90.

47. The more scientific terminology of the "negative reference group" seems to apply to the artificial division between the "us" and the "them." Perhaps the view of regarding the incumbents and the holders of power on all levels as politically "significant others" *ipso facto* means that a negative orientation is attached to the incumbents by the citizenry.

48. Almond and Verba, *The Civic Culture*, p. 15.

49. Jozsef Lick, *Az erkolcs: kenyszer vagy dontes* [Morals: Compulsion or Decision] (Budapest: Kossuth, 1970), p. 205.

50. Otto Kovacs, "Demokratikus centralizmus es kadermunka" [Democratic Centralism and Cadre Work], *Tarsadalmi Szemle* 25, no. 10 (1970), 70–89.

51. Ivan Volgyes, "The Hungarian Tightrope," *East Europe* 21 (May 1972), pp. 2–4.

52. In the 1971 Hungarian parliamentary elections, 12.6 percent of all electoral seats were contested by two candidates. Only in one electoral district did three candidates run for one seat.

53. In Hungarian, the term *valasztani* (to choose) also means to elect.

54. Ferenc Santa's characterization of a Communist as a person who "is serious about that 'what-do-you-call-it'

ideal," is an accurate description of the few believers in Hungary. Santa, *Husz Ora*, p. 80.

55. The vast majority of all representatives to the Hungarian Parliament are Party members. The exact breakdown according to Party membership of the five Hungarian parliaments elected between 1953 and 1975 is as follows: 1953–1958, 69.12 percent; 1958–1962, 81.63 percent; 1963–1967, 74.11 percent; 1967–1971, 74.22 percent; the percentage of Party members among the representatives to the 1971–1975 Parliament is estimated variously at between 72 and 74 percent.

56. Taken from his "Magyar vagyok" [I am Hungarian], in Sandor Petofi, *Osszes Koltemenyei* [Collected Poems] (Budapest: Atheneum, n.d.), p. 23.

57. Ferenc Kunszabo, *Parazson piritani* [Roasting on Embers] (Budapest: Magveto, 1970), p. 398.

58. "Nem birta hat" [He Could Take it No More], in *Hazadnak renduletlenul* [Faithfully for your homeland . . .] (Budapest: Ifjusagi, 1955), p. 297.

Chapter 12

1. Mihaly Sukosd, "Ertelmiseg a kuszobon" [Intelligentsia at the Doorstep], *Valosag*, no. 3 (1965), 36.

2. Ivan Volgyes, "Hungary in the Seventies: The Era of Reform," *Current History* (May 1973), 219.

3. "A KB novemberi hatarozatanak vegrehajtasa" [The Execution of the November Decisions of the Central Committee], *Partelet* 18, no. 6 (1973), 22.

4. "Az MSZMP Kozponti Bizottsaga Titkarsaganak 1973. majus 14-i hatarozata" [The May 14, 1973 Decision of the Secretariat of the Hungarian Socialist Workers Party's Central Committee], *Partelet* 18, no. 6 (1973), 44.

5. Central Statistical Office, *Magyar Statisztikai Zsebknoyv, 1972* [Statistical Pocketbook, 1972] (Budapest: Statisztikai Kiado, 1973), p. 185; *Az energiatermeles es az energiafelhasznalas szerkezete/Nepgazdasagi energiamerlegek/1964–1968* [The Structure of Energy Production and Utilization/Energy Balances of the People's Economy/1964–1968] (Budapest: Kozponti Statisztikai Hivatal, 1970, 1972), pp. 7, 9; I. Kovacs, "Az energiagazdalkodas elemzese az energiamerlegek segitsegevel" [Analysis of Energy Input and Output Using Energy Balances], *Statiszikai Szemle*, March 1971, 223. According to *Nepszabadsag*, August 15, 1972, p. 1, in 1971, 22.7 percent of Hungary's consumption of electricity was provided for through import, and 91 percent of all imports of electricity came from the USSR.

6. Once again, we would like to caution the reader concerning the documentation for our interpretation of the Hungarian political culture. The scarce and confidential opinion surveys conducted by the Hungarian state agencies are of little help. The attitude of the people as expressed in their political humor, whether in the forms of jokes, bon mots, or bittersweet statements in novels and plays, provides the most exact measure possible of their political orientations. For more information on this subject, see Arthur Koestler, *Insight and Outlook* (New York: Macmillan, 1949), particularly pt. I.

7. For information on the latest reorganization designed to insure greater productivity see *Nepszabadsag*, June 30, 1973.

8. "A KB novemberi hatarozatanak vegrehajtasa" [The Execution of the November Decisions of the Central Committee], *Partelet* 18, no. 6 (1973), 22–23, esp. 23–27.

9. *Ibid.*, 27.

10. Gyorgy Moldova, *Titkos zaradek* [Secret Protocol] (Budapest: Magveto, 1973), p. 76.

11. *Ibid.*, p. 52.

12. According to well-informed sources, it was Kadar himself who immediately ordered that Suto be demoted within 24 hours of his anti-Semitic speech. Suto was transferred from his job in the Central Committee Offices to the Foreign Ministry where he was assigned to the position of desk officer.

13. For these formal statements, see, "Az MSZMP Központi Bizottsága Titkarsaganak 1973 majus 14-i hatarozata" [The May 14, 1973 Decision of the Secretariat of the Central Committee of the HSWP], *Partelet* 18, no. 6 (1973), 44; and "Az MSZMP mellett mukodo kulturpolitikai munkakozosseg ALLASFOGLALASA nehany tarsadalomkutato antimarxista nezeteirol" [The Position of the Cultural Policy Collective Attached to the Central Committee of the HSWP Concerning the Anti-Marxist Views of Some Social Scientists], *Szociologia* 1, no. 1 (1973), 45–55.

14. "ALLASFOGLALAS," 45.

15. "Az MSZMP KB hatarozata," 44.

16. One reason, perhaps, why the trial was postponed was the presence of the "nation's widows" (Mrs. Mihaly Karolyi, Mrs. Laszlo Rajk and Ilona Duczynska) at the scheduled trial. Their presence, in our view, however, was just one of the manifestations of a mobilized public opinion that feared the return of purge trials and other forms of repression associated with Stalinism.

17. Moldova, *Titkos zaradek* p. 132.

18. *Ibid.*, p. 39.

Selected Bibliography

Books

Aczel, Tamas, ed. *Ten Years After*. New York: Holt, Rinehart & Winston, 1967.

Bain, Leslie Balogh. *The Reluctant Satellites*. New York: Macmillan, 1960.

Bako, Elemer. *Guide to Hungarian Studies*. Stanford, Calif.: Hoover Institution, 1973.

Balassa, Bela A. *The Hungarian Experience in Economic Planning*. New Haven, Conn.: Yale University Press, 1959.

Barber, Noel. *Seven Days of Freedom: The Hungarian Uprising, 1956*. New York: Stein & Day, 1974.

Baross, Gabor. *Hungary and Hitler*. Astor, Fla.: Danubian Press, 1970.

Berend, Ivan Tibor, and Gyorgy Ranki. *Hungary: A Century of Economic Development*. New York: Barnes & Noble, 1974.

Brown, J. F. *The New Eastern Europe*. New York: Praeger, 1966.

Csicsery-Ronay, Istvan. *The First Book of Hungary*. New York: Watts, 1967.

Czerwinski, E. J., and Jaroslaw Piekalkiewicz, eds. *The Soviet Invasion of Czechoslovakia: Its Effects on Eastern Europe*. New York: Praeger, 1972.

Davidson, Basil. *What Really Happened in Hungary*. U.D.C. Publications, 1957.

Endrey, Anthony. *The Future of Hungary*. Melbourne: Hawthorne Press, 1972.

Erdei, Ferenc, et al., eds. *Information Hungary*. New York, London, Budapest: Pergamon Press, 1968.

Fejto, François. *Behind the Rape of Hungary*. New York: David McKay, 1957.

Fel, Edit, and Tamas Hofer. *Proper Peasants*. Viking Fund Publications in Anthropology, Series no. 46, 1969.

Fenyo, Mario D. *Hitler, Horthy, and Hungary*. New Haven, Conn.: Yale University Press, 1972.

Fischer, Lewis A., and Philip E. Uren. *The New Hungarian Agriculture*. Montreal and London: McGill-Queen's University Press, 1973.

Fryer, Peter. *The Hungarian Tragedy*. London: Dennis Dobson, 1956.

Gado, Otto. *Reform of the Economic Mechanism in Hungary, 1968–71*. Budapest: Akademiai Kiado, 1972.

Gati, Charles, ed. *The Politics of Modernization in Eastern Europe: Testing the Soviet Model*. New York: Praeger, 1974.

Gyorgy, Andrew, ed. *Issues of World Communism*. Princeton, N.J.: Van Nostrand, 1966.

Halasz de Beky, I. L., comp. *A Bibliography of the Hungarian Revolution, 1956.* Toronto: University of Toronto Press, 1963.

Heller, Andor. *No More Comrades.* Chicago: Regnery, 1957.

Helmreich, Ernst Christian, ed. *Hungary.* New York: Published for the Mid-European Studies Center of the Free Europe Committee by Praeger, 1957.

Hungarian National Commission for UNESCO. *Cultural Policy in Hungary.* Paris: UNESCO Press, 1974.

Ignotus, Paul. *Hungary.* New York: Praeger, 1972.

Juhasz, William. *The Hungarian Revolution: The People's Demands.* New York: Free Europe Press, 1957.

Kecskemeti, Paul. *Social Patterns in the Hungarian Revolution.* Santa Monica, Calif.: Rand Corporation, 1960.

———. *The Unexpected Revolution: Social Forces in the Hungarian Uprising.* Stanford, Calif.: Stanford University Press, 1961.

Keefe, Eugene K. *Area Handbook for Hungary.* Washington, D.C.: Superintendent of Documents, U.S. Government Printing Office, 1973.

Kemeny, Gyorgy. *Economic Planning in Hungary, 1947–49.* London and New York: Royal Institute of International Affairs, 1957.

Kiraly, Bela, and A. F. Kovacs. *The Hungarian Revolution of 1956.* New York: Hungarian Freedom Fighter's Federation, 1960.

Kornai, Janos. *Mathematical Planning of Structural Decisions.* Amsterdam: North Holland Publishing Co., 1967.

Kovacs, Imre. *Facts About Hungary.* New York: Hungarian Committee, 1966.

Kovrig, Bennett. *The Hungarian People's Republic.* Baltimore: Johns Hopkins University Press, 1970.

———. *The Myth of Liberation.* Baltimore: Johns Hopkins University Press, 1973.

Kozponti Statisztikai Hivatal. *Statistical Pocketbook of Hungary.* Budapest: Statisztikai Kiado Vallalat, 1975.

Lauter, Geza Peter. *The Manager and Economic Reform in Hungary.* New York: Praeger, 1972.

Lasky, Melvin J., ed. *The Hungarian Revolution: A White Book.* Freeport, N.Y.: Books for Libraries Press, 1970.

Laszlo, Ervin. *The Communist Theory in Hungary.* New York: Reidel, 1966.

Lendvai, Paul. *Anti-Semitism Without Jews.* Garden City, N.Y.: Doubleday, 1971.

Lettis, Richard, and William E. Morris, eds. *The Hungarian Revolt, October 23–November 4, 1956.* New York: Scribner, 1961.

Macartney, Carlil Aylmer. *Hungary: A Short History.* Chicago: Aldine, 1962.

Marton, Endre. *The Forbidden Sky.* Boston: Little, Brown, 1971.

Meray, Tibor. *That Day in Budapest, October 23, 1956.* New York: Funk & Wagnalls, 1969.

———. *Thirteen Days that Shook the Kremlin.* London: Thames & Hudson, 1959.

Meray, Tibor, and Tamas Aczel. *The Revolt of the Mind.* London: Thames & Hudson, 1960.

Michener, James Albert. *The Bridge at Andau.* New York: Random House, 1957.

Mikes, George. *The Hungarian Revolution.* London: Deutsch, 1957.

Molnar, Miklos. *Budapest 1956: A History of the Hungarian Revolution.* London: Allen & Unwin, 1971.

Montgomery, John Flournoy. *Hungary, The Unwilling Satellite.* New York: Devin-Adair, 1947.

Nadanyi, P. *The Revolt that Rocked the Kremlin.* Washington, D.C.: Hungarian Reformed Federation of America, 1963.

Nagy, Ferenc. *The Struggle Behind the Iron Curtain.* New York: Macmillan, 1948.

Nagy, Imre. *On Communism: In Defense of the New Course.* London: Thames & Hudson, 1957.

Neuburg, Paul. *The Hero's Children.* New York: Morrow, 1973.

Pryce-Jones, David. *The Hungarian Revolution.* London: Benn, 1969.

Radvanyi, Janos. *Hungary and the Superpowers.* Stanford, Calif.: Hoover Institution, 1972.

Robinson, William F. *The Pattern of Reform in Hungary.* New York: Praeger, 1973.

Sartre, Jean Paul. *The Ghost of Stalin.* New York: Braziller, 1968.

Schramm, Wilbur Lang, ed. *One Day in the World's Press.* Stanford, Calif.: Stanford University Press, 1959.

Seton-Watson, Hugh. *The East European Revolution.* London: Methuen, 1956.

———. *Nationalism and Communism.* London: Methuen, 1964.

Shawcross, William. *Crime and Compromise: Janos Kadar and the Politics of Hungary Since Revolution.* New York: Dutton, 1974.

Sinor, Denis. *History of Hungary.* New York: Praeger, 1959.

Soviet Survey (editors of). *Hungary Today.* New York: Praeger, 1962.

Szasz, Bela Sandor. *Volunteers for the Gallows: Anatomy of a Show-Trial.* London: Chatto & Windus, 1971.

Sztaray, Zoltan. *Bibliography of Hungary.* New York: Kossuth Foundation, 1960.

Toma, Peter A., ed. *The Changing Face of Communism in Eastern Europe.* Tucson, Ariz.: University of Arizona Press, 1970.

Torok, Lajos. *The Socialist System of State Control.* Budapest: Akademiai Kiado, 1974.

United States Office of Geography. *Hungary: Official Standard Names.* Washington, D.C.: U.S. Government Printing Office, 1961.

Urban, George. *The Nineteen Days.* London: Heinemann, 1957,

Vajda, Imre, ed. *Foreign Trade in a Planned Economy*. Cambridge: Cambridge University Press, 1971.

Vali, Ferenc A. *Rift and Revolt in Hungary*. Cambridge, Mass.: Harvard University Press, 1961.

Veres, Janos, ed. *The Experiences of Building a New Society*. Budapest: Pannonia Press, 1964.

Volgyes, Ivan, ed. *Environmental Deterioration in the Soviet Union and Eastern Europe*. New York: Praeger, 1975.

————. *The Hungarian Soviet Republic, 1919*. Stanford, Calif.: Hoover Institution, 1970.

————, ed. *Hungary in Revolution 1918–1919*. Lincoln, Neb.: University of Nebraska Press, 1971.

————. ed. *Political Socialization in Eastern Europe: A Comparative Framework*. New York: Praeger, 1975.

Volgyes, Ivan, and Mary Volgyes. *Czechoslovakia, Hungary, Poland: Crossroads of Change*. New York: Thomas Nelson, 1970.

The World and Its Peoples: Austria, Hungary, Czechoslovakia, Poland. New York: Greystone Press, 1970.

Zinner, Paul E. *Revolution in Hungary*. New York: Columbia University Press, 1962.

Zsoldos, Laszlo. *The Economic Integration of Hungary in the Soviet Bloc: Foreign Trade Experience*. Columbus, Ohio: Bureau of Business Research, College of Commerce and Administration, Ohio State University, 1963.

Journal Articles

Aczel, Tamas. "Spokesmen of Revolution." *Problems of Communism* 18 (June–September 1969), 60–66.

Balint, Jozsef. "On the Unfolding of the Economic Reform." *Eastern European Economics* 9 (Fall 1970), 3–41.

Bass, R. "East European Communist Elites: Their Character and History." *Journal of International Affairs* 20, no. 1 (1966), 106–117.

Borbandi, Gyula. "Istvan Bibo: Hungary's Political Philosopher." *East Europe* 13 (October 1964), 2–7.

————. "Dealing with Hungary's Minorities." *East Europe* 18 (January 1969), 32–42.

Fischer-Galati, Steven, ed. "East Central Europe: Continuity and Change." *Journal of International Affairs* 20, no. 1 (1966), 1–171.

Fock, Jeno. "Economic Planning and International Co-operation." *New Hungarian Quarterly* 12, no. 43 (1971), 3–21.

————. "Hungary and the CMEA's Comprehensive Program." *Current Digest of the Soviet Press*, June 7, 1972, 8–10.

Friss, Istvan. "Practical Experiences of the Economic Reform in Hungary." *Eastern European Economics* 2 (September 1973), 3–26.

Gabor, Otto, and Gede, Miklos. "Role of the Engineering Industries in the Development of the Hungarian Economy." *Economics* 12 (Fall 1973), 82–104.

Gati, Charles. "Hungary: The Politics of Reform." *Current History* 60 (May 1971), 290–294.

Ginsburgs, G. "Demise and Revival of a Communist Party." *Western Political Quarterly* 12 (September 1960), 780–802.

Gleitman, H., and J. Greenbaum. "Hungarian Socio-Political Attitudes and Revolutionary Action." *Public Opinion Quarterly* 24 (Spring 1960), 62–76.

Gosztony, P. I. "General Maleter: A Memoir." *Problems of Communism* 15 (March 1966), 54–61.

Gripp, R. C. "Eastern Europe's Ten Years of National Communism: 1948–1958." *Western Political Quarterly* 13 (December 1960), 934–949.

Held, Joseph. "Hungary: Iron Out of Wood." *Problems of Communism* 15 (November 1966), 37–43.

Helmreich, Ernst C. "Kadar's Hungary." *Current History* 43 (March 1965), 142–148.

Janos, A. C. "Mass Revolution and Totalitarianism." *World Politics* 14 (April 1962), 542–547.

Jotischky, Laszlo. "Hungary, Fifteen Years After." *Political Quarterly* 42 (April–June 1971), 150–163.

Kadarkay, Arpad A. "Hungary: An Experiment in Communism." *Western Political Quarterly* 26 (June 1973), 280–301.

Kethly, Anna. "The Hungarian Dilemma." *East Europe* 17 (September 1968), 11–14.

Kiraly, Bela K. "Parallels and Contrasts." *Problems of Communism* 18 (July–September 1969), 52–60.

Kiss, Sandor. "The Kadar Imprint on the Hungarian Party." *East Europe* 18 (March 1969), 2–9.

————. "Soviet Troops in Hungary." *East Europe* 13 (October–November 1964), 8–13.

Kovacs, Imre. "Hungary: The Quest for Respectability." *East Europe* 14 (December 1965), 2–8.

Lendvai, Paul. "Budapest and Vienna—a Thaw?" *East Europe* 14 (May 1965), 16–20.

————. "Hungary: Change vs. Immobilism." *Problems of Communism* 16 (March 1967), 11–17.

Marczali, T. A. "Criminal Law in Communist Hungary." *Slavic Review* 23 (March 1964), 92–102.

Morgan, J. "Withering Class Struggles." *New Statesman*. August 20, 1965, 241.

Mueller, G., and H. Singer. "Hungary: Can the New Course Survive." *Problems of Communism* 14 (January 1965), 32–38.

Nagy, Karoly. "The Impact of Communism in Hungary." *East Europe* 18 (March 1969), 11–17.

————. "New Incentives in Hungary." *International Labour Review* 96 (November 1967), 529.

Paal, Ferenc. "Hungarian Foreign Policy in 1965: Principles and Achievements." *Hungarian Survey* 1 (1966), 81–87.

Peter, Janos. "The Foreign Policy of Hungary and Current Questions of European Cooperation." *New Hungarian Quarterly* 6 (Autumn 1965), 3–15.

Portes, Richard D. "The Strategy and Tactics of Economic Decentralization." *Soviet Studies* 23 (April 1972), 629–658.

Racz, Barnabas A. "Assessing Hungary's Economic Reforms." *East Europe* 17 (December 1968), 2–9.

———. "Political Changes in Hungary After the Soviet Invasion of Czechoslovakia." *Slavic Review* 29 (December 1970), 633–650.

Robinson, William F. "Hungary's Turn to Revisionism." *East Europe* 16 (September 1967), 14–17.

Savarius, Vincent. "Janos Kadar: Man and Politician." *East Europe* 15 (October 1966), 16–21.

Schopflin, G. A. "Hungary Today: The Balance Sheet of Kadar's Ten Years in Power." *World Today* 22 (November 1966), 455–459.

Shaffer, Harry G. "Progress in Hungary." *Problems of Communism* 19 (January–February 1970), 48–60.

Szabados, Joseph. "Hungary's NEM: Reorganization or Basic Reform?" *East Europe* 17 (June 1968), 13–18.

Timar, J. "High Level Manpower Planning in Hungary and Its Relation to Educational Development." *International Labour Review* 96 (October 1967), 364–387.

Toma, Peter A. "Revival of a Communist Party in Hungary." *Western Political Quarterly* 14(March 1961), 87–103.

Ujhelyi, T. "Foreign Trade in Agricultural and Food Products—The Hungarian National Economy and the World Market." *Acta Oeconomica* 2, no. 1 (1973), 3–17.

Urban, George. "Polycentrism and the Appeal of Communism." *Virginia Quarterly Review* 41 (Winter 1965), 18–39.

Volgyes, Ivan. "The Hungarian Tightrope." *East Europe* 21 (May 1972), 2–4.

———. "Hungary in the Seventies: The Era of Reform." *Current History* 64 (May 1973), 216–219.

———. "Political Socialization in Eastern Europe: A Comparative Framework." *Journal of Political and Military Sociology* 1 (Fall 1973), 261–277.

Index